The Mughals – descendants of Timur and Genghiz Khan with strong cultural ties to the Persian world – seized political power in north India in 1526 and became the most important artistically active Muslim dynasty on the subcontinent. In this richly illustrated book, Dr Milo Beach shows how, between 1555 and 1630 in particular, Mughal patronage of the arts was incessant and radically innovative for the Indian context. The Mughals also profoundly altered the character of painting in the Hindu areas of north India over which they ruled. These initially independent territories belonged to Rajputs, Hindus of the warrior caste. The author reveals how Mughal painting was defined by the styles and subjects popular at the imperial court, whereas Rajput painting consisted of many local court styles, corresponding to the various Hindu kingdoms, each with different tastes and artistic inspirations. Deeply rooted in Indian artistic traditions, Rajput paintings were also closely allied to imagery popular with Indian villagers and to works made for temple use throughout the subcontinent.

By reproducing nearly 200 examples in this study, Milo Beach traces the interplay of the traditions of Mughal and Rajput painting from the sixteenth to nineteenth centuries. He demonstrates the tolerance each showed towards outside influence and change and thus helps to define a uniquely Indian attitude towards the arts. The author also expands his narrative by listing, in an appendix, important dated manuscripts and related publications.

Mughal and Rajput Painting makes a major contribution to the study of north Indian painting. This work will be widely read by students and specialists of art history, Indian history and South Asian studies as well as by anyone interested in Indian art.

THE NEW CAMBRIDGE HISTORY OF INDIA

Mughal and Rajput Painting

THE NEW CAMBRIDGE HISTORY OF INDIA

General editor Gordon Johnson
Director, Centre of South Asian Studies, University of Cambridge, and Fellow of Selwyn College

Associate editors C. A. Bayly
Professor of Modern Indian History, University of Cambridge, and Fellow of St Catharine's College

and John F. Richards
Professor of History, Duke University

Although the original *Cambridge History of India*, published between 1922 and 1937, did much to formulate a chronology for Indian history and describe the administrative structures of government in India, it has inevitably been overtaken by the mass of new research published over the last fifty years.

Designed to take full account of recent scholarship and changing conceptions of South Asia's historical development, *The New Cambridge History of India* will be published as a series of short, self-contained volumes, each dealing with a separate theme and written by a single person, within an overall four-part structure. As before, each will conclude with a substantial bibliographical essay designed to lead non-specialists further into the literature.

The four parts are as follows:

I The Mughals and their Contemporaries.

II Indian States and the Transition to Colonialism.

III The Indian Empire and the Beginnings of Modern Society.

IV The Evolution of Contemporary South Asia.

A list of individual titles already published and in preparation will be found at the end of the volume.

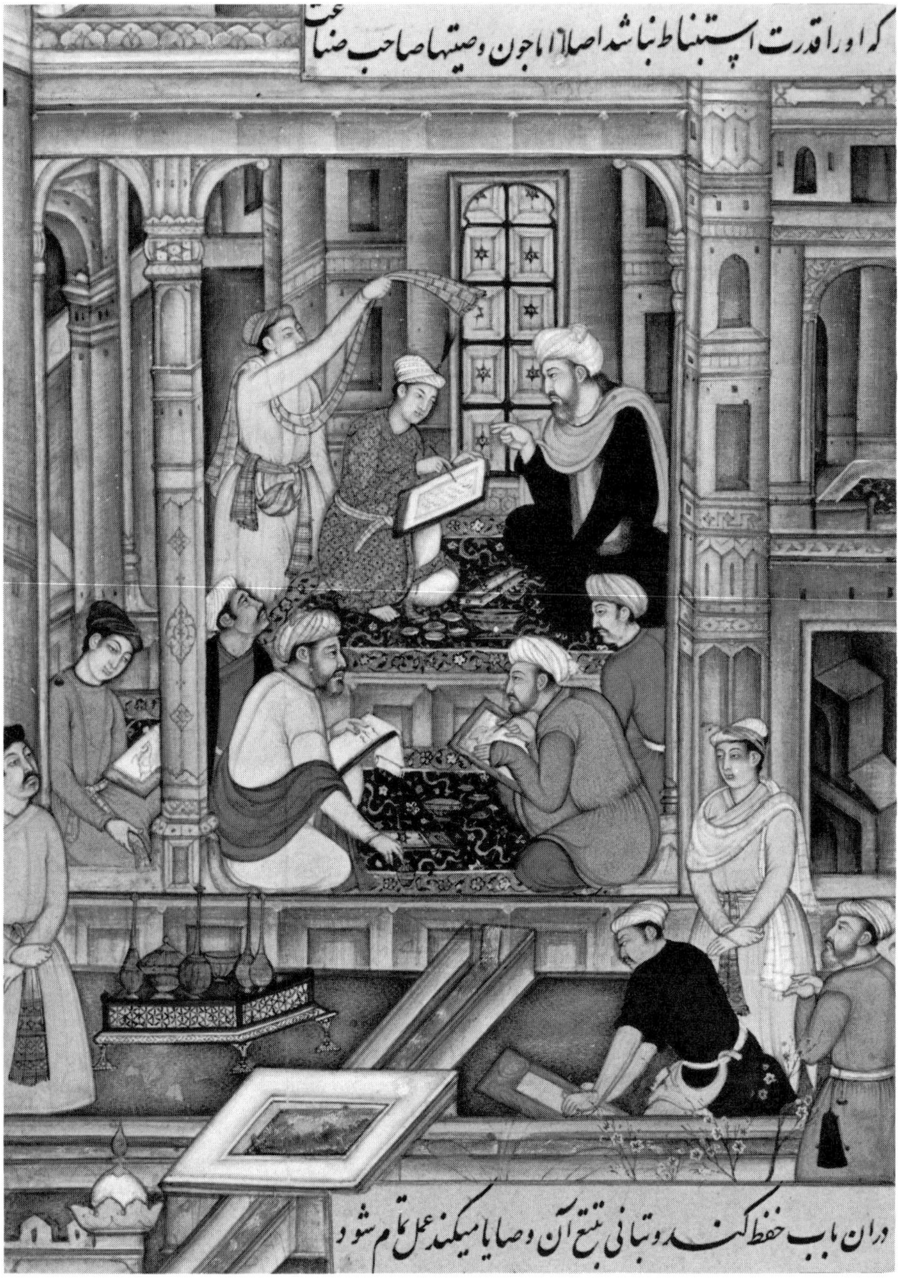

1. A Manuscript Atelier (detail). From an *Akhlaq-i-Nasiri* manuscript, Mughal, ca. 1590–1595

THE NEW CAMBRIDGE HISTORY OF INDIA

I : 3

Mughal and Rajput Painting

MILO CLEVELAND BEACH

DIRECTOR, FREER GALLERY OF ART AND ARTHUR M. SACKLER GALLERY,
SMITHSONIAN INSTITUTION, WASHINGTON DC

CAMBRIDGE
UNIVERSITY PRESS

PUBLISHED BY THE PRESS SYNDICATE OF THE UNIVERSITY OF CAMBRIDGE
The Pitt Building, Trumpington Street, Cambridge, United Kingdom

CAMBRIDGE UNIVERSITY PRESS
The Edinburgh Building, Cambridge CB2 2RU, UK http://www.cup.cam.ac.uk
40 West 20th Street, New York, NY 10011–4211, USA http://www.cup.org
10 Stamford Road, Oakleigh, Melbourne 3166, Australia
Ruiz de Alarcón 13, 28014 Madrid, Spain

First published 1992
Reprinted 2000

Printed in the United Kingdom at the University Press, Cambridge

A catalogue record for this book is available from the British Library

Library of Congress Cataloguing in Publication data
Beach, Milo Cleveland
Mughal and Rajput painting / Milo Cleveland Beach.
p. cm. – (The New Cambridge History of India)
Includes bibliographical references and index.
ISBN 0-521-40027-9
1. Painting, Mogul. 2. Painting, Islamic – India. 3. Rajput
painting. I. Title. II. Series.
DS436.N47 1987
[ND1002]
954 s – dc20 91–26573
[759.954] CIP

ISBN 0 521 40027 9 hardback

WD

CONTENTS

ILLUSTRATIONS

COLOR PLATES

Printing Defect

Due to a problem with the colour films, the colour plates in this book has been printed in Black and White only. The price therefore has been substantially reduced.

GENERAL EDITOR'S PREFACE

The New Cambridge History of India covers the period from the beginning of the sixteenth century. In some respects it marks a radical change in the style of Cambridge Histories, but in others the editors feel that they are working firmly within an established academic tradition.

During the summer of 1896, F. W. Maitland and Lord Acton between them evolved the idea for a comprehensive modern history. By the end of the year the Syndics of the University Press had committed themselves to the *Cambridge Modern History*, and Lord Acton had been put in charge of it. It was hoped that publication would begin in 1899 and be completed by 1904, but the first volume in fact came out in 1902 and the last in 1910, with additional volumes of tables and maps in 1911 and 1912.

The *History* was a great success, and it was followed by a whole series of distinctive Cambridge histories covering English Literature, the Ancient World, India, British Foreign Policy, Economic History, Medieval History, the British Empire, Africa, China and Latin America; and even now other new series are being prepared. Indeed, the various Histories have given the Press notable strength in the publication of general reference books in the arts and social sciences.

What has made the Cambridge Histories so distinctive is that they have never been simply dictionaries or encyclopedias. The Histories have, in H. A. L. Fisher's words, always been 'written by an army of specialists concentrating the latest results of special study'. Yet as Acton agreed with the Syndics in 1896, they have not been mere compilations of existing material but original works. Undoubtedly many of the Histories are uneven in quality, some have become out of date very rapidly, but their virtue has been that they have consistently done more than simply record an existing state of knowledge: they have tended to focus interest on research and they have provided a massive stimulus to further work. This has made their publication doubly worthwhile and has distinguished them intellectually from other sorts of reference book. The editors of the *New Cambridge History of India* have acknowledged this in their work.

The original *Cambridge History of India* was published between 1922 and 1937. It was planned in six volumes, but of these, volume 2 dealing with the period between the first century A.D. and the Muslim invasion of India never appeared. Some of the material is still of value, but in many respects it is now out of date. The last fifty years have seen a great deal of new research on India, and a striking feature of recent work has been to cast doubt on the validity of the quite arbitrary chronological and categorical way in which Indian history has been conventionally divided.

The editors decided that it would not be academically desirable to prepare a new *History of India* using the traditional format. The selective nature of research on Indian history over the past half-century would doom such a project from the start and the whole of India history could not be covered in an even or comprehensive manner. They concluded that the best scheme would be to have a *History* divided into four overlapping chronological volumes, each containing about eight short books on individual themes or subjects. Although in extent the work will therefore be equivalent to a dozen massive tomes of the traditional sort, in form the *New Cambridge History of India* will appear as a shelf full of separate but complementary parts. Accordingly, the main divisions are between I. *The Mughals and their Contemporaries*, II. *Indian States and the Transition to Colonialism*, III. *The Indian Empire and the Beginnings of Modern Society*, and IV. *The Evolution of Contemporary South Asia.*

Just as the books within these volumes are complementary so too do they intersect with each other, both thematically and chronologically. As the books appear they are intended to give a view of the subject as it now stands and to act as a stimulus to further research. We do not expect the *New Cambridge History of India* to be the last word on the subject but an essential voice in the continuing debate about it.

PREFACE

The majority of recent book-length studies of Indian painting have been exhibition catalogues, and the works discussed and illustrated have inevitably been examples of particular subjects or styles chosen for their distinctiveness. This study, in contrast, has more frequently decided to examine works that closely relate to other works. Its interest is not in singularity, but in interrelationships. Nor is the text encyclopedic; it cannot be, given its length. It seeks instead to provide a continuous narrative that can be expanded by additional, more specific readings cited in the bibliographic essay. The author is greatly indebted to all the scholars, volumes, and articles listed there, although he takes full responsibility for the text of this volume.

Two artistic systems are investigated in this study. The first concerns artists working for the Hindu Rajput rulers of north India, while the second centers on painters working for the Rajputs' overlords the Mughal emperors (who were Muslim). Of these, Mughal painting has been more frequently studied, and is the tradition better understood by European and American viewers. Mughal images reached Europe at least as early as Sir Thomas Roe's return to London in 1619, and four decades later they were copied and made known by Rembrandt. Mughal painting in turn was influenced in important ways by European art, and seems to use familiar and traditionally European visual techniques – figures are modelled with light and shade, for example, and space often seems (in some fashion) to recede. The central period, the century beginning about 1550, can also be discussed using the established methods of European art history. For example, the determination of dates for specific pictures and the arrangement of chronological sequences is important to the understanding of Mughal works, since changes in style show a consistent evolution and development of artistic thought. The identification and comparison of the distinctive styles of different artists is equally significant, for it reveals a respect for artistic individuality familiar to modern viewers.

Rajput works, the products of many different courts, are far more abundant than Mughal paintings in public and private collections in India and elsewhere. First introduced to Europe and America in 1923 through Ananda Coomaraswamy's great study *Rajput Painting*, these works have proved immensely popular but more difficult to discuss. The traditional Rajput patron seldom recognized the expressive contribution possible through an artist's personal style, and – as will be discussed in the text – styles seldom developed in meaningful linear sequences. Changes of style in Rajput paintings seem more often to be the result of circumstance than of conscious decision, and traditional European art historical methodologies have seldom produced meaningful information. It is then necessary to ask, of course, whether the European or American scholar's search for dates and attributions has skewed understanding of Mughal traditions by concentrating on those aspects most easily dealt with and discussed, albeit through the imposition of methodologies established for quite different works.

More than any single person, Stuart Cary Welch has inspired a generation of students, scholars, and collectors; in fact, many of the private collections that have been formed in America and Europe during the last three decades have been directly affected by his enthusiasm. The exhibitions he has assembled, and his published and unpublished studies of various aspects of the arts of India have provided a firm foundation for contemporary scholarship. This book is heavily indebted to his previous work, although he has nothing to do with its inadequacies. I am grateful also to Professor John Richards for his comments and support. His own scholarship continually sheds light on aspects of Indian paintings too frequently ignored by art historians.

INTRODUCTION

If the title *Mughal and Rajput Painting* suggests a simple historical tradition to be investigated through its year to year development, then it is misleading. The subject is, instead, a rich interweaving of varied and sometimes contradictory interests and traditions.

An initial unity is provided by format, for the earliest paintings to concern us were book illustrations. This means that the works were small (although books can, of course, vary dramatically in size), usually on paper, and closely linked to a literary narrative. The physical arrangement of volumes, however, evolved from two quite distinct sources: the cultural traditions that surrounded Hinduism and Islam. These were the major religious systems in India during the years included in this study, approximately 1500–1850. The earliest Hindu books, and related Buddhist and Jain volumes, were usually on pages made from leaves of the talipot palm; long and horizontal in format, the pages were pierced and threaded onto cords tied between wooden covers. The occasional illustrations were small and usually square. Islamic books, on the other hand, were on paper, bound along a spine, and often encased in leather covers. They were almost exclusively vertical, and were close to the shape of European books, except that they were read from right to left – the reverse of the European system. While paper became plentiful in India after about 1400, so entrenched were traditional attitudes that Hindu artists and craftsmen only slowly took advantage of the freedom that the new material allowed, to vary the size and shape from the severely restricted palm-leaf format. And even then the folios were seldom bound. Kept in stacks, the loose paper pages were wrapped in cloth and tied in bundles.

Hinduism was indigenous to India, whereas Islam arrived in the eighth century, growing to dominate the north politically by the thirteenth century. Muslims arrived on the subcontinent from throughout the Near East, bringing with them different cultural backgrounds and expectations, and an often militant antagonism to Hinduism. This was one reason why the existing mural tradition of painting in north India, public proclamations of Hindu identity, rapidly declined. Books were portable and easily hidden, however, and at a time when Hindu temples were being attacked and razed, manuscripts served as hideable repositories of doctrine and imagery for the worshipper. As the Hindu–Muslim relationship became more complicated and subtle, the Muslim love of books, especially elaborately illustrated books, inspired Hindu patrons and artists to be more inventive. When the patrons of either group were particularly eager or sensitive, this could include borrowing from the distinctive styles evolved within each other's cultures. Muslim and Hindu artistic ideals, after all, were very different.

The works we will discuss here are almost totally confined to court patronage. While folk and village traditions existed, such works were seldom saved or "collected," and little material earlier than the nineteenth century remains today. We are also excluding significant reference to the magnificent earlier tradition of Buddhist, Hindu, and Jain wall-painting, of which the caves at Ajanta provide the most profuse and brilliant examples (fig. 2). While these relate to book illustrations, they should properly be studied separately, along with the architecture that they decorated.

The most important artistically active Muslim dynasty was that of the Mughals, who ruled from 1526 to 1858 and almost unified the subcontinent. The name is a variation of Mongol and, between 1555 and about 1630 especially, Mughal patronage of the arts was incessant and radically innovative for the Indian context. The Mughals also profoundly altered the character of painting in the Hindu areas of north India. These initially independent territories were ruled by Rajputs, Hindus of the warrior caste, and this name is given to the second of the major artistic complexes that we will discuss. Whereas Mughal painting is defined by the styles and subjects popular at the imperial court, Rajput painting consists of many different court styles, corresponding to the various Hindu kingdoms, each with different tastes and aspirations. Geographically, too, Rajput painting is more scattered. The imperial court centered on Delhi or the Agra area, with a brief interlude in Lahore, whereas the Rajput kingdoms were found throughout Rajasthan, the Punjab Hills, and Central India. Each of these areas forms a separate subdivision of Rajput painting, which can then be further divided into individual states and, later, even into baronial holdings within these states. It is complicated, but while the complexities will be noted, a full definition and study is hardly appropriate here.

Rajput and Mughal, then, can be equated with Hindu and Muslim, or even with indigenous and foreign: and the study of these paintings allows us to see how two quite different cultural systems react to the same visual stimulus – to India – as well as to each other. Other complexes are referred to briefly, but only for comparative purposes. The kingdoms of the Deccan, south of the Mughal heartland, for example, were Muslim, but not Mughal; and they combine traditional Islamic attitudes, receptivity to Hindu India, and awareness of Mughal taste into yet another distinctive type of painting, which in turn influenced both Mughal and Rajput artists. Other regional artistic styles existed throughout the subcontinent, each with its own balance between local characteristics and awareness of pan-Indian traits. Gujarat, Orissa, and Bengal provided particularly important centers. And as if this were not enough, we must deal separately, and at the beginning, with types of book-painting in India preceding the Mughal arrival. This too will provide comparative material against which the achievements of Mughal and Rajput artists can be judged.

CHAPTER 1

PAINTING IN NORTH INDIA BEFORE 1540

At the beginning of the sixteenth century, painters in India were already heirs to an unbroken artistic tradition of great antiquity and extraordinary brilliance. Hindu, Buddhist, and Jain religious sanctuaries had long been decorated with carved and painted figures, and these were often accompanied by illustrative wall murals and ornamental designs. The libraries and treasuries of these temples usually housed religious manuscripts; often illustrated and decoratively embellished, these books preserved religious teachings for the use of devotees. As early as the fifth century, the *Kama Sutra* had mentioned that painting was an established and expected social accomplishment,[1] and contemporary paintings at the Buddhist site of Ajanta are among the most sensuous and sophisticated visual images known from any source (fig. 2). Even today, both unpretentious village houses and royal palaces are decorated with paintings on ceremonial occasions, a longstanding practice, while village storytellers continue to perform in front of narrative scrolls painted in traditional style. Painting, therefore, was never an exclusive or elitist activity, nor one limited to a particular social or religious community.

The majority of the paintings from Ajanta evoke that sense of three-dimensional volume that is so distinctive of Indian sculpture. By the sixteenth century, however, the wall-paintings at such shrine sites as Lepakshi (near Vijayanagar) were instead most expressive through two-dimensional surface design (fig. 3). This was due in part to the relative decline of the sculptural tradition in India, as well as to greater specialization among artists – painters no longer felt obliged to create sculptural effects. The Indian climate has not been kind to wall-paintings, however, so the vast majority of the paintings remaining to us today were made to illustrate books, even though books too were a fragile medium. With the acceptance of paper and its greater flexibility of format, the potential, even the need, for compositional innovation was increased. Changes, however, were achieved slowly. For centuries, the painters of Jain manuscripts on paper placed decorative circles on still horizontal pages to approximate the threading holes once necessary for palm-leaves (plate A).

A second important stimulus to innovation in this later period was the

[1] *The Kama Sutra of Vatsyayana*, translated by Sir Richard Burton and F. F. Arbuthnot, New York, 1966, p. 75.

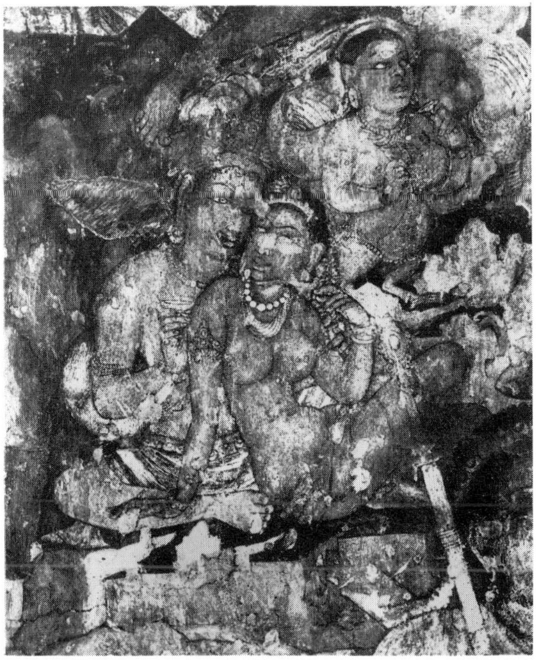

2. Lovers. Wall-painting from Ajanta (Cave no. 1), ca. 475

patronage provided by the Muslim rulers who came into north India after the late eleventh century. Indigenous Indian religious communities had been highly conservative in their artistic attitudes, often encouraging painters to repeat faithfully illustrations and compositions as familiar and unalterable as the texts to which they related. The Muslims, however, were interested in illustrated copies of Persian texts, and in styles of painting that recalled their homelands. They therefore commissioned – sometimes from these same painters – illustrated volumes of texts unfamiliar to the artists, thereby forcing them to abandon their familiar formulas. Moreover, these rulers provided a new class and type of patronage. Painting was a court art for the Muslims; and being created for a class conscious of its superiority, books became a prestigious emblem of wealth and power. Muslim patrons often demanded opulence of materials (papers and pigments), fine craftsmanship, and continual stylistic and narrative novelty, for painting was also a form of personal entertainment. We have no evidence that Hindu or Jain painters had earlier worked exclusively for particular or single patrons; this may not have been economically feasible. The Muslim rulers, however, formed *kitabkhanas* (library workshops) within their palaces, and artists and artisans often worked exclusively for specific employers. (A sixteenth-century Mughal *kitabkhana* is depicted in fig. 1, and a Persian example is shown in fig. 8.) Thus they painted to please a single person, rather than to reflect the general needs of a community, and this demanded sensitivity and responsiveness to a patron's individual and often highly idiosyncratic taste. The interplay of these differing attitudes towards patronage continues throughout subsequent developments. It is of major importance for any understanding of the varying traditions in India.

The artistic style developed by one specific Muslim dynasty, the Mughals, eventually came to dominate, even if briefly, the arts of north India. It drew from and unified earlier, highly diversified, local traditions. These local types of painting are most usefully termed "pre-Mughal," and can be divided into three basic categories: Hindu, Jain, and Muslim – the Mughals were the most important, but not the first of the Muslim dynasties in India – and particular stylistic traits are associated with each of these culturally distinct communities. This factor can be as important to the style of the works as geographic provenance. Jain paintings made at different times and places may have more in common with one another, for example, than with illustrations to Muslim and Hindu texts made contemporaneously in the same city. Furthermore, styles indigenous to India, but of differing cultural affiliation, share traits not found in the early, imported Muslim traditions of the subcontinent.

Pre-Mughal Hindu painting is best represented by a series of *Bhagavata Purana* illustrations datable to about 1540. The text is among the most popular of all Hindu works, and this specific copy can be compared eventually to other versions of the same text from different provenances and periods. The narrative recounts the adventurous career of the god Vishnu. The most popular episodes, however, relate to his incarnation of Krishna, seen first as a mischievous child, then as an amorous youth, and finally as an ideal princely ruler.

Illustrations in this sixteenth-century series relate to specific passages of the story, but several sequential episodes are often combined as one illustration: *Krishna Defeats the Demon Whirlwind* (plate B) is an example. In an especially dynamic composition, Krishna is shown both in the whirlwind's power and returning to his mother after defeating the demonic force. The architecture, tree, and figures are placed in compartmentalized units, bordered by solid lines and filled with unmodulated, flat planes of strong color. (These background areas are as positive and strong in shape as the figures of the narrative.) There is no attempt at a three-dimensional space, and there is nothing extraneous to the defining elements of the narrative. All figures are in profile. They are strong, angular shapes whose gestures (important to the story) are emphasized and easily read, and each figure is constructed according to the same formula. We are dealing with types, not individualized depictions, and the execution is rough. The artist is indifferent to technical expertise or the subtlety and variety of colors. And while we are presented with multiple moments or aspects of the event, the successive episodes are not in a visually linear sequence. The Hindu

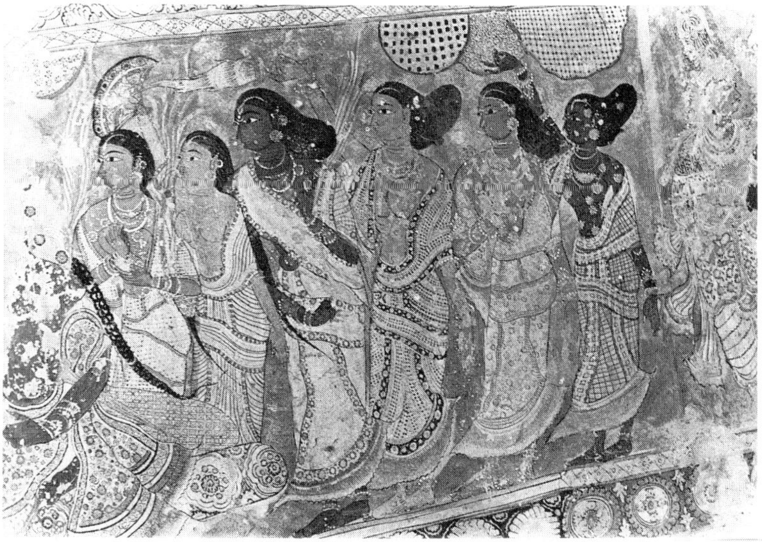

3. A Group of Women. Wall-painting from Lepakshi, ca. 1540

artist is not attempting to make the moment seem unique, nor to separate and distinguish individual forms in an empty space.

A second series of illustrations has given its name to this broad stylistic category of pre-Mughal Hindu painting in art-historical writings, however; it was the first of this group of works to be discovered, and it remains the most often discussed. The *Chaurapanchasika* (Fantasies of a Love Thief) (fig. 4) is an illustrated volume of erotic verses, and can be dated to about 1550. The text, by Bilhana, was written in the eleventh century, and while it has no overt religious meaning, neither is it purely secular. The page reproduced here illustrates the following verse: "At this moment of my death, nay, even in my next birth, I shall ever remember that swan in the cluster of lotuses of love, with her eyes closed in the ecstacy of love, all her limbs relaxed, while her garments and the tresses of her hair were strewn in disorder."[2]

In this scene, too, the visual elements do not stress a single or unique moment in time. They celebrate instead an amorous situation, and not even in the most dramatic way possible. Space is used metaphorically, not to provide a convincing physical setting. The lotus leaves that outline the architecture emphasize and intensify the beauty and fertility of the heroine, whose enormous breasts, tiny waist, and ample hips perfectly accord with traditional Indian ideals of physical beauty. The scene is spatially flat, but we are nonetheless aware – as

[2] Leela Shiveshwarkar, *The Pictures of the Chaurapanchasika – A Sanskrit Love Lyric*, New Delhi, 1967, p. 26.

we are in the murals from Ajanta (fig. 2) – that the figures have substantial volume.

The geographic origin of the style represented by these two sets is highly disputed, but information given in the colophon of a manuscript closely related in style to the *Bhagavata Purana* is important. The *Aranyaka Parvan* (Forest Book) is one section of the great Sanskrit epic *Mahabharata*. In a copy dated 1516 and made near Agra, the inscription names the patron who commissioned the work as "Bhanadasa Chaudhuri of Chandrapuri."[3] While not otherwise known, his name indicates that he was the headman or foreman of a *pargana* or other small administrative unit or market area. It seems, therefore, that the general *Chaurapanchasika* style was not necessarily or exclusively royal in origin or execution. However, while the *Bhagavata Purana* is very close in style and conception to the *Aranyaka Parvan*, the *Chaurapanchasika* seems to be from a different (if related) workshop. Many of its pages are far more sophisticated – even self-conscious – in style than the *Aranyaka Parvan* or the *Bhagavata Purana*, and lack the roughness and resulting power of those sets. Here again we do not have enough information to know whether these differences are due to historical development, to a difference of provenance, or to variations in the level and type of patronage. (These are essential questions to keep in mind for comparisons made throughout this study.) It is the *Bhagavata Purana*, rather than the *Chaurapanchasika*, however, that was eventually most influential at the Mughal court.

A second localized stylistic category is usually termed Jain, or Western Indian. While Gujarat (on the west coast, north of Bombay) is the major center of production, the style is in fact geographically far more wide-ranging. The texts illustrated usually relate to Jainism, a religion that grew up in India contemporaneously with Buddhism. However, a few illustrated manuscripts to Hindu texts in this style are also known.[4]

The Siege of Ujjain and the Magic She-Ass comes from a Jain *Kalpasutra* and *Kalakacharyakatha* (Scripture of Right Conduct and Story of Kalaka) manuscript, dated 1411 (plate A). The narrative relates a tale in which the heroic Kalaka defeats the evil King of Ujjain, whose power resides in a mechanical donkey placed on the walls of his fortress; the donkey's brays force any enemy to fall to the ground vomiting blood. Kalaka's troops, however, fill the donkey's mouth with arrows before it can make any noise, and thereby defeat its master.

As in the *Chaurapanchasika* style (fig. 4), colors are very limited and applied in flat, clearly bounded areas; profiles, postures, and gestures are sharp and

[3] Karl Khandalavala and Moti Chandra, *An Illustrated* Aranyaka Parvan *in the Asiatic Society of Bombay*, Bombay, 1974, p. 24.

[4] See W. Norman Brown, *Vasanta Vilasa*, New Haven, 1962, for a manuscript dated 1451–1452.

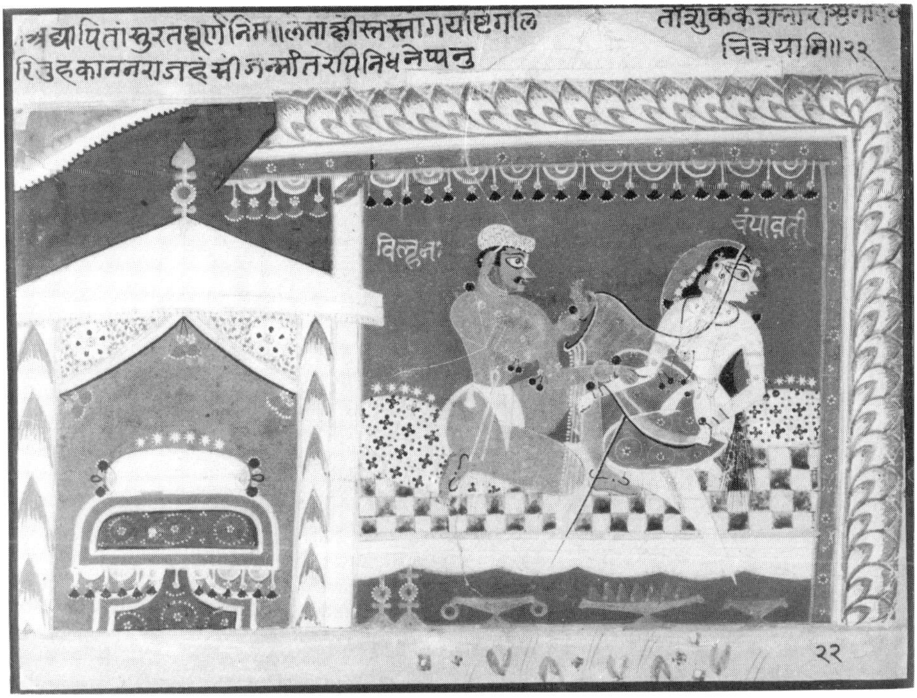

4. Bilhana Makes Love with Champavati. From a *Chaurapanchasika* series, ca. 1550

angular; and compositions are broken down into small compartments with strongly colored flat backgrounds. These can be taken as general characteristics of indigenous Indian painting styles of the time, however, for the *Chaura-panchasika* style could be described with the same terms. Distinctive traits of Western Indian painting include the wiry, and at its best extremely vital, line drawing; compositions and colors far less robust and energetic than those of the *Chaurapanchasika*; and the very repetitive character of the scenes in many manuscripts.

There is only modest variety in the choice of texts illustrated within the Jain tradition. Copies of the *Kalpasutra* and *Kalakacharyakatha* were commissioned most often, especially by wealthy merchants wishing propitious gifts for temple presentation. Few of these reveal any distinctive character. In addition to the 1411 *Kalpasutra* and *Kalakacharyakatha* (plate A), important exceptions are a *Kalpasutra*, dated 1439, from Mandu – illustrated in a style very close to that of the 1411 manuscript – and a *Kalpasutra* copied and illustrated at Jaunpur (Uttar Pradesh) in 1465. (See the Appendix for further references for all dated manuscripts mentioned here.) Within the context of Western Indian painting as traditionally understood, these three volumes are uncommonly lively and vital in effect. This is due less to compositional inventiveness, however, than to the enthusiasm, talent, and freshness with which an established style and compositional format were executed. That painters were nonetheless familiar with other styles is proven by the figures of West Asians demanded by the narrative illustrated in plate A. In the battle shown, Kalaka has been joined by an army of West Asians or Scythians (*sahis*). These foreign men are depicted with the three-quarter profile and formulaic facial features common in Persian painting (see fig. 6). Jain painters were therefore sufficiently aware of other styles to draw upon such sources when useful to the narrative. However, this did not necessarily lead to the development of new attitudes to pictorial space or compositional format.

While Jain or Western Indian painting generally kept its distance from Muslim styles, recent important research by Dr. Saryu Doshi has transformed understanding of the overall character of painting for Jain patrons.[5] By gaining access to Jain temple repositories (*bhandars*), Dr. Doshi has extended awareness of the range of stylistic variation that did in fact exist, especially for copies of manuscripts less central to the faith than the *Kalpasutra* or *Kalakacharyakatha*. Manuscripts dated 1441, 1454, 1540, 1596, and 1606 show a slow but inevitable interplay of traditional Jain and pre-Mughal Hindu styles. Just as Jain and Hindu temple sculpture was often stylistically interrelated so Jain and Hindu paintings in some areas were also inextricably intertwined.

Western Indian painting – and thus the Mandu *Kalpasutra* – is not to be considered a court art. Mandu was the capital of an important sultanate (or pre-Mughal Muslim kingdom) in the area of Central India called Malwa, however, and a contemporary Muslim court art did exist there. Its character, very different from the Western Indian style, allows us to discuss the third pre-Mughal category: sultanate painting.

The most important royal manuscript from Mandu is the *Niʿmatnama* (Book of Recipes) (figs. 5 and 7), an illustrated collection of recipes begun for Sultan Ghiyath ad-Din Khalji (r. 1469–1501) and finished by his son Nasir ad-Din (r. 1501–1512). The Sultan was one of the most eccentric rulers in India, his court the perfect model for an Arabian Nights fantasy. Khwaja Nizamuddin Ahmad, a sixteenth century historian, allows us to glimpse the social milieu within which the work was created. He wrote of the events following Ghiyath ad-Din's accession to the throne:

> When he had finished the festivities and rites of the accession, he sent for the amirs one day, and said, "As I have spent 34 years at the stirrups of my father in labours and expedition, it now comes to my mind, that I should endeavour to guard what has come to me from my father, and should not give myself the trouble to acquire more; and should open the door to peace and rest, and pleasure and enjoyment on me, and those depending on me. It is better to keep

[5] *Masterpieces of Jain Painting*, edited by Saryu Doshi, Bombay, 1985.

> the territories in peace and quiet, than to strike one's hand on those of others." He commenced to endeavour to collect musicians; and they came to his threshold from all directions. He filled his seraglio with beautiful slave girls and daughters of Rajas and zamindars; and in this matter made very great exertions. He taught an art and a profession to each of the beautiful girls; and taking their fitness into consideration, taught some the arts of dancing and singing; and others those of reading and recitation and playing on the flute; and a small number the art of wrestling. He had five hundred Abyssinian slave girls dressed in male attire . . . [and] five hundred Turki slave girls in Turki dress . . . He also established a market in his harem, so that whatever went to the market of the city for sale was also sold there. Altogether sixteen thousand slave girls were collected in his harem.[6]

In the paintings of the manuscript, Ghiyath ad-Din is surrounded by these harem ladies, many of them wearing male dress.

The style of the *Ni'matnama* illustrations derives in part from contemporary painting in Iran. *The Sultan Samples Milk Used for Pastry* (fig. 5), for example, is immediately comparable to *Abu'l Mihjan and Sa'd ibn abi Wakkas Before a Ruler* (fig. 6), from a Persian *Khavarnama* manuscript of about 1480. Both show a ruler, surrounded by courtiers, enthroned in a room decorated with tile patterns and architectural details, and both compositions are flat and densely patterned. The *Khavarnama*, however, is clear and spatially coherent, while the *Ni'matnama* is compositionally confused. The areas of pattern described in the Indian work seem almost arbitrarily placed on the surface, and the architectural niches are unrelated forms, like postage stamps glued at random to the surface. One aspect of the *Ni'matnama*, therefore, and an important one, is its provincialism; some pages seem simply naive continuations of Iranian style, probably by Indian artists who did not fully understand the Iranian visual conventions they were directed to adopt.

Other *Ni'matnama* folios present a far more important combination of Iranian and Indian stylistic traits, and seem to predict the artistic character of early Mughal manuscripts. They also provide a model against which to judge the originality of Mughal attempts to synthesize these same pre-existing traditions. The composite stylistic nature of the manuscript overall can be easily seen in the use of both Iranian and Hindu figure types, which are quite distinct. In *Gruel for the Sultan* (fig. 7), the three-quarter profiles and flowing lines popular in Iran (fig. 6) combine with the dark-skinned, angular, and strongly gesturing full profile forms of the Hindu tradition (plate B). The *Ni'matnama*, like the *Kalpasutra* and *Kalakacharyakatha* (plate A), uses different figure types when narratively appropriate; the profile figures in the *Ni'matnama* are presumably Indian attendants. Nonetheless, the presence and

[6] Khwajah Nizamuddin Ahmad, *Tabaqat-i-Akbari*, translated and annotated by Brajendranath De, Calcutta, 1939, pp. 544–545.

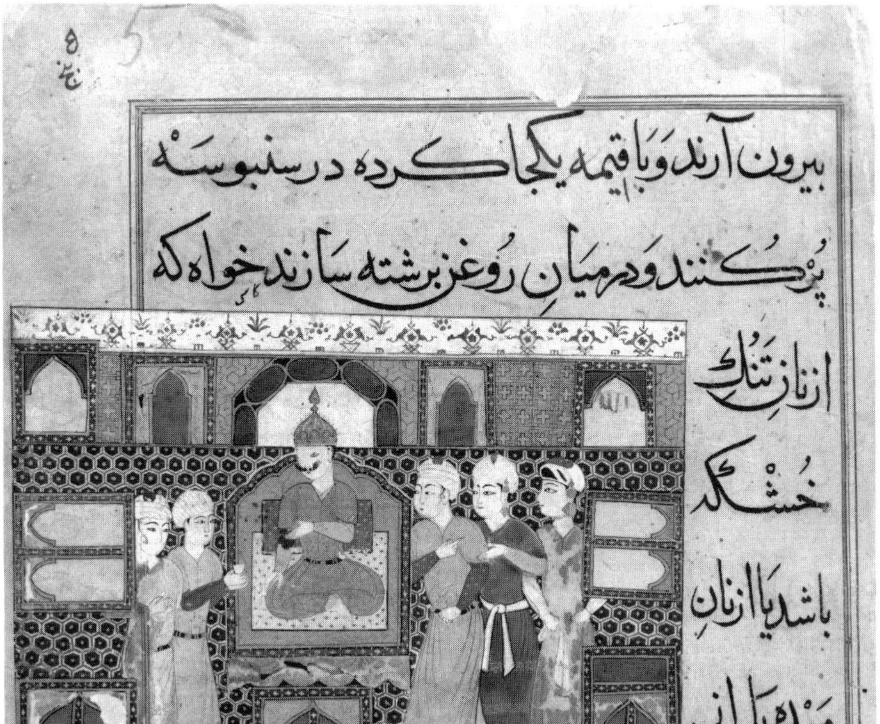

5. The Sultan Samples Milk Used for Pastry. From a *Niʿmatnama* manuscript, Sultanate, Mandu, ca. 1500–1505

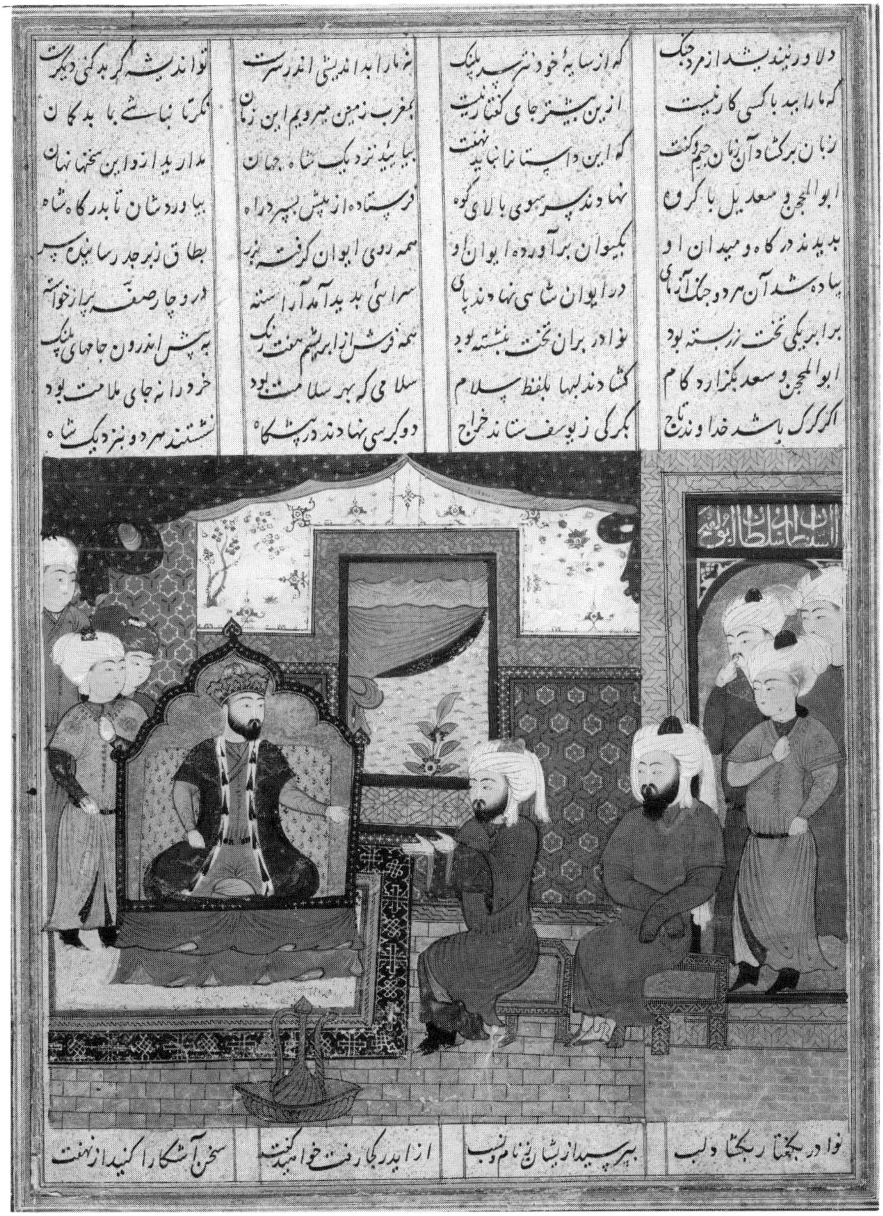

6. Abu'l Mihjan and Sa'd ibn abi Wakkas Before a Ruler. From a *Khavarnama* manuscript, Iran, probably at Shiraz, ca. 1480

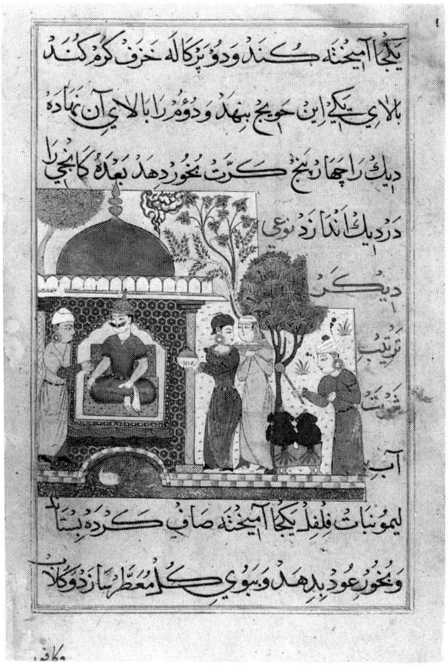

7. Gruel for the Sultan. From a *Ni'matnama* manuscript, Sultanate, Mandu, ca. 1500–1505

rich mixture at Mandu of these three styles, each associated with a particular cultural community, failed to produce any influential new style or attitude. The best *Ni'matnama* illustrations are, however, extremely animated, both visually and narratively. As character types, the mustachioed sultan and his harem ladies are among the liveliest figures in Indian painting.

CHAPTER 2

1540–1580: PAINTING AT MUSLIM COURTS

> The king undressed, and ordered his clothes to be washed, and in the meanwhile he wore his dressing gown; while thus sitting, a beautiful bird flew into the tent, the doors of which were immediately closed, and the bird caught; his Majesty then took a pair of scissors and cut some of the feathers off the animal; he then sent for a painter, and had a picture taken of the bird, and afterwards ordered it to be released.[1]

Jauhar, a private servant of the Mughal Emperor Humayun (r. 1530–1540; 1555–1556) made these observations while describing a moment during Humayun's flight from the Indian subcontinent. In 1540, a brilliant and able Afghan, Sher Shah, seized control of the kingdom in India established by Humayun's father Babur in 1526, and Humayun was ousted from power. That a painter was among the few people who accompanied him into exile certainly indicates the importance of painting at his court; while information that the artist was asked to observe and record aspects of the natural world allies Mughal painting to the innovative, if more fanciful, documentary interests of such works as the *Niʿmatnama*. However, painting as precise record of specific events, personalities, or objects is not known among the pre-Mughal Indian traditions we have discussed.

Humayun's retreat from India was slow. In 1542, he was in the deserts of Sind (now within Pakistan) where his fifteen-year-old empress Hamida Banu Begam gave birth to a son. This child, the future Emperor Akbar, was then left with guardians and attendants while Humayun continued to the court of the Safavid Shah Tahmasp of Iran to ask help in regaining his territories. Successful, and wildly impressed by the splendor of the court he had visited, Humayun returned east with military reinforcements. He captured Kabul (presently the capital of Afghanistan) after a series of battles with his brother Kamran, who had taken advantage of Humayun's misfortunes to proclaim his own independence and power. Humayun then used Kabul as a base for his campaign to return to India. An aesthete and voluptuary, he enjoyed himself there, creating gardens and pavilions, writing poetry, studying astrology, and drinking. It was only after ten years, in fact, that he descended through the passes of Hindu Kush and reclaimed his patrimony.

While at the Iranian court, Humayun hired several artists and craftsmen.

[1] Jauhar, *Tezkereh al Vakiat*, translated by Charles Stewart, New Delhi, 1970 (reprint), p. 43.

Shah Tahmasp had been among the very greatest of all Iranian connoisseurs and patrons of painting and book illustration, and his discussions with Humayun were held in rooms newly decorated with wall-paintings. He was becoming increasingly orthodox, however, and strict Muslims had long looked on image-making as a blasphemous attempt to usurp the creative powers of God. Many of Tahmasp's artists were thus seeking work elsewhere. The painters Mir Sayyid Ali and Abd as-Samad joined Humayun in Kabul in 1550, followed soon by Mir Musavvir and Dust Muhammad. The illustrations that these men made there are among the earliest identifiably imperial Mughal paintings. They, of course, brought knowledge of the latest Iranian artistic techniques and styles to Humayun's court, and as former members of the Shah's entourage, their acceptance of the Mughal's patronage must have seemed fitting acknowledgment to Humayun of his own (albeit temporarily suspended) imperial rank. We cannot be sure how novel the style practiced by the Iranian painters was in its new setting, however, because we do not yet know the style of the artist mentioned by Jauhar; but the quality of workmanship that they represented must certainly have exceeded what was then otherwise available to Humayun. Following this visit to Iran, Mughal court painting was dominated by the accepted artistic standards of the Iranian court.

A painting attributed to Mir Sayyid Ali in the years before he entered Humayun's employ serves both to define some aspects of what we will continually refer to as Iranian taste, and to give information about the organization of the imperial studios. *School Scene* (fig. 8) describes, with vivid attention to detail, activities at a gathering of apprentices in a manuscript workshop. Craftsmen are preparing dyes at the bottom of the scene, for example, and then coloring paper and hanging it on a line to dry. Above, to the right, one youth is being punished, while his comrades burnish paper, practice calligraphy, and recite. To the left, cooks prepare noodles for a meal.

As a narrative, *School Scene* should also be seen in conjunction with *A Manuscript Atelier* (fig. 1), a later Mughal work which also documents a workshop of painters; together they give important information about the organization of the imperial studios. In each scene, the preparation of manuscripts – the polishing of paper, the writing of calligraphy, the grinding and mixing of pigments, and the painting of illuminations and illustrations – is a communal activity under the supervision of a senior master. Because the physical materials were expensive, it is not surprising that artists worked for wealthy patrons rather than independently, and in both scenes mentioned the setting is a palace building. The apprenticeship system was usual, and in both the Persian and Mughal worlds sons frequently continued their father's occupation – Mir Sayyid Ali was himself the son of Mir Musavvir.

In *School Scene* especially, the painter's attention to descriptive detail extends far beyond narrative necessity. In niches at the workshop entrance, for

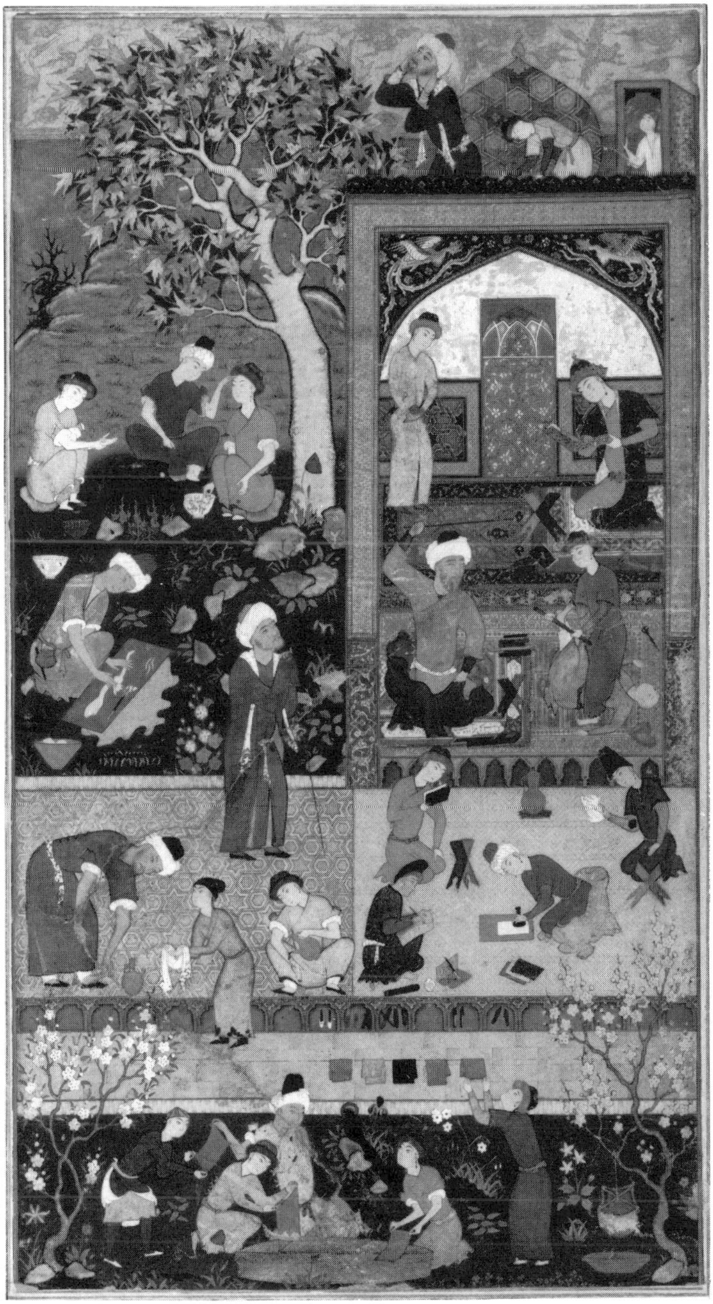

8. School Scene. Attributed to Mir Sayyid Ali; Iran, probably at Tabriz, ca. 1540

example, shoes are neatly lined up, and the architectural tilework is an exact representation of decorative patterns of the period. This is a *tour de force* of miniaturistic technique and careful observation, presented in such a way that no single detail or episode dominates. Visual interest is evenly distributed over the entire surface of the work, and only slowly does the painting reveal its power. This style will be continually evoked in comparison when defining the new character of Mughal painting.

We know now that Humayun and Kamran both employed artists, and books belonging to Hamida Banu Begam, Akbar's mother, have also survived. Babur must certainly have patronized artists too, although no direct visual or literary evidence for this has yet been found. A library was expected of any ruling Muslim household, and rather than simple repositories these often served as book-making centers as well, with resident staffs of paper-makers, calligraphers, illuminators, gilders, illustrators, and binders. Books were frequently presented or exchanged on ceremonial occasions, and they formed a desirable part of the spoils of war. In his lively and very informative memoirs, the *Baburnama* (History of Babur), the emperor himself described an episode in his victorious battle against Sultan Ibrahim Lodi of Delhi in 1526: "After spending two nights on the rise, I inspected the fort. I went into Ghazi Khan's book-room; some of the precious things found in it, I gave to Humayun, some sent to Kamran . . . There were many books of learned contents."[2] Books, being both scarce and items of luxury, were seen as evidence of wealth and power, especially when elaborately decorated or illustrated. They also fulfilled more personal tastes, and an even more convincing reason to assume that Babur patronized painters is his own visual sensitivity and love of close observation. This is shown throughout the *Baburnama* text, which not only chronicles the major events in his life, but quite frankly reveals more individual enthusiasms and reactions. Most interesting among these for us here are the careful and exact descriptions of flora and fauna he encountered, verbal precedents for the visual record of the intrusive bird ordered by Humayun in 1542. Babur describes a peacock, for example, as follows:

> The peacock is . . . a beautifully coloured and splendid animal . . . Its form is not equal to its colouring and beauty. Its body may be as large as a crane's but it is not so tall. On the head of both cock and hen are 20 to 30 feathers rising some 2 or 3 inches high. The hen has neither colour nor beauty. The head of the cock has an iridescent collar; its neck is of a beautiful blue; below the neck, its back is painted in yellow, parrot-green, blue and violet colours . . . [3]

[2] Zahir'd-din Muhammad Babur Padshah Ghazi, *Babur-nama*, translated by A. S. Beveridge, London, 1922, p. 460.

[3] Babur, *Babur-nama*, p. 493.

Among the earliest known books attributable to a Mughal patron is the Fitzwilliam Album, a scrapbook of paintings and calligraphies, one of which is inscribed as having been written "in Kabul, the capital of the empire," and dated H 953/1546–1547.[4] (In that year, Kabul was Humayun's interim capital.) Accounts of Humayun's reign describe the elaborate decoration of the palace and its gardens during the great Mystic Feast celebrated soon after that emperor's accession in 1530. Turkish and European cloths decorated the walls of rooms that were "the envy of Chinese picture galleries."[5] And further, "In the second room, called the House of Good Fortune, an oratory had been arranged, and books placed, and gilded pen-cases, and splendid portfolios, and entertaining picture-books [*muraqqa'*] written in beautiful character."[6] The Fitzwilliam Album (or *muraqqa'*) was therefore a well-accepted type of decorative volume.

Only a few pages separated from the original volume are now known, but they are important to understanding the early stages of Mughal patronage; they reveal varied stylistic sources. There are paintings by artists trained at Bokhara (now in the Republic of Uzbekistan), where Uzbeq rulers – rivals of the Mughals – continued to patronize styles typical of painting in Iran under the earlier rule of the Timurid dynasty in the fifteenth century. (Painters at Bokhara must have been organized into commercial as well as court workshops; evidence of artistic mass-production there is profuse.) There are also adaptations – rather than copies – of familiar Bokharan compositions.[7]

In *A Young Prince Riding* (fig. 9), the figure is derived from a generic and ever-popular Persian compositional type, although the cap identifies the youth with Humayun's court. Inscriptions on the work are words of advice; across the book held by the rider, for example, it is written: 'May the world grant you success and the celestial sphere befriend you. May the world-creator protect and preserve you."[8] Given that it is a young prince in Humayun period headgear, it is almost inevitable that the figure should be understood as the young Akbar.

A Young Prince Riding derives its vigor from a roughness of execution quite different from the refinements of *School Scene* (fig. 8). *Cow and Calf* (fig. 10), also from the Fitzwilliam Album, presents even bolder and more innovative brushwork. The vegetation is drawn with a freedom unprecedented in the Islamic world; unlike in *School Scene*, we sense here the weight and texture of the pigment, and the artist's movements as he applied color to paper. (Some of

4 Milo Cleveland Beach, *Early Mughal Painting*, New York and London, 1987, fig. 33.

5 Khwandamir, *Qanun-i-Humayuni*, translated by B. Prasad, Calcutta, 1940, pp. 64–65.

6 Gulbadan Begam, *Humayun-nama*, translated by A. S. Beveridge, Delhi, 1972 (reprint), p. 124.

7 See Beach, *Early Mughal Painting*, pp. 37–48.

8 Across the top of the page it further states, "I'll give you some good advice. Listen and do not make excuses: Accept whatever a compassionate adviser tells you" (translated by Wheeler Thackston).

this spontaneity of execution is found too in *Krishna Defeats the Demon Whirlwind* [plate B], although this is the only page from that Hindu set painted in this manner. The interrelationship of these traditions needs further study.) Both the technique and the subject would appear to result from direct observation of the natural world were the central animal motif not based on a very familiar Hindu compositional formula (fig. 11), and did the technique not correspond so closely to German works of the early sixteenth century of a type known to have circulated at the Mughal court. The seemingly novel elements present in the album thus arise from new combinations of motifs from distinct traditions, and it is clear that painters were allowed to experiment.

The most important page in the Fitzwilliam Album is *Prince Akbar Hunting a Nilgae* (fig. 12). It must be an exact depiction of an event which occurred on July 20, 1555, as Humayun returned to Delhi following his exile:

> His Majesty [Humayun] . . . alighted at Salimgarh which is on the north of Delhi and on the bank of the Jamuna . . . On this day and while on the march His Majesty the Shahinshah [Prince Akbar] struck a nilagao [an antelope] with his sword and took it as prey . . . His Majesty Jahanbani [Humayun] who . . . had given up the eating of animals now turned his thoughts towards the making of a beginning [of eating flesh]. On this day he rejoiced exceedingly and ordered that a piece of the nilagao be dried and kept in order that when . . . he should be disposed to eat animal food, he might make his first meal from this flesh. He then returned thanks to god.[9]

The narrative details of the scene, the Humayun period turban on the young princely hunter, the distant fortress, and the nearby river all correspond to the event as described in the verbal passage. This is therefore a documentary image of an historical subject, and there is no reason to doubt that it was painted at the time of the hunt. Mughal historical painting, with its profusion of specific details and lively interplay of actions and personalities, was therefore initiated by the time of Humayun's rule, no surprise when the emperor was already commissioning visual records of interesting fauna.

However, the Fitzwilliam Album is not the only work known from Humayun's reign. Several paintings signed by or attributable to Abd as-Samad during these years have survived, as has a major depiction of the emperor attributed to Dust Muhammad.[10] Important recent research by James L. Wescoat has revealed that this latter scene depicts a specific historical event, further confirming Humayun's interest in documentary illustrations.[11] Such

[9] Abu'l Fazl Allami, *Akbar Nama*, translated by H. Beveridge, Delhi, 1971–1972 (reprint), vol. II, p. 634.

[10] See Stuart Cary Welch, *India – Art and Culture 1300–1900*, New York, 1985, no. 85, although the picture is reproduced in reverse.

[11] James L. Wescoat, "Gardens of invention and exile: the precarious context of Mughal garden design during the reign of Humayun (1530–1556)," *Journal of Garden History*, vol. 10, no. 2, pp. 106–117.

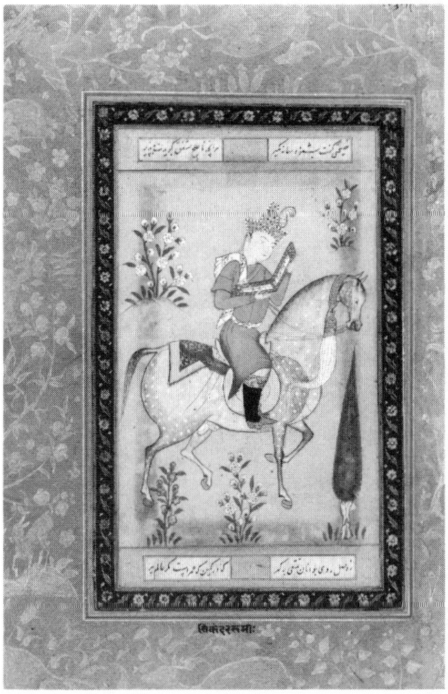

9. A Young Prince Riding. From the Fitzwilliam Album, Mughal, ca. 1555

works introduced a fully imperial Persian style into the Mughal ateliers, and this expanded the artistic aspirations of some of those painters already in Humayun's employ.

A few months after he regained Delhi, his legs enfeebled by alcohol and opium addiction, Humayun fell down the steep stairs of his library and died. Akbar, therefore, was only thirteen when he came to the throne. He had had no practical experience of ruling, and the power he inherited was more potential than actual; there had been little time for Humayun to consolidate or expand his control. It was due to Akbar's personal energy and intelligence, therefore, that the Mughal empire so quickly became the most powerful kingdom in India's history.

Along with the other trappings of kingship, Akbar inherited the artistic workshops that his father had established. The earliest manuscript that can be attributed to his reign is a *Tutinama* (Tales of a Parrot) (figs. 13, 14, and 29). It is an anthology of short stories, ostensibly told by a parrot to its mistress on each of 52 successive nights. By continually catching her interest with a new and intriguing tale, he prevents her departure to meet with a lover during her husband's absence. It is best read as sheer entertainment.

Like the Fitzwilliam Album, the *Tutinama* illustrations lack stylistic unity – which is not to say that the volume does not have a distinctive character. Many

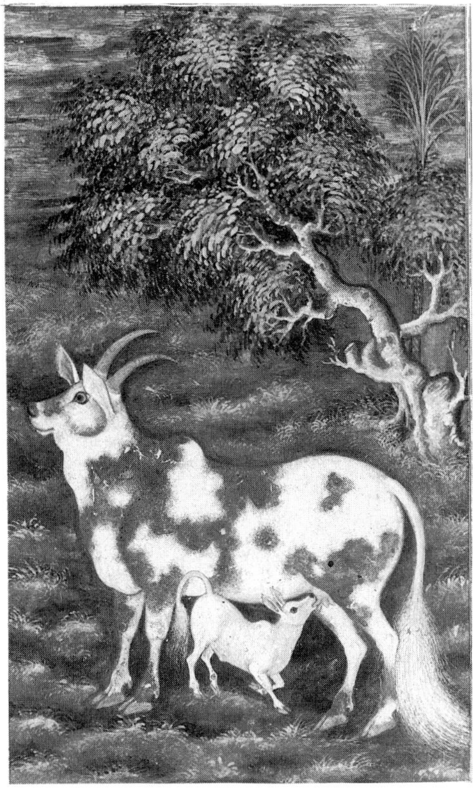

10. Cow and Calf. From the Fitzwilliam Album, Mughal, ca. 1555–1560

of its pages are virtually unaltered examples of a variety of local Indian styles, while others are comparable to the new and distinctive style shown in *Prince Akbar Hunting a Nilgae*. For example, *The Merchant's Daughter with Her Companions Meets the Gardener* (fig. 13), with its strong colors, flatly silhouetted figures, angular gestures and profiles, composition arranged in horizontal bands, and clear presentation of narrative, is closely related to the pre-Mughal Hindu tradition of *Krishna Defeats the Demon Whirlwind* (plate B). The slightly softer outlines and more organic proportions of the female figures in the *Tutinama* show that the earlier style is being adjusted to a new taste, a development equally clear when comparing the trees in the *Bhagavata Purana* (plate B), the *Tutinama* (fig. 13), and an *Anwar-i-Suhaili* manuscript of 1571 (fig. 19) to be discussed further below.

The Devotee's Daughter Restored to Life (fig. 14), also from the *Tutinama*, seems to have nothing in common stylistically with *The Merchant's Daughter*

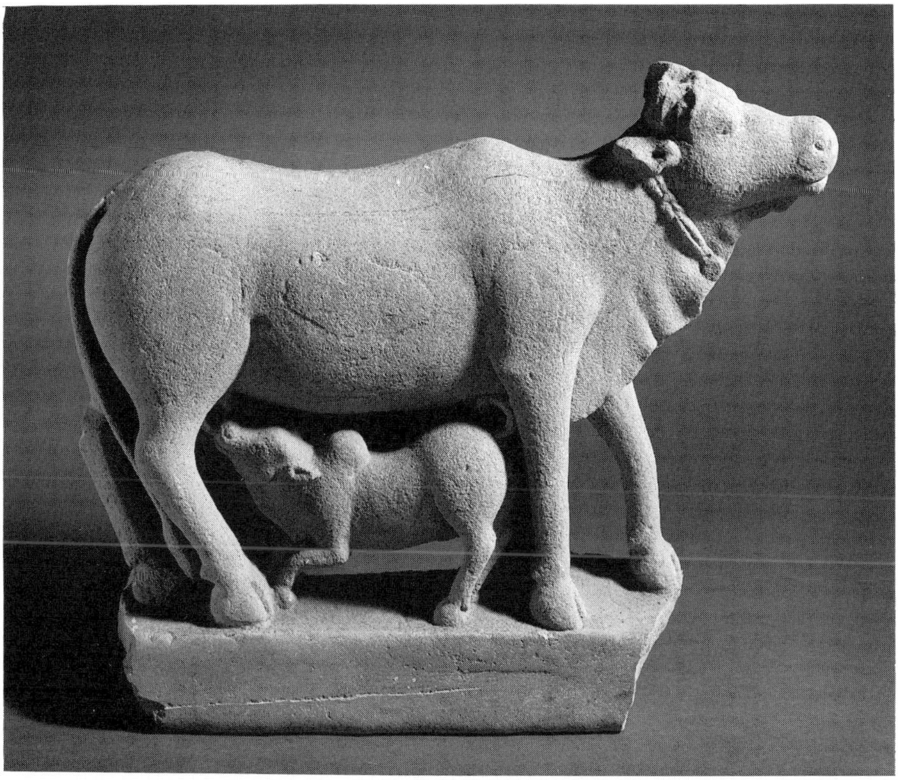

11. Cow and Calf. Uttar Pradesh, 7th century, sandstone

(fig. 13). Instead, it indicates the arrival at the Mughal workshop of an artist who had previously worked in the style of an early sixteenth-century *Laur-Chanda* manuscript (fig. 15), a traditional Muslim love story copied and illustrated for an as yet unidentified pre-Mughal Muslim ruler, perhaps at Malwa. The shape of the horizon line, the placement of the tree, and the pale colors in each are sufficient proof of their relationship. Again the artist of the *Tutinama* page is quickly incorporating traits that would become Mughal conventions: the insertion of a mountainous landscape in the foreground, the abolition of the decorative and space-denying background, and the shading of figures – all leading to a greater sense of substance in the forms, and of depth to the space.

Other equally informative comparisons can be found throughout the book, and a unified and novel stylistic development – first isolated and discussed by Pramod Chandra – quickly becomes apparent. An examination of the *Tutinama* illustrations shows that those new imperial painters trained in pre-Mughal styles were constantly attempting to adjust their work to conform to

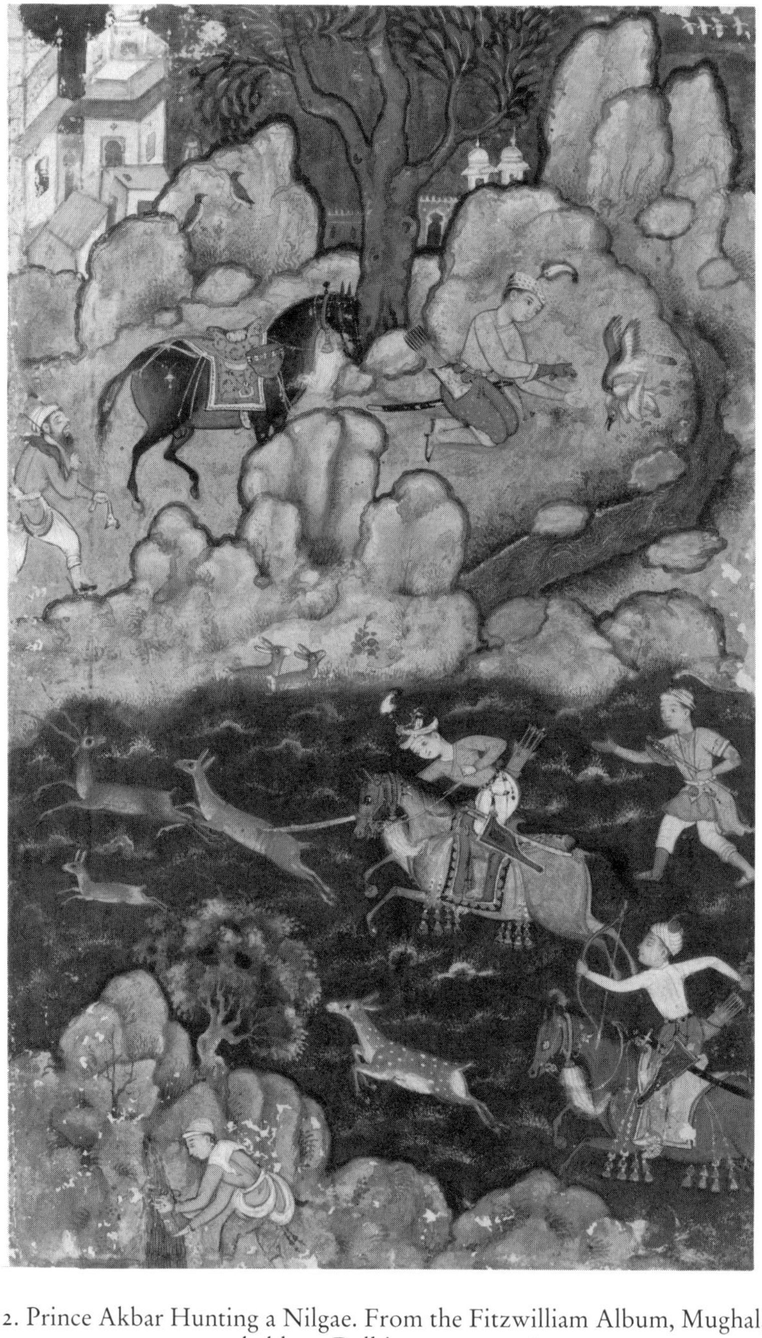

12. Prince Akbar Hunting a Nilgae. From the Fitzwilliam Album, Mughal, probably at Delhi, ca. 1555–1560

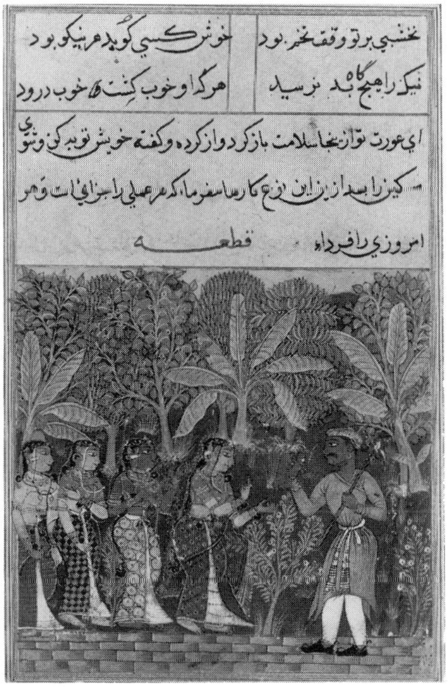

13. The Merchant's Daughter with Her Companions Meets the Gardener. From a *Tutinama* manuscript, Mughal, ca. 1560

the new direction already defined by the Fitzwilliam Album. The coordination of these efforts was controlled by the workshop directors, whose demands increasingly took precedence over individual artistic initiative and past training.

There is some visual evidence that both of the older Persian masters were involved in the making of the *Tutinama.* Contemporary historical accounts state explicitly, however, that they served in turn as supervisors of the *Hamzanama* (or *Dastan-i Amir Hamza*) manuscript project (fig. 16 and plate C), begun probably about 1562. We will discuss the work at length, for it is of the greatest importance for understanding the evolution of Mughal painting and its relationship to other traditions within India. It is also one of the most exciting and visually inventive works within the entire tradition of Islamic manuscript illustration.

Akbar was illiterate; that is, he could neither read nor write. This was not an unusual situation for Muslim rulers with attendant scribes, however, and he employed readers to keep himself informed and entertained. In the *A'in-i-Akbari* (Annals of Akbar), a continuation of the *Akbarnama* describing the administrative organization of the empire, Abu'l Fazl discusses the character of the imperial library, and then says of the books:

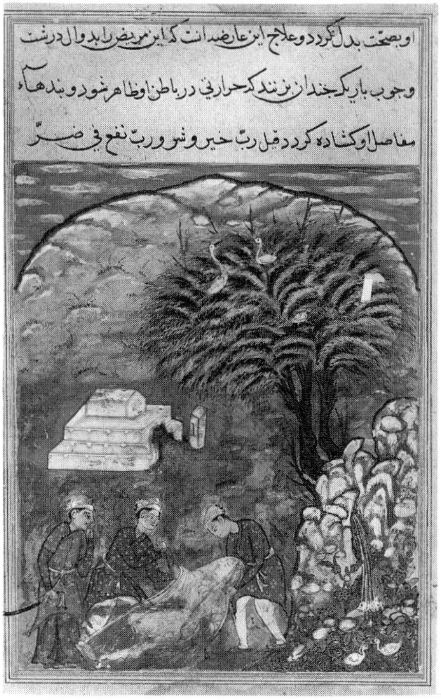

14. The Devotee's Daughter Restored to Life.
From a *Tutinama* manuscript, Mughal, ca. 1560

> Experienced people bring them daily and read them before His Majesty, who hears every book from the beginning to the end. At whatever page the readers daily stop, His Majesty makes with his own pen a sign, according to the number of the pages; and rewards the readers with presents of cash, either in gold or silver, according to the number of pages read out by them. Among books of renown, there are few that are not read in His Majesty's assembly hall.[12]

More specifically, after an exciting elephant hunt in 1564, we read:

> When the world-warming sun had sate on the throne of the horizons, H.M. the Shahinshah [Akbar] with the desired prey in his net and the cup of success at his lip sate on that auspicious throne and graciously ordered the courtiers to be seated. Then for the sake of delight and pleasure, he listened for some time to Darbar Khan's recital of the story of Amir Hamza.[13]

The *Hamzanama* is an adventure story based partly on fact, but incorporating local legends and popular tales. It centers on the purported adventures of Amir Hamza, an uncle of the Prophet Muhammad who sought to convert the world

[12] Abu'l Fazl Allami, *A'in-i-Akbari*, translated by H. Blochmann, Calcutta, 1938–1939, vol. I, p. 110.
[13] Abu'l Fazl, *Akbar Nama*, vol. II, pp. 343–344.

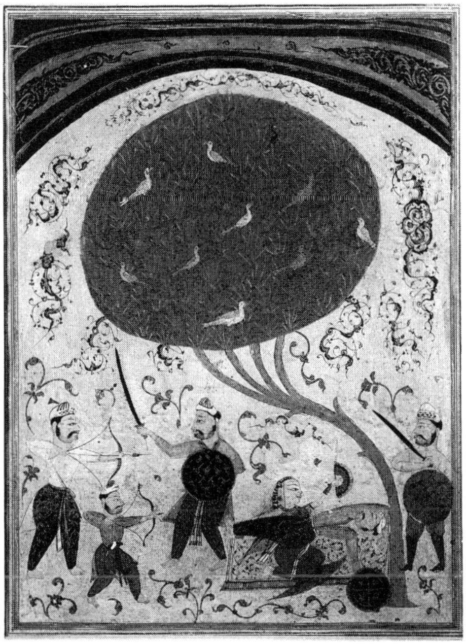

15. Chandra Fanning Laur on the Battlefield.
From a *Laur-chanda* manuscript, Sultanate,
probably Central India, ca. 1540

to Islam. The narrative is a series of action-packed tales about love affairs, murders, kidnappings, and battles, and its cast of characters includes giant magicians, demons, and dragons – as well as heroic warriors and beautiful maidens. Babur considered the story "one long farfetched lie, opposed to sense and nature,"[14] but it must have been very immediate to his grandson, himself trying to spread Islam among the varied communities of India.

The copy of the story made for Akbar was famous in its own time, for contemporary historical records refer to the project.[15] The manuscript consisted of fourteen volumes, each with one hundred illustrations of relatively large size (about 27 inches high and 20 inches wide). At least fifty painters were employed on the work, and about one hundred men overall. The workshops, therefore, had become very large very quickly, evidence both of the extent of Akbar's interest in book production, and of the ability of the Mughal court to attract artists and craftsmen to its employ. That the book's illustrations are far more uniform in style than those of the *Tutinama* confirms that the workshops were under increasingly strong central control.

14 Babur, *Babur-nama*, p. 280.

15 For a summary of these texts and further references see Milo Cleveland Beach, *The Imperial Image – Paintings for the Mughal Court*, Washington, 1981, pp. 58–68.

This is not a manuscript in which paintings occasionally appear to ornament the text. Instead, since there is an illustration for every opening of the volume, the paintings are integrally involved in the unfolding of the narrative. And unlike *School Scene* (fig. 8), with its many areas of visual interest evenly distributed over the surface of the page, the visual impact of these *Hamzanama* illustrations is controlled by one narratively central episode. This links the work with the *Tutinama*, from which it also derives many of its compositions.[16] A further source for these compositions lies in another aspect of the richly varied Islamic painting traditions of Iran. A *Falnama* manuscript, possibly painted at Tabriz about 1550, is an important precursor of the *Hamzanama*. One of its pages, *Adam and Eve* (fig. 17), can be directly compared to *Amr Fights the Dragon* (fig. 16), from the *Hamzanama*. Not only is it similar in composition, with peripheral figures observing and framing the single central episode, the size of the pages in both volumes is unusually large.

The rather rough workmanship of the *Hamzanama*, as well as its limited but dramatically manipulated palette of earth and mineral colors (see plate C), is different from the varied, subtle, finely ground colors, and intensely controlled technique found in the Mir Sayyid Ali *School Scene* or even *Adam and Eve*. This was not completely a matter of choice. The sources from which artists in Iran had obtained their pigments and papers – zinc white came from Kashgar, for example, and many of the finest papers from Samarkand – were simply not available initially to the Mughals in India, and this obviously affected the way they could paint, the style. The rough surfaces and bolder colors seen in the *Hamzanama* were therefore not necessarily the result of artistic decisions. Furthermore, Akbar did not recruit painters from Iran alone. Many elements of the *Hamzanama* – like those cited for the *Tutinama* – can only be explained by the actual presence in the imperial workshops at this time of Indian artists, men trained in local styles for which such standards of craftsmanship were simply not important. One strength of the *Hamzanama* pages, in fact, lies in the resulting vigor and energy of the workmanship.

Neither the *Tutinama* nor *Hamzanama* manuscript contains a contemporary colophon or date. The earliest Akbari manuscript with such an inscription is the *Deval Rani Khizr Khan* of 1568, a romance by the poet Amir Khusrau Dihlavi (1253–1325) which now contains two illustrations. *A Fiery Horse Is Brought to Prince Khizr Khan* (fig. 18) remains closer to Persian tradition than the more innovative *Hamzanama* scenes, but the gesticulating

[16] Compare, for example, *Khorshid Sails to Mecca*, from the *Tutinama* (Stuart Cary Welch, *A Flower from Every Meadow – Indian Paintings from American Collections*, New York, 1973, no. 54b) with *The Search Party Departs*, from the *Hamzanama* (Gerhard Egger, *Hamza-nama*, Graz, 1974, no. v.14). We regret that it has not been possible to reproduce these works here.

figures, or the horse and groom, betray a distinctively Mughal interest in physical action.

A second dated manuscript, an *Anwar-i-Suhaili* (Lights of Canopus) of 1571 (figs. 19 and 54), contains 27 illustrations made for a translation from Sanskrit into Persian of a series of moral fables which also inspired Aesop. Two scenes in the volume are in almost unadulterated Bokharan style, although the rest are in the most advanced imperial Mughal style of the time. Much smaller in size than the *Hamzanama*, the *Anwar-i-Suhaili* manuscript is more easily compared to the similarly scaled *Tutinama*. (The design solutions and levels of workmanship possible in illustrations on the scale of wall-paintings is necessarily different from those in a book easily held in the hand.) *The Bear's Attack* (fig. 19), for example, develops compositionally from *The Merchant's Daughter with Her Companions Meets the Gardener* (fig. 13). In each the upper half is background jungle, and the lower half has isolated figural activity against a plain foreground. The later work uses diagonal lines and overlapping forms to lead us into space, however; its forms have greater volume, and the physical distance of the jungle is more easily experienced.

During the decade of the 1570s, the need to complete the *Hamzanama* may have overwhelmed painters, for few other manuscript projects are known. During this decade the new city of Fatehpur-Sikri was also under construction, and evidence still exists (although barely visible) that many of its walls were painted with scenes in *Hamzanama* style. True portraits, studies of specific physical appearance and character, are also known from these years. Babur had shown astute perception of physical appearances in his memoirs, although the first Mughal portrait studies that still exist can only be dated to the reign of Humayun. Akbar found this category of imagery of especial interest. According to Abu'l Fazl, "His Majesty himself sat for his likeness, and also ordered to have the likenesses taken of all the grandees of the realm. An immense album was thus formed: those that have passed away have received a new life, and those who are still alive have immortality promised them."[17]

The study of an extraordinarily stout courtier (fig. 20), possibly Mota Raja ("Fat Raja") Udai Singh of Jodhpur (r. 1583–1595), is a very perceptive presentation of personality. Nothing is idealized; there is a specific man whom we could recognize in a crowd, and both color and line are used only to understand better his individuality. Udai Singh had been displaced by a younger brother in 1562 as heir to the Jodhpur kingdom, and formally allied himself with the Mughal court in 1570, eventually marrying a daughter to Prince Salim, the future Emperor Jahangir. He was a well-known member of the court circle, therefore, and this is only one among many such portraits of a distinctively Mughal type. Comparably specific depictions of physical appearance are

[17] Abu'l Fazl, *A'in*, vol. I, p. 115.

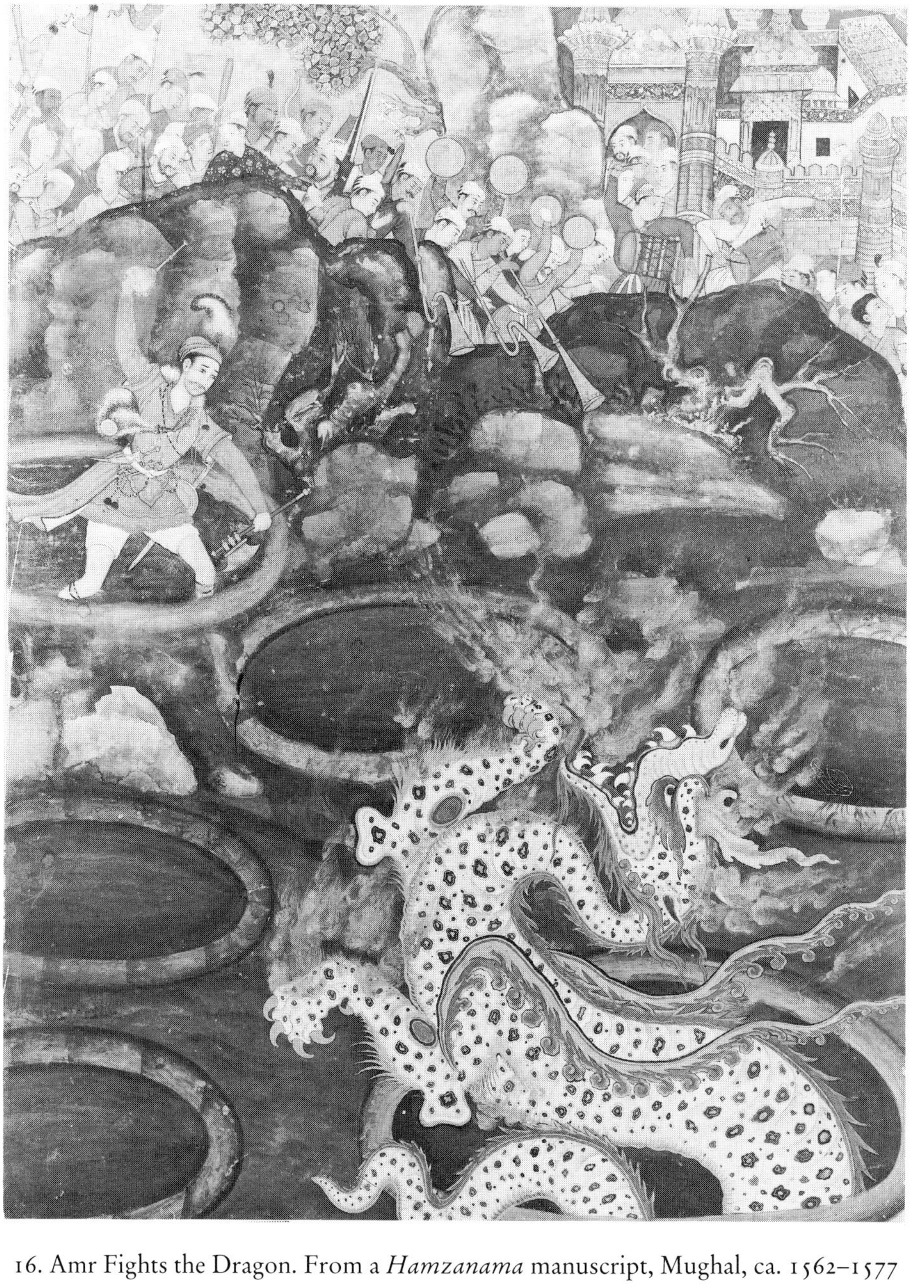

16. Amr Fights the Dragon. From a *Hamzanama* manuscript, Mughal, ca. 1562–1577

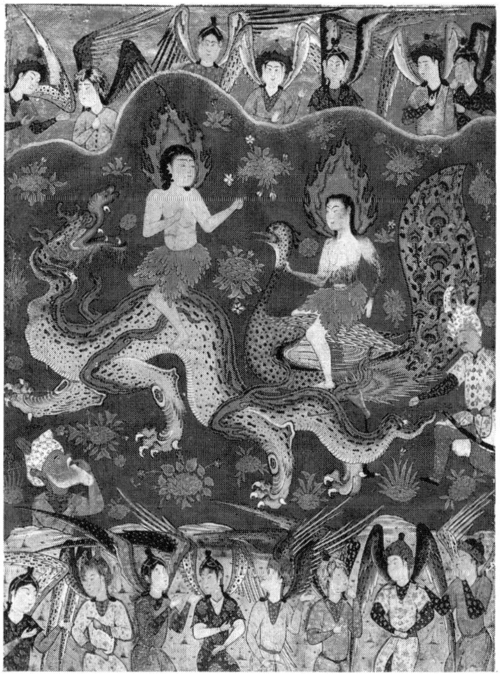

17. Adam and Eve. From a *Falnama* manuscript, Iran, ca. 1560

known from Iran as well, but they are found among artists' sketches, or as studies of courtiers and lesser nobility;[18] the rulers themselves were almost always presented as ideal types. Here too Mughal interests follow well-established precedents. It is not radical change, therefore, but new choices in the emphasis and importance given to existing practices that distinguishes these earliest Mughal works.

It is clear that when Akbar decided to patronize book production and the arts in a major way, he attracted artists and craftsmen from both local and distant centers of production. These men brought the established traditions in which they had been trained to the Mughal workshops, where they were adapted to the existing style developed initially under Humayun's patronage and exemplified by *Prince Akbar Hunting a Nilgae* (fig. 12). The process is shown to us in the pages of the *Tutinama*, while the *Hamzanama* and the 1570 *Anwar-i-Suhaili* are the first fully fledged results of the synthesis. The creation of a unified and distinctive artistic style from this combination of Iranian court and provincial styles with disparate but active regional Indian traditions is among the most fascinating episodes of Indian or Islamic art. The profound

[18] See Stuart Cary Welch, *Wonders of the Age*, Cambridge, Massachusetts, 1979, nos. 72 and 80.

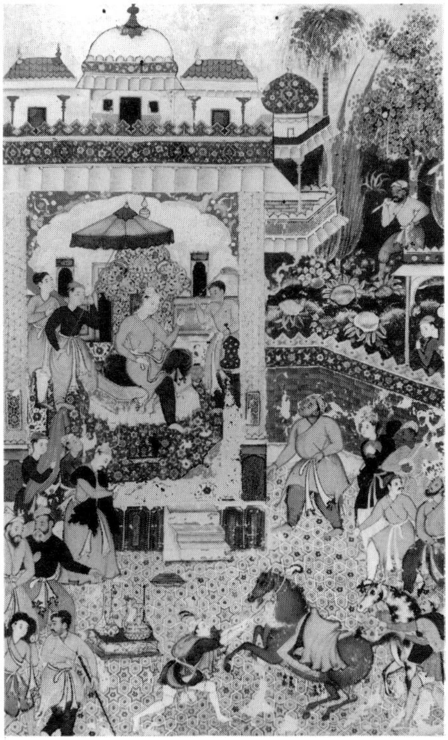

18. A Fiery Horse is Brought to Prince Khizr Khan.
From a *Deval Rani Khizr Khan* manuscript, Mughal, dated 1568

influence that this new Mughal style had on the various geographically, culturally, and religiously distinct regions of the subcontinent demands our initial concentration on Mughal painting when exploring painting within India generally.

Just as Humayun's defeat by Sher Shah Afghan and his retreat into exile created the circumstances that eventually brought Mir Sayyid Ali and Abd as-Samad from Iran to India, so certain historical events of these later years are important to understanding the development of the arts. The murder of the regent Bairam Khan in 1561, for example, marked the beginning of Akbar's political maturity, and his power over north India increased steadily with the defeats of the Rajput capital at Chitor in 1568, of Gujarat in 1573, and of Bengal three years later. The emperor encouraged marriage alliances with defeated royal families – the Kachhwahas of Amber (later known as Jaipur) being the most prominent – and members of the newly subservient courts were brought, often as virtual hostages, for extended residence in the imperial capital. Mughal contact with

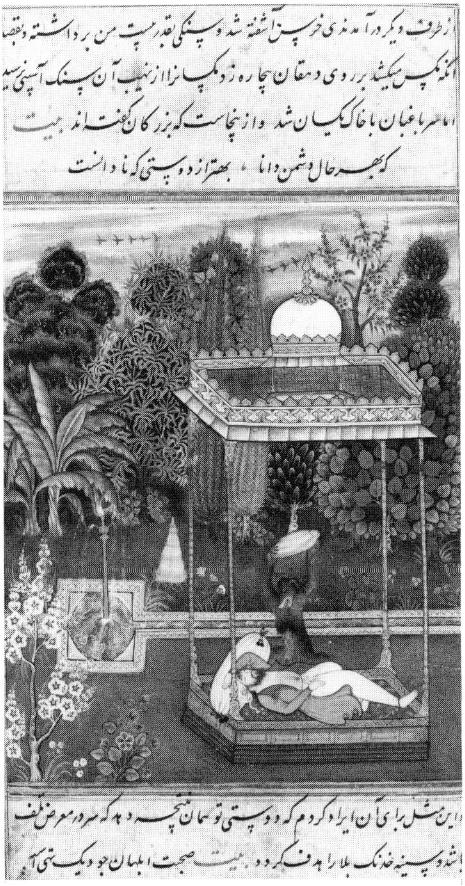

19. The Bear's Attack. From an *Anwar-i-Suhaili* manuscript, Mughal, dated 1571

the peoples and regional cultural traditions of India was thereby vastly increased, and a system for contacts and interrelationships among these distinctive traditions was established, based on the unavoidable centrality of Mughal power.

Akbar's personal power was further bolstered with the birth of three sons between 1569 and 1572 and the dynastic security that this provided. Much of his energy during the ensuing decade was directed towards the construction of the new imperial capital at Fatehpur-Sikri, and paintings show him inspecting and directing the builders' work. Within the walls of the new palace he built a gathering-place for people of different intellectual beliefs, the *Ibadat Khana* (House of Worship), to which men of different religions (including Christianity) were invited for discussions. Reports of these meetings would certainly have spread widely among the intelligentsia of India and the Islamic world. The intellectual, as well as the artistic, interests of the Mughal emperor and his court therefore were continually placed in fruitful contact with peoples from other regions within India.

The intellectual experimentation of those years, together with the undeniable power now wielded by the emperor, led Akbar to proclaim a new religious system, the *Din-ilahi* (Divine Faith). This attempted to reconcile various of the beliefs he had explored, but also stated that the emperor was the ultimate authority in the interpretation of religious doctrine – a claim not easily acceptable to the orthodox clergy. This situation parallels that experimentation which we have already seen in painting at the same time, and a change in the nature of the texts being illustrated will show clearly that art would soon be used to proclaim as well as to reinforce Akbar's authority. While the *Tutinama* and *Hamzanama* manuscripts were at least nominally adventure stories and thus sheer entertainment, historical subject matter and texts related to the religious and literary traditions of both Islam and Hinduism were to be given special prominence in the royal library after 1580.

A completely different spirit pervades the schools of painting in the Deccan, a series of Muslim kingdoms south of Mughal territories against whom the Mughals continually fought. In a process of increasing fragmentation, the Deccan had become independent of the Delhi Sultanate in the mid fourteenth century, and was ruled first by Bahman Shah, whose descendants were known as the Bahmanid dynasty. By the late fifteenth century, this region had further split into five separate sultanates: Ahmadnagar, Bijapur, Golconda, Berar and Bidar. Their rulers brought diverse cultural, historical, and geographic backgrounds to each kingdom. Ahmadnagar was established by Ahmad I Nizam Shah, the son of a Hindu slave converted to Islam, for example; the rulers of Bijapur, who took the title Adil Shah, were descended from Ottoman Turks; while Sultan Quli Qutb Shah of Golconda was a Black Sheep Turkman (Qara Qoyunlu), whose family had sought refuge in India in 1467, when the White Sheep Turkmen (Aq Qoyunlu) conquered their kingdom in western Iran. The region, therefore, was wildly cosmopolitan.

In 1565, the Deccani Sultans together defeated the powerful Hindu kingdom of Vijayanagar, on the southern fringes of Bijapur. The Lepakshi murals (fig. 3) are just one indication that Vijayanagar had been important and active artistically, and many of its painters – once that patronage had ceased – brought their talents to the sultanate courts. Incidentally, 1565 is the date proposed for the earliest identified Deccani manuscript, the *Tarif-i-Husain Shahi*, a history of Husain Shah (r. 1554–1565) of Ahmadnagar, which was probably made at his court. As an historical chronicle, and because of its style, its precursors should be sought in Ottoman Turkey.

Sultan Husain Nizam Shah of Ahmadnagar Enthroned (fig. 21) comes from

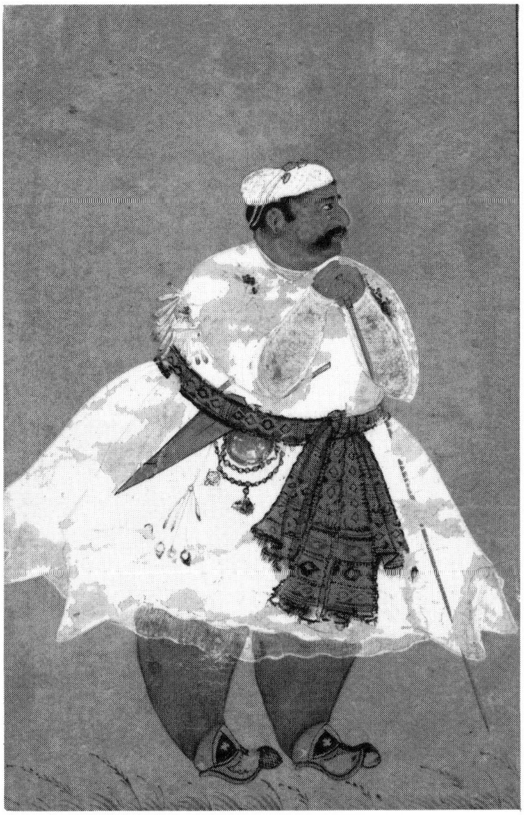

20. Mota Raja Udai Singh. Mughal, ca. 1575

this volume. While it bears no colophon, a date of circa 1565 has long been accepted; not only was this the year of the victory over Vijayanagar, it was also that of Husain Shah's death. The book should be compared to both the pre-Mughal Hindu *Bhagavata Purana* (plate B) and the *Ni'matnama* (figs. 5 and 7), although it is most closely associated stylistically with the latter. Whereas the Hindu manuscript creates excitement by contrasting broad areas of pure strong color, in the Deccani work compartments of vivid but often intricate pattern are juxtaposed; and certain colors (pink, lilac, or chartreuse) have no place in the Hindu set. In all three volumes the space is absolutely flat, without even a diagonal to lead us back from the picture surface.

Aspects of the style of the *Tarif-i-Husain Shahi* contributed to Akbar's *Tutinama* (figs. 13, 14, and 29), although *Sultan Husain Nizam Shah of Ahmadnagar Enthroned* has no interest in the naturalistic or technically experimental tendencies of the imperial manuscript. The figures there are also less animated than those in either the *Ni'matnama* or the *Tutinama*. With the

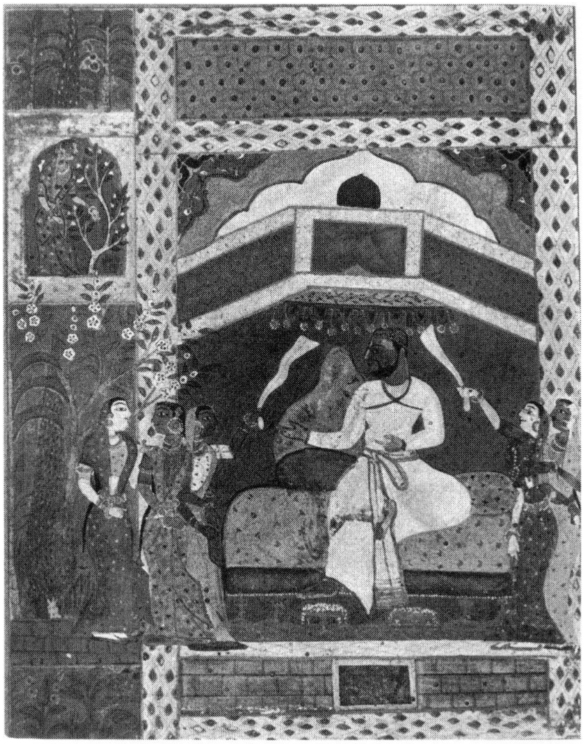

21. Sultan Husain Nizam Shah of Ahmadnagar Enthroned.
From a *Tarif-i-Husain Shahi* manuscript, Deccani, at Ahmadnagar, ca. 1565

exception of the Shah – the shadowy figure next to him was originally Queen Humayun, but she fell from favor and was painted out – the human forms are important only as areas of pattern, and no more (or less) expressive than the blossoming trees or the tiled wall surfaces.

If Ahmadnagar is the first Deccani Muslim court known to have patronized painters, its activity was also the briefest, for the kingdom fell in 1600 to attacking Mughal troops. The *Tarif-i-Husain Shahi* also seems to bear no direct relationship to later Ahmadnagar works, which must be the products of a new artistic personality at the court. The greatest portrait attributed to the school has been identified recently as Sultan Murtaza Nizam Shah (r. 1565–1588; fig. 22), and dated circa 1575.[19] It depicts three male figures attendant on an enthroned ruler, all against a plain background; but its seeming simplicity belies its richness. The background, for example, is gold, and while it denies rational

[19] See Mark Zebrowski, *Deccani Painting*, London, 1983, pp. 21–22 and plate II.

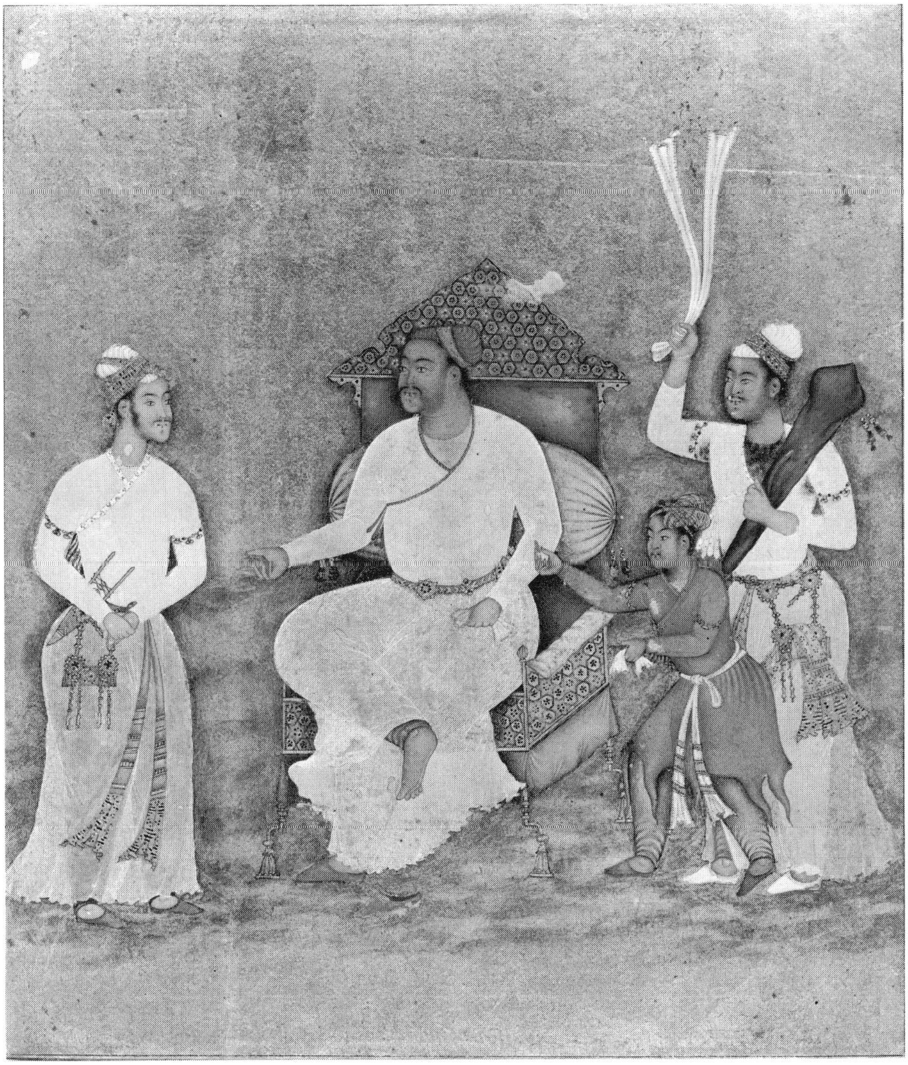

22. Sultan Murtaza Nizam Shah. Deccani, at Ahmadnagar, ca. 1575

space, it creates opulence and brilliant light. The figures are not true portraits, yet the gestures are dramatic, and the painter is intensely interested in the patterns created by jewels and cloth. Released from the need for explicit description, such details as the Sultan's hem turn into breathtaking visual cadenzas. If this is really of the date proposed, then the otherworldliness evoked here predicts several of the great Mughal imperial portraits of the early seventeenth century.

Deccani painting is not a subject of this study. Awareness of its rich traditions, however, is necessary when explaining the sources of Mughal style, and for a sharper perception of the distinctive traits of both the Mughal and Rajput traditions.

CHAPTER 3

1580–1600: THE NEW IMPERIAL STYLE AND ITS IMPACT

In the *A'in-i-Akbari*, Abu'l Fazl named the major painters at Akbar's court, beginning with Mir Sayyid Ali and Abd as-Samad. Third on this list, which seems to be hierarchic, is Daswanth, of whom it was written:

> Then there was Daswanta [Daswanth], the son of a palanquin-bearer (*kahar*), who was in the service of this workshop and, urged by a natural desire, used to draw images and designs on walls. One day the far-reaching glance of His Majesty fell on those things and, in its penetrating manner, discerned the spirit of a master working in them. Consequently, His Majesty entrusted him to the Khwaja [Abd as-Samad]. In just a short time he became matchless in his time and the most excellent, but the darkness of insanity enshrouded the brilliance of his mind and he died, a suicide. He left several masterpieces.[1]

The *Akbarnama* narrative dates the death of the painter to 1584, and corroborates his insanity and suicide.[2]

The character of Daswanth as an artist is elusive, for few of his works exist. A signed and certainly authentic page is found in the *Tutinama* and provides further evidence for that manuscript's imperial origin and Akbar period date; the illustration is early and immature, however. While he must have worked on the *Hamzanama* as well – its dates coincide with the years of his greatest activity in the court workshops – successful attributions to his hand have yet to be made. The greatest, fully mature illustrations by Daswanth known to us are in a *Razmnama* (Book of Wars) manuscript begun in 1582. These are paintings that he designed, but did not fully execute. Contemporary workshop methods often divided responsibility in this way between a major painter, who designed the composition, and a younger or less prestigious man who executed the work under the master's supervision. Sometimes a specialist in portraiture drew the heads of the major figures. While this defines logical stages in the apprenticeship system, such strict and well-defined divisions of responsibility had not been usual in Iran. This procedure may have been inspired instead by the communal methods familiar in Indian folk and village tradition, where individualized contributions to artistic images were deemed inappropriate and groups of artists often shared the necessary tasks.

[1] Translated by C. M. Naim and quoted in Pramod Chandra, *The Tutinama of the Cleveland Museum of Art and the Origins of Mughal Painting*, Graz, 1976, p. 183.

[2] Abu'l Fazl, *Akbar Nama*, vol. III, p. 651.

Daswanth's compositions in the *Razmnama* are extraordinarily powerful, and of a particular character, often so visually irrational as to seem nightmare visions. *A Night Assault on the Pandava Camp* (fig. 23), designed by Daswanth, shows the ghoulish Kal-ratri emanating from a corpse and drinking the blood of battle victims. A vision related to Tibetan and Tantric imagery, it possesses extraordinary power and directness. The demoness wears a necklace of freshly severed heads, and the skins of flayed animals. These are iconographic traits, however; it is the style that creates the impact. Here there is no defined or definable space, but neither is it flat. Kal-ratri hovers suspended, and even the surrounding encampment does not anchor the scene. At every point where a horizontal or vertical might create stability, overlapping forms instead cause spatial ambivalence. It is a perfectly conceived presentation of an otherworldly being, and its technical and aesthetic complexity defines the highest level of imperial painting at the time.

The *Razmnama* text is a translation into Persian of a great Hindu epic, *Mahabharata* (literally "Great India"), originally written in Sanskrit. The project, commissioned by Akbar, began with the assembling at Fatehpur-Sikri of learned Hindus, who could recite the text orally. They were set to work with scribes and translators, one of whom, the orthodox Muslim Abdu-l-Qadir ibn-i-Muluk Shah *al Badaoni*, was appalled at the task. The text, he wrote, was full of "puerile absurdities at which the eighteen thousand creations might well be amazed."[3] Several men made a rough translation, which was then handed over to a major poet – in this case Faizi, brother of Abu'l Fazl – to form a final polished version. As the translation was proceeding, painters were set to work planning and executing the illustrations. This particular manuscript, reportedly with 176 illustrations, was finished by 1586. Akbar then ordered the chief nobles to make copies for their own libraries, assuring that knowledge of and familiarity with this important Hindu text would spread throughout Mughal territories; a contemporary chronicle states: "When fairly engrossed and embellished with pictures, the Amirs had orders to take copies of it, with the blessing and favour of God."[4] A comparable project for another great epic, the *Ramayana* (The Story of Rama), was initiated about 1584.

Copies of *Ramayana* and *Razmnama* manuscripts made for various Mughal nobles have survived, and some contain illustrations that are close in style to those in the imperial volumes. On the whole, however, they are both conceptually and qualitatively simpler. A dispersed *Razmnama*, dated 1598, contains illustrations by many of the junior painters in the imperial workshops, although the specific patron is unknown. Were it not for the presence of

[3] Abdu-l-Qadir ibn-i-Muluk Shah *al Badaoni*, *Muntakhabut-t-Tawarikh*, translated by W. Haig, Patna, 1973 (reprint), vol. II, p. 330.

[4] Abdu-l-Qadir ibn-i-Muluk Shah, *Muntakhabut-t-Tawarikh*, pp. 330–331.

Kal-ratri, the scene of *A Night Assault on the Pandava Camp* (fig. 24) from that second manuscript might describe an historical battle. The unearthly aspect of Daswanth's work, therefore, is due to the artist's particular interpretive skills; it is not an inevitable response to the text. (Indeed, the majority of illustrations of mythological or other ahistorical events are presented even in the imperial *Razmnama* as everyday, contemporary occurrences.)

This is one indication of the growing acknowledgment of individual artistic initiative in the development of the Mughal style. However, this delight in originality comes into conflict both with the need for artistic unity among the artists assigned to any single manuscript production project, and with the traditional Indian indifference to expressions of individual artistic personality. It is also a result of the growing dominance of a secular artistic tradition, that made works to delight and continually surprise the viewer, over a more traditionally Indian attitude that saw artists as mere vehicles for the expression of sacred and eternal truths.

Unlike the copying of the text, in which accuracy to the original would have been prized, the compositions for the illustrations in these sub-imperial volumes seem little affected by those in the emperor's book. While the figure of the demoness in the 1598 *Razmnama* is certainly modelled on the general type of source used also for Daswanth's earlier illustration, the painting is otherwise an independent work. Since the latter volume is clearly not of the highest imperial level of quality, it may have been commissioned by a member of the nobility, although it could also have been made to be given as an imperial gift. In any case, it had direct and immediate impact.

Brihispati Greeting Bhimasena and His Friends (fig. 25), also from the 1598 manuscript and by Bhagwan, provides in turn – by its landscape and human forms, and its pale colors – the stylistic prototype for *Nata Ragini* (fig. 26), from a *Ragamala* series made almost certainly for a Rajput patron. (The text is written not in Persian, but in *devanagari* script.) The *Ragamala* is the single most popular text illustrated for Hindu patrons, and when Rajput rulers became interested in commissioning paintings of such familiar subjects, they sought artists and compositional models wherever available. When they were interested in confirming their links with Mughal power, those models were most often Mughal. Paintings like those in the 1598 *Razmnama* must have provided one accessible and imitable prototype. And what is thereby established by a comparison of these various works is a clear artistic hierarchy, extending in steps from the highest level of imperial taste through increasingly distant political and social circles.

Another *Ragamala*, painted at Chunar and dated 1591 (figs. 27 and 120), was also made for an important member of the nobility. The size and shape of the illustrations found in the Chunar set, as well as the arrangement of the compositions, form the model for numerous later *Ragamala* series painted

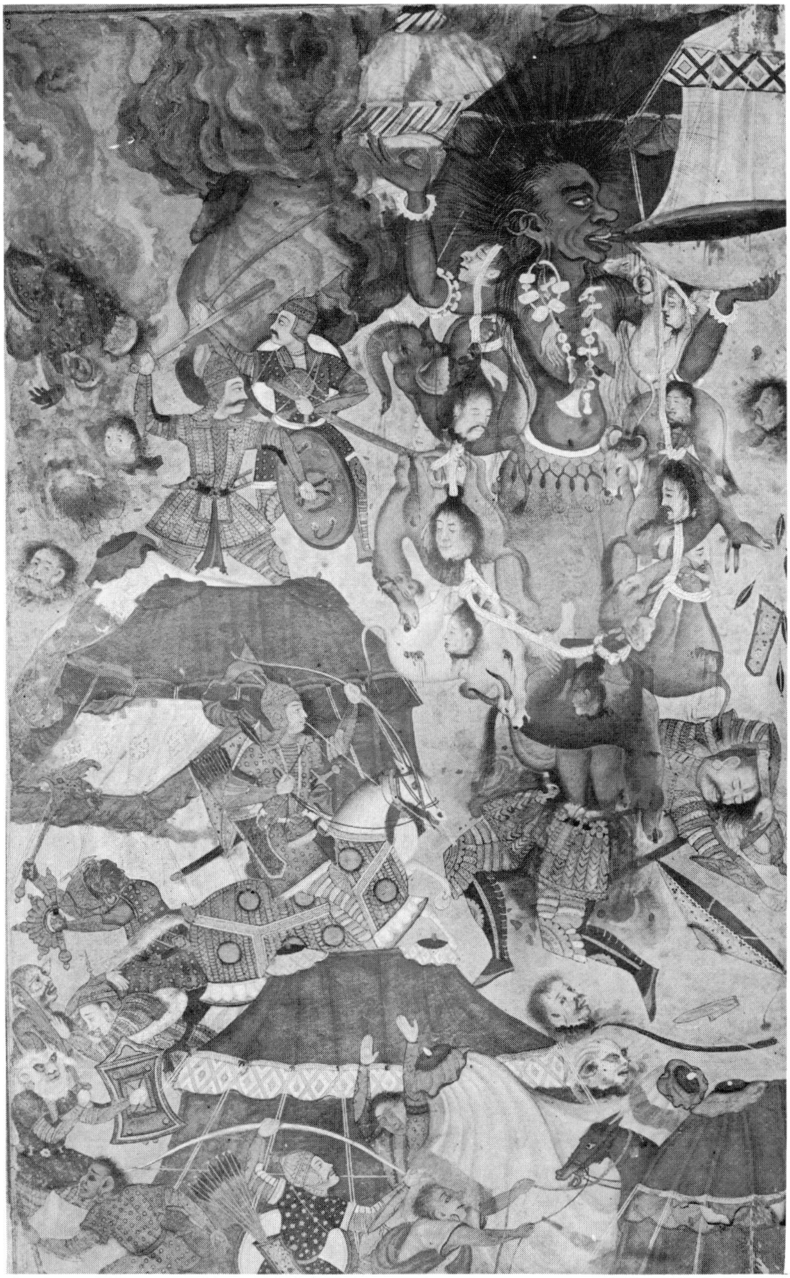

23. A Night Assault on the Pandava Camp. Designed by Daswanth, painted by Sarwan; from a *Razmnama* manuscript, Mughal, ca. 1582–1586

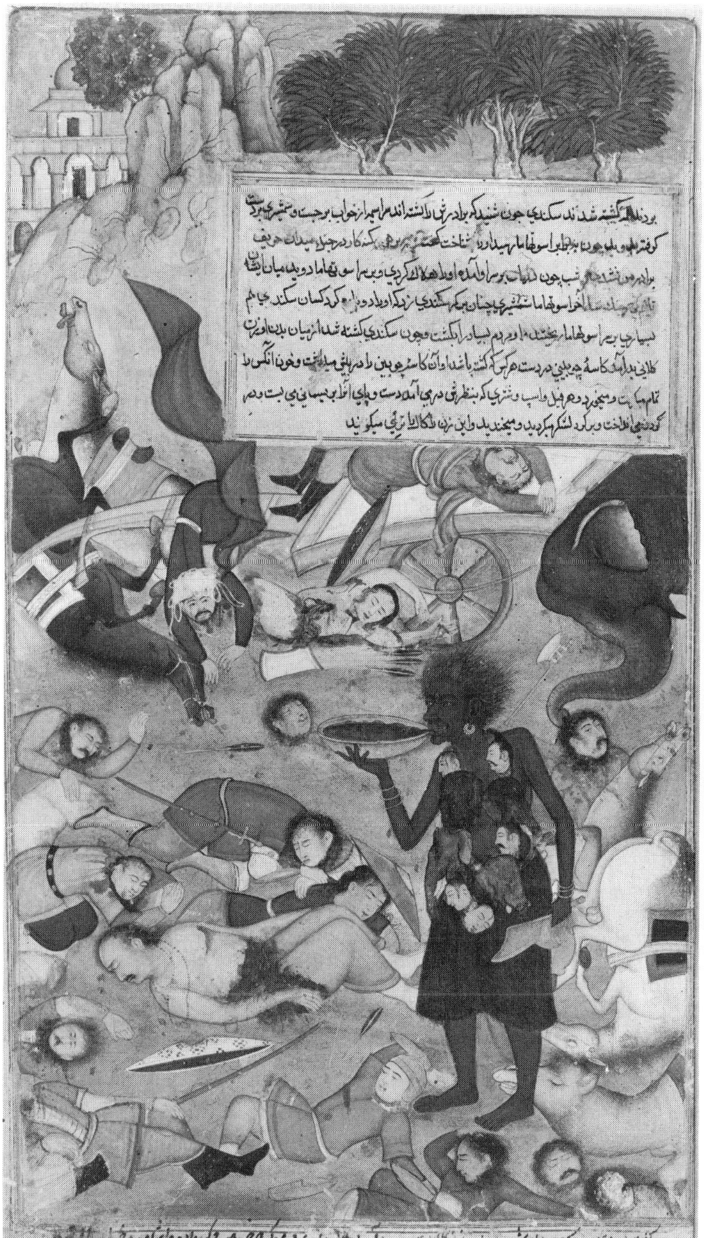

24. A Night Assault on the Pandava Camp. From a *Razmnama* manuscript, Mughal, dated 1598

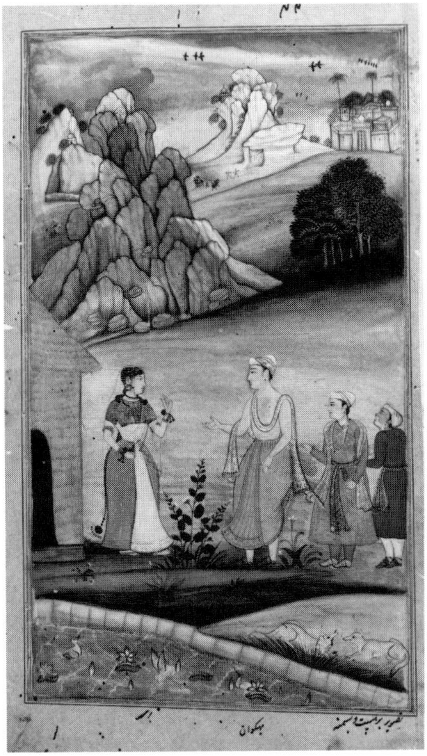

25. Brihispati Greeting Bhimasena and His Friends.
By Bhagwan; from a *Razmnama* manuscript, Mughal,
dated 1598

exclusively in the Bundi area of Rajasthan continuously into the nineteenth century. Chunar was a Mughal territory on the Ganges, near Benares, but its governor in the later Akbar period was the Hindu Rao Surjan (r. 1554–1585), ruler of the Rajput kingdom of Bundi. (Rajputs were frequently given such posts far from their homelands to remove them from natural bases of power should they ever entertain thoughts of rebellion.) It seems reasonable, therefore, to suppose that the Chunar set was commissioned or purchased by (or perhaps presented to) a member of the Bundi family, and that it then became a model for painters from that state.

The vertical proportions of the set, together with the marginal decorations around several of the folios, can only be explained by the painters' awareness of the format of Islamic books. Within individual scenes, there are also tentative attempts at spatial depth. Forms are strongly modelled, and skies are atmospheric, streaked with color and light, successfully evoking dawn or dusk. *Bhairava Raga* (fig. 27), from the Chunar set, should be compared to an earlier

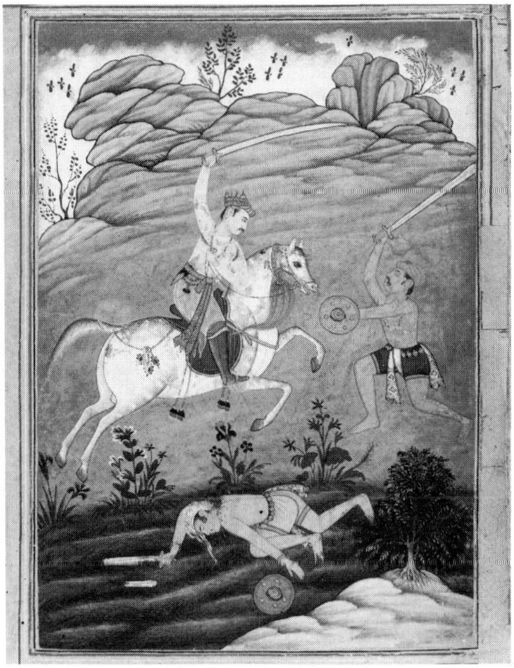

26. Nata Ragini. From a *Ragamala* series, sub-imperial Mughal, ca. 1600

version of the same subject (fig. 28), one contemporary with the pre-Mughal *Bhagavata Purana* series (plate B). The *Ragamala* text metaphorically explores possible relationships between a worshipper and the divinity through romantic imagery. Each of these illustrations shows a woman worshipping at a shrine to the god Shiva, but in the later scene the phallic emblem of the god has been replaced by Shiva himself.

The compositions used in the Chunar *Ragamala* did not develop directly out of the pre-Mughal tradition of the early set – the formulas used for human figures and the strong primary colors of the early scene are unrelated to the 1591 page – nor does there seem to be any very specific relation to the style of *Nata Ragini* (fig. 26). Instead, the Chunar *Bhairava Raga* is an offshoot of such work as *The Deceitful Wife Assaults her Erring Husband* (fig. 29), from the *Tutinama* of circa 1560. The architectural setting in each is similarly arranged, with both works trying to show spatial depth through diagonal lines, unlike the totally flat space or simple overlapping of the circa 1540 illustration. The female figures in the *Tutinama* and the Chunar series are almost interchangeable in style and shape, and have more realistic proportions than the earlier ladies. Even the dark sky dotted with stars, and the distant palm tree in each, are directly comparable. One major difference is that the Mughal work is full of

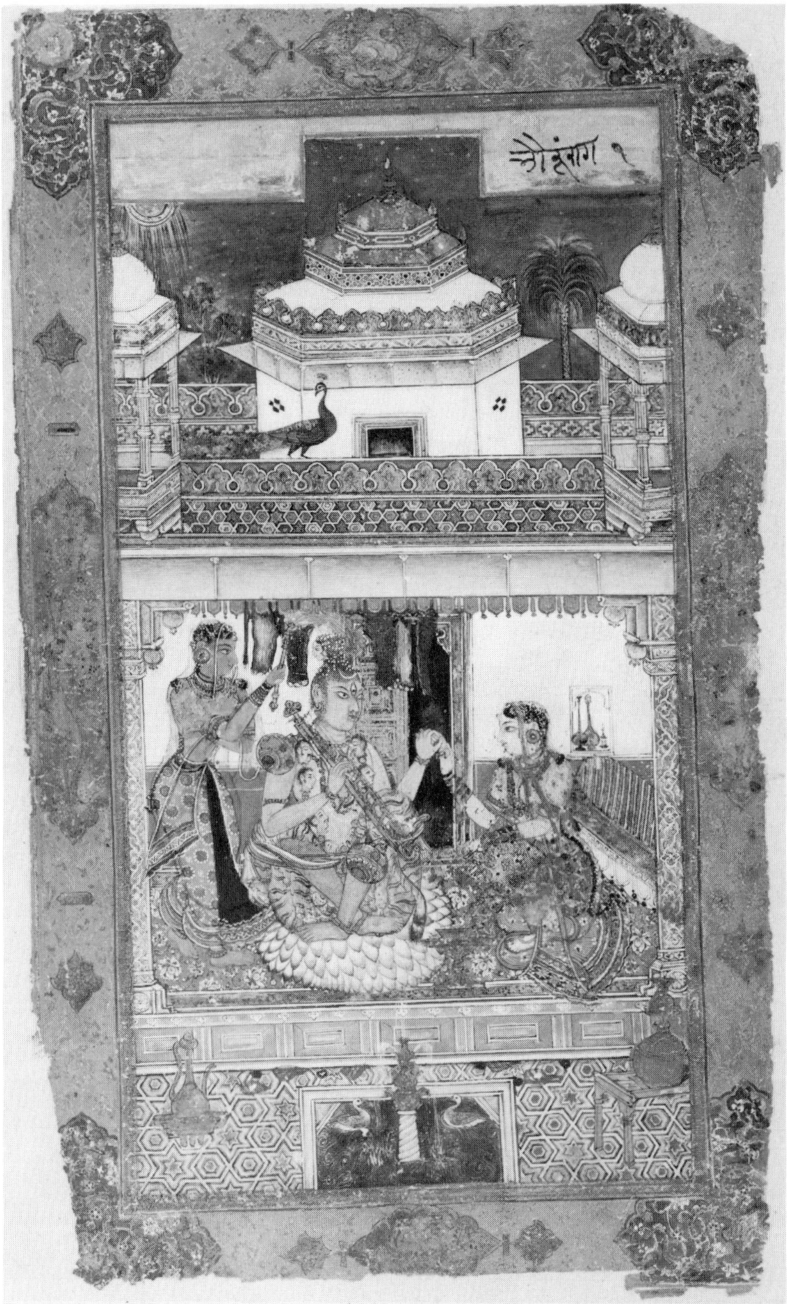

27. Bhairava Raga. From a *Ragamala* series, Rajput or sub-imperial Mughal, at Chunar, dated 1591

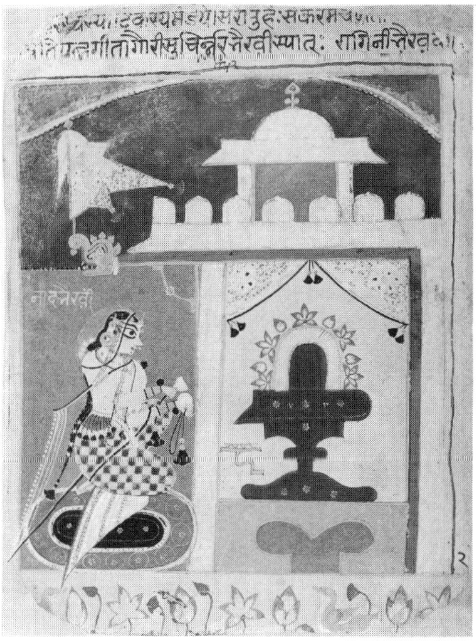

28. Bhairava Raga. From a *Ragamala* series, Delhi area or Rajasthan, ca. 1540

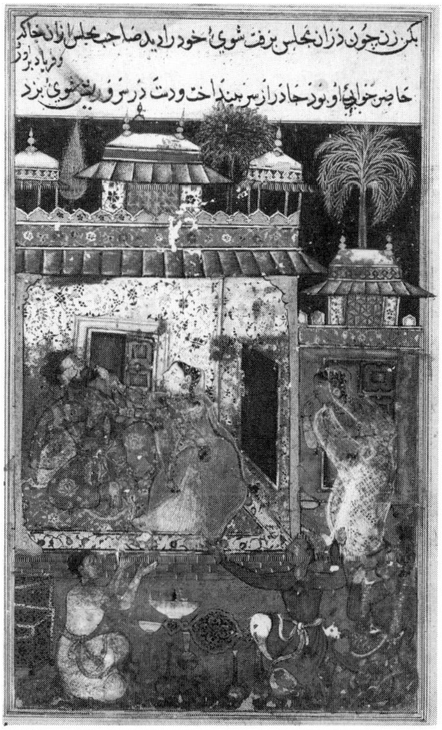

29. The Deceitful Wife Assaults Her Erring Husband. From a *Tutinama* manuscript, Mughal, ca. 1560

action. One gets a sense of the moment; this is one of a continuous sequence of events. The Hindu *Ragamala* scene, whether the early or later version, depicts instead an atemporal situation, for no action or even movement is really implied. Its liveliness – and each version is a very animated scene – is formal, rather than narrative. This is a valid and important general distinction between Mughal and Rajput styles.

An inscription found on the Chunar *Ragamala* is translated in the Appendix. The passage names three painters and implies that they had studied in the Mughal workshops. If by the early 1590s their styles had not progressed much beyond that of the *Tutinama*, then it is no wonder that they were no longer in Akbar's employ. Those artists and models available to the lesser nobility were inevitably either historically or qualitatively distant from contemporary imperial taste. Even had they wished, few members of the nobility could have had copies of Akbar's *Razmnama* or *Ramayana* made that were as faithful in their illustrations as in their text.

The imperial *Razmnama* project was transitional to a new direction which Mughal manuscript painting took in the 1580s, when Akbar was no longer primarily interested in the fantasy adventure stories of his youth – the *Hamzanama* or *Tutinama*, for example. It was the rational and historical that was henceforth to dominate his interest. In 1582, he ordered explicitly that "the rational contents of different religions and faiths, should be translated in [from] the language of each, and that the rose garden of the traditional aspects of each religion should, as far as possible, be cleared of the thorns of bigotry."[5] His interest in the *Razmnama*, therefore, perfectly balanced his wish to learn about traditional India and his waning concern for fantastic or mythological narratives.

During these years he commissioned a new history of the first thousand years of Islam, the *Tarikh-i-Alfi* (History of a Thousand), and an illustrated chronicle of the life of Timur, the *Timurnama*, from which *Timur Lays Siege to the Fort of Sari* is reproduced here (fig. 30). The latter manuscript was particularly important. Babur was a fifth generation descendant of Timur, a leader of such importance that the Mughals continually proclaimed themselves Timurids. The text and illustrations for this history of Timur's life describe briefly his descendants as well, ending with Akbar. The legitimacy of that emperor's power, and his direct continuation of Timur's accomplishments and heritage, could not be more clearly stated, nor the political uses of artistic imagery more clearly understood. The compositions used in the *Timurnama* provide present-day viewers with the first known models and standards for the illustration of a sequence of historical events. Earlier historical manuscripts almost certainly existed, but they are presently unknown.

A particularly important artist during these years was Basawan, whom Abu'l Fazl placed fourth – following Daswanth – in his *A'in-i-Akbari* list: "In designing, painting faces, colouring, portrait painting, and other aspects of this art, Basawan has come to be uniquely excellent. Many perspicacious connoisseurs give him preference over Daswanta."[6] The last phrase is significant, and visual evidence also indicates that Daswanth and Basawan painted in quite different styles. This was obviously recognized and appreciated by their contemporaries, and with the death of Daswanth and the emperor's increased interest in historical or documentary subjects, Basawan becomes the most prominent artist in the studios.

Unlike Daswanth, Basawan was particularly skillful in evoking the myriad character types found on the subcontinent, and in exploring their

[5] S. A. A. Rizvi, *Religious and Intellectual History of the Muslims in Akbar's Reign*, New Delhi, 1975, pp. 354–355.
[6] Chandra, *Tutinama*, pp. 183–184.

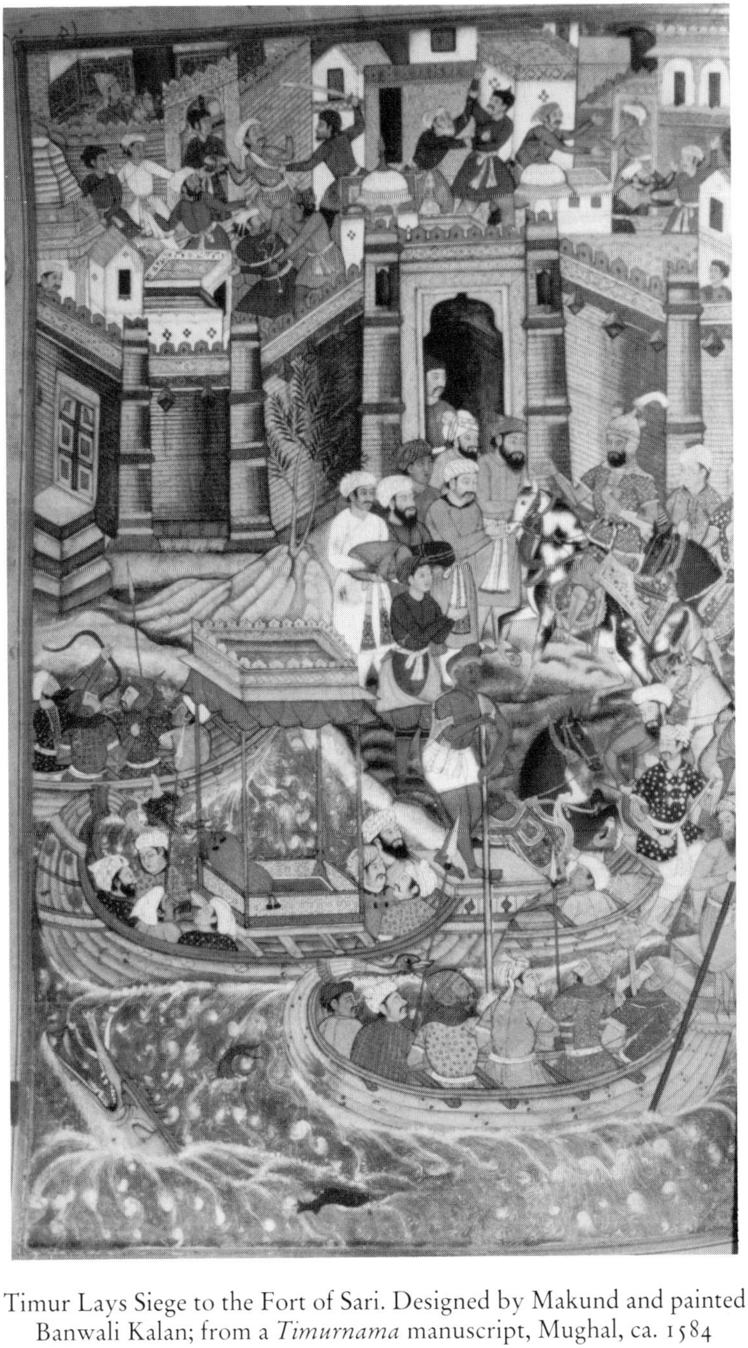

30. Timur Lays Siege to the Fort of Sari. Designed by Makund and painted by Banwali Kalan; from a *Timurnama* manuscript, Mughal, ca. 1584

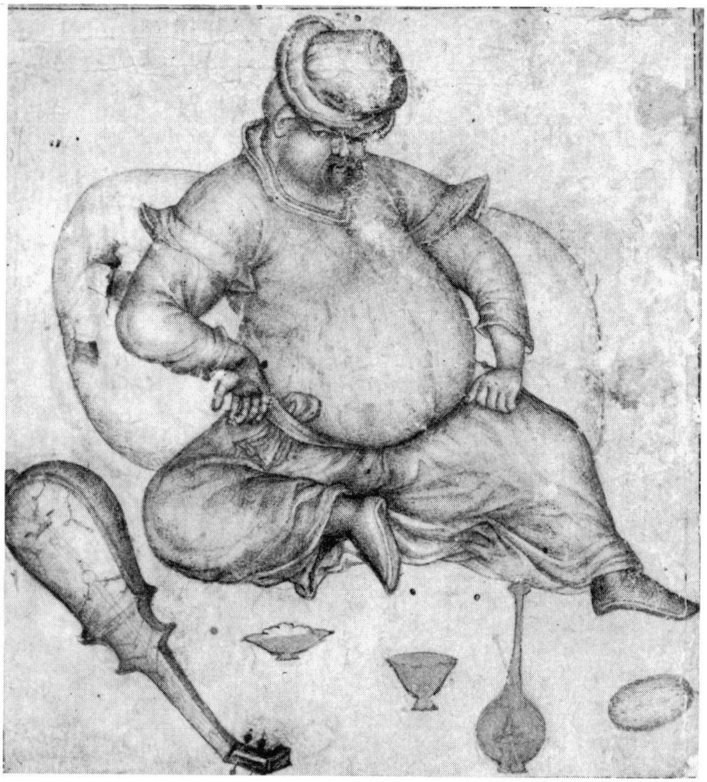

31. Seated Man. By Basawan; Mughal, ca. 1580

physiognomies and characters, the texture of their clothing, or the way they positioned themselves in space. The drawing *Seated Man* (fig. 31) reveals that Basawan's interests are very different from those of Mir Sayyid Ali, under whose supervision he may have spent his early years in the imperial studio. *Seated Youth* (fig. 32), by the Persian master, uses the figure as an excuse to explore the aesthetic beauty and independent expressiveness of line. For the younger Mughal artist, however, the lines are there as tools to interpret a jovial, Falstaffian personality. Like the *Timurnama*, with which it is contemporary, *Seated Man* seems intent on increasing awareness of the day-to-day world of experience.

At a time when members of the nobility were developing increased patronage of the arts – one way, certainly, to link themselves with imperial power – a new refinement and elegance of taste is seen in Akbar's own workshops. One example is the illustrations added at the Mughal court about 1585–1590 to a copy of the *Khamsa* of Nizami written at Yazd (in Iran) at the beginning of the century. *Khusrau and Shirin in Bed* (fig. 33), by Basawan and Dharm Das

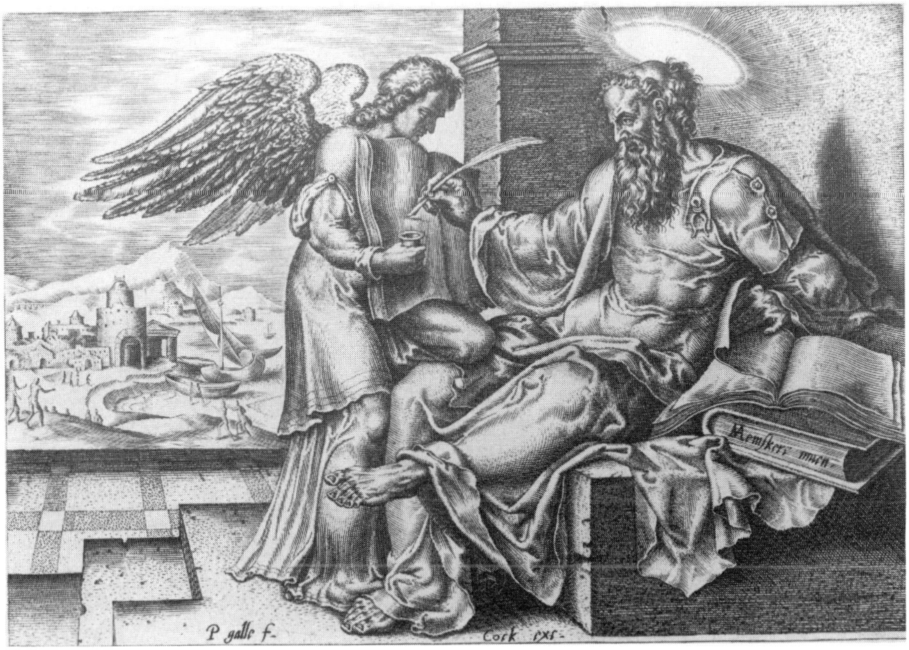

36. St. Matthew. By Philip Galle after Maarten van Heemskerk; Flemish, ca. 1565

which were quickly absorbed into Mughal painting. A small self-portrait by the artist (fig. 37) reveals a far less overtly European-influenced style, but betrays Kesu Das' interest in using fabric to define physical volumes.

That European influences reached the court long before the Jesuits arrived in 1580 is now evident. Even chronicles of Humayun's reign mention European textiles displayed at court, indication that lines of communication and trade were already then openly active.[9] Abu'l Fazl recognized the importance of European example to the developing Mughal style. He wrote:

> Such excellent artists have assembled here that a fine match has been created to the world-renowned unique art of Bihzad [the greatest Timurid artist in Iran] and the magic-making of the Europeans. Delicacy of work, clarity of line and boldness of execution, as well as other fine qualities have reached perfection, and inanimate objects appear to have come alive. More than one hundred persons have reached the status of a master and gained fame; and they are numerous who are near to reaching that state or are half-way there.[10]

By the 1590s, therefore, when the passage was written, Iran and Europe were held up as standards against which Mughal paintings were to be judged. There

[9] Khwandamir, *Qanun-i-Humayuni*, pp. 37, 46, 49, etc.
[10] Chandra, *Tutinama*, p. 183.

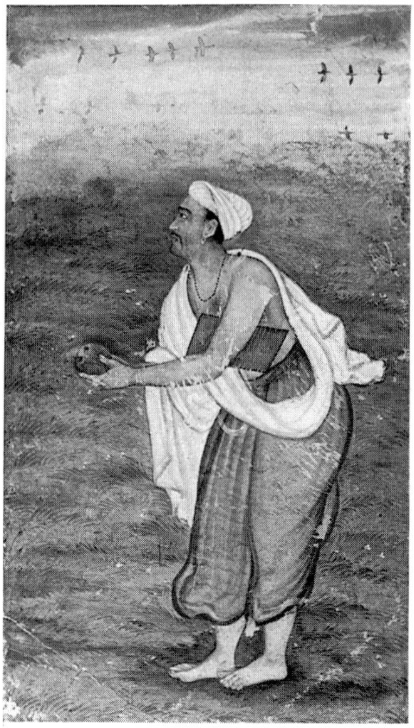

37. Self-portrait. By Kesu Das. Mughal, ca. 1570

is no mention of Hindu works; indeed, the Hindu stylistic traits noted in the early manuscripts are no longer present. Illustrations now perfectly embody a new and far more sophisticated taste. Subtle color transitions have replaced those bold juxtapositions found in the *Hamzanama*; technical prowess is celebrated – seen best in the detailed representations of architecture or textiles; and pigments are rich, varied, and expensive.

The most luxurious level of imperial style during these years, which we associate with the city of Lahore, where Akbar lived between 1585 and 1598, is best defined by a series of volumes of poetical texts, one of which would certainly be the 1588 *Diwan* of Anwari (fig. 34). *Majnun Consoled by His Father* (fig. 38), from the *Khamsa* of Amir Khusrau Dihlavi, dated 1597–1598, is by Lal, the most prolific of Akbar's artists. Its concern for human interaction, sympathetic depictions of animal life, and spatial depth, and its insistent visual activity over every area of its surface, is typical of these Lahore works. The technique too is immaculate, full of tightly controlled brushstrokes and continual modulations of color.

A second page from this manuscript, *Laila and Majnun at School* (fig. 39), by Dharm Das, should be compared to *Sa'di and the Youth of Kashgar* (fig. 40), from a *Gulistan* of Sa'di, dated 1486 and attributed to Bihzad, the painter

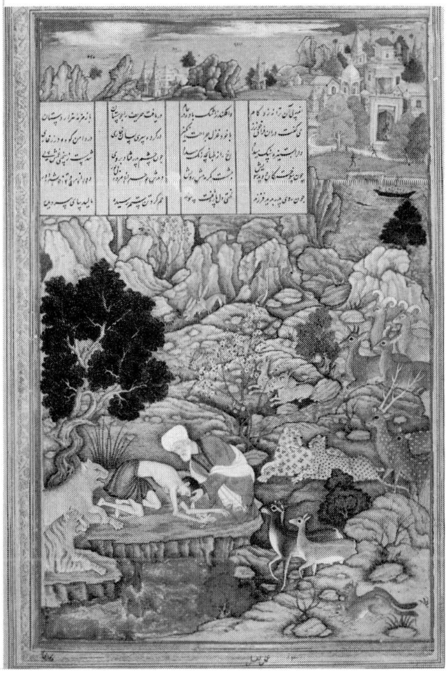

38. Majnun Consoled by his Father. By Lal; from a *Khamsa* of Amir Khusrau Dihlavi manuscript, Mughal, dated 1597–1598

lauded by Abu'l Fazl. Each shows a schoolroom with people outside the doorway, and a distant landscape. Each is a faithful reconstruction of architectural forms and of the placement of humans within the space. And each shows the highest level of technical skill. The results, however, are very different.

The Persian painting is dominated visually by surface patterns; for example, the fluid, serpentine movement which unites the shapes of the children is obviously contrasted to the tight, geometric circles which enliven the wall surfaces. This is a formally idealized world existing in a space separate from our own, for we could not experience the interrelationships of these patterns in this way at the actual scene. Dharm Das, by contrast, gives dramatic immediacy to the figures in *Laila and Majnun at School.* We immediately notice their actions, not their placement. And because the forms are shaded, giving them volume and weight, we are not conscious of boundary lines and flat surfaces. These figures move of their own volition within a deep spatial ambient similar to our own; they are not – as they are in Bihzad's work – primarily the means to arrange colors, lines, and shapes for our delectation. Abu'l Fazl expressed Akbar's admiration for Bihzad, and by the 1590s Mughal painting had indeed developed a technical expertise, formal elegance, and emotional

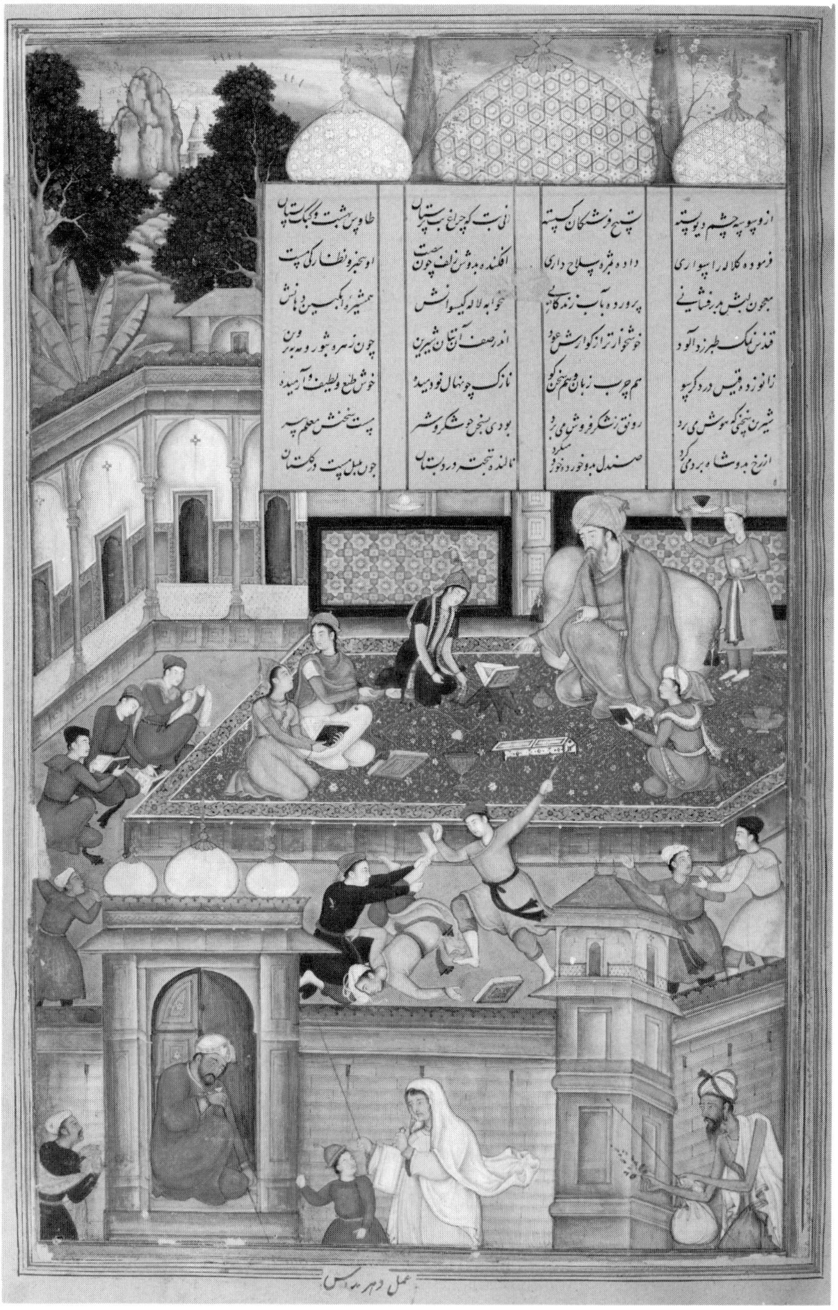

39. Laila and Majnun at School. By Dharm Das; from a *Khamsa* of Amir Khusrau Dihlavi manuscript, Mughal, dated 1597–1598

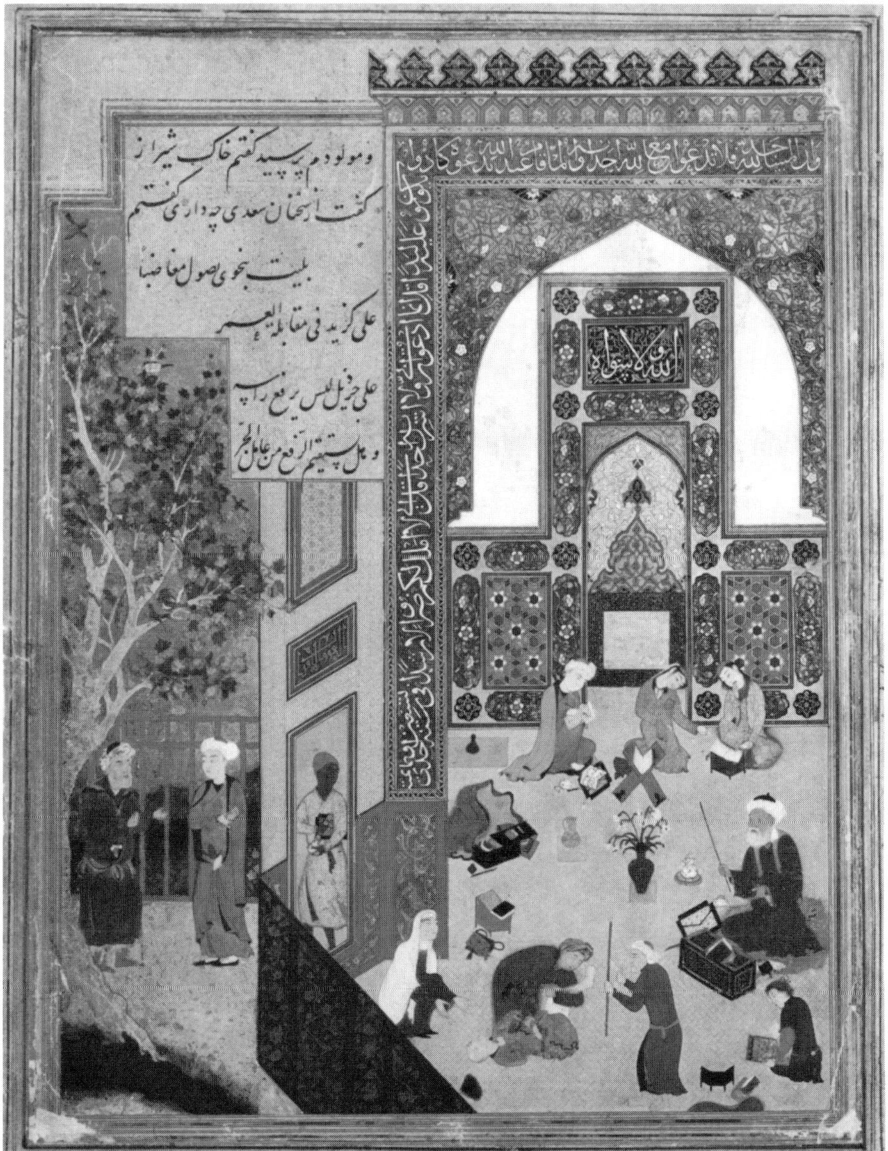

40. Sa'di and the Youth of Kashgar. Attributed to Bihzad; from a *Gulistan* of Sa'di manuscript, Iran, at Herat, dated 1486

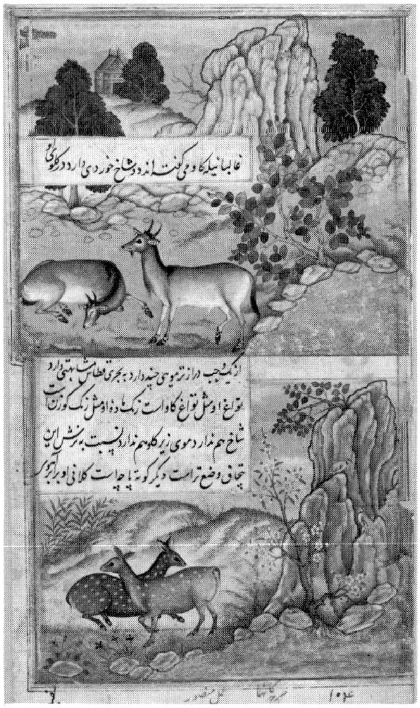

42. Two Blue Bulls and Two Hog Deer. Designed by Kanha, painted by Mansur; from a *Baburnama* manuscript, Mughal, ca. 1589

animals can all be considered rather reticent in effect. The use of thin washes of pigment rather than heavily layered, burnished color, and the quick, sketchy quality of the execution, imply that these were not works meant to impress by the richness of the materials used, or by the obvious time spent in their execution – important factors to such projects as the imperial *Razmnama*. Clearly a formula for illustrations of animals had developed that was used at this time no matter what the character of the text was. The similarities discussed here may also indicate that the *Kitab-i-Saat* was illustrated in the imperial studios, although the text had been copied earlier elsewhere.

The most important of the historical projects, however, were unquestionably the *Timurnama* (fig. 30), and the two known *Akbarnama* manuscripts. The *Akbarnama* is a history of the emperor's own reign, for which he asked his confidant Abu'l Fazl in 1590–1591 to begin composing a narrative – a text from which we have already quoted liberally. In 1574, Akbar had established a Record office, where fourteen clerks kept note of the events and details of the emperor's life; he also asked older courtiers and court servants to assemble their memoirs of earlier years. All of this material was made available to Abu'l Fazl.

The first volume of text for the *Akbarnama* was finished and presented to the

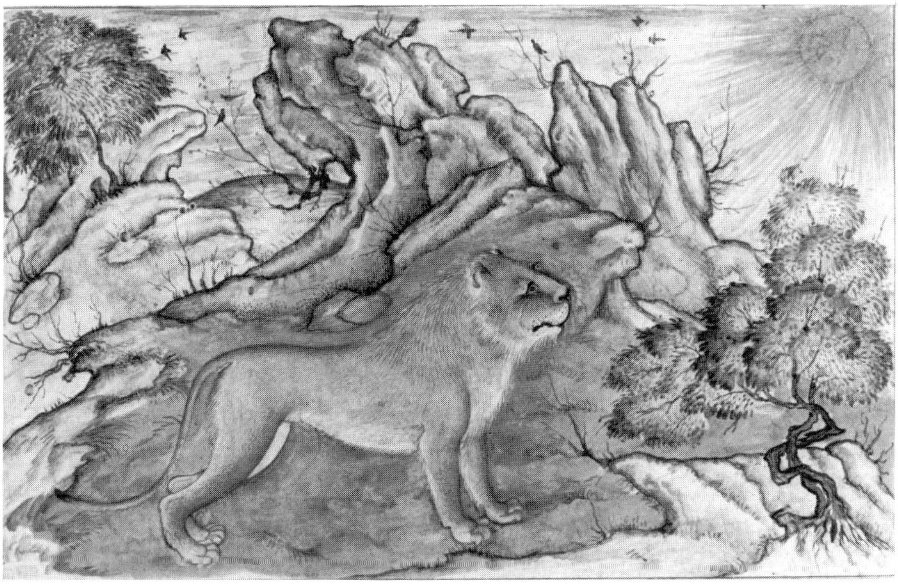

43. The Constellation Leo. From a *Kitab-i Saat* manuscript, Mughal, dated 1583

emperor in 1596. It covered the years up to 1572, and included an extensive description of the foundation and loss of empire under Babur and Humayun. Two years later a second volume was completed, bringing the account up to date. The total project had then taken seven years, according to information that comes from Abu'l Fazl's own narrative.

The copy of this *Akbarnama* with the earliest illustrations includes only those episodes occurring between 1560 and 1578, so that it cannot be considered complete. The manuscript is nonetheless extraordinary visual evidence for Akbar's character and physical vitality. Its illustrations show him hunting, watching Hindu yogis slaughtering a rival sect, riding a wild elephant, viewing men who catch fish with their teeth, at war, and in the relative peace of the darbar. One of the finest of the few known dispersed pages of the book illustrates *The Arrest of Abu'l-ma'ali* (fig. 44), a handsome youth, the favorite of Humayun, who had become arrogant and demanding to Akbar. On the third day after the emperor's accession, Abu'l-ma'ali was seized in open court assembly by servants of the regent, Bairam Khan, seen standing just in front of the enthroned Akbar. The *Akbarnama* recounts the event:

> At this time the stupefying wine of thoughts and caprices overpowered Shah Abu'l Ma'ali, whose brain had been ruined by the worship of his own beauty and the intoxication produced by the world . . . After making his attendance [at court] conditional on certain things which were of no value, he attended . . . He sate down on H.M. the Shahinshah's [Akbar's] right hand. It was the time when the festive board was about to be spread, and when he put out his

> hands to wash them, Tolag Khan Qucin, who was strong and nimble, behaved dextrously, and coming from behind seized both of Shah Abu'l Ma'ali's arms and made him a prisoner. Others who stood at the foot of the throne came forward to assist . . . [12]

Designed by Basawan and executed by Shankar, the scene is full of the bustle and agitation which such a sensational act would provoke. The clarity of the action and space, and the liveliness of the figures and the color, are elements found in the best pages from this manuscript. Historical events are usually presented in as factually authentic a manner as possible, clear here by comparing the historical narrative with the illustration. We find, as well, a new naturalism in the depiction of architecture and such details as textiles. On the other hand, many of the illustrations in this *Akbarnama* are simple adaptations of scenes in the *Timurnama*, sometimes made with the obvious intent of creating an identity between the two rulers.[13] John Seyller has recently confirmed the suggestion that the illustrations included in this manuscript were made before the compilation of Abu'l Fazl's text by discovering that an earlier historical narrative originally written on the pages was covered over by the new official history once it was written.[14] This, of course, has important implications for the continuing study of the relationship between text and image within the entire Mughal manuscript tradition.

A second major illustrated copy of the *Akbarnama* text is also known. Dr. Seyller and Wheeler Thackston have further suggested that the traditional date of 1604, hitherto accepted for the volume, is also incorrect, and that it was produced – or at least initiated – about 1597, a date found on one of the pages.[15] For the earlier *Akbarnama*, several artists usually collaborated on any single illustration. This later manuscript consists of paintings by the very greatest imperial painters working alone, however, a working method that became more dominant with Akbar's increasing appreciation of his artists' individual skills.

While several of the sequentially earlier illustrations in the book are less than full-page in size, the manuscript quickly took on a more lavish character, shown best by the frequent appearance of double-page illustrations. One specific depiction that would have had no compositional precedent shows *Akbar's Expedition to the Eastern Provinces* (fig. 45), when courtiers and even elephants sailed down the Ganges. The *Akbarnama* describes the scene:

> H.M. took along with him two mountain-like, swift-as-the-wind elephants. The first was Bal Sundar, who was put into one boat with two female elephants . . . Together with rank-breaking might, and strength to cast down mountains he was perfectly sedate and quiet . . . The spectacle was an astonishing one. The

[12] Abu'l Fazl, *Akbar Nama*, vol. II, pp. 27–29. [13] Beach, *Early Mughal Painting*, pp. 114–115.
[14] Seyller, "Codicological Aspects." [15] Seyller, "Codicological Aspects."

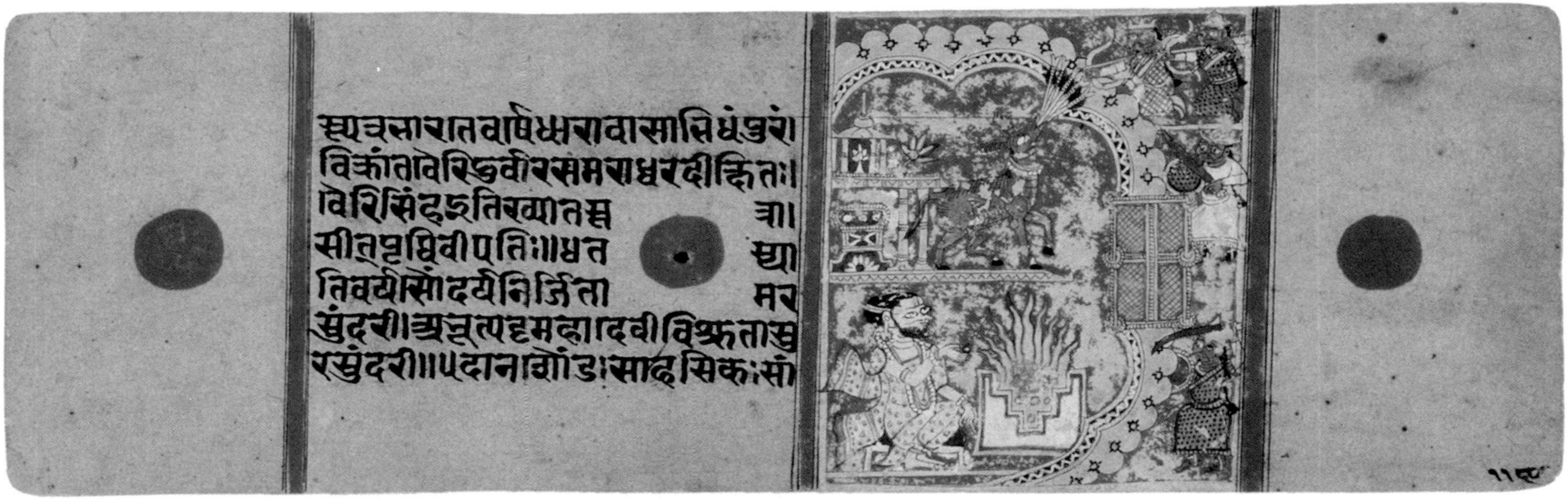

A The Siege of Ujjain and the Magic She-Ass. From a *Kalpasutra* and *Kalakacharyakatha* manuscript, Western or Central India, dated 1411

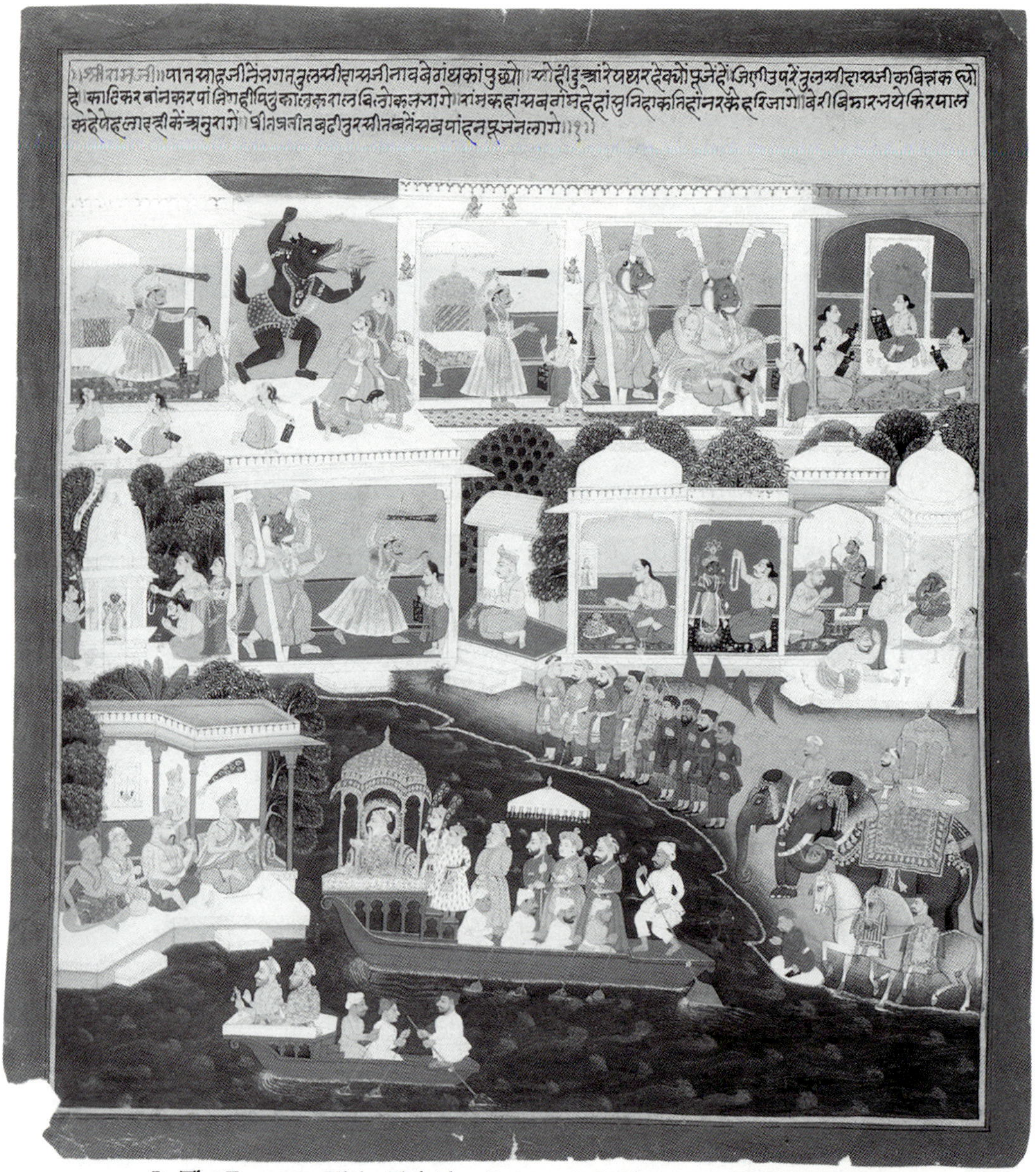

L The Emperor Visits Tulsidas. Rajput, Rajasthan at Udaipur, ca. 1710

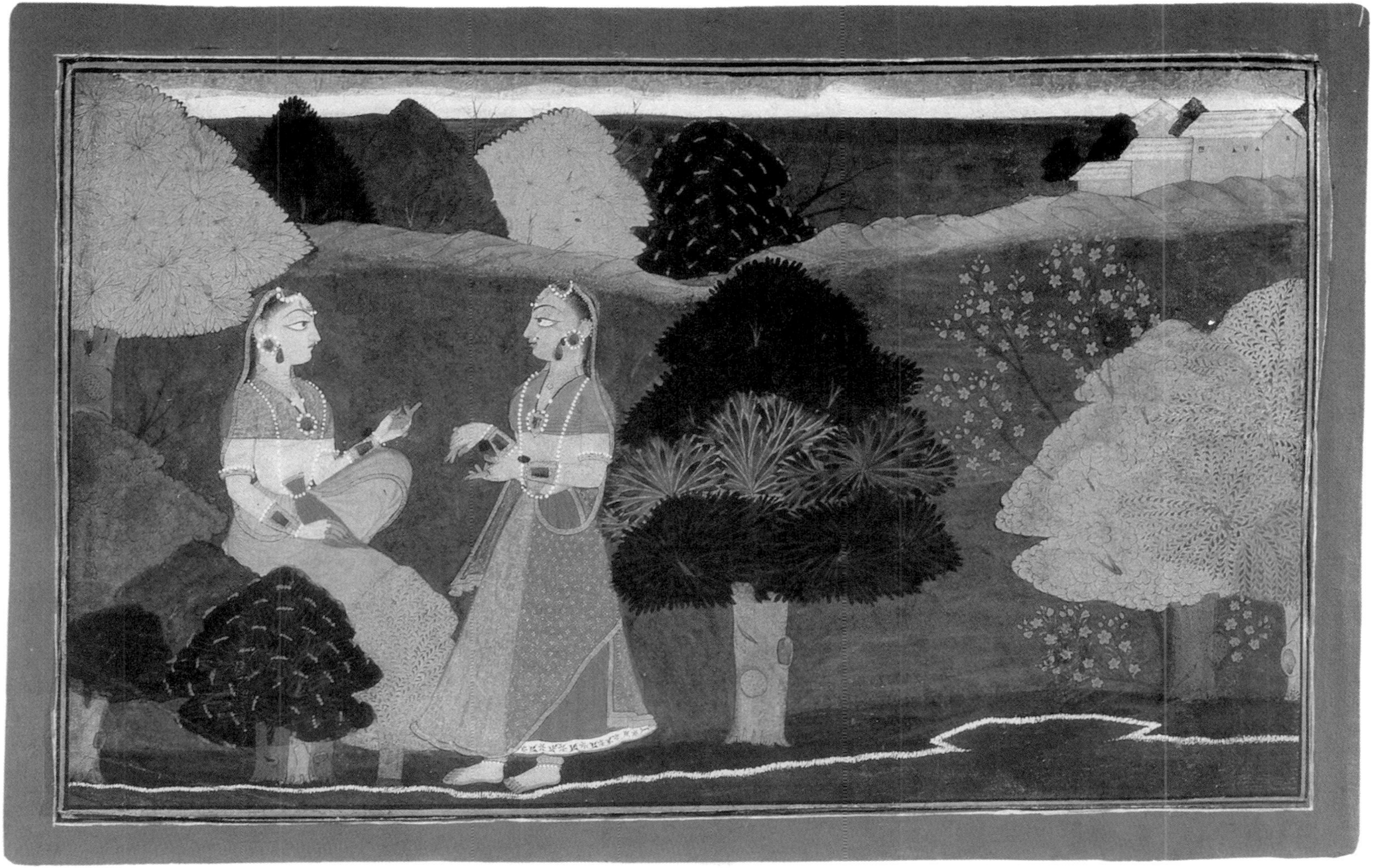

M Radha and a Confidante. From a *Gita Govinda* series, Rajput, Punjab Hills, dated 1730

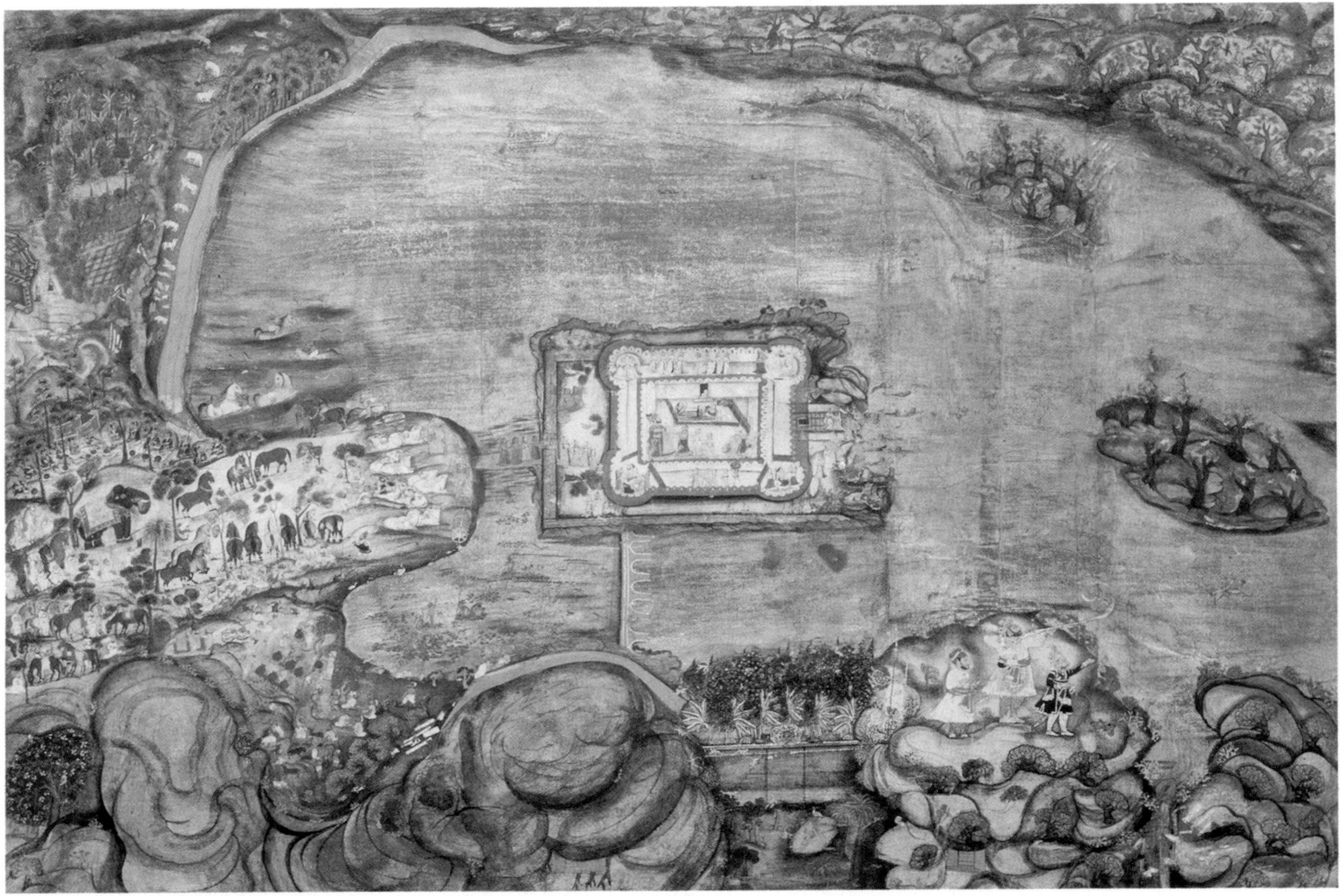

P Rawat Gokul Das of Devgarh at a Lake Palace. By Bagta; Rajput, Rajasthan at Devgarh, dated 1808

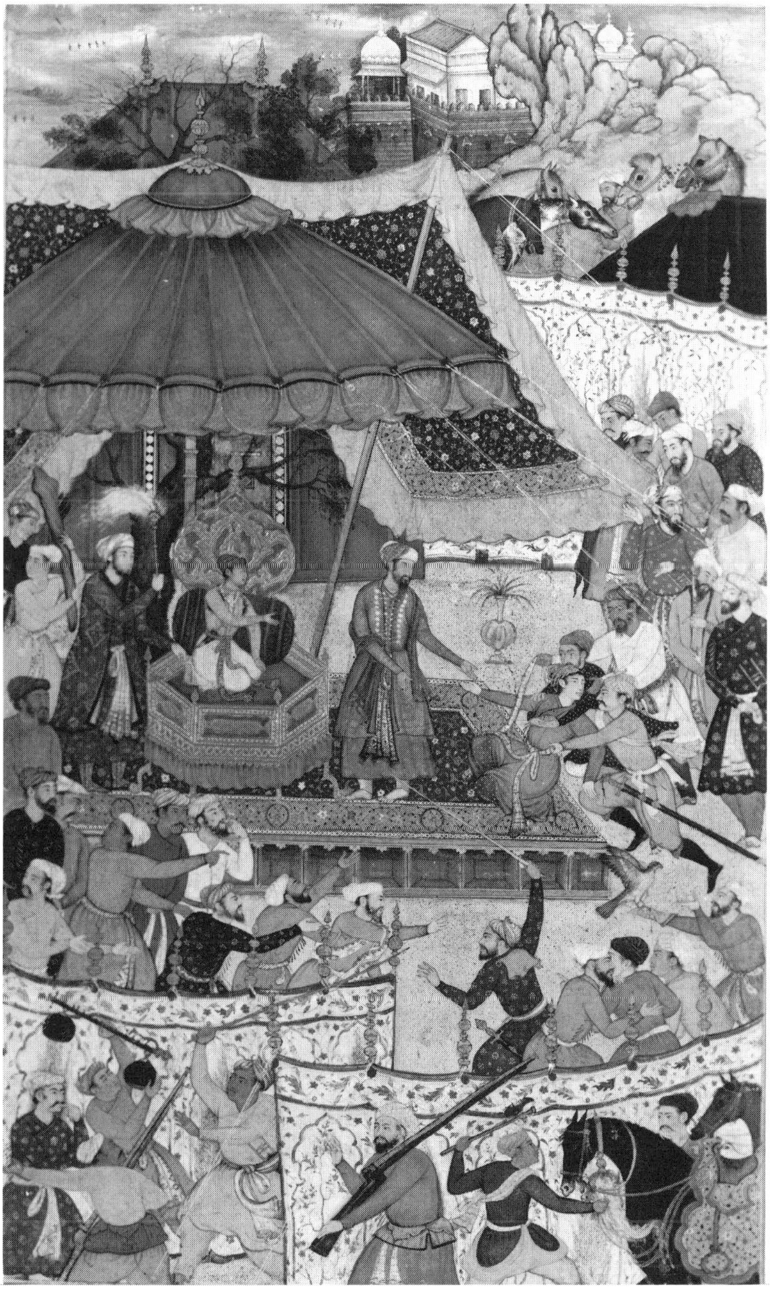

44. The Arrest of Abu'l-ma'ali. Designed by Basawan and painted by Shankar; from an *Akbarnama* manuscript, Mughal, ca. 1585

emperor, and the glance out of the frame by the courtier at the top right, certainly had a specific significance.) The pent-up energy of the emperor gives no doubt of his unflagging power – a problem for his eldest son, then in his thirties and allowed little responsibility.

Prince Salim finally acceded to the imperial throne as the Emperor Jahangir in 1605, but only after a longstanding rivalry with his father. As early as 1591, Akbar had accused the prince of attempting to poison him, and by the end of the century, the split had become so profound that Salim formally rebelled. He set up an independent court at Allahabad, and assumed the imperial title of Shah. This was a flagrant challenge to Akbar; and in other ways too Salim's behavior was outrageous and inflammatory.

> At this time it was reported by truthful and disinterested persons that the heart of that cypress of fortune's stream [Salim] had become excessively addicted to wine. He did not keep his lips from the wine-cup for a moment. When he got habituated to wine, he drank more, but the intoxication was less, and so he added opium . . . At the time when a double intoxication [of wine and opium] had taken hold of him, and when the brain was dried up, and his disposition unsettled, he for slight offences ordered unfitting, capital punishments. For instance, he had his Recorder flayed alive in his presence. And he castrated one of the pages . . . and had a khidmatgar beaten so that he died.[1]

Akbar protested in horror at these events; a reaction that should be taken with some cynicism, of course, considering the emperor's own career. Nonetheless, the two men themselves were clearly convinced that their own temperaments were quite different.

As part of his establishment at Allahabad, Salim supported painters. He had long been interested in the arts and, like his father, voraciously commissioned and collected works of art. An early seventeenth-century chronicler, paraphrasing the reports of Father Jerome Xavier, who led the Third Jesuit Mission to the Mughal Court in 1595, wrote that Salim

> was very angry with those who had conducted the Fathers, because they had not brought him any picture of our Lady from Goa; and speaking to another who was about to set out for those parts, he charged him to buy certain pieces which he desired to have, bidding him above all things not to forget to bring a beautiful picture of our Lady. As the Fathers had brought with them a Portuguese painter, the Prince straightaway ordered him to make a copy of the picture of our Lady which they had brought from Goa.[2]

The earliest work specifically attributable to Salim's patronage is the marginal design now on a page of the *Muraqqa Gulshan*, an extraordinary album of pictures and calligraphies which Salim began before his father's death, and of

[1] Abu'l Fazl, *Akbar Nama*, vol. III, p. 1242.
[2] Pierre du Jarric, *Akbar and the Jesuits*, translated by C. H. Payne, London, 1926, pp. 66–67.

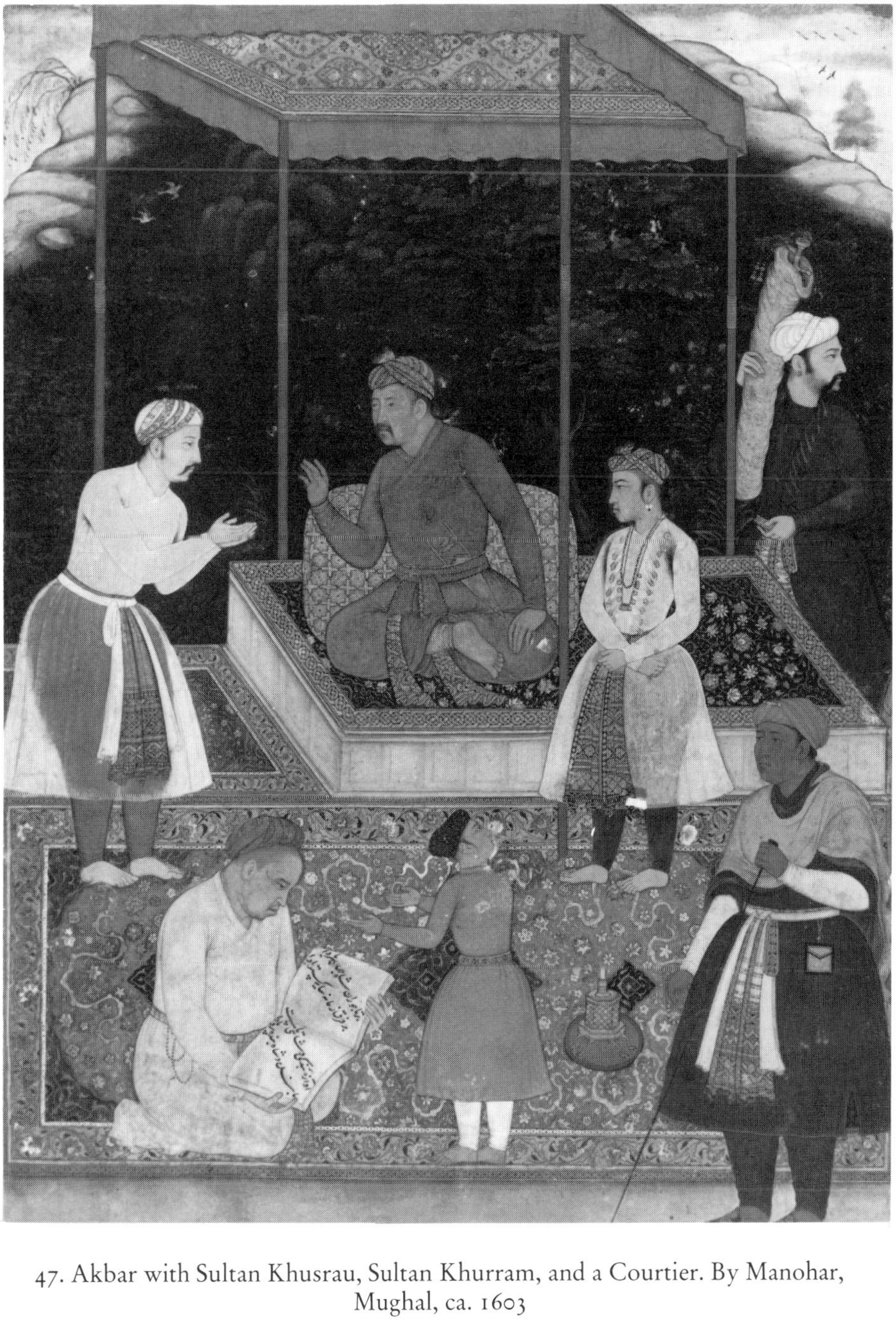

47. Akbar with Sultan Khusrau, Sultan Khurram, and a Courtier. By Manohar, Mughal, ca. 1603

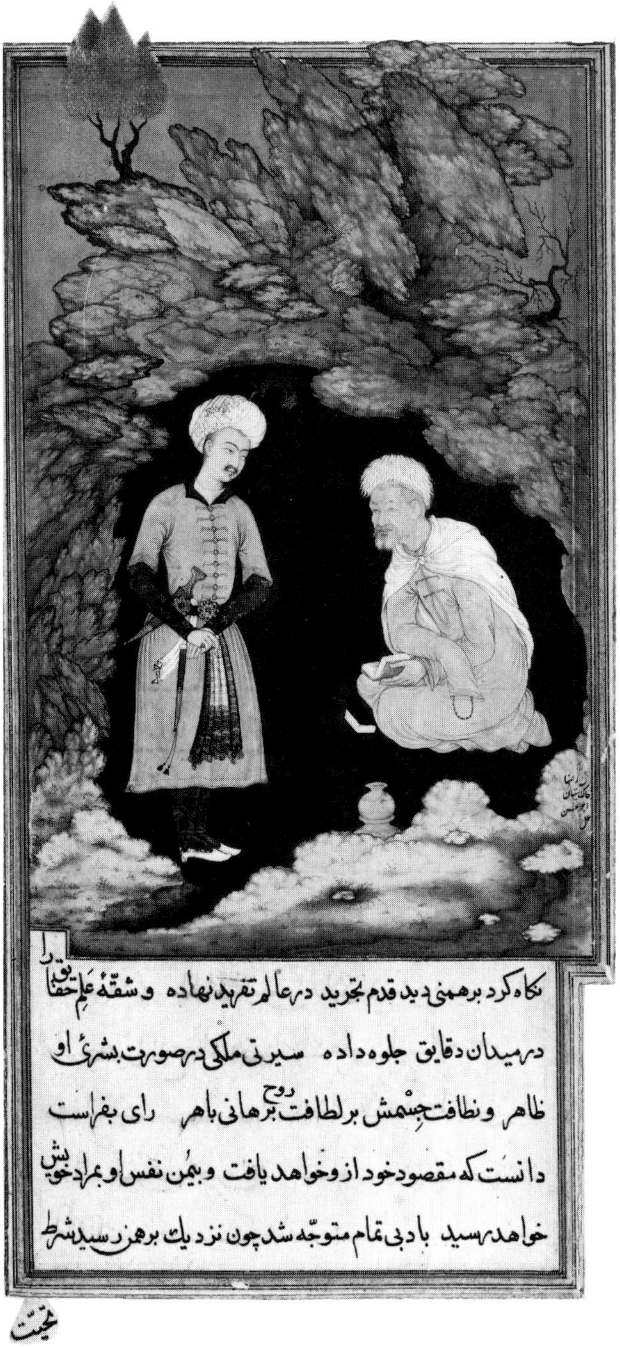

49. King Dabshalim and the Sage Bidpai. By Abu'l Hasan; from an *Anwar-i-Suhaili* manuscript, Mughal, dated 1604–1610

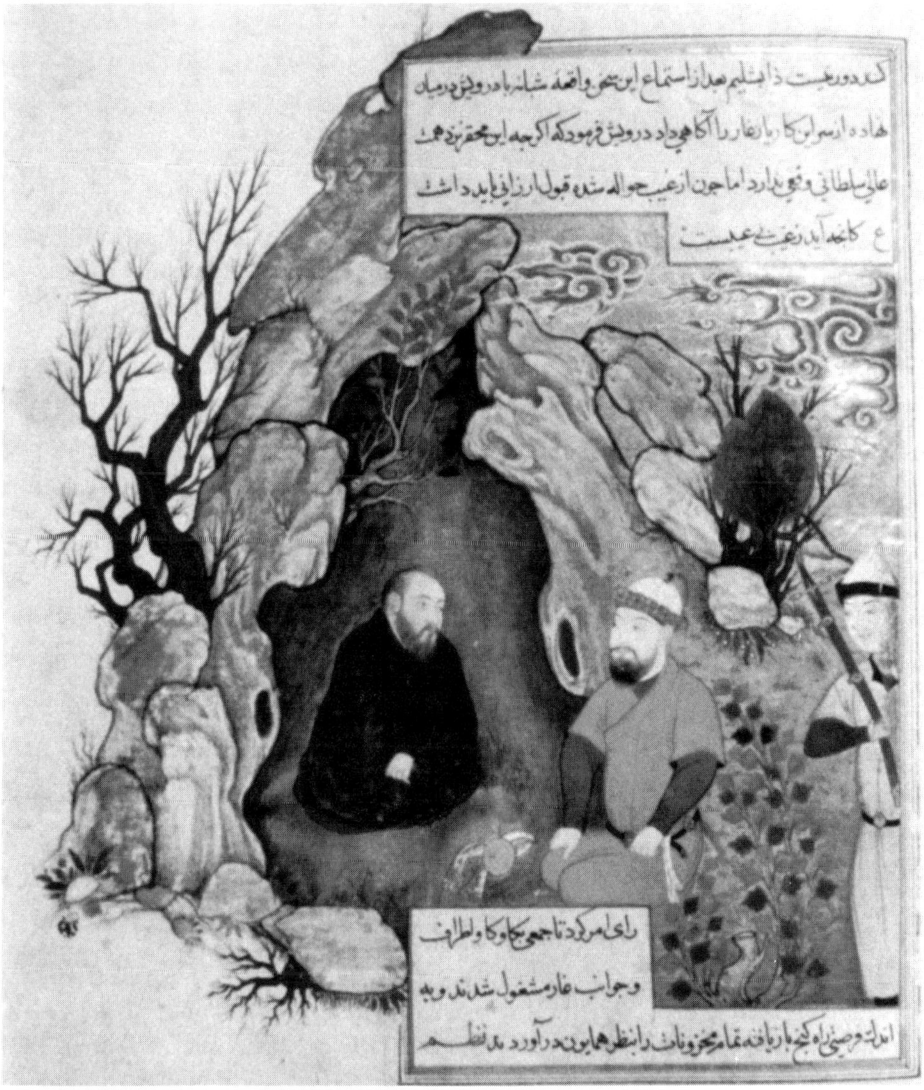

50. A King Visits a Hermit. From an *Anwar-i-Suhaili* manuscript, Iran, at Qazwin, dated 1593

The 1604–1610 *Anwar-i-Suhaili* manuscript contains elements of this distinctive Allahabad style, together with a continuation of the type of painting which had developed at Akbar's court. And a comparison of three versions of the same episode from different copies of the *Anwar-i-Suhaili* helps to define the artistic developments of the early seventeenth century. The scene chosen tells of a woman attacked by a lion. She had been married to an old man, but deserts him to run off with a handsome young prince – who flees ungallantly when she is mauled. The tale is an excuse for moral injunctions against infidelity.

As presented in the copy dated 1571, *The Lion, the Unfaithful Wife, and the Prince* (fig. 54) also includes a second episode to create a continuous narrative. (To the right, the prince and his love picnic before the attack.) The surface is loosely compartmentalized, and space segmented; as well, the technique is sketchy, and the colors strong: red and orange dominate. For these reasons, the work is still heavily in debt to pre-Mughal Hindu styles. More emphasis is placed on the background in a Lahore period manuscript dated 1596–1597 (fig. 55), for it is packed with mountains and a distant town, and this diffuses our interest. A single instant is shown, and the technique is smoother, just as colors are more subdued and space more fluid and continuous. In the 1604–1610 *Anwar-i-Suhaili* (fig. 56), the composition is reduced to the most basic elements: woman, prince and lion against a minimal landscape which serves only as a screen to keep our interest on the story. The depiction of the attack is far more graphic and painful to behold, for nothing draws our attention away from the event. The move from the excitement of several narrative episodes to the visual stimulation of a crowded composition to the concentration on the pain of the lion's attack perfectly coordinates with shifts in the most basic elements of Mughal painting over four crucial decades. On the other hand, the ultimately narrow range of difference among the works indicates just how conservative and traditional the treatment of frequently illustrated texts remained at the Mughal court.

Upon his accession in 1605, Salim had chosen the title Jahangir (Seizer of the World). He inherited his father's artists and ateliers, of course, along with imperial power, and his commissions inevitably took a new direction. While the Allahabad period can be isolated as a separate sub-style, it nonetheless predicts certain directions in which imperial painting immediately moved. Three manuscripts are especially important in the evolution of this new level and intensity of patronage: a *Kulliyat* ("Collected Works") of Sa'di; a *Bustan* of Sa'di (plate E); and a *Khamsa* of Mir Ali Shir Nava'i. Like the Lahore manuscripts made for Akbar a decade earlier, these are volumes of poetry and are supremely sumptuous. Specifically dated 1605, the *Bustan* is central to the group. It includes pages attributable to the Allahabad artists Aqa Riza, Mirza

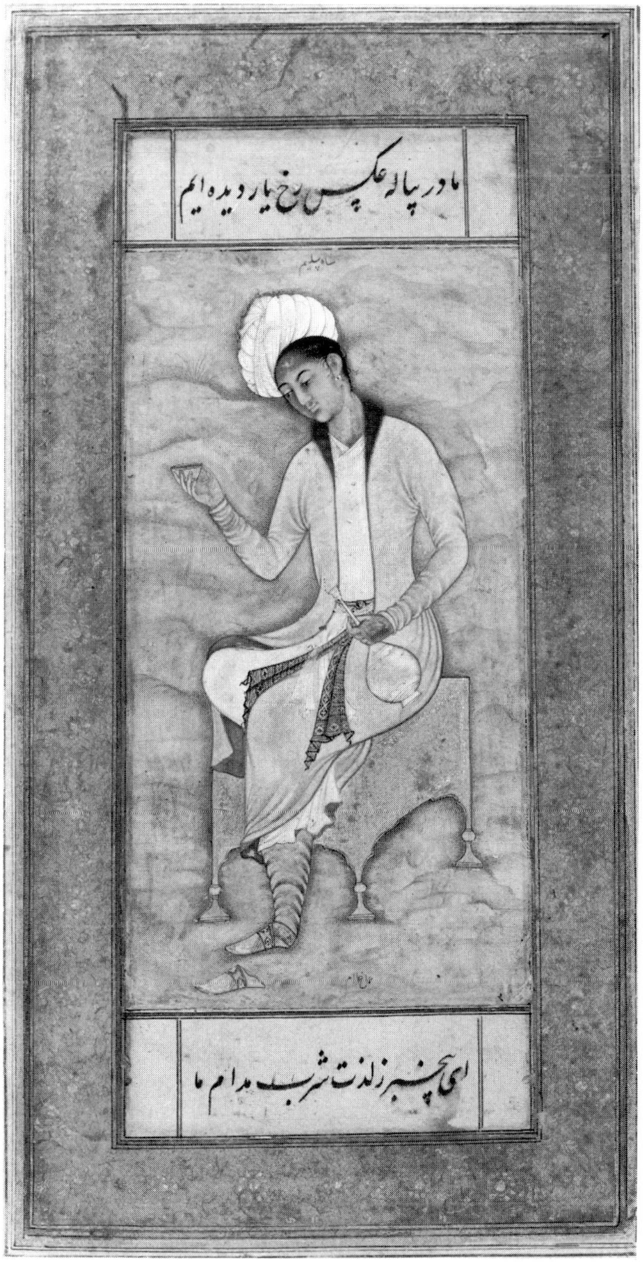

53. Seated Youth. By Ghulam; from the Salim Album, Mughal, ca. 1600–1605

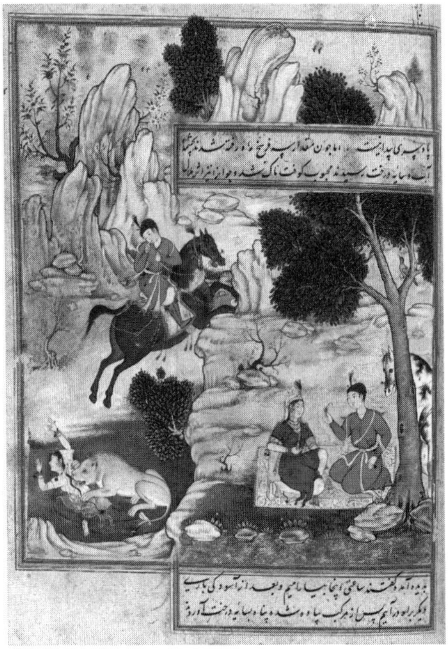

54. The Lion, the Unfaithful Wife, and the Prince. By Nanha; from an *Anwar-i-Suhaili* manuscript, Mughal, dated 1571

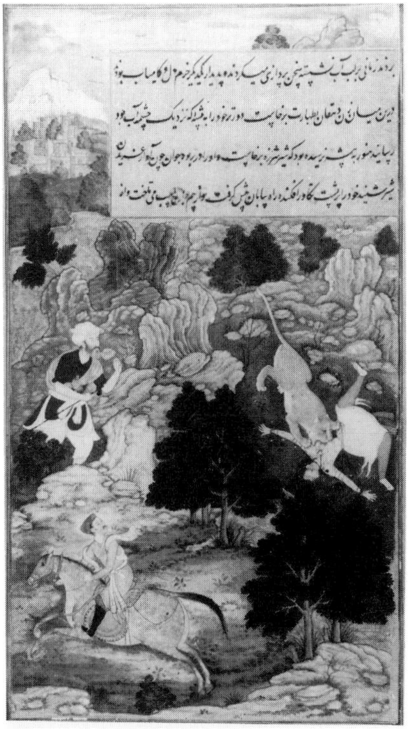

55. The Lion, the Unfaithful Wife, and the Prince. From an *Anwar-i-Suhaili* manuscript, Mughal, at Lahore, dated 1596–1597

Ghulam and Abu'l Hasan, as well as the imperial Akbari painters Govardhan, Daulat and Sur Das Gujarati. The other two books are so closely related to the *Bustan* in style that together they define a particular and important moment in Mughal painting, a time when new standards were again being established.

The Muezzin and the Drunkard (plate E), from the *Bustan*, is set in and around a small mosque: one of the most vivid, exact depictions of architecture in all Mughal painting. The building is placed at a slight diagonal, and this makes us acutely aware of space and both the placement and interrelationship of the figures. The scene is full of quietly revealed details, none of which overpower the central encounter (and quiet is not a word one could apply to many Akbari paintings of a decade earlier). The drunkard, turban askew, is a model of stubborn resistance, and faces throughout are absorbed, thoughtful, and convincingly individualized.

Jahangir's earliest imperial commissions continue the trend which developed in painting for Akbar during the Lahore period. Compositions are simpler and

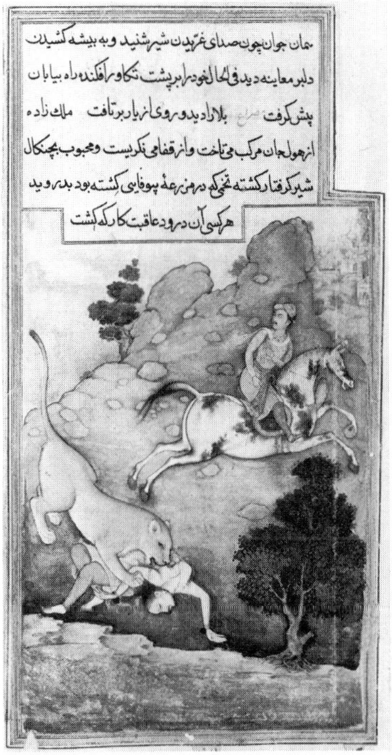

56. The Lion, the Unfaithful Wife, and the Prince.
From an *Anwar-i-Suhaili* manuscript, Mughal, dated 1604–1610

the amount of activity is lessened. We no longer concentrate on actions and events, which humans simply carry out. Instead, what is of interest is the revelation and interplay of human personalities: here the men in conversation or prayer, or the worshipper performing his ablutions. This distinguishes Jahangir's imperial patronage from the works he commissioned as a prince. On the other hand, the interest he showed at Allahabad in refined, controlled technique and the importance of surface design now mixes with his Akbari inheritance, and his painters apply those skills to an ever more precise investigation of human individuality. This is quickly achieved.

One of the greatest manuscripts, a *Gulistan* ("Rose Garden") of Sa'di, is known only through illustrations now removed from the original book and mounted on album pages. The volume is otherwise lost. *The Salvation of One Brother* (fig. 57), by Daulat, tells of a boatload of men who come upon two drowning brothers; since they are able to save only one, they choose the man who is known for his past generosity and kindness.

There is nothing inessential, or inexpressive, in the illustration. The basic narrative necessities are present: the deluged boat of the brothers, one man drowning, a turban floating off on the waters. Interest concentrates on the

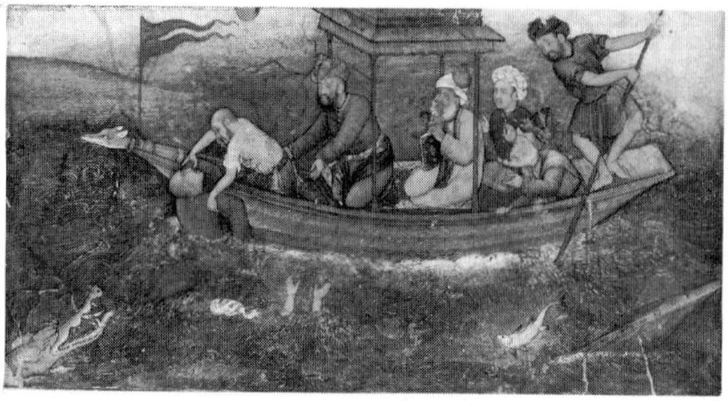

57. The Salvation of One Brother. By Daulat; from a *Gulistan of* Sa'di manuscript, Mughal, ca. 1610

faces, especially of the man in the bow. The drawing of that figure is technically masterful, with extraordinary attention paid to the effects of the thin muslin shirt over his dark skin, for example. (This should be viewed together with knowledge of the size of the painting; it is 2⅝ inches high, and thus the man is painted with true miniaturism.) Such careful observation never distracts us into a concentration on detail for its own sake, however; it is completely at the service of the story.

A superb culmination of the trends we have noted is found on a page from one of the emperor's albums (fig. 58). Painted in 1609–1610 by Govardhan, the figures in the marginal decoration are executed with extreme finesse. Yet Govardhan is not content simply with technical feats. The figures of the men are extraordinarily powerful character studies. They are quite clearly specific portraits, and one senses the interaction of the figures across empty space. This flesh and blood quality continues to separate Mughal painting from its Iranian roots, for however superficially similar the two traditions have again become by the seventeenth century, it is Mughal painting alone that consistently recognizes, acknowledges, and investigates the individuality and personal uniqueness of the people it portrays; and it becomes more and more exclusively an art of portraiture.

Jahangir's albums are the best way to judge that ruler's taste and sensitivities. Much less interested in manuscripts than his father, and certainly not interested in volumes with hundreds of illustrations made as virtual state documents – the Akbari system – Jahangir more frequently commissioned and collected individual pictures, and then had them placed in elaborate and beautiful albums (*muraqqas*). We find Iranian and Turkish paintings and drawings, Deccani illustrations, actual European prints and paintings, and Mughal copies and adaptations of all these, included together with contemporary and earlier Mughal works. The volume was bound so that two facing pages of calligraphy were followed by two related illustrations (see especially figs. 59 and 60), and the elaborate marginal decoration was continuous over both folios of the open

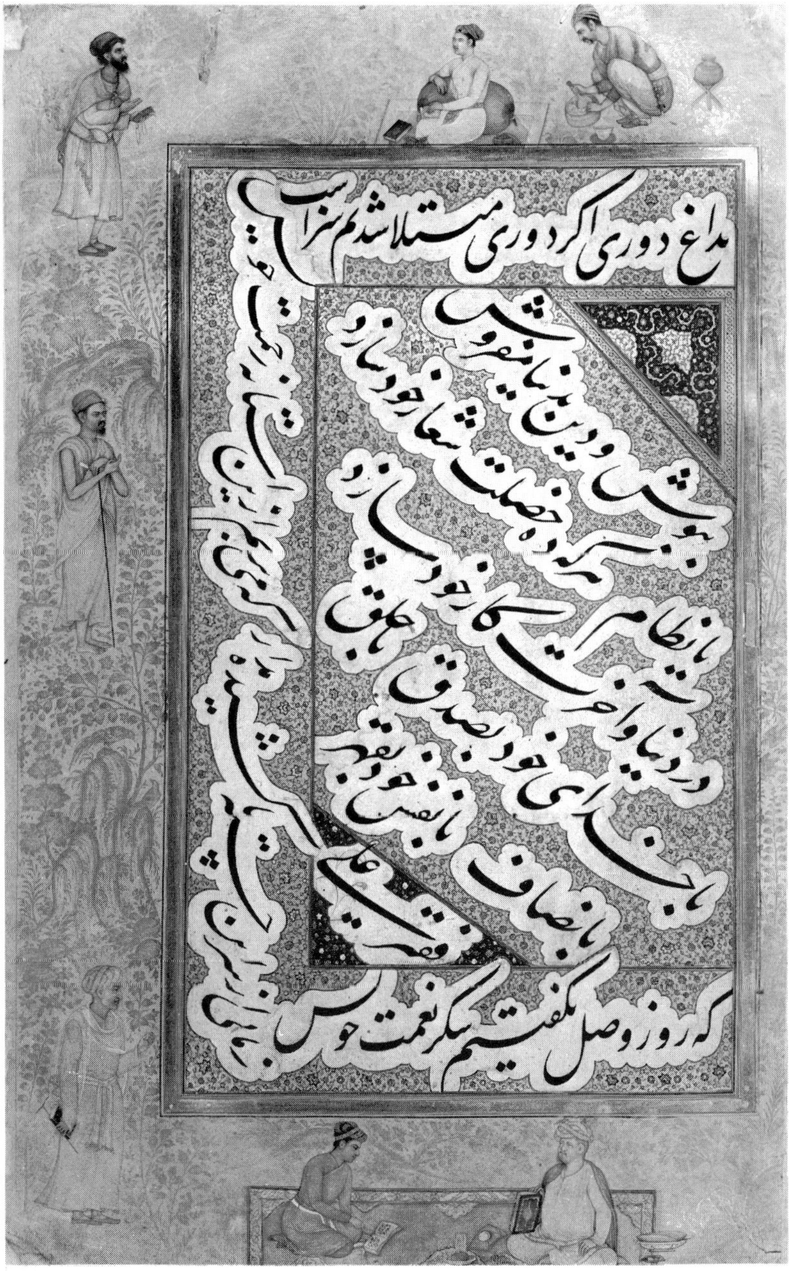

58. Album Page. Marginal decorations by Govardhan; from the Berlin Album, Mughal, dated 1609–1610 (H.1018)

volume. The variety of works that Jahangir knew, his support for his artists to study and learn from this repository, and the taste and care with which illustrations were placed and framed in the albums certainly attests to the epicurean enthusiasm with which Jahangir treated painting. Sometimes several quite disparate illustrations were placed on one page, and a Mughal artist then added a background to relate them visually. Figures 59 and 60, for example, each contain four quite separate paintings that were not originally intended to be combined.

For each single folio in the volumes, therefore, there was an illustration (or illustrations) on one side and calligraphic panels on the other. The border designs surrounding the calligraphies are generally figural (for example fig. 61), unlike the floral or arabesque illuminations that frame the illustrated folios (for example figs. 59 and 60), and they are among the very greatest Mughal works. They not only show imperial or noble figures, they detail the activities of astrologers, hunters, gardeners, or craftsmen and painters at work. In fact, they provide an invaluable guide to Mughal life. The Jahangiri album borders develop from the marginal designs found in the Lahore manuscripts of the 1590s, which themselves are adaptations of earlier Iranian borders. Mughal margins evolve quite differently from their prototypes, however. While the earliest Mughal borders seem to be almost exclusively in gold, as were most Iranian borders, the figures soon came to be elaborately colored and modelled – figs. 58 and 61 provide excellent examples – separating themselves spatially and expressively from the gilding, which then becomes a true background. These later border figures are, in fact, complete portraits and often compete with the central panel for the viewer's attention.

The continually important role of Europe is also made clear in the albums, as well as in fragmentary remaining wall-paintings at sites such as Lahore Fort. Ebba Koch has recently published one series of European-influenced images from that site, but the murals in a small building in the so-called Jahangiri Quadrangle remain unstudied (figs. 62 and 63). The European prints or their copies that are found especially abundantly among album folios include one group of works by Dürer and his circle (including especially the Beham brothers and Georg Pencz), and this is the source for several of the figures shown in the borders of fig. 61.[4] Another source, however, is the Antwerp printmakers (for example Jan Wiericz, Philip Galle, and the Sadeler brothers) of the later sixteenth century. While the German images may have come early in the century, even before Akbar developed a personal interest in such illustrations, the Antwerp group certainly came primarily with the missionaries and traders who arrived in increasing numbers after 1580. Antwerp, the major

[4] For sources, see Ernst Kuhnel and Hermann Goetz, *Indian Book Painting*, London, 1926, plate facing p. 50.

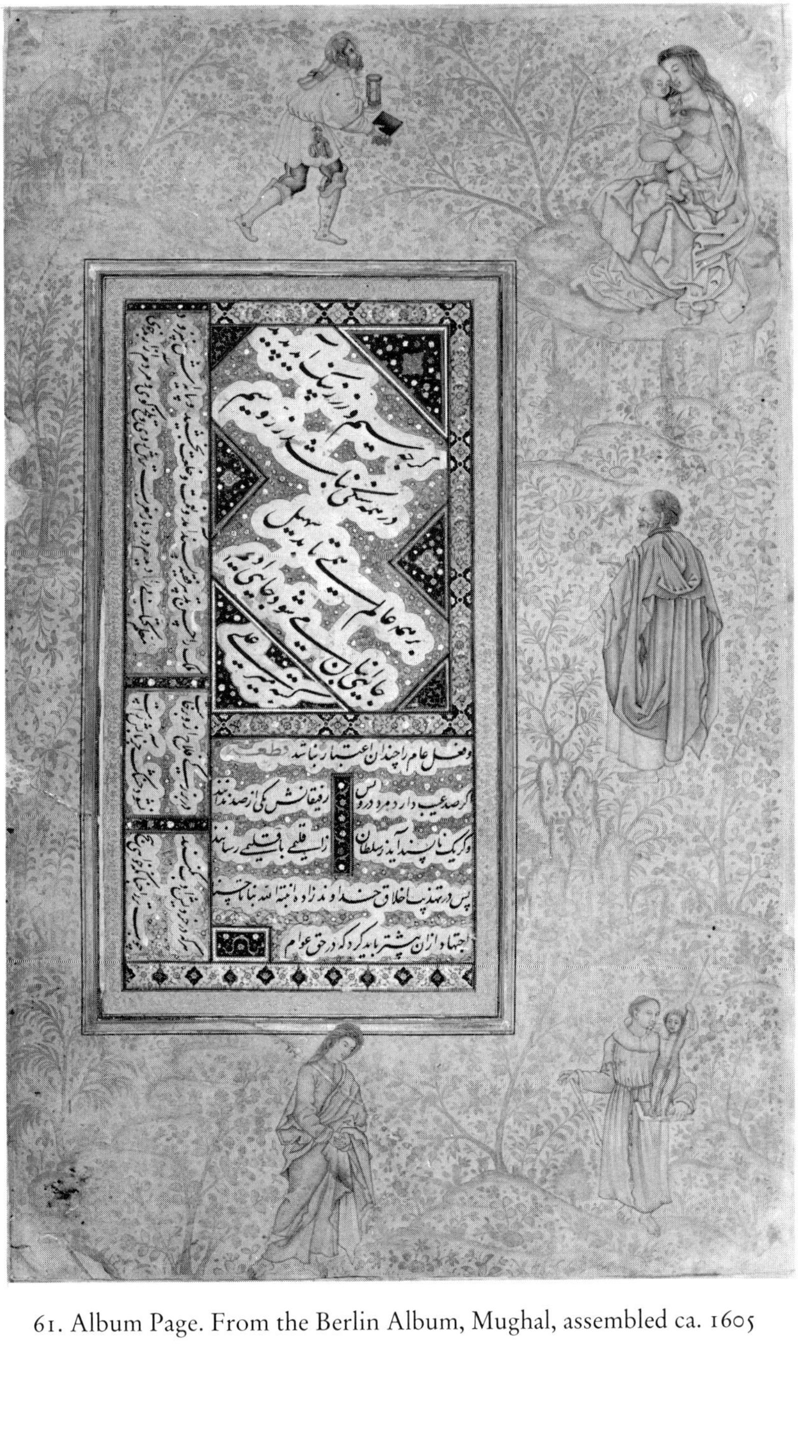

61. Album Page. From the Berlin Album, Mughal, assembled ca. 1605

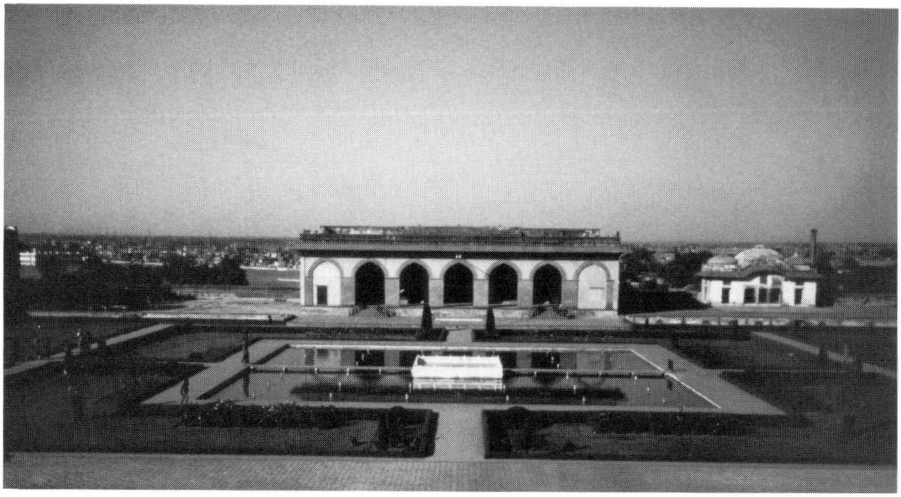

62. The Jahangiri Quadrangle, Lahore Fort

printmaking center in Europe, was also the main port from which ships sailed east.

As if the albums were not sufficient proof of his involvement as patron and connoisseur, Jahangir made an important statement about painting in his memoirs (the *Jahangirnama*, or *Tuzuk-i-Jahangiri*):

> As regards myself, my liking for painting and my practice in judging it have arrived at such a point that when any work is brought before me, either of deceased artists or of those of the present day, without the names being told me, I say on the spur of the moment that it is the work of such and such a man. And if there be a picture containing many portraits, and each face be the work of a different master, I can discover which face is the work of each of them. If any other person has put in the eye and eyebrow of a face, I can perceive whose work the original face is, and who has painted the eye and eyebrow.[5]

Such a claim of connoisseurship, whether true or not, is our best evidence of Jahangir's personal absorption in the achievements of his painters. That individual artists' styles should be considered recognizable and important is as novel a concept within India as the introduction of true portraiture – and not all painters could develop the necessary expressive skills to satisfy the emperor's particular taste. Those painters capable of easily absorbing new influences and of developing individual artistic personalities might remain at court if their work was of sufficient quality. Others, for whom communal

[5] Jahangir, *The Tuzuk-i-Jahangiri; or Memoirs of Jahangir*, translated by A. Rogers and edited by H. Beveridge, London, 1968 (reprint), vol. II, pp. 20–21.

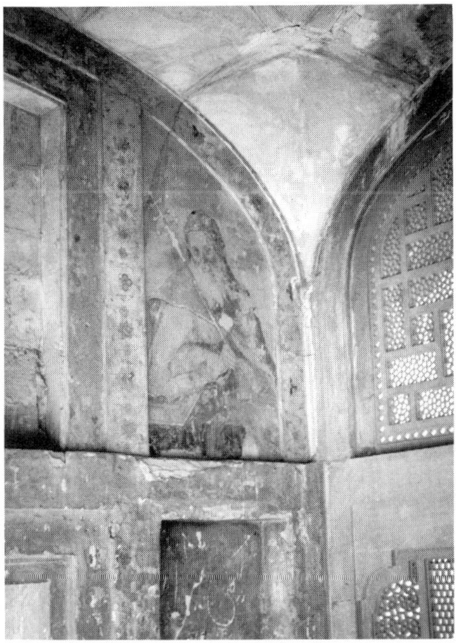

63. Wall-painting in Jahangiri Quadrangle.
Mughal, late 16th or early 17th century

identity and established tradition were more important, sought work in more congenial surroundings.

The *Jahangirnama* text is revealing in other ways also, for in it the emperor chronicles his personal interests, and his reactions to the world around him. Like Babur, he noted curious flowers and animals:

> Although King Babar has described in his Memoirs the appearance and shapes of several animals, he had never ordered the painters to make pictures of them. As these animals appeared to me to be very strange, I both described them and ordered that the painters should draw them in the Jahangir-nama, so that the amazement that arose from hearing of them might be increased. One of these animals in body is larger than a peahen and smaller than a peacock. When it is in heat and displays itself, it spreads out its feathers like the peacock and dances about. Its beak and legs are like those of a cock. Its head and neck and the part under the throat are every minute of a different colour. When it is in heat it is quite red – one might say it had adorned itself with red coral – and after a while it becomes white in the same places and looks like cotton. It sometimes looks of a turquoise colour. Like a chameleon it constantly changes colour . . . [6]

The bird so carefully described is a turkey, a specific animal which arrived from Goa in 1612, and two related paintings – one of which is reproduced as fig. 64

[6] Jahangir, *Tuzuk*, vol. 1, pp. 215–216.

survive. In style, the work is as clinically descriptive as Jahangir's prose. It develops directly out of the depictions of flora and fauna found in the Akbar-period *Baburnama* manuscripts (fig. 42), as well as those of the Fitzwilliam Album (fig. 10). It is also a forerunner of the natural history studies which form such a major aspect of painting during the British period (fig. 175).

Jahangir, a man of immense visual alertness, was also possessed of a mercurial temperament. We have referred to it already in the account of the Allahabad years, and there are other important incidents as well. During that rebellious period, his eldest son, Prince Khusrau, was being forwarded by powerful factions as the legitimate heir-apparent, to succeed Akbar upon his death, and he is the prince in attendance on the emperor in *Akbar with Sultan Khusrau, Sultan Khurram, and a Courtier* (fig. 47). Once Jahangir had returned to court and safely succeeded to the throne, there was a temporary reconciliation before Khusrau again rebelled. Jahangir then had his son blinded with hot needles, and his followers impaled alive, to prevent any challenge to his rule.

Jahangir was thirty-six when he became emperor, and he had grown up amidst political and physical security, and immense wealth. His situation, therefore, was completely different from that of his father in 1556. As he grew older, he became increasingly dependent on opium and alcohol, an addiction already noted at Allahabad, and eventually he could no longer continue even the writing of his memoirs. Much of the administration of the country was assumed by Nur Jahan, his independent and ambitious wife. It is no surprise, therefore, that it is not action and energy that animate Jahangiri painting, but subtlety of perception, delectation of style, and the judgments of the connoisseur.

Jahangir's interest in the particular and recognizable character of the work of each of his artists led to the intense cultivation of individual artistic styles. (He had little interest in the earlier procedure of allowing several artists to work on single paintings.) Certain painters developed recognizable areas of expertise: Mansur as an animal and flower painter, Abu'l Hasan and Bishan Das as imperial portraitists, and Govardhan as a painter of holy men, musicians, and eccentrics.

Mansur is mentioned in the *Jahangirnama* more frequently than any other artist. For example:

> At this time the King of Persia has sent with Pari Beg Mir Shikar one falcon . . . What can I write of the beauty and color of this falcon? There were many beautiful black markings on each wing, and back, and sides. As it was something out of the common, I ordered Ustad Mansur, who has the title of *Nadiru-l-asr* [Wonder of the Age] to paint and preserve its likeness.[7]

[7] Jahangir, *Tuzuk*, vol. II, pp. 107–108.

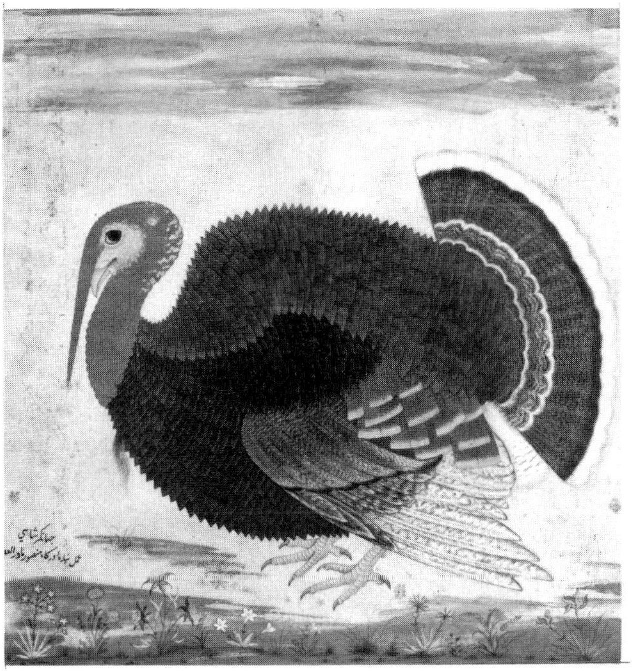

64. A Turkey Cock. By Mansur; Mughal, ca. 1612

A Turkey Cock (fig. 64) is a perfect example of Mansur's style. He was a careful, precise, and probably slow draftsman; and his color is applied in small areas that are meant to describe scientifically the physical surface of the subject. Backgrounds are often visually empty, frequently left as untouched paper, with a few simple plants to lend rhythm to the composition. Since this is true also in the earlier *Two Blue Bulls* and *Two Hog Deer* (fig. 42), designed by Kanha, as well as the illustrations to the *Kitab-i-Saat* (fig. 43), Mansur's talent represents skillful accomplishment of an established style. He was no innovator; his interest was in presenting work that was visually accurate and useful. He was also an illuminator for the frontispieces and decorative panels in manuscripts, and a painter of decorative marginal designs, an art demanding careful craftsmanship rather than insightful perceptions. His earliest known work of this type is in the *Khamsa* of Amir Khusrau Dihlavi of 1597–1598.

The best-known work of Abu'l Hasan is the enigmatic *Squirrels in a Plane Tree* (fig. 65). The squirrels are the most natural and closely observed animals ever painted by a Mughal artist, although it has been suggested that they are a species unknown in India or Iran.[8] Set against a gold sky, the tree, together with

[8] Toby Falk and Mildred Archer, *Indian Miniatures in the India Office Library*, London, 1981, pp. 59–60.

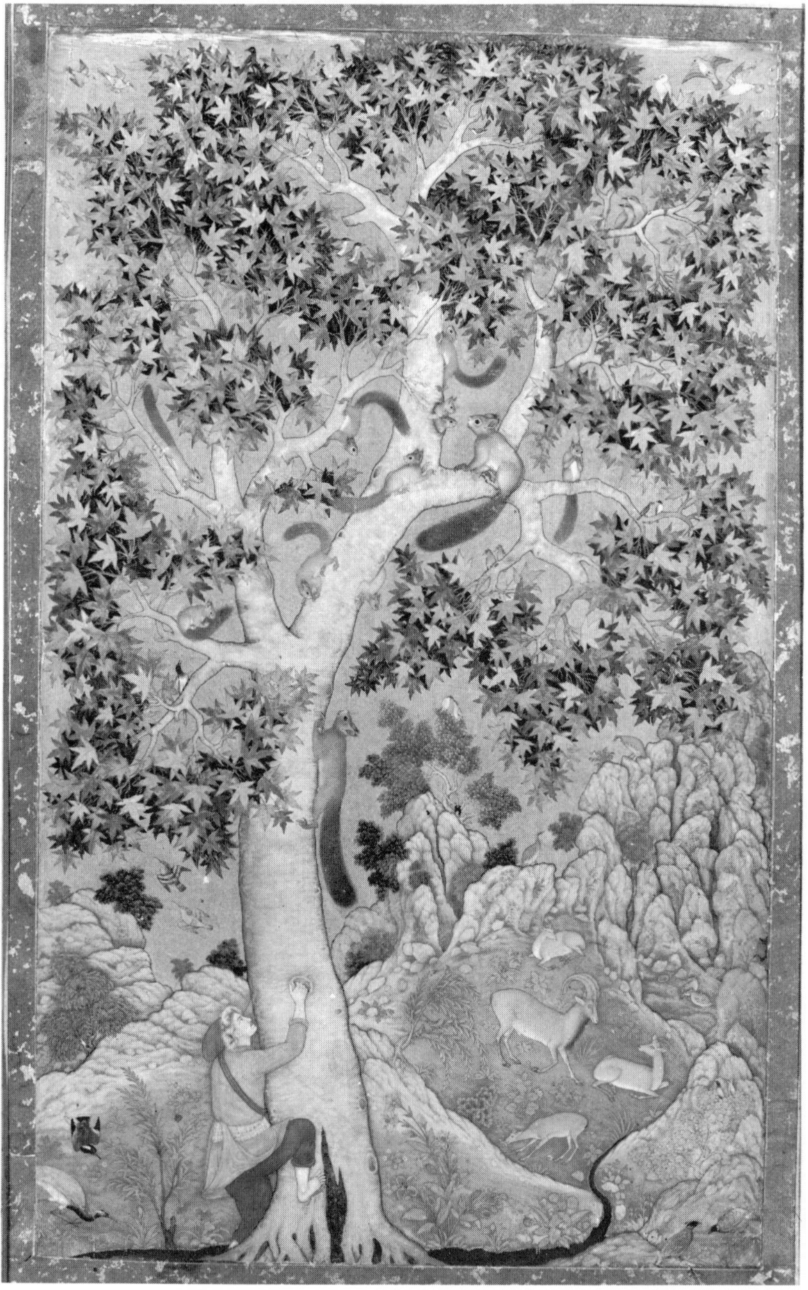

65. Squirrels in a Plane Tree. By Abu'l Hasan; Mughal, ca. 1615

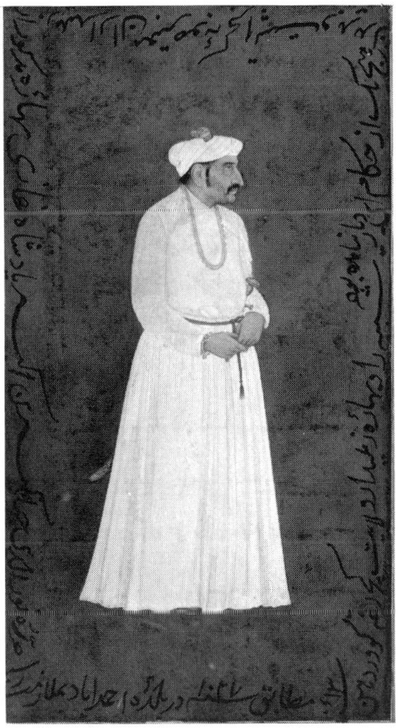

66. Rao Bharah. By Govardhan; from the Berlin Album, Mughal, dated 1617–1618

the pattern created by the squirrels' tails, also creates a superbly decorative surface composition. The work, therefore, consummately combines the Bihzadian (Iranian) and European ideals evoked by Abu'l Fazl as standards for Mughal painting; Bihzadian because of the controlled and consciously decorative surface arrangement, and European because of the intense semblance of realism, and the use of light and shadow to enhance the physical shapes and textures of the animals.

We have discussed Govardhan's marginal figures of 1609–1610 (fig. 58). Like both Abu'l Hasan and Mansur, Govardhan began painting at the end of Akbar's reign, contributing pages to the second *Akbarnama*. These were immature works, however, for his figures there lack the naturalness of gesture and the depth of personality that so distinguish his greatest paintings. A portrait of *Rao Bharah* (fig. 66), dated 1617–1618, has a sense of three-dimensional corporeality as intense as that created by Abu'l Hasan; the figure seems so palpable and full of life that it could walk off the page.

A fourth artist, Bishan Das, was "unequalled in his age for taking likenesses," according to the emperor.[9] In 1613, Jahangir sent an embassy to the court of

[9] Jahangir, *Tuzuk*, vol. II, p. 116.

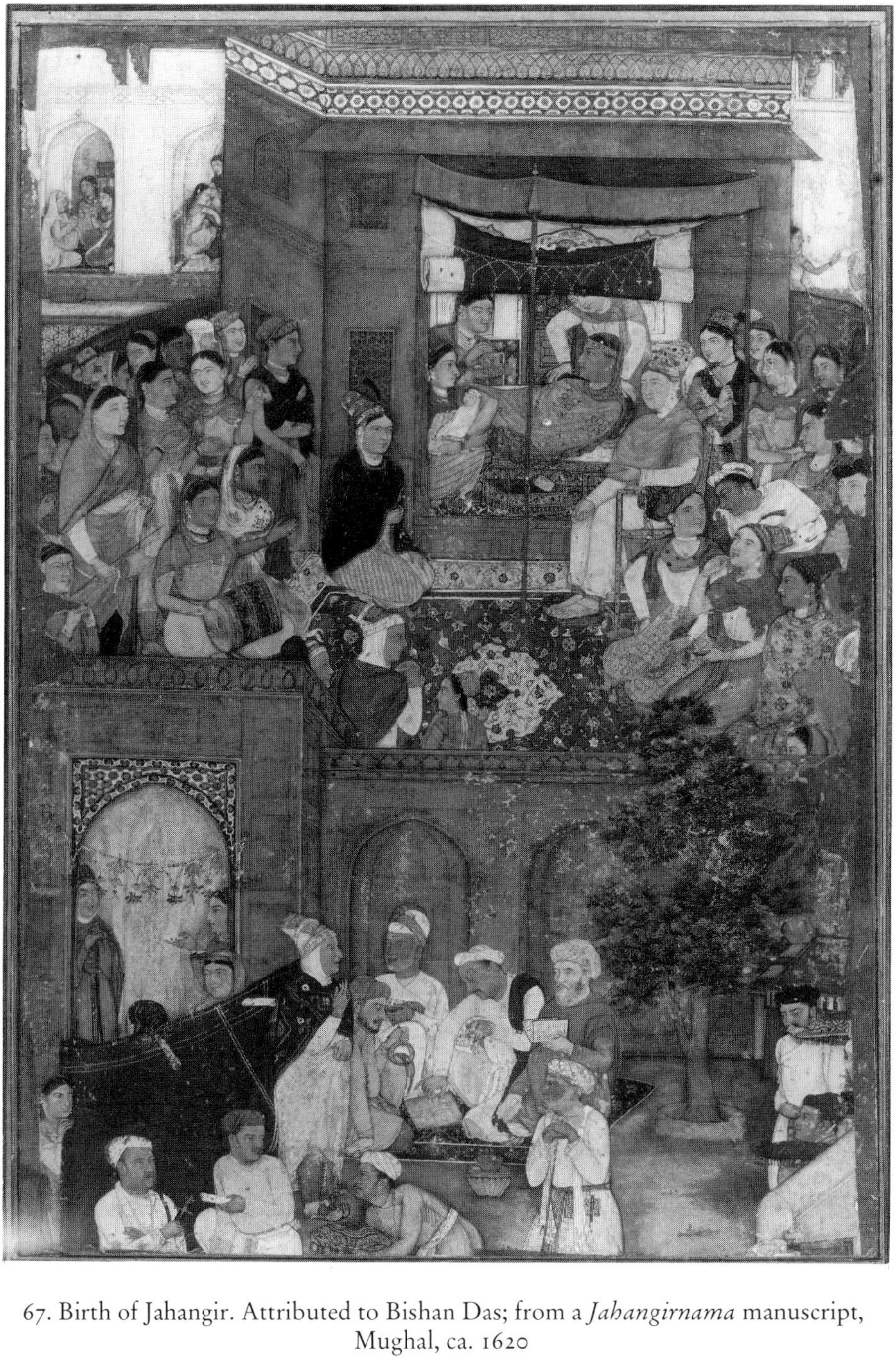

67. Birth of Jahangir. Attributed to Bishan Das; from a *Jahangirnama* manuscript, Mughal, ca. 1620

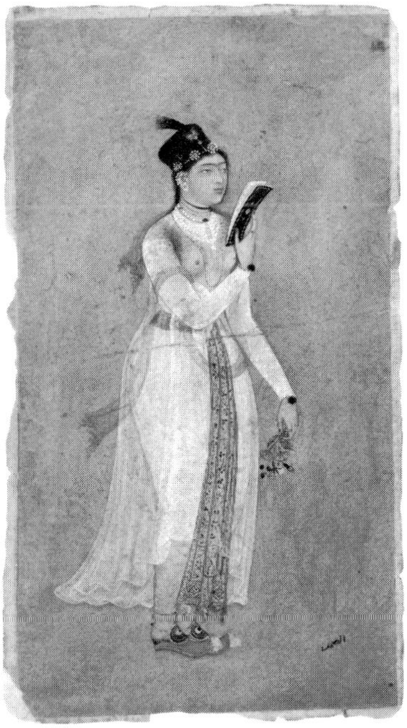

68. A Court Lady. Attributed to Bishan Das;
Mughal, ca. 1620

Shah Abbas at Isfahan, and Bishan Das accompanied the party to make portraits of the shah and members of his court. The *Birth of Jahangir* (fig. 67) further attests to the artist's skill as portraitist, especially of women. In the major historical manuscripts such as the *Akbarnama*, women had usually been shown as general types, whether in scenes within the harem (for example birth scenes) or as dancing girls. There could have been no alternative, for ladies at court were kept in strict seclusion and did not publicly attend major court functions, although they were allowed to keep watch on the ceremonial events through screened windows. (A Rajput illustration which includes a woman hidden by screens is reproduced as fig. 141.) This segregation is sensed here, for the only male figures present, other than the child, are astrologers and servants placed below, outside the well-guarded harem enclosure. Bishan Das includes informative and lively details, such as the woman looking around the curtain at the lower left. This is no rigid line-up of stock types, but the depiction of an excited throng of ladies at a major harem event. Yet, while studies of particular women are almost unknown, this is precisely what we seem to find in Bishan Das' painting. The women convince us that they are based on observation, for they have clearly defined and individualized personalities; some can be recognized in other works by different artists. *A Court Lady* (fig. 68), attributable to

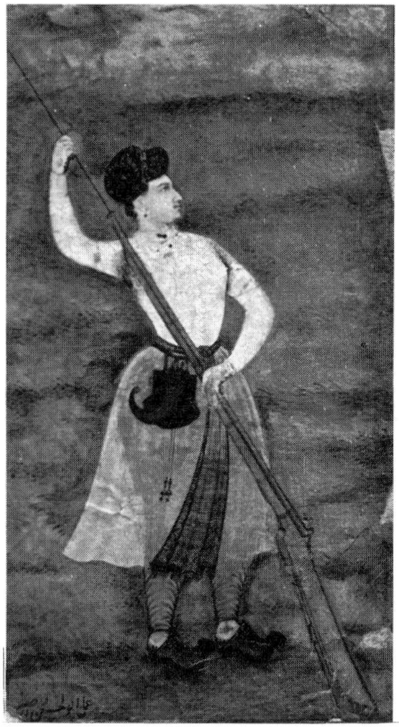

69. Nur Jahan with a Rifle. By Abu'l Hasan;
Mughal, probably dated 1612–1613 (H. 1021)

the same artist, is one of several further examples. The most important female portrait, however, is by Abu'l Hasan and has been convincingly identified by Dr. Arshizadeh as the Empress Nur Jahan (fig. 69), whom Jahangir married in 1611. In his memoirs he wrote of watching her hunt during the spring of 1617:

> She shot two tigers with one shot each and knocked over two others with four shots. In the twinkling of an eye she deprived of life the bodies of these four tigers. Until now such shooting was never seen, that from the top of an elephant and inside of a howdah six shots should be made and not one miss, so that the four beasts found no opportunity to spring or move. As a reward for this good shooting I gave her a pair of bracelets of diamonds worth 100,000 rupees and scattered 1,000 ashrafis [over her].[10]

Her refusal to follow convention allowed her to invite the Rajput Prince Karan Singh into the harem quarters for an audience in 1615, for example, and her insistence on greater freedom for women seems to have had its impact on the arts as well. *Nur Jahan with a Rifle* depicts a woman of undoubted power, and it is unprecedented in either Indian or Islamic art. Another relatively informal portrait of Jahangir, probably painted slightly earlier, shows the emperor

[10] Jahangir, *Tuzuk*, vol. 1, p. 375.

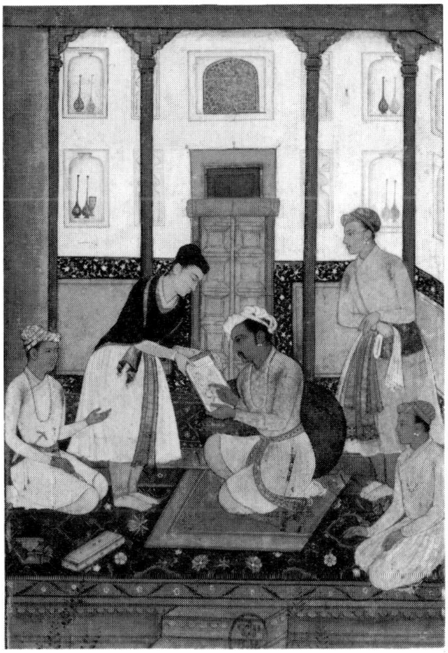

70. Abu'l Hasan Presenting a Painting to Jahangir.
Attributed to Abu'l Hasan; Mughal, ca. 1605

inspecting a painting being presented by a young artist (fig. 70). This is almost certainly Abu'l Hasan, whose portrait by Daulat is in the Gulshan Album.[11]

The only important identified historical manuscript made for Jahangir is the illustrated version of his memoirs, the *Jahangirnama*, and The *Birth of Jahangir* may have been made for inclusion in the imperial copy. The text was probably begun at the time of Jahangir's accession, and the emperor was concerned with illustrations for the work by at least 1612, when an entry in the memoirs notes a commission for the volume in that year.[12] There is no bound contemporary illustrated version of the work still extant, and it is possible that the single pages which have been located in various collections were never actually mounted into a final copy. Several major illustrations were in Iran by the mid eighteenth century, when they were probably taken as loot at the sack of Delhi by Nadir Shah in 1739. They were mounted in albums in Iran, which suggests that they were not already in a bound volume when dispersed. In any case, the known illustrations range widely in date of execution, although none

[11] See Milo Cleveland Beach, *The Grand Mogul – Imperial Painting in India 1600–1660*, Williamstown, Massachusetts, 1978, fig. 4. The identification was first made in *A la Cour du Grand Moghol*, catalogue of an exhibition organized by the Bibliothèque Nationale, Paris, 1986, no. 8.

[12] Jahangir, *Tuzuk*, vol. 1, p. 215.

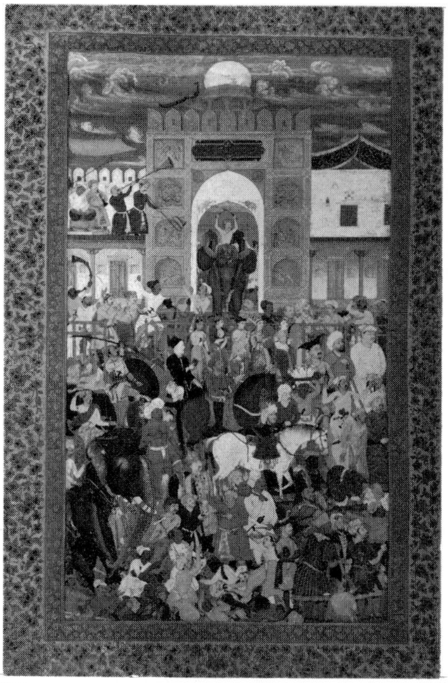

71. The Accession of Jahangir (left half). By Abu'l Hasan; from a *Jahangirnama* manuscript, Mughal, ca. 1618

is dated by inscription. Many of the pages are badly rubbed and areas of the surface have disappeared, while others have been extensively repainted. Irrelevant signatures have often been added, further confusing our ability to judge the manuscript reliably, and many proposed *Jahangirnama* pages may in fact come from later copies, or may have illustrated other texts. It is another topic that would richly repay careful study.

The greatest of the *Jahangirnama* illustrations include two folios (figs. 71 and 72) which almost certainly formed the frontispiece of the manuscript, as mentioned by Jahangir during his account of the year 1618:

> On this day Abu-l-Hasan, the painter, who has been honoured with the title Nadiru-z-zaman, drew the picture of my accession as the frontispiece to the Jahangir-nama, and brought it to me. As it was worthy of all praise, he received endless favours. His work was perfect, and his picture is one of the chefs d'oeuvre of the age.[13]

The scene is lavish and animated. Jahangir, surrounded by courtiers, is enthroned within a tent enclosure in the fort at Agra, and above him are two

[13] Jahangir, *Tuzuk*, vol. II, p. 20.

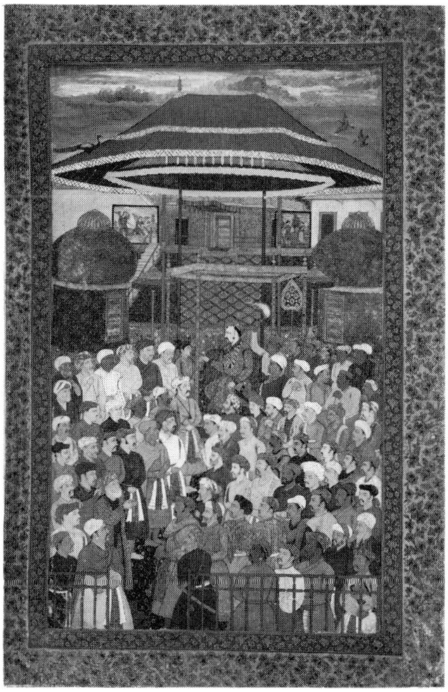

72. The Accession of Jahangir (right half). By Abu'l Hasan; from a *Jahangirnama* manuscript, Mughal, ca. 1605

large paintings of European subjects. On the left, inside a gateway, is a crowd of spectators, which includes a black-robed Jesuit priest and a dandified European gentleman (at the bottom right). As men bring gifts and kneel in homage, a superbly self-satisfied courtier tosses out a shower of gold and silver coins, causing frenzied scrambling. It is an amusing and boisterous scene. While presented to the emperor in 1618 – if the *Jahangirnama* reference is correct – the two halves of the double-page were not painted at the same time. The right half must have been painted just before the presentation, but the left half is recognizably in Abu'l Hasan's youthful style. That it was executed at the time of the coronation is indicated too by the fact that Abu'l Hasan perfectly conveys an immediate reaction to the emotions of the moment. Moreover, an inscription above the gateway on this half states "Happy be your conquest of realms. Blessed be your enthronement. Year 1014 [= 1605–1606]."

Within the context of historical manuscripts, the depiction of the emperor in these *Jahangirnama* pages marks a subtle change from the manner in which Akbar had been shown in the *Akbarnamas*. In each case, the emperor is just one among many courtiers at any chosen event, but no scenes of action are known in the *Jahangirnama*. Every illustration shows Jahangir in full control of an already established power; his figure is serene, untroubled, and often isolated. There is no suggestion of challenge to his rule, and consequently he is most often shown holding an audience, meeting with holy men, or inflicting punishment on rebels already captured. One misses the brio and energy of Akbar's encounters with the world.

With single portraits, too, there are important innovations. The great *Jahangir with His Three Sons* (fig. 73) can be dated to 1605–1606, just before Khusrau fell from favor. It is by Manohar, whose portrait of *Akbar with Sultan Khusrau, Sultan Khurram, and a Courtier* (fig. 47) has been discussed, and it is an immediate continuation of types of portraiture begun in the Akbar period. A second major double-page portrait, *Jahangir Greeting the Poet Sa'di* (figs. 74 and 75), is by Abu'l Hasan and can be dated 1615. Here the emperor, surrounded by his younger sons and various courtiers, is being presented with a book by the great Iranian mystic poet Sa'di. It is not an historical episode, however, for Sa'di lived in the thirteenth century, and the symbolic nature of the work is extended by the manner in which Jahangir himself is shown. He sits European fashion (rather than cross-legged, as the throne behind would demand) with his feet on a globe – an obvious proclamation of world dominance which is enhanced by the keyhole in the globe and the key hanging from the imperial belt. There is an inscription on the globe stating that the work was painted at Ajmer, where Jahangir had taken residence from 1613 to 1616, while his son Sultan Khurram (the future Shahjahan) fought and eventually defeated the Rajput rana of Mewar. The rana's son and heir, Prince Karan, is seen at the upper left, the dark-skinned man in attendance on the emperor. He came to court at Ajmer early in 1615, while the emperor left that city in November 1616, suggesting a fairly exact date for the historical underpinnings of the scene. (The Turkish and Iranian rulers at the bottom of the left half are modelled on such European depictions of oriental types as Gentile Bellini's *Portrait of Mehmet I*.[14])

The two paintings that form the scene would have been placed on facing folios in the original album or book for which they were intended. The nobles form an oval around the emperor and poet, so that the scene seems to have two major focuses of interest. It thus shows an affinity or identification between the emperor as world ruler and the poet as ruler of the spirit. Akbari scenes continually proclaim Akbar's military and political might, whereas Jahangir, for whom this power was unquestionable, was concerned instead with establishing his own spiritual and religious credentials.

This is further shown in *Jahangir Prefering a Sufi Shaikh to Kings* (fig. 76). The emperor sits on an hourglass throne, and to counteract the passing of time,

[14] Milo Cleveland Beach, "The Mughal painter Abu'l Hasan and some English sources for his style," *Journal of the Walters Art Gallery*, vol. 38 (1980), fig. 12.

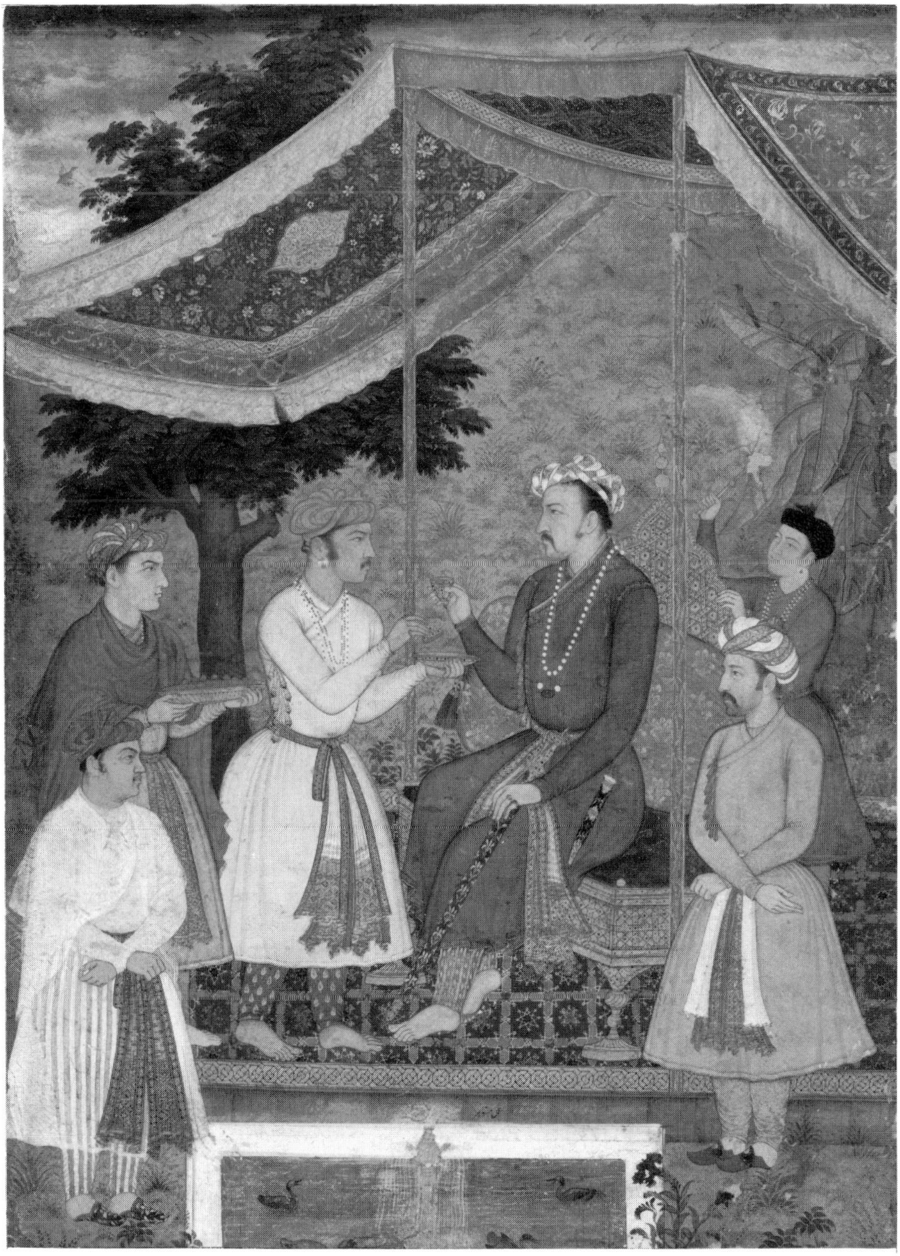

73. Jahangir with His Three Sons. By Manohar; Mughal, ca. 1605

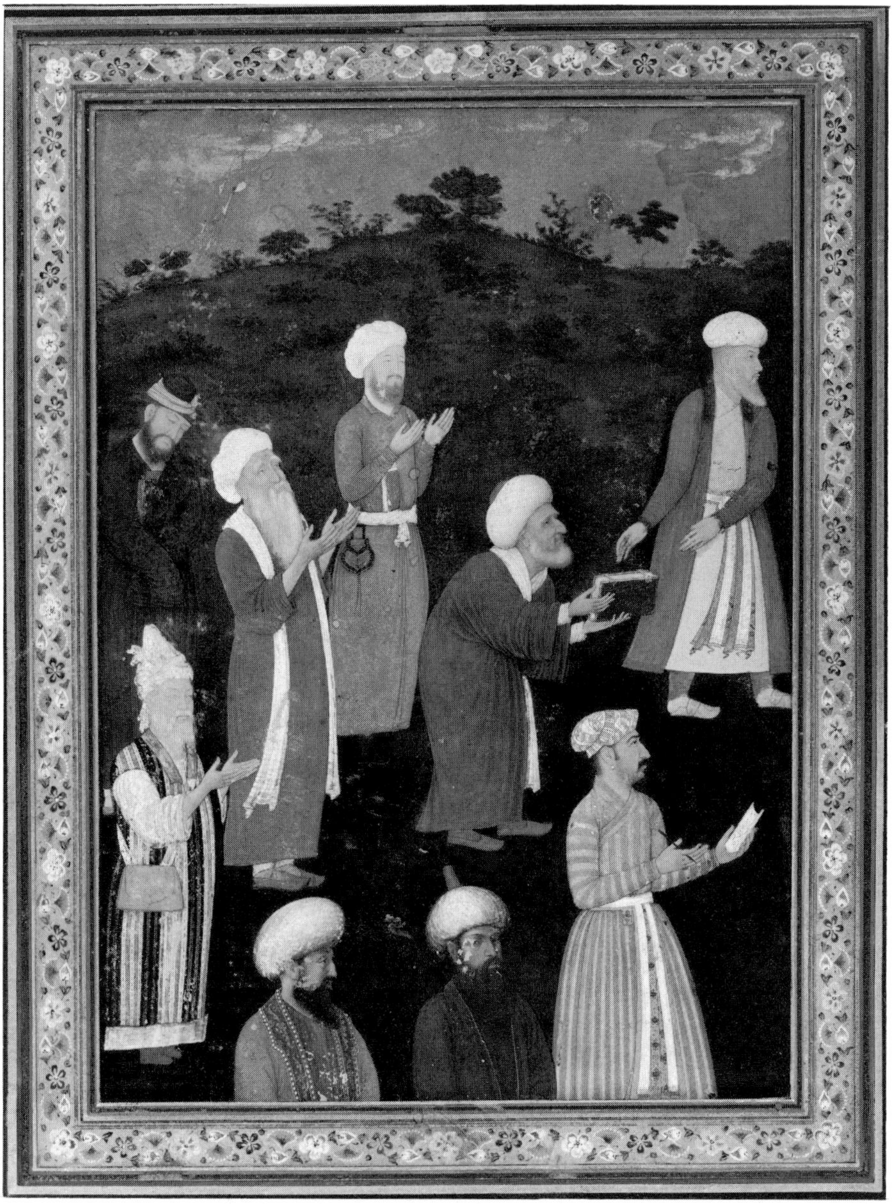

74. Jahangir Greeting the Poet Sa'di (left half). Attributed to Abu'l Hasan; Mughal, ca. 1615

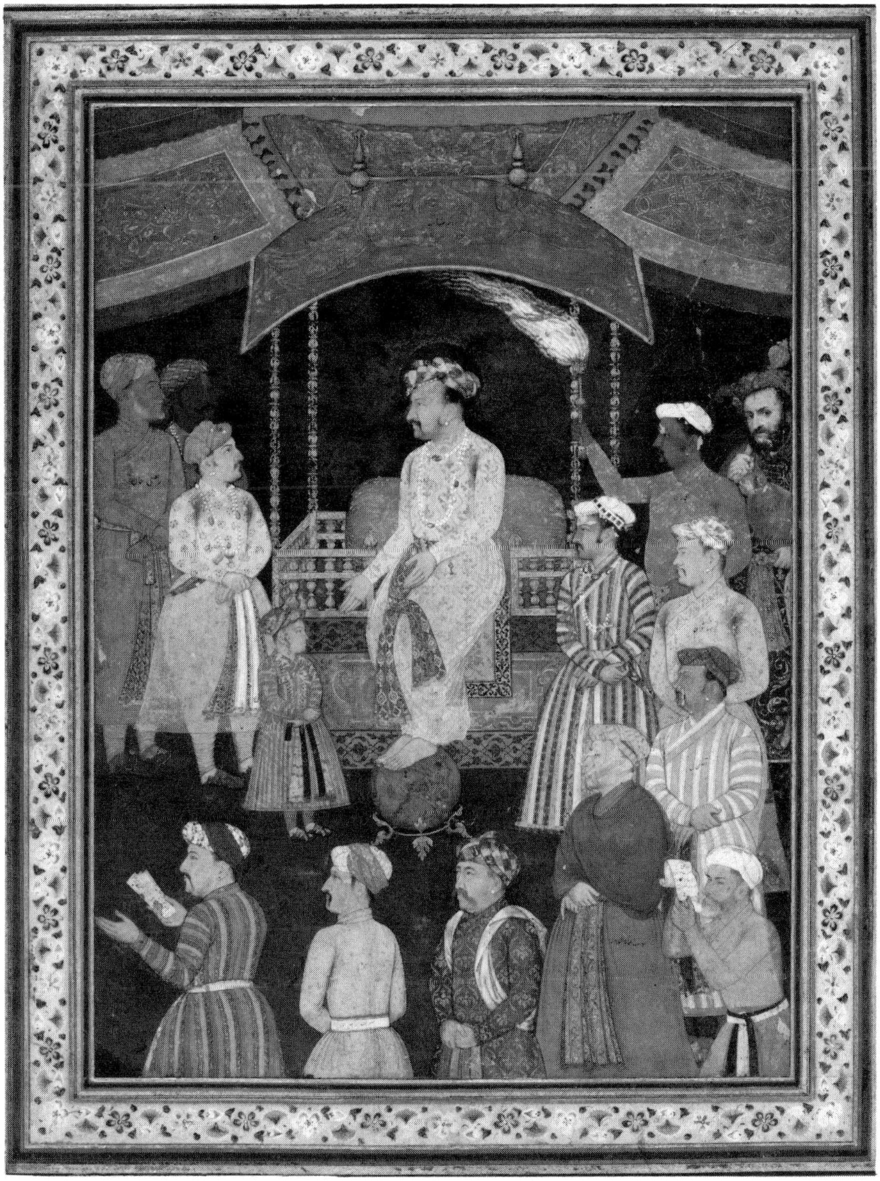

75. Jahangir Greeting the Poet Sa'di (right half). By Abu'l Hasan; Mughal, ca. 1615

angels at the base inscribe: "O Shah, may your reign last a thousand years." Along the left edge of the work are four figures: a Sufi mystic (who may be Shaikh Husain Chishti, head of the great shrine at Ajmer, a religious center for the Mughal imperial family); a Turkish sultan (again derived from a European portrait rather than observation); King James I of England; and a modest Hindu. As interpreted by Richard Ettinghausen, the work would symbolize Jahangir's disdain for worldly power and his preference for spiritual matters, for it is the religious leader upon whom the emperor concentrates. Ettinghausen further states that the manner in which James I looks away from the emperor may have been an allusion to "the independent attitude of Sir Thomas Roe," the first English ambassador then in residence at court. And the Hindu placed at the lower left is purposely of low rank because Jahangir placed Hinduism "in the lowest rank in the hierarchy of religions."[15]

Possible alternate interpretations of details of the work force us to question so controlled a political meaning, however. The depiction of James I is simply an exact copy of a portrait by the English king's official portraitist John de Critz,[16] and the Turkish sultan is almost certainly an equally literal copy of a European portrait of a Turk. The poses, therefore, are determined by the prototypes. Moreover, we now know, from similar figures with identifying inscriptions, that the Hindu must be a portrait of the artist – its presence in this position was soon to become a cliche of Mughal painting. One would be hard-pressed to explain the painter's inclusion of himself alongside the great political and spiritual leaders of the world were the significance of the symbolism so specific. The enormously innovative composition – for which a source has not yet been identified – may therefore have been more experimental than has previously been thought.

In many ways, the interest in portraiture and the identifiable European sources make this the most "European" of all Jahangiri portraits. However, it is simultaneously more traditionally Indian than any earlier Mughal work. A figure seated on a symbolic throne, his head at the center of a circular aureole towards which cherubic divinities approach, is the formula developed for the seated Buddha image by the second century A.D. (fig. 77), and it was used as well, with variations, for Hindu deities. The physical volume and impact of the figure of the emperor also corresponded more closely to the emphasis on volume found in earlier Indian sculpture than to the weightless, bodiless figures of Persian or early Mughal art.

By 1615, the major Mughal painters were no longer interested in those aspects of European works that had previously held their attention: the

[15] Richard Ettinghausen, "The emperor's choice," in *De Artibus Opuscula XL – Essays in Honor of Erwin Panofsky*, edited by Millard Meiss, New York, 1961, pp. 98–120.

[16] Beach, *Imperial Image*, p. 30 and fig. 4.

sense of spatial depth, for example, or exotic Christian subject-matter. These interests have certainly helped to make Mughal painting popular and seemingly comprehensible outside of India, but they must have remained foreign exoticisms to viewers in India at the time. What continued to remain of serious interest to artists were the new techniques that allowed human figures to take on weight and volume. The resulting physical presence of the figures provided a reinterpretation of Islamic artistic traditions in terms instinctually comprehensible to an Indian viewer; this explains in part just why Mughal artists had been so interested in experimenting with European imagery. European works would have had no impact on Mughal traditions if they had not presented forms and ideas to which the artists and patrons were willing and eager to respond. European prints, and sometimes the same European prints, were taken also to China and Japan, for example, where they had little comparable effect.

English influences are found also in *Jahangir Embracing Shah Abbas I* (fig. 78), again by Abu'l Hasan. His portrait of the emperor with Sa'di (figs. 74 and 75) was still relatively traditional in composition, for it was presented within a narrative, albeit ahistorical, context. Here the presentation is symbolic, and truly imperial. Jahangir embraces the Iranian Shah with regal condescension, and whereas Jahangir stands on a lion, Shah Abbas is supported by a lamb. This is pure wish fulfillment on Jahangir's part, for the Shah, whom he had never met, was a troublesome and threatening neighbor. Nonetheless, it is the isolation of figures in a symbolic context rather than the depiction (or intimation) of a specific moment that is innovative here. The best parallel for such a composition comes not from earlier Mughal or Iranian works, but from English painting: the great Ditchley portrait of *Queen Elizabeth I*, by Marcus Gheerarts, for example.[17]

The earliest known use of such symbols, and the roots of this universally imperial imagery, are found in *Jahangir Greeting the Poet Sa'di* of circa 1615, the year in which Sir Thomas Roe arrived at the court at Ajmer on an Embassy from James I. Roe was a cousin of the great English miniaturist Isaac Oliver, and is known to have taken English paintings, presumably including a presentation portrait by John de Critz, to India. His memoirs chronicle the emperor's fascination with these works, which so perfectly matched his interest in imagery that expressed and promoted his imperial authority. It is from the time of Roe's visit that symbolic imperial imagery replaces the earlier narrative scenes of imperial life, transforming the character of Mughal portraiture.

Roe eventually brought a group of Indian illustrations back to England. An engraving, *The Emperor Jahangir with Prince Khurram* (fig. 79), was published

[17] Beach, *Imperial Image*, p. 31 and fig. 5.

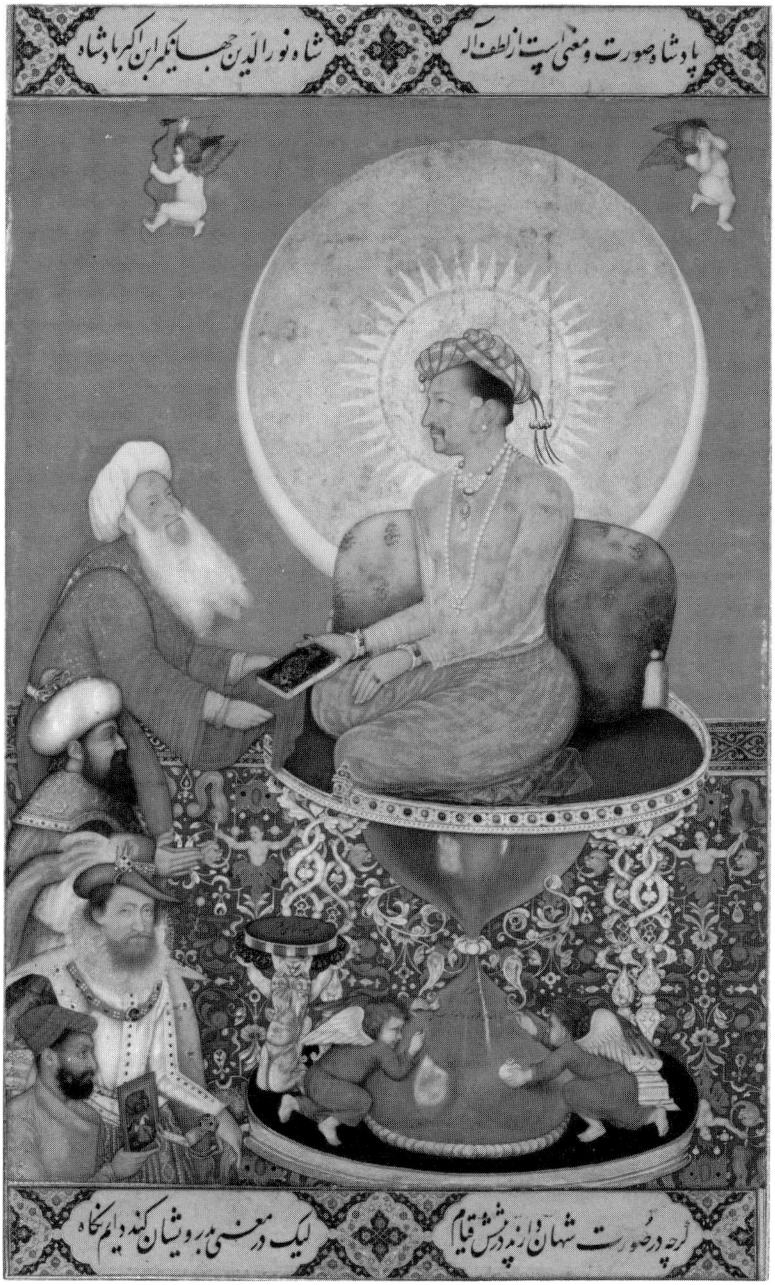

76. Jahangir Prefering a Sufi Shaikh to Kings. By Bichitr; Mughal, ca. 1615–1618

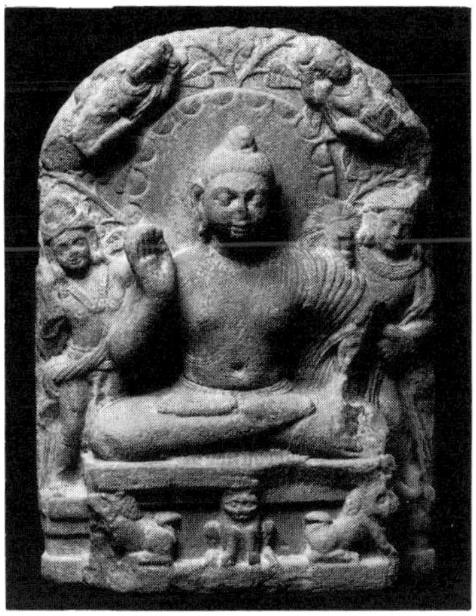

77. Seated Buddha and Attendants. India, Kushan dynasty, ca. 3rd century, red sandstone

in London in 1625, almost certainly as a copy of a Mughal image belonging to Roe. The inscription allows us to know that the original was by Manohar, although the date is illegible. Seen as a curiosity by the English, it had no immediate impact on the traditions of English artists.

Jahangir had inherited an established style. Painting during his reign does not show the swift and dynamic evolution of the Akbar period. Nonetheless, Mughal painting of the early seventeenth century developed an intensified interest in technical precision and craftsmanship, coupled with a concern for depictions of personalities and personal interrelationships, rather than historical events. It was a period of transformation, rather than innovation. One aspect of Jahangir's importance as a patron can be summed up by the most extraordinary of all Mughal portraits, *The Dying Inayat Khan* (fig 80). The emperor has left us an astonishing verbal account of its commission.

> On this day news came of the death of Inayat Khan. He was one of my intimate attendants. As he was addicted to opium, and when he had the chance, to drinking as well, he became maddened with wine. As he was weakly built, he took more than he could digest, and was attacked by the disease of diarrhoea, and in this weak state he two or three times fainted. By my order Hakim Rukna applied remedies, but whatever methods were resorted to gave no profit. At the same time a strange hunger came over him, and although the doctor exerted himself in order that he should not eat more than once in twenty-four hours, he could not restrain himself . . . At last he became dropsical, and exceeding low and weak. Some days before this he had petitioned that he might go to Agra [his home]. I ordered him to come into my presence and obtain leave. They put him into a palanquin and brought him. He

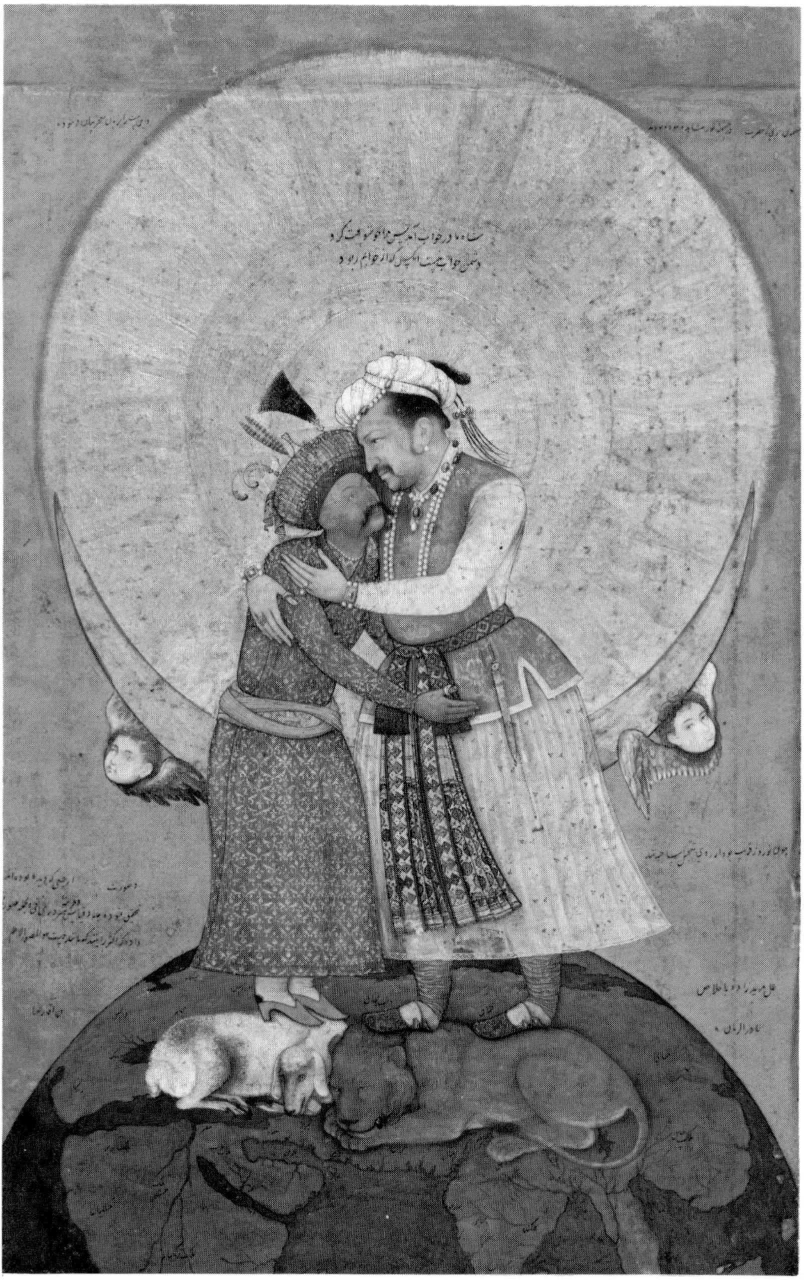

78. Jahangir Embracing Shah Abbas I. By Abu'l Hasan *Nadir al-Zaman*; Mughal, ca. 1615

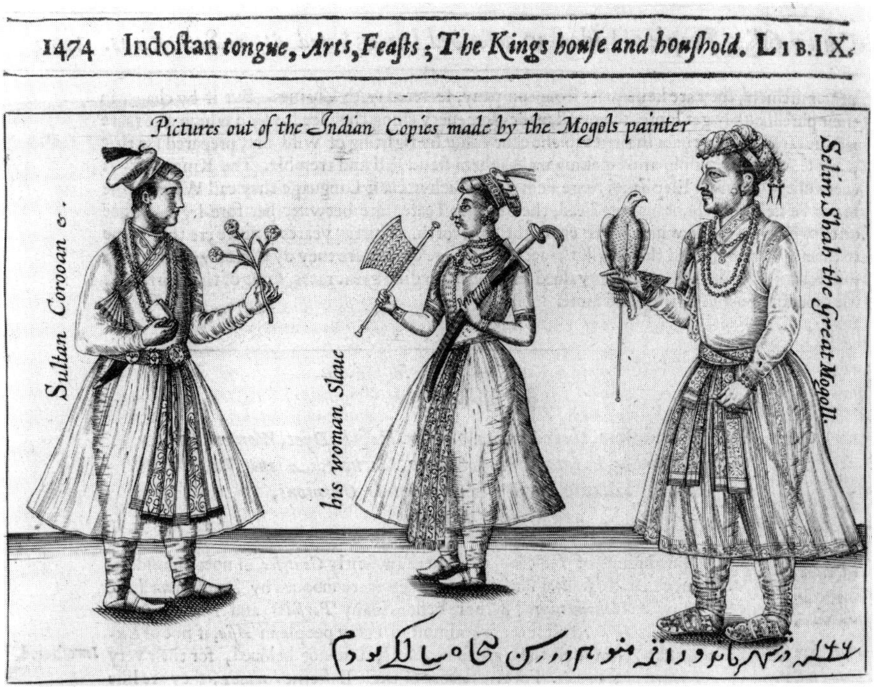

79. The Emperor Jahangir with Prince Khurram. From *Purchas his Pilgrimes* (vol. II), engraving, published in London, 1625

> appeared so low and weak I was astonished . . . Though painters have striven much in drawing an emaciated face, yet I have never seen anything like this . . . As it was a very extraordinary case I directed painters to take his portrait . . . Next day he travelled the road of non-existence.[18]

While the finished painting has also survived,[19] the preliminary drawing reproduced here is the more powerful work. It has an intensity and immediacy unparalleled in Mughal art. The entire episode, in which a dying man is made to appear at court and then – because of his curious appearance – to pose for his portrait, however, tells us as much about Jahangir's personal character and aesthetic taste as the drawing tells of Inayat Khan's emaciation.

Because of the passage in the *Jahangirnama* text, we can date *The Dying Inayat Khan* to the years 1618–1619, the mid-period of Jahangir's rule. A powerful drawing of Jahangir (fig. 81) must have been made at the same time. Both works indicate the split that had developed between official art and these more intimate, personal studies, images never meant for public display. The

[18] Jahangir, *Tuzuk*, vol. II, pp. 43–44.
[19] Laurence Binyon, *The Court Painters of the Grand Moguls*, London, 1921, pl. xxiv.

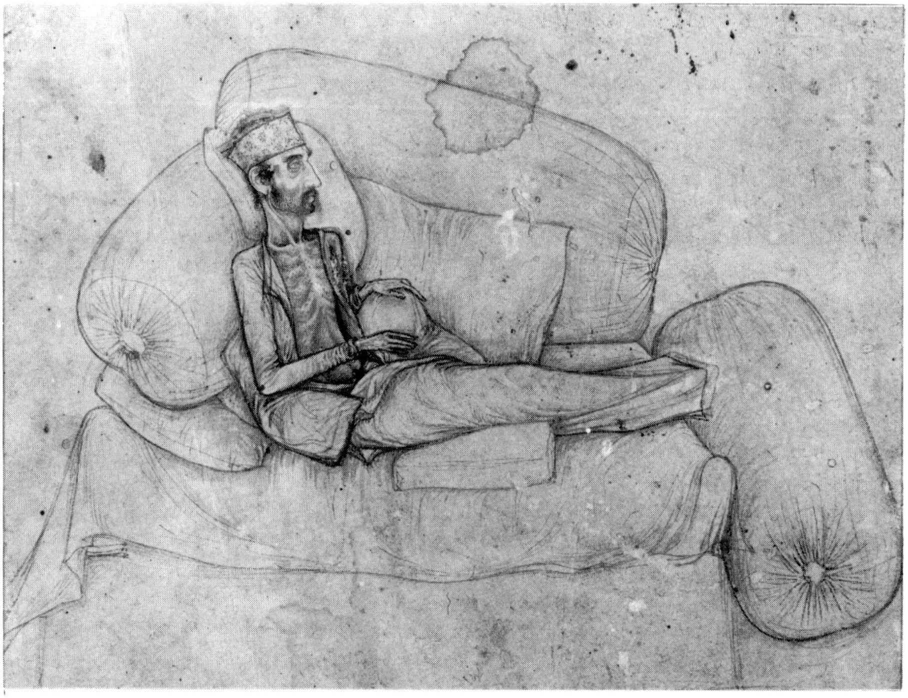

80. The Dying Inayat Khan. Attributed here to Hashim; Mughal, ca. 1618–1619

study of Jahangir can be attributed to the artist Hashim,[20] an artist whose drawings are often more powerful than his paintings; *The Dying Inayat Khan* is probably by him as well.

B. REGIONAL DEVELOPMENTS

The developing Mughal penchant for psychologically probing portraiture and for greater realism in figural proportions or natural textures affected painting in other areas of India in different ways. Unlike the Rajput states of the north, the Deccani sultanates usually remained politically independent of the Mughal court, although there was continual contact. Deccani patrons commissioned portraits, almost certainly following Mughal example, but the descriptive qualities of appearance and personality were not usually of major interest, as we have seen already at Ahmadnagar (for example fig. 22).

A Prince Reading a Book (fig. 82), by Abd al-Karim, is among the most

[20] It is closely related to an extraordinary painting of Jahangir, signed by Hashim, in the Minto Album; see T. W. Arnold and J. V. S. Wilkinson, *The Library of A. Chester Beatty – A Catalogue of Indian Miniatures*, London, 1936, vol. III, pl. 61.

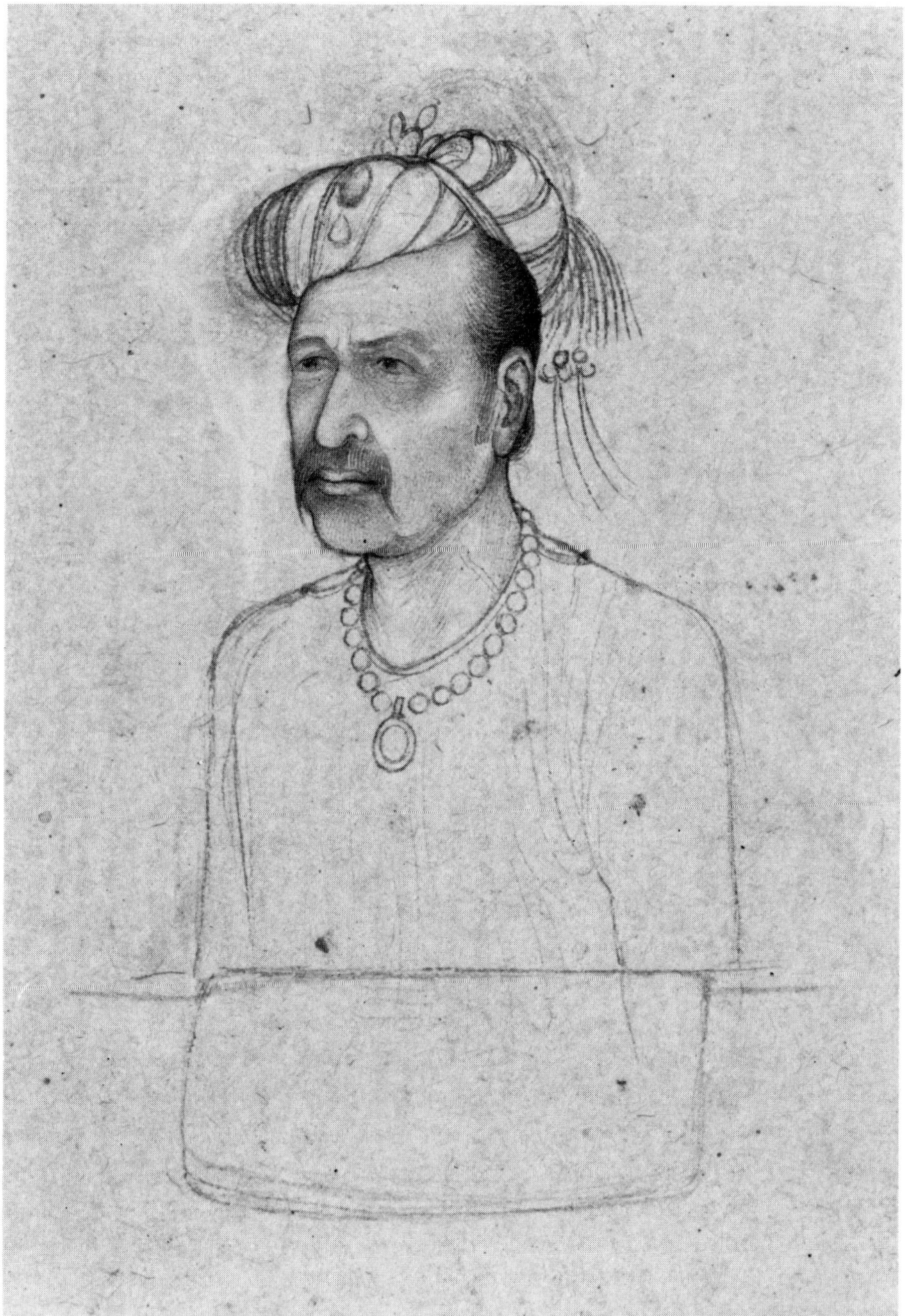

81. Jahangir. Attributed here to Hashim; Mughal, ca. 1620

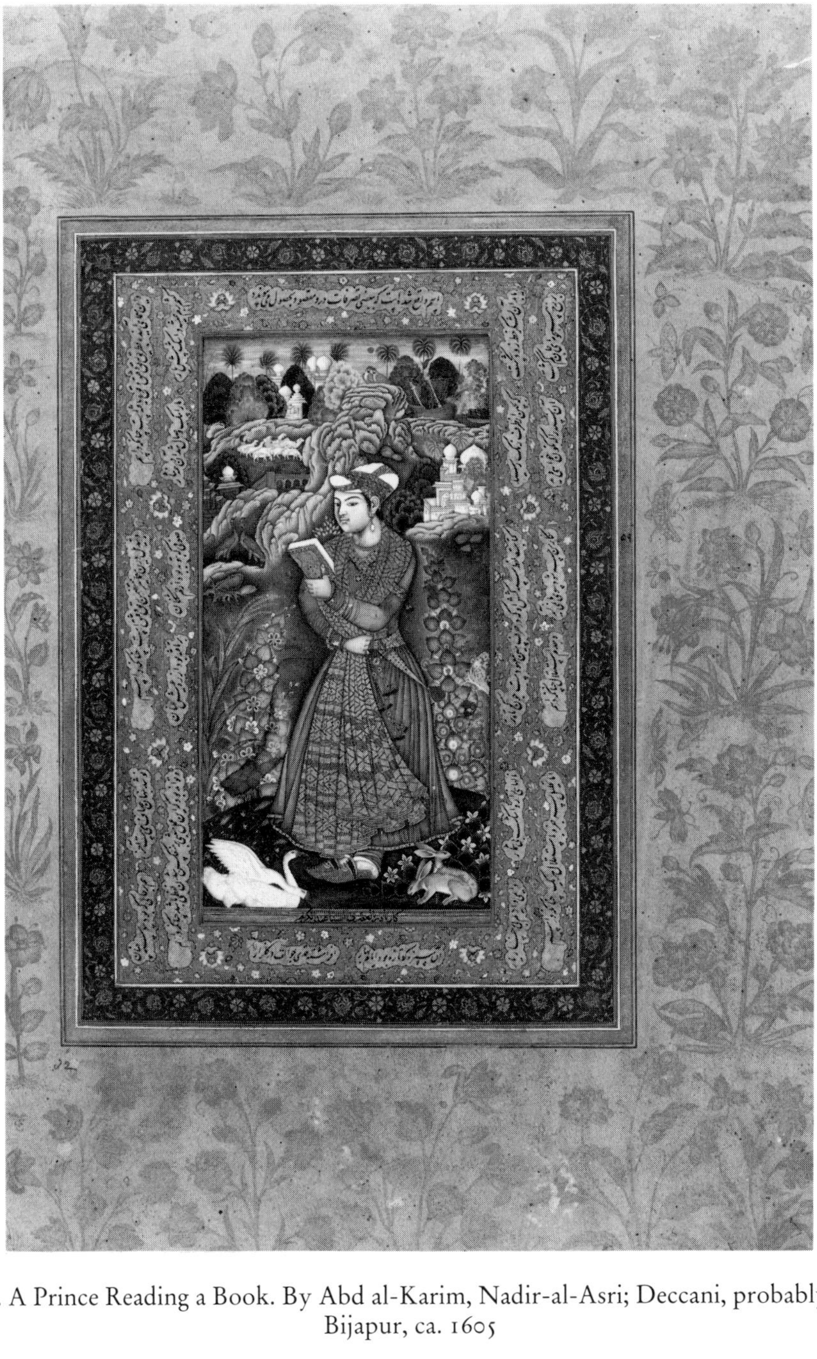

82. A Prince Reading a Book. By Abd al-Karim, Nadir-al-Asri; Deccani, probably at Bijapur, ca. 1605

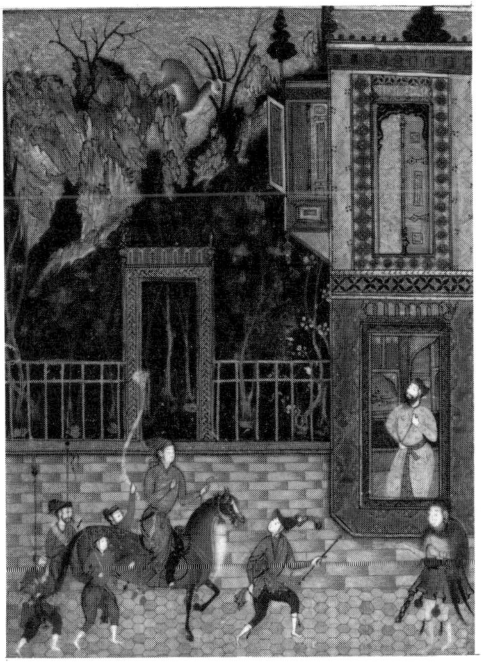

83. The Arrival of a Prince. By Jan Quli. Deccani, at Bijapur, ca. 1600

brilliant of all Deccani paintings. It is impossible to know whether the illustration was inspired by a specific person, however, so distant is it from the kind of personal and spatial realism at its height in contemporary Mughal court works. The illustration is instead an excuse for unashamedly aesthetic indulgence: we are affected by colors and lines, not by personalities. It is a powerful and sophisticated painting, made for an epicurean, elitist taste. It presumes considerable technical expertise, self-confidence, and expressive originality; and it is a tradition with different goals than those of the Mughal court.

While much of the technical refinement and subtlety of color seen here, as well as the spirited landscape, comes from a reassertion of Iranian interests – Bijapur had strong political and religious links with the Safavids – such details as the heavy shading on the prince's face indicate awareness of the expressive possibilities of European modelling. This was seen earlier in the contemporary Allahabad-period portrait by Mirza Ghulam (fig. 53), and it is found too in *The Arrival of a Prince* (fig. 83), which is inscribed to the painter Jan Quli. However, despite the seemingly everyday subject, the combination of interest in shading with disinterest in portraiture produces an otherworldly quality. Nowhere in Bijapur works are the artists interested in simulating the physical textures of flesh or cloth. Yet despite such differences of emphasis, the two

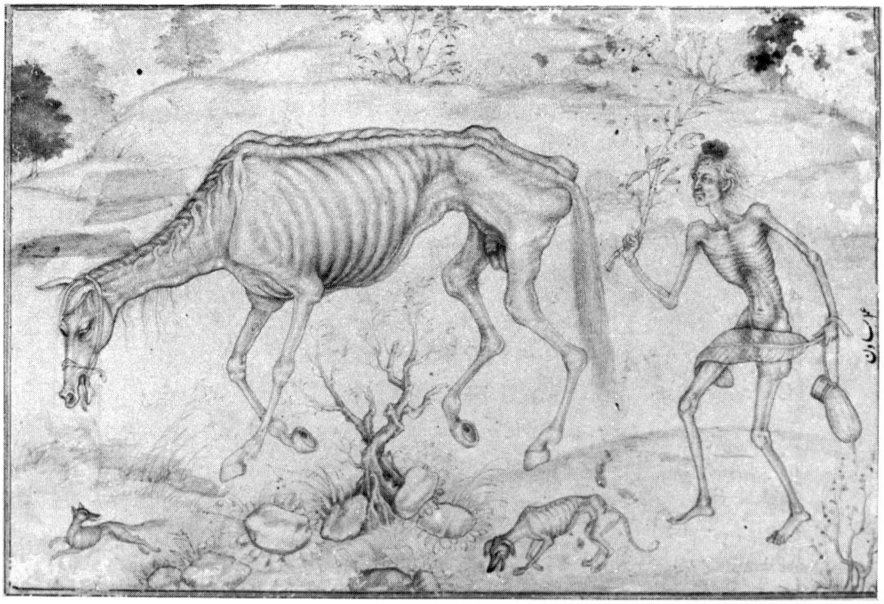

84. Emaciated Horse and Groom. By Basawan; ca. 1595

areas of patronage were in continual contact; poets and painters travelled between the various courts, and the Mughals collected Deccani paintings – several are found inserted into Jahangir's albums. As well, two thousand volumes, many of them illustrated, were sent from Bijapur to the Mughal court in 1601, in connection with the arrangements for the marriage of Sultan Ibrahim's daughter to Sultan Daniyal, Jahangir's son. And such Mughal artists as Farrukh Beg, Muhammad Ali, Mirza Ghulam, and Hashim either copied Bijapuri compositions or worked in styles heavily influenced by the Deccan.

A comparison of two versions of an almost identical subject and composition is instructive when comparing the character of north Indian Muslim painting and the more southern Deccani styles. *Emaciated Horse and Groom* (fig. 84), by Basawan about 1590, presents us with a study of physical decrepitude; everything about the image stresses the earthly plight of both the man and the animal – it is a forerunner of *The Dying Inayat Khan*. In a Bijapuri image, *Ascetic Riding a Nag* (fig. 85), we are instead presented with a scene made unearthly by the extraordinary marbelized background. This immediately removes from the scene any sense of physical reality. The image has been interpreted as a metaphor for the power of asceticism and self-denial, and throughout Deccani painting the unearthly is continually revealed.

On the other hand, Deccani painting can also be a celebration of worldly pomp. *Sultan Abdullah Qutb Shah of Golconda Watching a Celebration*

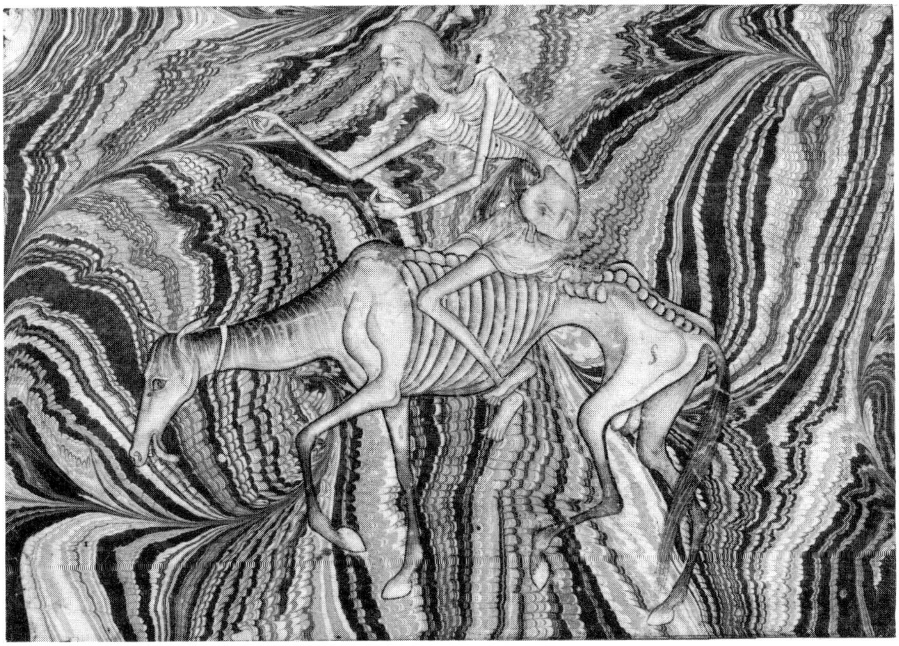

85. Ascetic Riding a Nag. Deccani, Bijapur, mid 17th century

(fig. 86) is one of five illustrations bound into a copy of the *Diwan* of Hafiz but not originally intended for the volume. It can be dated to about 1630 because of the presence of recognizable personalities. In the illustration reproduced, the Sultan (who ruled between 1626 and 1672) sits in an alcove decorated with wall-paintings, and this is only one of the details which assert the opulence and wealth of the court. Gold is used everywhere: in the clothing, for the numerous metal vessels found in all the illustrations, and to define the lines of the architecture. The scene is flat, and none of the technical refinements of contemporary Bijapuri works is in evidence. Its stylistic primitivism, coupled with the quantity of people and material objects, suggests that the work is as much a declaration of wealth as a fulfillment of artistic sensibility.

The patronage of painting at Deccani courts may have been intensified by the known activity of the rival Mughal workshops, a situation increasingly true also in the Rajput states. Rajput princes were frequently assigned to Deccani campaigns by their Mughal overlords, and they were affected by local Deccani artistic traditions. Certainly some Rajput princes had painters with them when they were resident in the Deccan, and commissioned works there. A group of illustrated manuscripts – copies of the *Gita Govinda*, *Rasamanjari*, and *Ragamala* are known – was made at Aurangabad, and one is inscribed to Mohan Singh Shaktavat, evidently a minor prince related to the rulers of

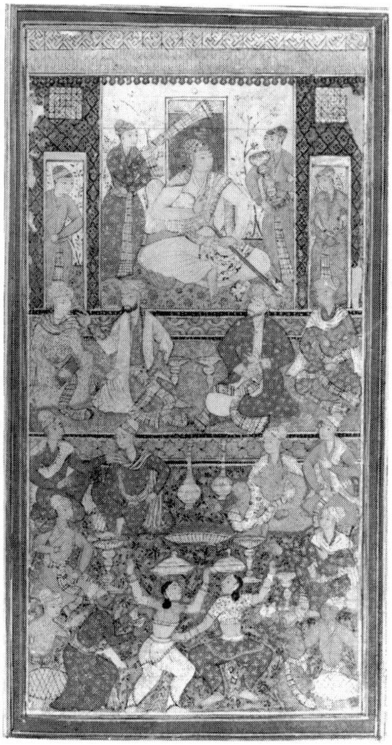

86. Sultan Abdullah Qutb Shah of Golconda Watching a Celebration. From a *Diwan* of Hafiz manuscript, Deccani, at Golconda, ca. 1630

Mewar. *Krishna Fluting* (fig. 87) exemplifies the style, in which a traditional Hindu subject is enlivened by brilliant pattern and color. To identify this as a Deccani style on the basis of the place of execution, rather than a Rajasthani style because of the patron, however, is difficult. One *Rasamanjari* volume is dated 1650, but the style continued with only minor adjustments – plus a decided decline in quality of execution – until at least 1723, the date on a *Gita Govinda* series.

Rajput contact with Mughal artistic taste and standards was also often direct, for Rajput rulers and princes were frequently in residence at the imperial court. *Jahangir Greeting the Poet Sa'di* (figs. 74 and 75), for example, showed Karan Singh of Mewar in attendance on the emperor. The son of Maharana Amar Singh, Karan Singh was also a grandson of the heroic Rana Pratap, whose refusal to accept Mughal overlordship remains today an active model of Hindu heroism. The final capitulation of the Mewar kingdom was thus of great symbolic importance to the Mughals. And Jahangir was impressed by the prince, who attended the imperial court in token of this submission.

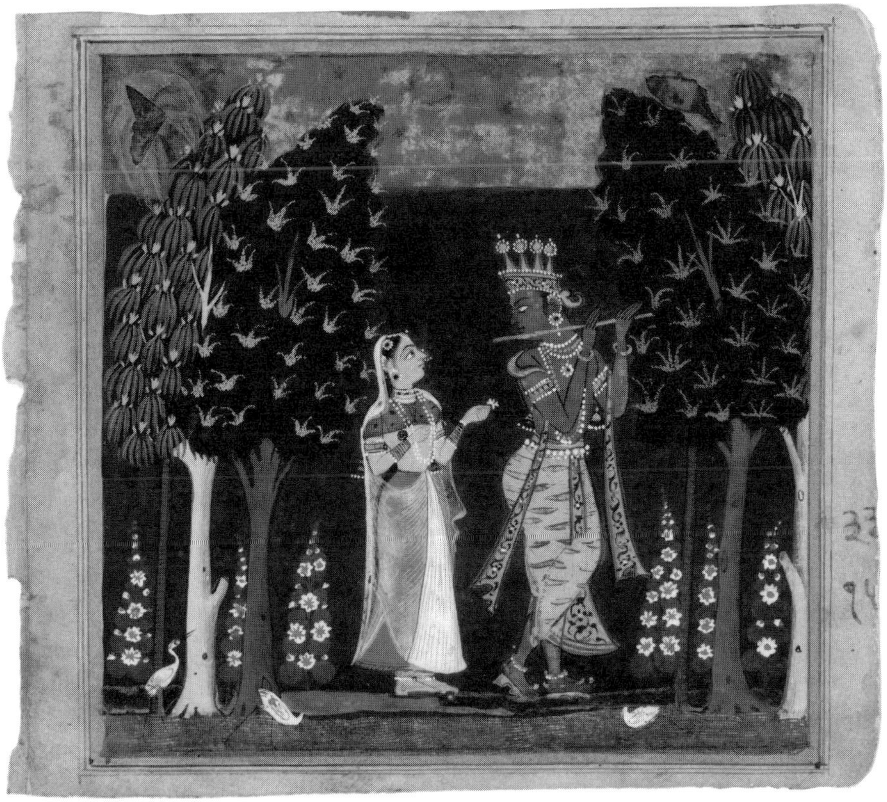

87. Krishna Fluting. Rajput, Deccan at Aurangabad, ca. 1650

> As it was necessary to win the heart of Karan, who was of a wild nature and had never seen assemblies and had lived among the hills, I every day showed him some fresh flavour, so that on the second day of his attendance a jewelled dagger, and on the next day a special Iraqi horse with jewelled saddle, were given to him. On the day when he went to the darbar in the female apartments, there were given to him on the part of Nur-Jahan Begam a rich dress of honour, a jewelled sword, a horse and saddle, and an elephant. After this I presented him with a rosary of pearls of great value.[21]

After such exposure to Mughal ideals and the seductive opulence of imperial taste, few Hindu princes could resist adopting the standards of fashion at the prestigious and politically powerful Mughal court. In terms of painting, this meant that Rajput court artists were often asked to paint in a Mughal manner, or to attempt portraits and records of historical events, instead of illustrating

[21] Jahangir, *Tuzuk*, vol. 1, pp. 277–278.

merely familiar texts extolling the gods, the subject matter that dominated Rajput traditions prior to the Mughal arrival. At each state the demands and expectations were different, however, and thus Rajput painting as a whole is a complex, disjointed tradition, lacking the single-minded focus and straightforward historical development of the classic Mughal style.

Among the earliest specifically inscribed and dated Rajput works is the well-known Chawand *Ragamala* (plate F), so named because a colophon states that Chawand, in Mewar, was the provenance. A small town south of Chitor Fort, Rana Pratap's capital, Chawand had served as the rana's home after the fort was seized by imperial troops in 1568. A partially obliterated date given in the inscription has been read as 1605.

The style of the Chawand *Ragamala* pages develops directly from the pre-Mughal illustration of *Bhairava Raga* (fig. 28). Both *Ragamala* pages have an almost square format, and in each the composition is divided into rectangular compartments of varying size and shape. Colors in both works are confined to a few bright hues, dominated by the primaries (red, yellow, and blue), together with white and green, applied as flat, unmodulated, clearly bounded areas placed edge to edge. The figures in each are unnaturally large in relation to the architecture, although the formula for women used in the Chawand set is slightly less angular than that in the earlier work; and the space, with its overlapping forms, is relatively more complex. The compositions are so close, within the context of Indian styles, however, that the Chawand artists must certainly have been trained in the style of that earlier *Ragamala*. Unlike painting for the neighboring Rajput rulers of Bundi, therefore, which began as a direct offshoot of the Mughal workshops (figs. 27 and 29), Mewari artists initially drew instead from deeply rooted pre-Mughal traditions.

Akbar's defeat of Chitor Fort in 1568 was a purely symbolic victory. Rana Pratap, who ruled Mewar between 1572 and 1597, refused to ally himself with the emperor, a man whom orthodox Hindus viewed as both infidel and outcaste. Pratap's title, rana, was unique within the Hindu system, and he was the most prestigious of all the ruling chiefs. Seeing himself as the standard-bearer for Rajput bravery and dynastic purity, he exhausted his kingdom's resources futilely fighting to remain independent of Muslim control. Mewar never regained the economic and military supremacy of its pre-Mughal days, but Pratap's resistance to Islam remains legendary. The one-eyed hero is a favorite subject of Rajput paintings, Hindi films, and modern Indian comic books.

In 1614, however, Prince Khurram (the future Shahjahan) finally defeated Maharana Amar Singh (r. 1597–1621). Karan Singh (r. 1621–1628) then extended the palace at Udaipur, one mark of Mewar's renewed prosperity. There was also now a willingness to learn from Mughal taste, even if Mewar never wholeheartedly adopted Mughal artistic styles. By 1628, the inscribed date on a *Ragamala* by the painter Sahibdin, the Mewar court had changed

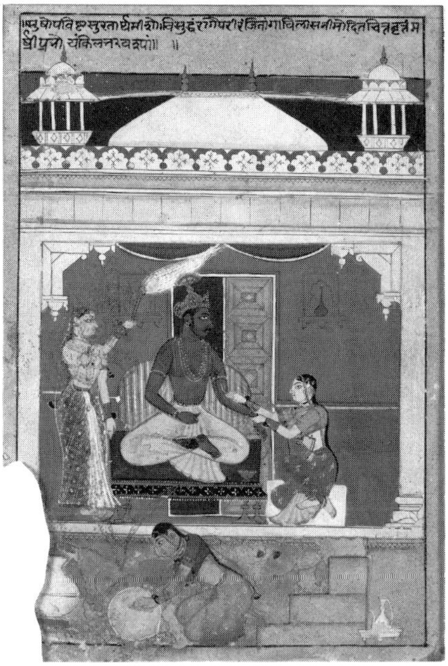

88. Bhairava Raga. By Sahibdin; from a *Ragamala* series, Rajput, Rajasthan at Mewar, dated 1628

dramatically, and undeniably under Mughal impact. In *Bhairava Raga* (fig. 88) – the same subject that we saw in the pre-Mughal *Ragamala* page (fig. 28), as well as in the 1591 Chunar *Ragamala* (fig. 27) – the figures fit the scale of the architecture; the clothing, no longer defined by angular flat shapes and sharp lines, is realistically soft and transparent; and the faces are shaded and three-dimensional. The figure of Shiva seems to be based on individualized physiognomy and is no longer simply a repeated generalized figural formula. No one could mistake this for a Mughal illustration, of course, but Mughal stylistic contributions are clearly recognizable.

The year 1628 is also that of the accession to the Mewar throne of Maharana Jagat Singh (r. 1628–1652), Karan Singh's son. The great nineteenth-century British historian James Tod wrote memorably of the ruler in his epic *Annals and Antiquities of Rajasthan*:

> The twenty-six years during which Juggut Sing occupied the throne passed in uninterrupted tranquility . . . This period was devoted to the cultivation of the peaceful arts, especially architecture . . . The palace on the lake (covering about four acres), called the Jugnewas [now the luxurious Lake Palace Hotel], is entirely his work . . . Parterres of flowers, orange and lemon groves, intervene to dispel the monotony of the buildings, shaded by the wide-spreading tamarind and magnificent ever-green kheenee; while the peaceful palmyra and

> cocoa wave their plume-like branches over the dark cypress or cooling plantain . . . Here they listened to the tale of the bard, and slept off their noon-day opiate amidst the cool breezes of the lake, wafting delicious odours from myriads of lotus-flower which covered the surface of the waters; and as the fumes of the potion evaporated, they opened their eyes on a landscape to which not even its inspiration could frame an equal . . . Amidst such scenes did the Sesodia [Mewar] princes and chieftains recreate during two generations, exchanging the din of arms for voluptuous inactivity.[22]

Jagat Singh's reign was fully as hedonistic as Tod's description indicates, and it produced an enormous output of painting. Many additional works by Sahibdin are known, including a dispersed *Bhagavata Purana* dated 1648. The largest project, however, was an extensive *Ramayana* series, of which the known volumes are dated between 1649 and 1653. By no means do we see a step-by-step process of Mughalization, however, as we might expect after comparing the *Ragamalas* of circa 1540, 1605, and 1628 (fig. 28, plate F, and fig. 88). In fact, *Mithila is Besieged by Sita's Disappointed Suitors* (fig. 89), from the first book of the *Ramayana*, dated 1649, seems a retreat from the definite interest in Mughal style found in Sahibdin's *Ragamala* (fig. 88). The composition is completely flat, with profile figures silhouetted against flat planes of strong color, and the fortress is a schematic diagram. (In this regard, the work maintains strong links with the battle scene in the Jain *Kalpasutra* manuscript of 1411, reproduced as plate A.) The scene is by Manohar, who is not to be confused with the Mughal painter of the same name. He is a more conservative artist than Sahibdin, but even in general Mewar painting in the mid seventeenth century still remains closer to pre-Mughal styles than to any contemporary Mughal works. (Compare the *Ramayana* illustration to a Mughal *Battle Scene* of about 1640, reproduced as fig. 100.)

The central Indian kingdom of Malwa, which borders Mewar on the southeast, was also an active center of the arts. It was a Muslim sultanate controlled by the Khalji dynasty until 1561, when Akbar's troops defeated Sultan Baz Bahadur. The capital city, Mandu, was indisputably the most active identified center of book-painting until at least the early sixteenth century. We have mentioned already the Mandu *Kalpasutra* of 1439, the *Ni'matnama* (figs. 5 and 7) of about 1500–1505, and an uninscribed *Laur-Chanda* (fig. 15); and additional manuscripts from the region are now known. Not only was the output of the state prolific, it was equally vital within distinct sub-styles: works made in the same region but not for the same patron or even the same religious community. It is no surprise, therefore, that paintings have also been attributed to Malwa, as well as central India more generally, under Rajput patronage in the

[22] James Tod, *Annals and Antiquities of Rajast'han or the Central and Western Rajpoot States of India*, London, 1829, vol. I, pp. 372–373.

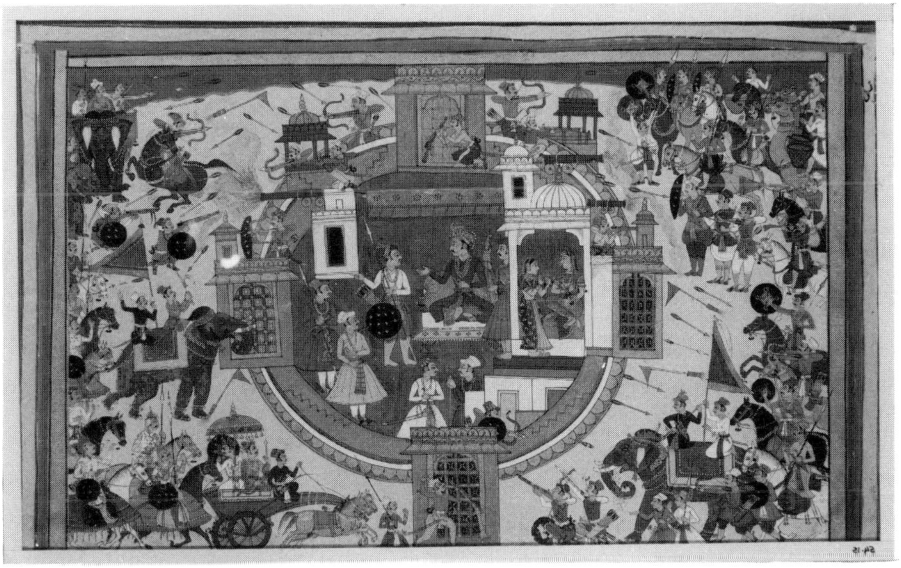

89. Mithila is Besieged by Sita's Disappointed Suitors. By Manohar; from a *Ramayana* series, Rajput, Rajasthan at Udaipur, dated 1649

seventeenth century. While the works are descendants of pre-Mughal Malwa styles, exact provenances are debated.

The earliest Rajput series from Central India is a *Rasikapriya* dated 1634. A *Ragamala* series shows the style at a slightly later and more assured stage. In *Malkaus Ragini* (fig. 90) the composition remains simple, and nothing distracts us from the episode: a couple shown making love at night while a peacock screeches. There is no spatial move into depth to dilute the immediacy of the work. The large size of the bird, and the vibrant form of the trees, are determined by their dramatic and emotional role in the scene, and not by disinterested visual naturalism.

The Rajasthani states of Bundi and Kota provide a further excellent example of the way in which regional artistic identities grew during this period. Kota did not exist as a separate state until 1624, when Jahangir seized part of Bundi territory (a prerogative of Mughal overlordship), presenting it to Madhu Singh, younger brother of the Bundi Maharao, as a reward for bravery and support (Madhu Singh is the Rajput warrior at the center of *The Death of Khan Jahan Lodi*, from the illustrated history of Shahjahan's reign, the *Padshahnama*; see plate G). This geographic and political surgery diminished Bundi's economic status and therefore its capacity for rebellion, and established enmity within the Hara family, further ensuring Mughal security – a conscious purpose of the tactic.

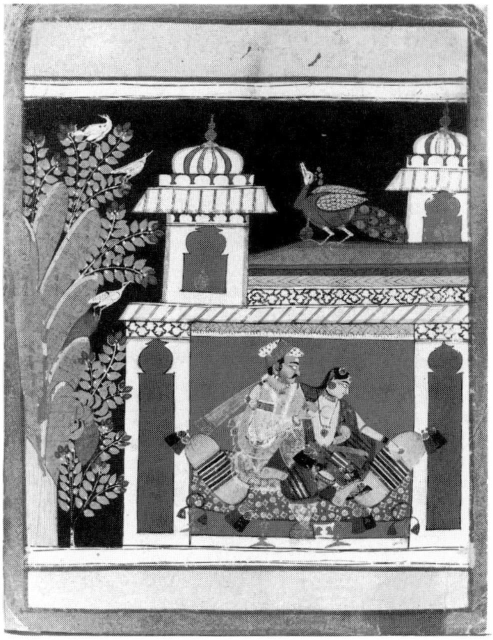

90. Malkaus Ragini. From a *Ragamala* series, Rajput, Central India, ca. 1640

We have discussed the Chunar *Ragamala* (fig. 27), a set dated 1591 and associated with the Bundi family. An unfinished and fragmentary *Bhagavata Purana* series has also long been attributed to Bundi, although the greater part is now in the collection of the former Kota maharao. In *Kamsa and his Demon Minister* (fig. 91), the composition – with figures walking along a wall towards a guarded doorway, and an interior garden with a pavilion in which an enthroned ruler talks with attendants – is a stereotypically Akbar-period composition; nothing in it indicates any awareness of the pre-Mughal *Bhagavata Purana* tradition. The lack of space and air within this scene, and the insistent division of the surface into almost rectangular units, however, is thoroughly Rajput. Also the figures, while animated, are types, whereas even with such non-historical subjects, imperial artists of this period usually created convincingly portraitlike characterizations. Probably attributable now to Kota, the set perpetuates a somewhat out-of-date phase of imperial style.

An important, recently discovered drawing, *A Royal Hunt* (fig. 92), is contemporary with the *Bhagavata Purana*, with which it shares figural and landscape formulas. Unlike the *ragamalas* and other traditional subjects that dominate Rajput painting before the later seventeenth century, this is a dynamically composed scene which almost certainly documents an actual event. Although clearly a fragment, it is an astonishingly vital and original work

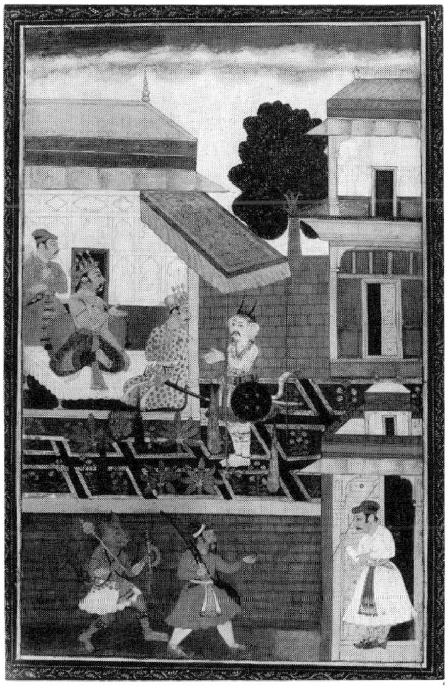

91. Kamsa and his Demon Minister. From a *Bhagavata Purana* series, Rajput, Rajasthan at Kota, ca. 1640

within the context of its time. As a type, the subject was certainly based on Mughal scenes, but the large size of the remaining fragment – it is about forty inches wide – and therefore its physical impact are unusual for a composition on paper. It may have been inspired by wall-paintings within the imperial palace, works with which favored Rajput princes might most easily have come into contact. Fragments of scenes of hunting and elephant combat remain on the walls of the palaces at Fatehpur-Sikri, for example.

The scene is broken into definite, carefully contrasted, units: horsemen dominate the left edge; hunters riding elephants the right; and a central mountain landscape separates two large elephants, one of which is being attacked by a lion. It is not simply the subject that produces excitement, but the enormous relative size of the central encounter compared to the attendant figures. Despite a profusion of detail, the central combat rivets our attention.

Within the three units, there is a variety of effects. The repetition of horses' heads at the left, each with a darkly shaded mane, produces rich surface rhythms, and contrasts with the curling lines defining the more volumetric elephant forms at the right. The twisting, rippling line of the central river gorge dominates, however. No previous Rajput painting had used this kind of fluid, linear energy. Earlier works are usually jagged and angular, while the line in

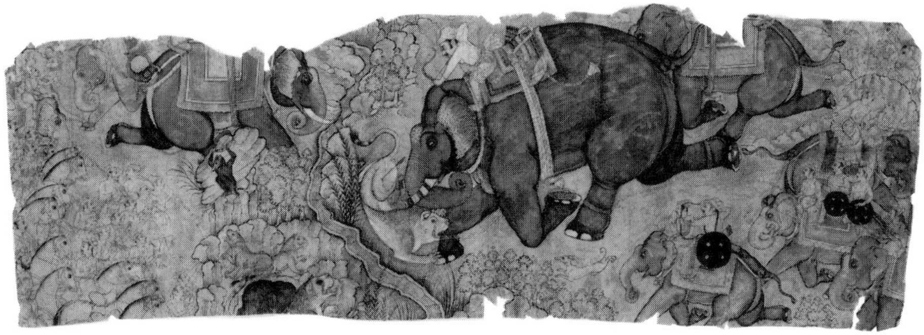

92. A Royal Hunt. Rajput, Rajasthan at Kota, ca. 1640

Mughal works is more descriptive than independently expressive (for example fig. 84). The landscape, while it derives from the basic shapes of Mughal rocks and mountains, is almost completely flat, a surface design rather than solid forms in a three-dimensional space. One clue to a source for the painter's style is the small bear, seen sitting on a mountain peak. It holds a rock over its head, prepared to hurl it at the approaching armies, and this is a favorite motif of Safavid Iranian painters. Contact with Iranian and Deccani models may prove to be an origin for the sophisticated linearism seen here.

Hunting scenes were especially popular at Kota, as was an appreciation for highly finished drawings. Since specific motifs, such as the large elephant, are found later repeatedly in definite Kota works (fig. 127), as we shall discuss further below, a Kota attribution for *A Royal Hunt* and the closely related *Bhagavata Purana* set seems inevitable.

Jodhpur (or Marwar) was ruled by the Rathor family, a branch of the Chauhan dynasty founded in 1212. The Rathors, like the Sesodias of Mewar, the Kachhwahas of Amber, and the Hadas of Bundi and Kota, ultimately traced their genealogy to the gods of the sun and moon. Jodhpur, in the deserts of northwestern Rajasthan, had been named for Rao Jodha, who moved the capital of his kingdom from Mandor to the present site in 1459. During Humayun's slow procession into exile, the Mughal ruler was briefly offered refuge at Jodhpur, and that may be one reason why Sher Shah, who had ousted Humayun from Delhi, attacked and claimed Jodhpur territories. Rao Maldeva Rathor (r. 1531–1562) recaptured the lands after Sher Shah's death, but immediately following Akbar's accession, the young emperor, in turn, seized the greater part of Jodhpur State. (This then included Ajmer, which was never returned and became the Mughal administrative capital in Rajasthan.) Akbar's attack had been encouraged by Ram Singh, the elder son of Maldeva. Before his death, Maldeva had chosen his third son as his successor, thereby making

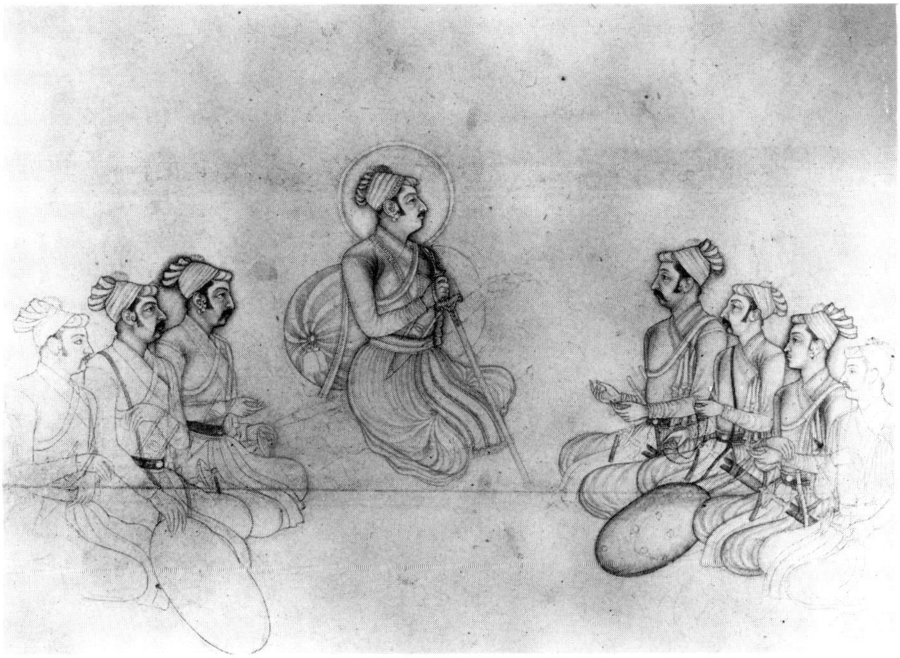

93. Raja Jaswant Singh of Jodhpur and Courtiers. Rajput, Rajasthan at Jodhpur, ca. 1645

deadly enemies of the three brothers. It was by a promised capitulation to the Mughals should he receive the throne that Ram Singh won the help of imperial troops and defeated his rival siblings. Akbar did not return Jodhpur Fort to the Rathors until 1583, however, at which point Udai Singh (fig. 20), Maldeva's second son, succeeded his younger brother. With his daughter's marriage to Salim, Udai Singh (r. 1583–1594) and his successors became important members of the Mughal inner circle. Raja Gaj Singh (r. 1619–1635) held the highest rank possible for a Hindu at the Mughal court under Jahangir. He is shown in *The Accession of Shah Jahan* (fig. 96), from the *Padshahnama*, standing just below and to the left of the imperial throne.

Maharaja Jaswant Singh (r. 1635–1678) of Jodhpur was an important patron of painting; while few works of his reign still exist, they are sufficiently original and distinctive to indicate that an active and sophisticated patronage was at work. Two examples are reproduced here. *Maharaja Jaswant Singh of Jodhpur and Courtiers* (fig. 93) is an unfinished sketch for a darbar scene, and this subject alone is evidence of important Mughal influence. Dating from about 1645, the style and technique are of almost imperial calibre. The portraits of the attending nobles are precisely observed and minutely detailed. If the even

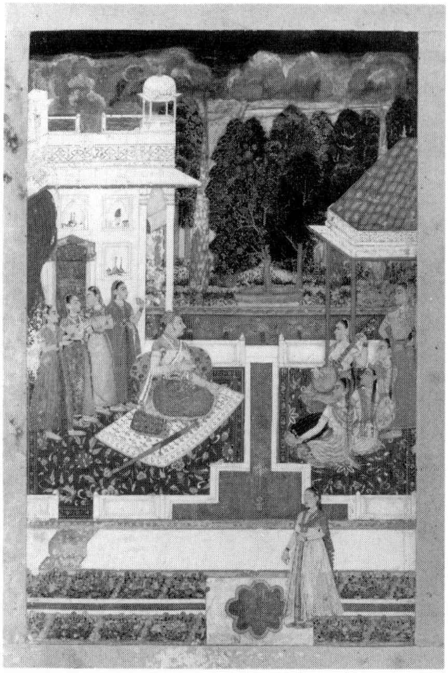

94. Maharaja Jaswant Singh of Jodhpur Listening to Music. Rajput, Rajasthan at Jodhpur, ca. 1660

and symmetrical line-up of the men is more rigid than usual in Mughal works, the scene is nevertheless an accurate approximation of mid-seventeenth-century imperial style. Clearly Jaswant Singh's artistic ideals and aspirations were quite different from those of Mewar.

A second illustration, *Maharaja Jaswant Singh of Jodhpur Listening to Music* (fig. 94), presents us with an older man seated on the carpeted terrace of a garden pavilion. (The scene can be dated to about 1660, and already shows a retreat from the earlier enthusiasm for Mughal taste.) Female attendants and musicians surround him, and the hedonism of the setting is matched by the visual opulence of the style. Rich and varied colors claim our attention, as does the variety of shapes and patterns throughout the scene. On the other hand, the entire surface is so lively that we do not see people emphasized by a less important background. Each area equally demands our time. Unlike the simpler but nonetheless compositionally comparable Mughal scene, *Lovers on a Terrace* (fig. 111), the background in the Jodhpur work is as intricate and detailed as the human figures; the women are no more important visually than the architecture, for example, or the rug on which they stand. Nor are we aware of differentiations of physical texture. The contrast of the floral rug and the formally arranged flowers of the garden is effective because of the surface

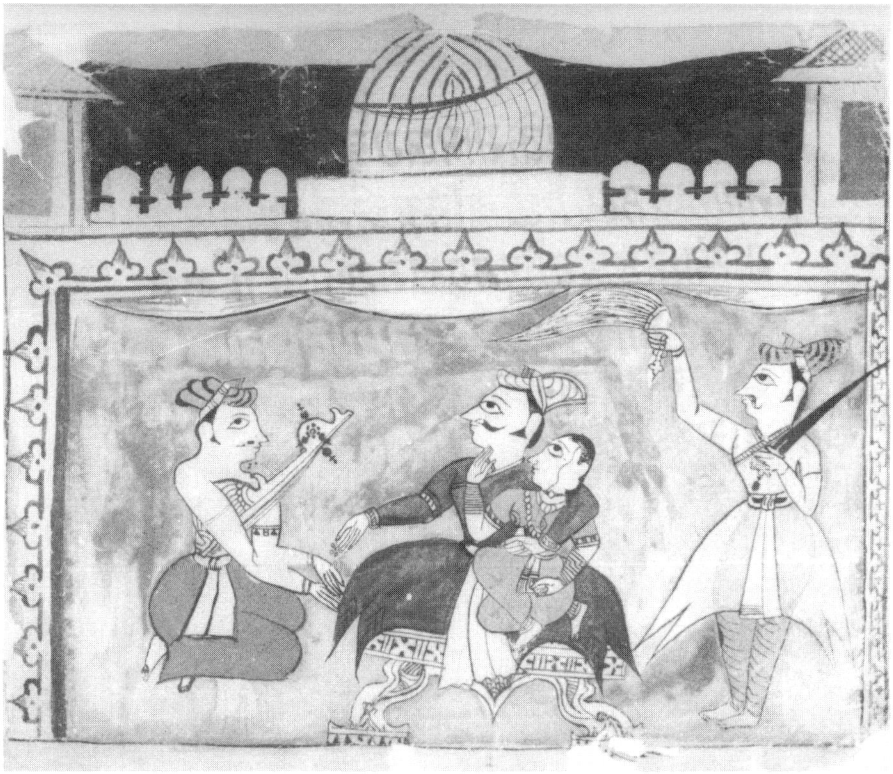

95. Pancham Ragini. By Virji; from a *Ragamala* series, Rajput, Rajasthan at Pali, dated 1623

pattern each creates, and the clothing does not arouse in us a sense of muslin or silk – as it does in *Lovers on a Terrace* – but simply of strong shapes and colors. This disinterest in any accentuation of human subjects or material textures separates the work from the most prominent and distinctive aspect of mid-seventeenth-century imperial style, by which it had nonetheless been profoundly influenced. Unlike contemporary paintings from Mewar, however, this seems to record a specific event and an identifiable setting in a style that is technically intricate and based on relatively close observation.

If Mughal style strongly affected works made for the Jodhpur court, paintings made elsewhere in the state retained recognizable pre-Mughal elements. A *Ragamala* made at Pali, a small land-holding (*thikana*) subsidiary to the Jodhpur court, is dated 1623 and inscribed with the name of the painter: Virji. As shown by *Pancham Ragini* (fig. 95), the set is in a local variant of the pre-Mughal *Chaurapanchasika* (fig. 4) and betrays no knowledge of imperial style. A *Meghaduta* manuscript, dated 1669, was illustrated at nearby Asani, probably for members of the Jain community and related stylistically to the Pali set rather than to the central court style.[23] This suggests that indigenous artistic attitudes remained well entrenched in areas not affected by high court fashion, and this may explain the ease with which familiar local styles reasserted themselves when interest in Mughal artistic standards eventually waned.

C. IMPERIAL PAINTING AT SHAHJAHAN'S COURT

Sultan Khurram, third son of Jahangir, was granted the title of *Shahjahan* (Ruler of the World) in 1617, in honor of his military victories in the Deccan and his earlier defeat of the Rajput rana of Mewar. Jahangir also ordered that Khurram be allowed to sit near the imperial throne when in attendance at court, an unusual acknowledgment of his status as heir apparent. Two years later, the prince again departed for the Deccan, and with distance the relationship with Jahangir became more difficult. Shahjahan grew increasingly aware that factions at court were moving against him, and in 1622 he rebelled, attempting to seize the royal treasury at Agra and establish himself as emperor. From that year onward, Jahangir referred officially to Shahjahan as *bi-Daulat*, or the wretched one.

Khurram's movement through the political and dynastic hierarchy can be chronicled in painting. The British Museum portrait *Jahangir with His Three Sons* (fig. 73) showed the imperial siblings in a clearly hierarchical ranking: Khusrau, the eldest, is closest to his father, while Parviz stands just behind his older brother; Khurram, the youngest, fans the emperor. Khusrau's personal history suggests that the work should be dated 1605, for during the next year he rebelled against Jahangir, and the emperor made it clear that Parviz would replace Khusrau as intended successor to the throne. This new relationship remains intact in *Jahangir Greeting the Poet Sa'di* (figs. 74 and 75) of 1615. Jahangir now faces Parviz, while Khurram (Shahjahan), in a striped robe, stands behind his father, in an undeniably subservient position. Khusrau is absent. Parviz, a dullard and voluptuary, however, proved himself incompetent militarily and politically. Jahangir lost patience, and later in 1615 raised Khurram to equal rank with Parviz. A year later, giving him a still higher position, Jahangir thereby signalled that now Khurram was intended to succeed.

When Shahjahan himself eventually rebelled against his father, he needed to

[23] Moti Chandra and U. P. Shah, "New documents of Jaina painting," in *Shri Mahavir Jaina Vidyalaya Golden Jubilee Volume (Part I)*, Bombay, 1968, pp. 389–391 and fig. 14. The identification of Asani there with a town near Jaunpur is not accepted here.

ensure that his power would remain intact. In 1622 Shahjahan arranged for Khusrau's murder, and Parviz's death four years later was at the time attributed to him as well. By the time of his accession, nephews, male cousins, and his blind and leprous brother Shahryar, had all been murdered – thus removing any effective challengers.

Shahjahan formally became emperor at an accession ceremony in 1628. One of his first acts was the commission of the Peacock Throne, an object made of heavy gold and jewels that – as a lavish display of vast wealth – came to symbolize Mughal imperial splendor. It also reveals Shahjahan's taste for the precious and finely crafted, which extended to painting and architecture also. Far more than his father, Shahjahan was interested in architecture, public monuments proclaiming his power and might. Unlike the red sandstone buildings made for Akbar, Shahjahan's buildings were predominantly of translucent white marble, a stone capable of being finely cut, highly polished, and precisely inlaid with colored stones – a technique especially popular at this time. As we shall see, this taste also affected the paintings the emperor commissioned.

Shahjahan's favorite wife was Mumtaz Mahal, the daughter of Asaf Khan, brother of Jahangir's wife Nur Jahan (fig. 69). (Shahjahan was himself born of a different wife, a Rajput princess from Jodhpur.) They were married in 1612, when she was nineteen, but she died in 1631 giving birth to their fourteenth child. The emperor was inconsolable. Until January 1633 the court was in mourning, although Shahjahan had by then begun to plan and build the Taj Mahal, Mumtaz Muhal's mausoleum. From 1639 to 1648 he was further involved in planning the building of a new capital city, Shahjahanabad, near Delhi.

In the eighth regnal year, Shahjahan commissioned an official history of his reign from Muhammad Amin Qazwini. Babur and Jahangir had written their own memoirs, of course, while Akbar, illiterate, had ordered a biography from Abu'l Fazl, a close friend. All of these were frank, enthusiastic, and personally revealing documents. The *Padshahnama* was clearly an official state document in both text and illustrations. Qazwini's text covered the first ten years of the reign and was finished in 1646. The project was then given over to Abd al-Hamid Lahori, who used Qazwini as the basis for a written account of this first decade, to which a volume was added covering the next ten years. A completion of the text up to 1656 was eventually commissioned from Muhammad Waris as a third volume.

A section of the imperial copy of Abd al-Hamid Lahori's *Padshahnama* has survived intact, and several illustrations which must have been intended for additional, now missing, volumes are in various public and private collections. Some bear dates (for example 1628, 1635, 1639) which indicate that certain illustrations were made before Abd al-Hamid Lahori's text was assembled, presumably with the intention that they illustrate another work.[24] (Both here and in the first *Akbarnama* there is clear evidence that illustrations – even for the most prestigious and important imperial manuscripts – were sometimes taken from other sources.)

Whereas the text and illustrations of the first *Akbarnama* were a revelation of Akbar's physical and intellectual vitality, and the *Jahangirnama* showed that emperor's curiosity about the world and spiritual matters, the *Padshahnama* is far less personally revealing. There are few scenes of action, and little tells us of any particularly personal enthusiasms of the emperor. The majority of the paintings show court ceremonials or great military victories. It was a book meant to assert the emperor's power – perhaps even his deification – and it is the most important manuscript of Shahjahan's reign.

One of the earliest pages made for the volume describes an event during the accession celebrations of 1628, when Shahjahan's four sons arrived at Agra to pay homage to their father (fig. 96). As Asaf Khan, their maternal grandfather, looks on, Dara Shikoh is embraced by his father, Shuja and Aurangzeb await their turns, and Murad, the youngest, stands behind the emperor. The color is clear and brilliant in the work, and line and composition are perfectly controlled. The artist, Bichitr, is obviously delighted with the contrasts of textile patterns, and the variety of people present, for the descriptions are intensely perceptive and highly differentiated. In these ways, the work develops directly out of Jahangiri painting, and gives us a basis for judging the more innovative aspects of other illustrations in the book.

If Bichitr's work is distinguished by the painter's accuracy in presenting physical characteristics of the people and objects he describes, other folios show a seemingly accurate presentation of architecture as well. *Festivities at the Wedding of Dara Shikoh* (figs. 97 and 98) takes place on the throne platform between the Diwan-i-Khas (Hall of Private Audience) and the Hamam (Baths) in Agra Fort (fig. 99). The entrance hall for the hamam, at the left, is now in London, and the arcade at the lower level in the photograph is a later addition. Indeed, the present Diwan-i-Khas was built in 1636 on the site of an earlier hall, and it is this that we presumably see in the manuscript page. The viewpoint of the painter is convincingly that from the still-existing raised platform on the other side of the open court in which the dancers and musicians are assembled, even if the painter has changed the actual central position of Shahjahan's throne platform so that it does not cross the spine of the book. Another characteristic of *Festivities at the Wedding of Dara Shikoh* is its almost excessive neatness. Despite the celebratory atmosphere, it is a scene of complete decorum. We are observing the enactment of a court ritual, rather than delighting in the quirks

[24] For further discussion, see Beach, *Grand Mogul*, pp. 78–85, and W. E. Begley and Z. A. Desai, *The Shah Jahan Nama of Inayat Khan*, Delhi, 1990, pp. xiii–xxxvii.

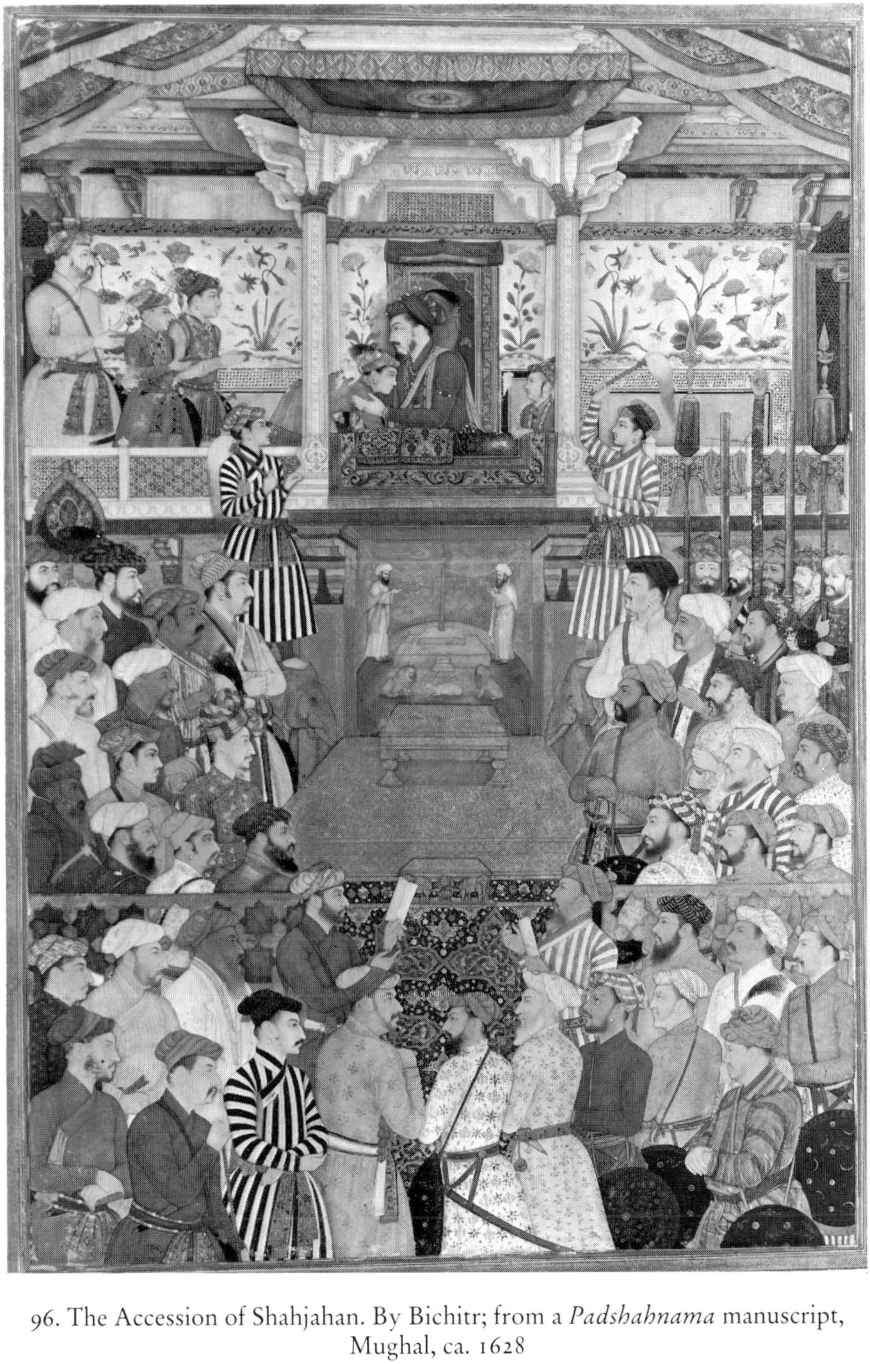

96. The Accession of Shahjahan. By Bichitr; from a *Padshahnama* manuscript, Mughal, ca. 1628

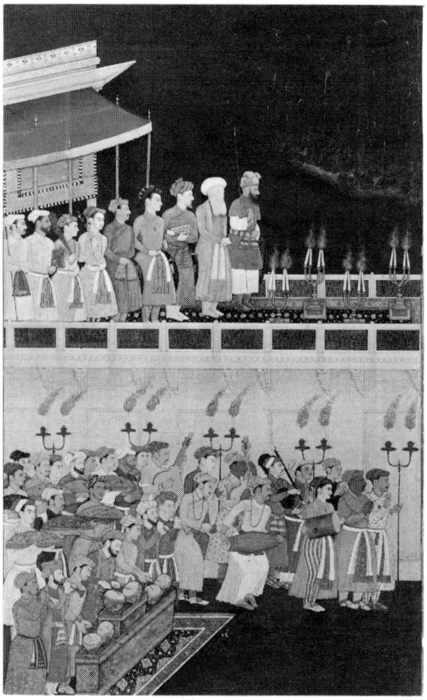

97. Festivities at the Wedding of Dara Shikoh (left half). Attributed to Bulaki, son of Hushang; from a *Padshahnama* manuscript, Mughal, ca. 1633

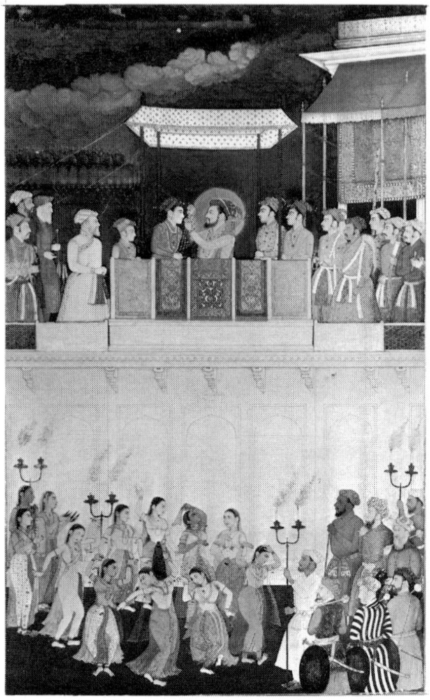

98. Festivities at the Wedding of Dara Shikoh (right half). Attributed to Bulaki, son of Hushang; from a *Padshahnama* manuscript, Mughal, ca. 1633

and unpredictability of humans in groups – which is precisely what attracted Abu'l Hasan in *The Accession of Jahangir* (figs. 71 and 72). The manuscript abounds with such ritual enactments of imperial power.

A quite different style is found in the *Padshahnama* illustration of *The Death of Khan Jahan Lodi*, an event of 1630 (plate G). It is signed by Abid, a brother of Abu'l Hasan. One of the very greatest of Mughal painters, few works can be attributed to Abid prior to his work on this volume, although he was probably among the artists working for Jahangir at Allahabad. In the darbar scene by Bichitr (fig. 96), or *Festivities at the Wedding of Dara Shikoh*, the space is totally rational – not scientific, by European standards, but easily comprehensible. Here, however, the space is dreamlike. Proportions neither diminish in depth, according to accepted Mughal practice of the time, nor remain consistent over the entire surface, as in Persian tradition. Instead, Abid manipulates proportions, and thereby space, for independently expressive ends. The figures in the foreground, and those behind the central mountain, are identical in size, despite their distance in space. Those behind the distant hills,

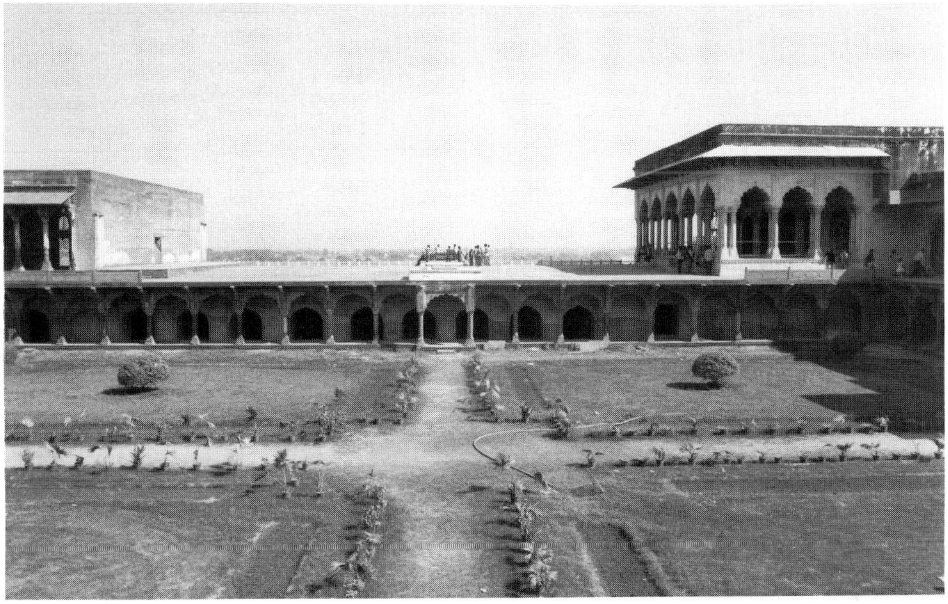

99. Diwan-i-Khas Platform, Agra Fort

however, are smaller, but arranged in an even row that gives them the role of choral commentations rather than participants in the scene (for an earlier example of this device, see fig. 16). The two facing horses and warriors, and the clear circular lines above and below, set up a very formal composition which gives structure to the scene. This forces greater concentration on the central and horrifying decapitation, and on the extraordinarily precise depictions of the individual men and their clothing. The color too, dominated by an acid green, is electrifying, whereas in Bichitr's *The Accession of Shahjahan* it is simply rich and opulent. In this work, Abid shows himself fully equal to his brother as a portraitist, and far more innovative as an artist. The irrationality is a new element in seventeenth-century Mughal painting, however, and is a move away from the overwhelming dominance of the naturalism demanded by Jahangir. (Again, it recalls earlier works, in this case those of Daswanth for the *Razmnama*, as seen in fig. 23.)

A further important folio is a *Battle Scene* (fig. 100). The episode, which has not been satisfactorily identified, depicts the siege of a fortress by massed armies in a heavily wooded and mountainous terrain. Like the Abid painting, this too marks a quite radical shift in seventeenth-century works. The characteristics can best be isolated by comparing it to *Travelers in a Landscape* (fig. 101), painted by Manohar about 1605. Both show foreground figures with distant mountains and buildings. The men remain flat on the surface in the

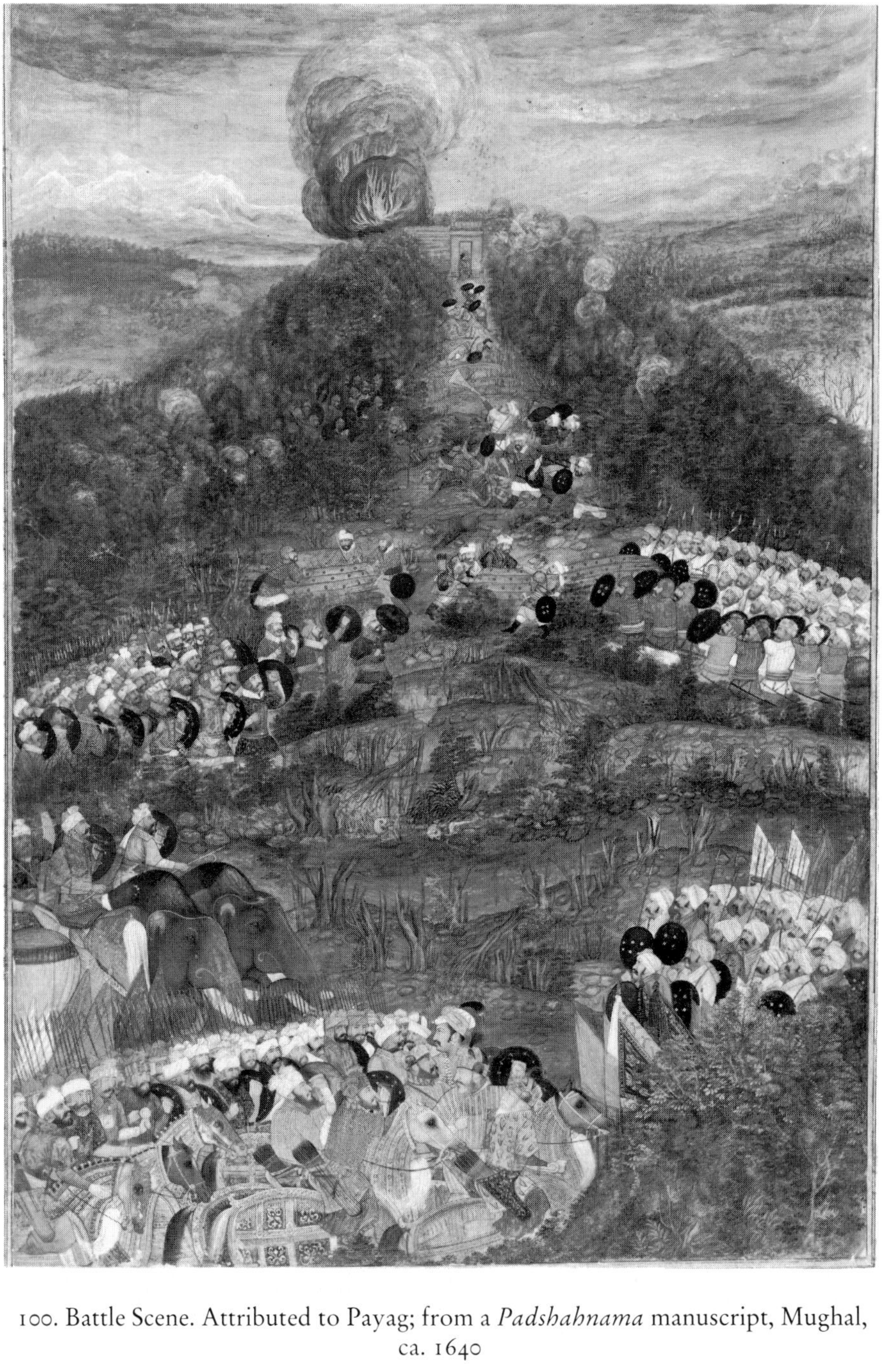

100. Battle Scene. Attributed to Payag; from a *Padshahnama* manuscript, Mughal, ca. 1640

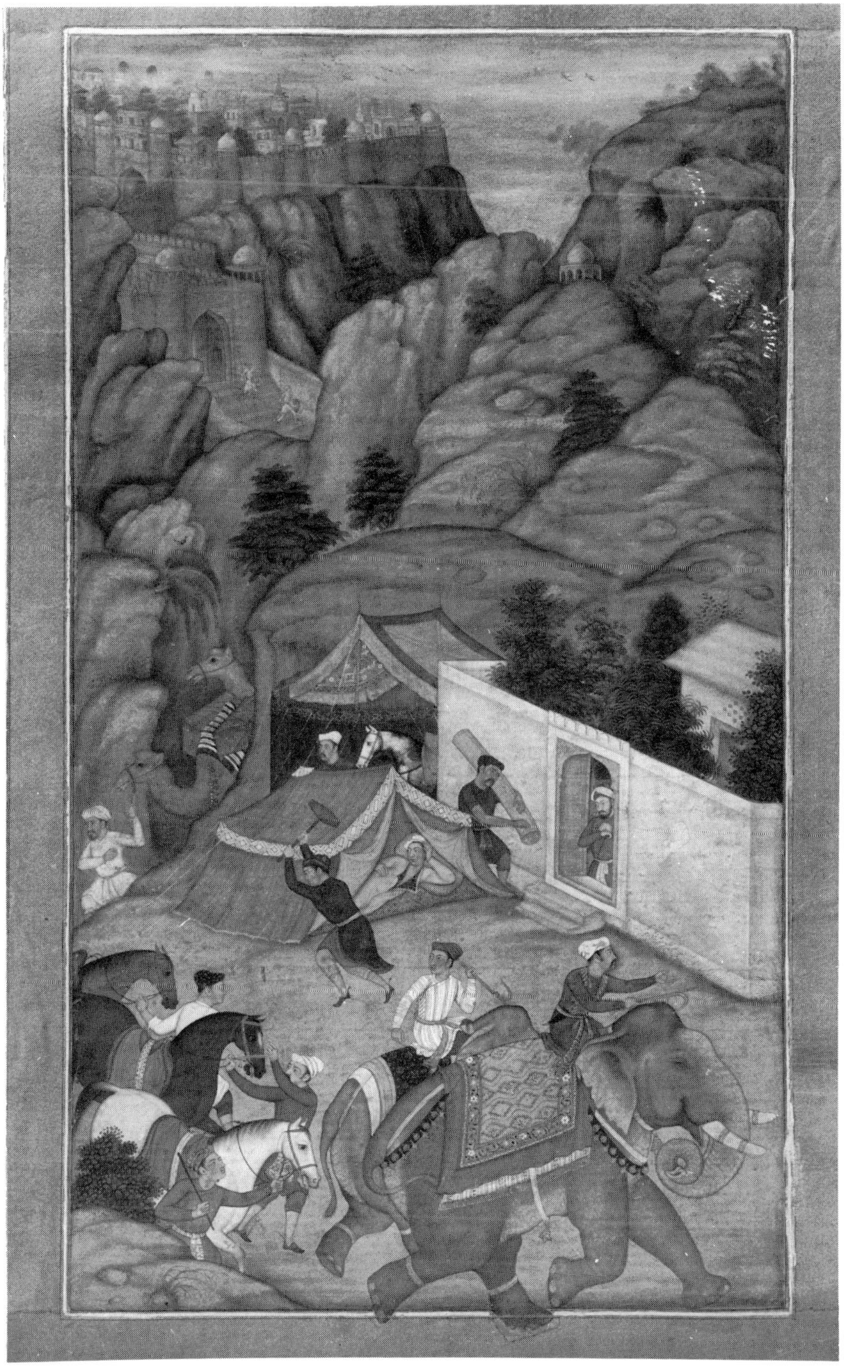

101. Travelers in a Landscape. Attributed to Manohar; Mughal, ca. 1605

earlier illustration, however, and they are carefully defined, with distant figures smaller in scale. In the later work, there is gradual diminution of scale throughout the scene, although it proceeds by steps rather than as a smooth and continuous movement. More importantly, despite the quantity of figures in the earlier illustration and the initial sense of bustling activity, each figure is carefully placed so that he is clearly visible, and there is an even diffusion of visual activity over the entire surface. Each figure in the Akbar period scene is thus treated with an identical degree of definition and given equal visual interest, while in the *Battle Scene* we are aware of masses of figures before we see individuals. The figures in front of each group in the *Padshahnama* illustration are carefully, indeed minutely, defined, but the men behind are simply indicated by turbans or lances. There being no individuation of these figures, it is the clearly defined and bounded groups that demand our attention. Rather than stressing the distinctness of each man, the artist, Payag, tells us that each warrior is a part of a mass greater than any individual. This is a clear return to more traditionally Indian ideas of the individual's subservience to an ultimate unity, and a major change of direction for the Mughal tradition. Like *The Death of Khan Jahan Lodi* (plate G), although in a different way, this too breaks with early seventeenth-century style.

The landscape in the *Battle Scene* is vast, and far more open and airy than in *Travelers in a Landscape*. In fact, there is nothing comparable to it in Mughal painting before this time. Once again, the closest visual analogy is a European work: Albrecht Altdorfer's *Battle of Darius and Alexander* (fig. 102), where both space and the massing of figures is extremely comparable. (The German work is not being cited as a specific source, however.) The brushwork in *Battle Scene* is looser than in earlier seventeenth-century Mughal painting. The pigments appear to be spontaneously and freely applied, a technique similar to that found in the earliest Akbari works (for example fig. 10), but here far more delicately handled. The technique, as well as the composition, was therefore almost certainly inspired by European oil paintings, or hand-colored prints.

The *Padshahnama* is stylistically a remarkably innovative manuscript. Since the mid sixteenth century, many Mughal artists had been trying to bring painting closer to empirically perceived reality. Until the end of Jahangir's reign in 1627, the creation of descriptive images of the rational, natural world in its most straightforward terms was still the concern of the majority of painters, and this was brought to its consummation in the portrait of Inayat Khan (fig. 80). Pre-Mughal Rajput painting, on the other hand, had had different goals, for the Hindu ideal was to find what was universal, rather than particular, in a world of impermanence and illusion. The Mughal concern for objective distinctiveness and human individuality was therefore a radical shift within both Islamic and Indian traditions. The first movement away from these concerns had occurred in the symbolic portraits made for Jahangir – works

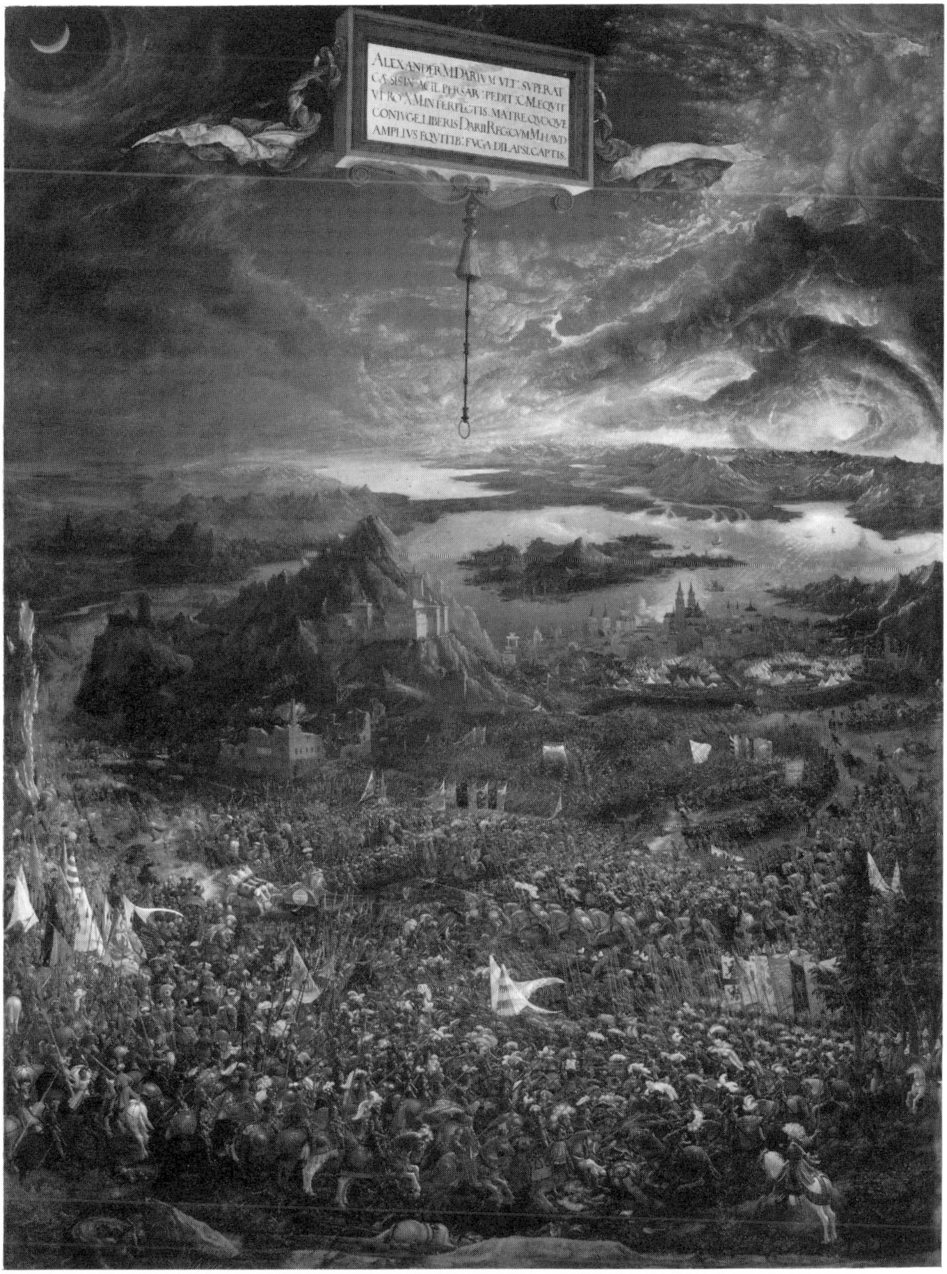

102. Battle of Darius and Alexander. By Albrecht Altdorfer; German, ca. 1529

contemporary with *The Dying Inayat Khan* – where the emperor is visually deified, or is presented as a universal monarch, and in the *Padshahnama* these new Mughal concerns are further developed. Even in narrative scenes, it is no longer what separates men but what unites them that is important. This is further acknowledgment of the degree to which Mughal culture was becoming integrated into Hindu India.

Three further manuscripts allow us to discuss other aspects of Shahjahan period court painting. A small *Gulistan* of Sa'di is the greatest of the poetical manuscripts. The text was written in Iran in the fifteenth century, and decorative illuminations were added somewhat later. About 1640, six illustrations were commissioned by Shahjahan, who then owned the book. These were to replace original Persian scenes which had been water damaged. The greatest imperial artists (including Abid, Balchand, Govardhan, and Payag) worked on the paintings, which are closely allied to the *Padshahnama* in style, although far more intimate in scale and effect.

Sa'di in the Rose Garden (fig. 103) illustrates a passage from the opening of the text:

> I saw that my friend had in his skirt collected roses, sweet basil, hyacinths, and fragrant herbs with the determination to carry them to town; whereon I said: "Thou knowest that the roses of the garden are perishable and the season passes away," and philosophers have said: "Whatever is not of long duration is not to be cherished." He asked: "Then what is to be done?" I replied: "I may compose for the amusement of those who look and for the instruction of those who are present a book of a *Rose Garden*, a *Gulistan*, whose leaves cannot be touched by the tyranny of autumnal blasts and the delight of whose spring the vicissitudes of time will be unable to change into the inconstancy of autumn . . . " After I uttered these words he threw away the flowers from his skirts, and attached himself to mine, saying: "*When a generous fellow makes a promise he keeps it.*"[25]

The painting is by Govardhan, late in his career, and it is a work of intense refinement. The two men stand against a purple hill, behind which the sky is gold. To the left is a thin and elegant tree with graceful pink blossoms; like the tree at the right, the leaves twist and turn in space, giving them life and animation. The glances of the two men, and their gestures, are as emotionally charged as the passage illustrated. The intimacy and intensity of the scene would be impossible with the subjects and scale of the *Padshahnama*. This work directly continues the mode of illustration found in the *Gulistan* of about 1610 (fig. 57).

A *Bustan* (Garden) of Sa'di, dated 1629, was presented to Charles I of England by Shahjahan in 1638. Its ten illustrations are small, horizontal panels

[25] *The Gulistan or Rose Garden of Sa'di*, translated by Edward Rehatsek, London, 1964, pp. 66–67.

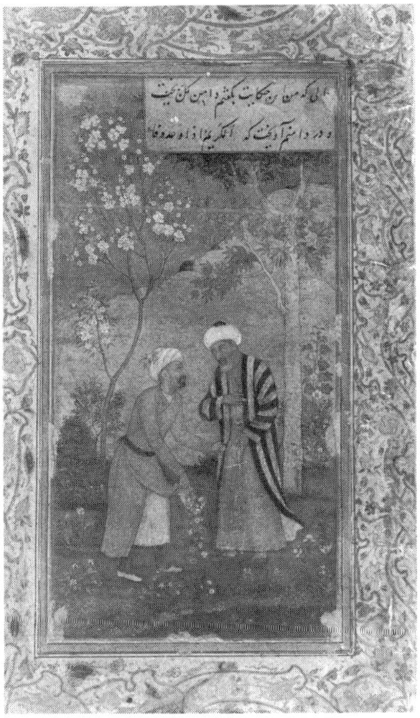

103. Sa'di in the Rose Garden. By Govardhan;
from a *Gulistan* of Sa'di manuscript, Mughal, ca. 1640

inserted into the text area, continuing a formula seen in the earlier Jahangiri *Gulistan*. The illustrations and text are surrounded by rich gold borders, visible in the reproduction of *An Old Man Rebukes a Young Girl* (fig. 104). In each of the paintings, the scenes are finely composed and precisely detailed: gestures are clear, and one can tell how the turbans or kamarbands (cummerbunds) are tied or the texture of different fabrics. If, despite this technique, the work fails to engage our interest, it is because there is little observation beyond the surface. Figures, while carefully modelled and convincingly observed, are stock types, and we cannot be involved with them as human beings – compare this illustration to those in the earlier manuscript (fig. 57). This basic simplicity also separates the volume from the almost contemporary *Gulistan* of circa 1640 (fig. 103), with its visual complexities and depth of characterization. Whether this was because the *Bustan* was originally intended as a diplomatic gift and therefore less worthy of full efforts is uncertain. This simplicity, however, made such works more easily imitable models for provincial and other courts. As we shall see, this style had considerable impact elsewhere in India.

A third manuscript, although not made for the emperor, is nevertheless imperial in calibre. This is the *Mathnavi* of Zafar Khan (fig. 105), a collection of verses by one of Shahjahan's leading nobles. The scenes show Zafar Khan

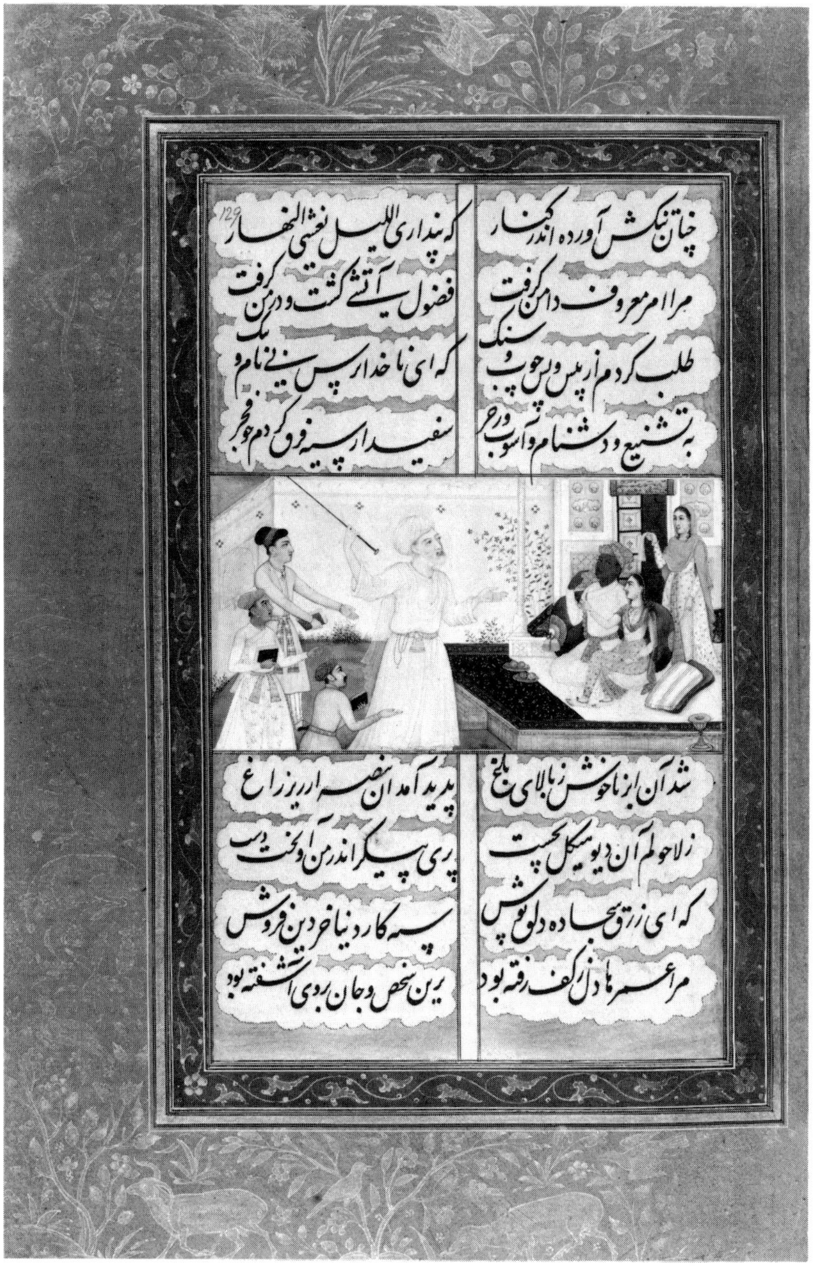

104. An Old Man Rebukes a Young Girl. From a *Bustan* of Sa'di manuscript, Mughal, dated 1629

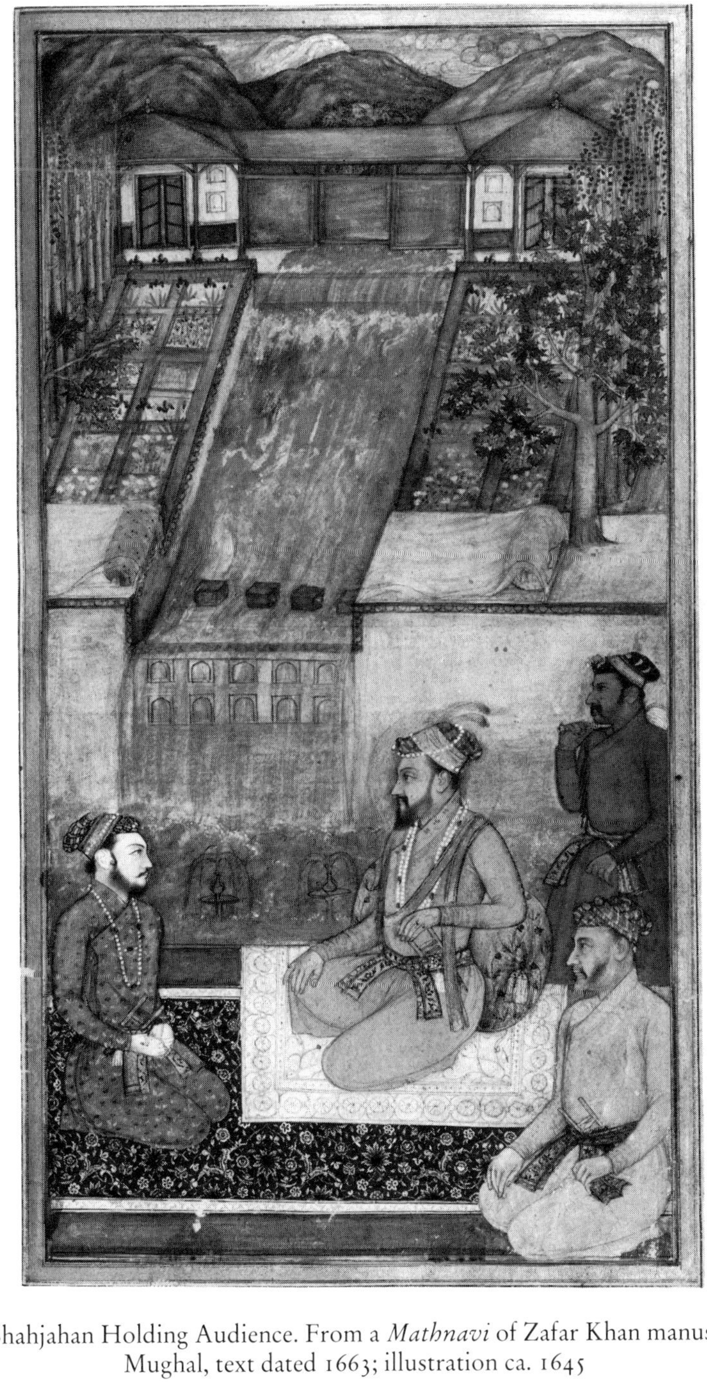

105. Shahjahan Holding Audience. From a *Mathnavi* of Zafar Khan manuscript, Mughal, text dated 1663; illustration ca. 1645

and his son, as well as Shahjahan and Dara Shikoh, and the illustrations were probably made to commemorate a visit that the emperor paid in 1645 to Zafar Khan, who had been given the governorship of Kashmir. This date would be confirmed by the ages of the men shown. The manuscript text is dated 1663, however, the year of Zafar Khan's death, and it seems that once again earlier paintings were reused to illustrate a later manuscript.

Like Akbar and Jahangir, Shahjahan also formed albums (*muraqqas*), but these were primarily assemblages of contemporary and Jahangir-period portraits (both single and group). The limitation in subject matter here must be compared to the wide-ranging diversity found in the collections of Jahangir. The greatest of the Shahjahani *muraqqas* is the Minto Album. Several other albums (for example, the Kevorkian Album, the Wantage Album) include late copies alongside early pages, and may have been assembled early in the nineteenth century.

The Minto Album includes works by the greatest artists of the first half of the seventeenth century: Bichitr, Govardhan, Hashim, and Mansur, among others; and these show a development akin to what we find in the *Padshahnama* pages. The portrait *Shahjahan Riding with Dara Shikoh* (fig. 106), by Govardhan about 1638, depicts the emperor and his eldest son as minute figures in a landscape that seems made of gold-dust and crushed jewels. Extreme elegance of style had replaced flesh and blood, and this stylistic self-consciousness extends to the facing page from the album, which depicts *Timur Riding with an Attendant*.[26] This double image not only proclaimed Shahjahan's link with his dynastic predecessor; the image of Timur was executed in a consciously archaistic and recognizably Timurid (that is, fifteenth-century Persian) style.

The many standing portraits also in the albums, however perceptive and technically controlled, lack the sheer energy of Akbar period works or the simplicity and directness of the greatest portraits made for Jahangir. Flawless technique and a concern for surface accuracy and beauty replaced insight into personality with increasing frequency. In Govardhan's border figures of circa 1609–1610 (fig. 58), for example, a first reaction would be empathy with the men shown, whereas in *Shahjahan Riding with Dara Shikoh* one notices first the brilliance of the surface, and only then the subject. This can be interpreted as a drying up of inspiration, but that would be unfair. When seen together with the *Padshahnama* pages, it can be interpreted equally validly as a retreat from naturalism, and a return to seeing the individual as type. And beauty of appearance is once again a metaphor for the beauty of the divine.

The margins of the Minto Album, and of several additional albums of the period, are most frequently formal floral designs (for example, fig. 107). Such

[26] Arnold and Wilkinson, *Library*, vol. III, pl. 55.

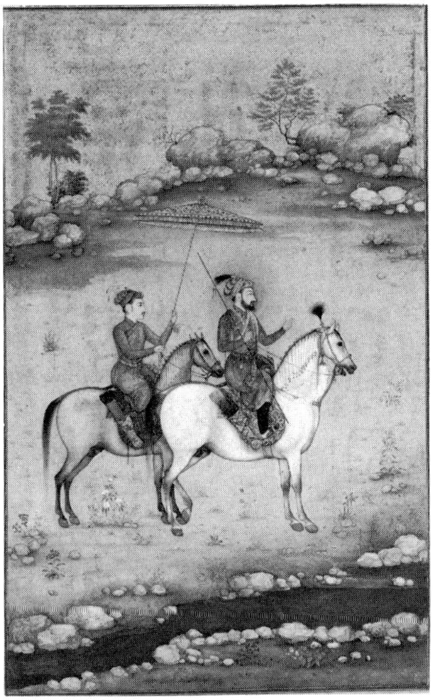

106. Shahjahan Riding with Dara Shikoh. By Govardhan; from the Minto Album, Mughal, ca. 1638

motifs were basic to architectural decoration of the period as well and are found throughout Agra, Delhi, and Lahore Forts, as well as at the Taj Mahal – the most famous example. As Robert Skelton has shown, many of the later examples are copied and adapted from European herbals imported into India, but the origin of this all-pervasive motif, which remained in vogue until the end of Mughal rule, seems to have preceded the arrival of such European sources.[27]

Quite unlike the seemingly freely sketched gold work and figures on Jahangir-period *muraqqa* margins, the formality of the flowers is compositionally matched by the style. While some plants are simply gold (often against a dark blue background, giving an extremely luxurious effect), others are colored; and those are often outlined with a gold line of even thickness, increasing the sense of richness, but diminishing the naturalism. Jahangir's borders, no matter how sumptuous, seem spontaneous sketches; Shahjahan-period examples are as self-consciously placed on the page as jewels in their mounts, and as formally posed as portraits of the emperor himself. Whereas even in the allegorical portraits of Jahangir, we sense the frailty and humanity

27 Robert Skelton, "A decorative motif in Mughal art," in *Aspects of Indian Art*, edited by P. Pal, Leiden, 1972, pp. 147–152.

of the emperor beneath the surface, images of Shahjahan are virtual icons. Surface perfection is all-important.

In *Shahjahan* (fig. 107), by Payag, the emperor stands on a globe, holding a rifle, and behind him are faint scenes of a mountain fortress being subdued. This is an aggressively brilliant portrait. Shahjahan's dark robe accentuates the light emanating from the gold decoration and the rich collection of necklaces, armlets, and turban ornaments; his pose is powerful and unflinching, and his expression lively and involved. Based on the English portrait formulas we have discussed, this is among the most imperial of all Mughal illustrations. But it also recalls the rigidly posed, aureoled icons of Hindu deities. A further portrait of the emperor surrounded by his sons (fig. 108) leaves no doubt about the power and opulence of his court. So minutely decorated is every architectural or ornamental surface that the effect is almost claustrophobic. The painting can be compared to the earlier portraits of Akbar and Jahangir with their sons (figs. 47 and 73) to understand the degree to which painting has become increasingly concerned with the proclamation of wealth and power.

Non-imperial portraits, however, retain their greater informality and experimentalism. Payag's range of both styles and subjects is far greater than that of any other Shahjahan-period painter, and a group of further works represents his most novel achievement. These are night scenes, often showing shaikhs or holy men around a fire – as in *A Gathering of Mystics* (fig. 109). Payag is interested here in exploring lighting effects, showing figures illuminated by candles or flames, and otherwise surrounded by darkness except for dusky or moonlit skies. Later versions of the type of scene he evolves tend to make the darkness a flat area of black, whereas Payag is successful here in giving us a sense of brooding, mysterious space and atmosphere. (This is certainly true as well of his *Battle Scene* in fig. 100.) Despite their suggestion of close observation of actual natural effects, however, these works derive from such European chiaroscuro scenes of the first half of the seventeenth century as the paintings of Adam Elsheimer.[28]

Shahjahan himself was passionate about jewels – the notorious Peacock Throne is only one piece of evidence of this. He was also frequently painted holding or inspecting jewels, and so many of his paintings seem themselves like artificial gems that the more inventive and original pages of the *Padshahnama* or the works of Payag, for example, are particularly unexpected products of his patronage.

A favorite theme developed in Akbar-period painting was that of a prince visiting a holy man in his retreat and discussing spiritual matters with him – an obvious reference to the spiritual, as well as secular, role that rulers played.

[28] *Alte Pinakothek Munchen – Kurzes Verzeichnis der Bilder, Amtliche Ausgabe 1958*, Munich, 1957, Abb. 94.

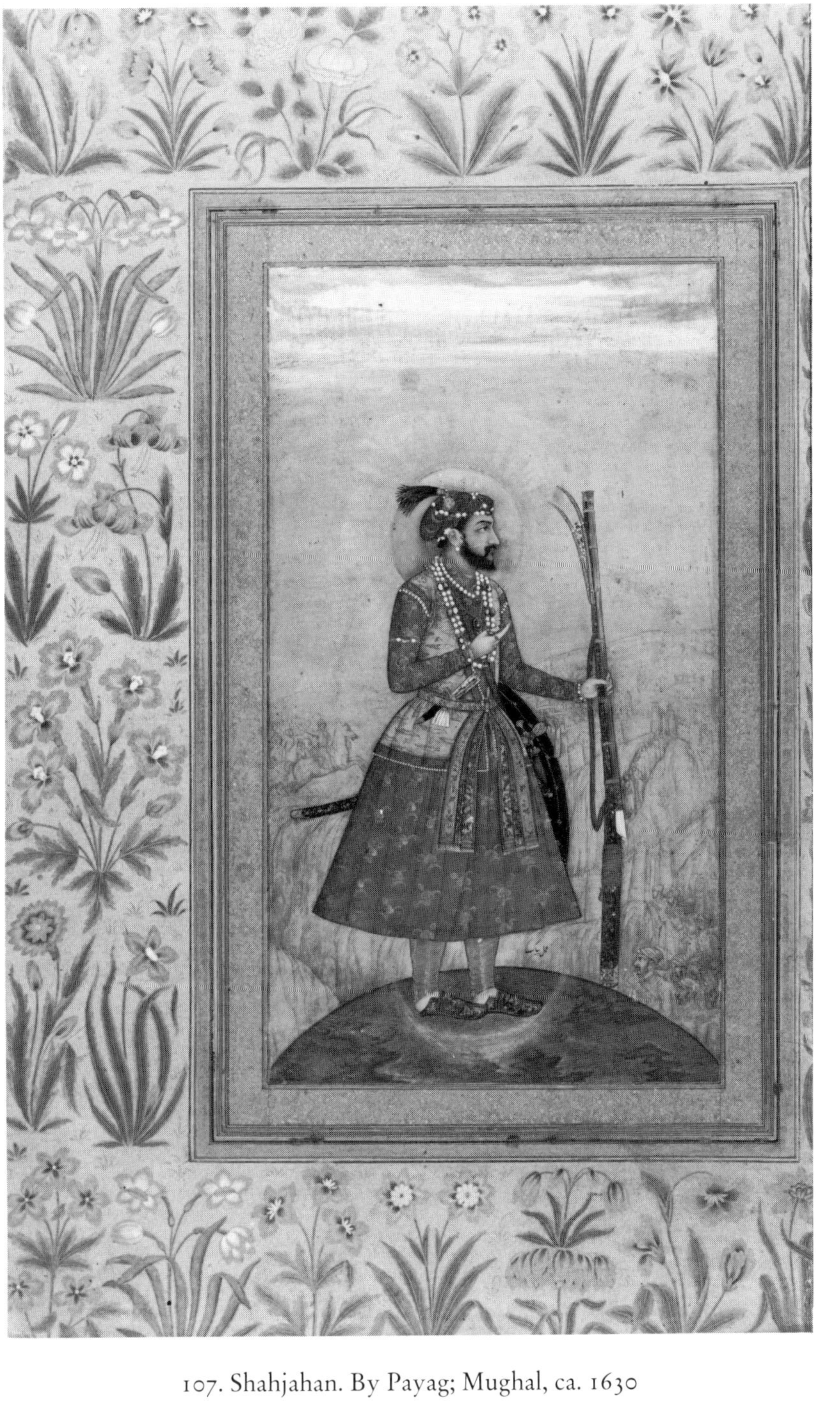

107. Shahjahan. By Payag; Mughal, ca. 1630

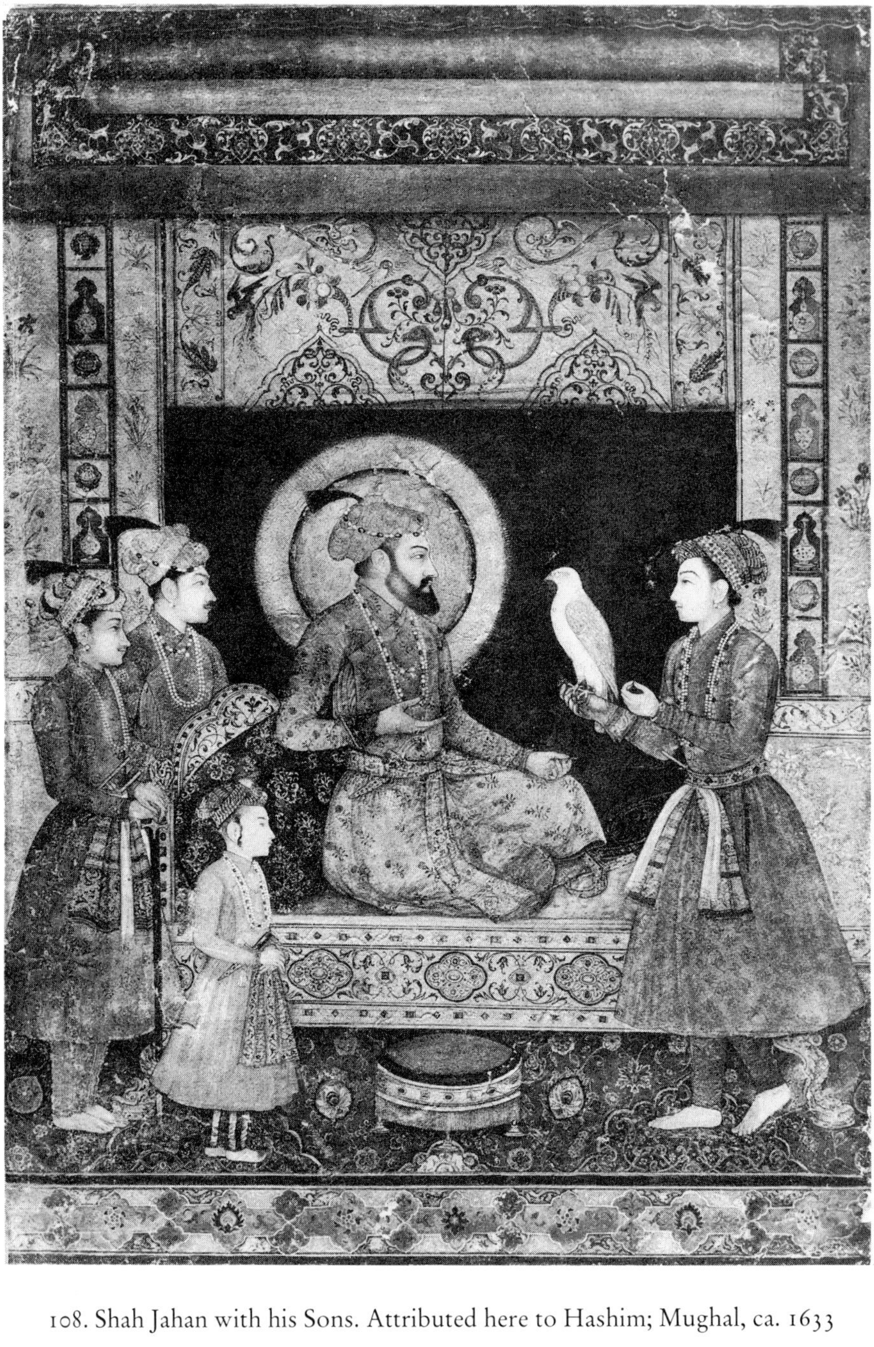

108. Shah Jahan with his Sons. Attributed here to Hashim; Mughal, ca. 1633

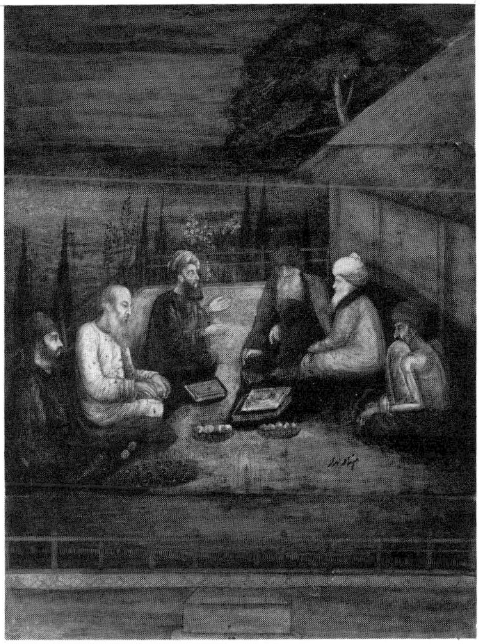

109. A Gathering of Mystics. Attributed to Payag; Mughal, ca. 1640

(The theme is an ancient one in both India and the Islamic world.) Jahangir himself is shown in a *Jahangirnama* page visiting the Hindu sage Jadrup, who lived almost naked in an isolated cave, and several discussions with the ascetic are recorded in the imperial memoirs. Shahjahan seldom visited holy men, but he did entertain them at court, although he was far more sympathetic to Muslim than to Hindu sages. His relative orthodoxy certainly was important in creating a climate whereby artists again presented the world as a metaphor for universal values, but it may have been Dara Shikoh, his eldest son, who inspired several studies of divine teachers, in many of which the prince himself is included. Unlike his father, Dara was an eclectic and a mystic; like Akbar, he sought to reconcile Islam and Hinduism, and as a scholar he translated Hindu texts into Persian and provided commentaries.

Dara Shikoh and a Holy Man (fig. 110) is a lightly colored drawing probably made about 1635. Well-established techniques of shading are used, perhaps most visibly in the hands, but we are more conscious of the large, angular shapes of the holy man's robe and their contrast with the soft fabric worn by Dara. The figures as a whole are curiously bodiless, and their spiritual character dominates the scene.

Throughout Shahjahan's reign, Dara was recognized as the emperor's favorite son and intended successor. It is Dara whom, Shahjahan is embracing

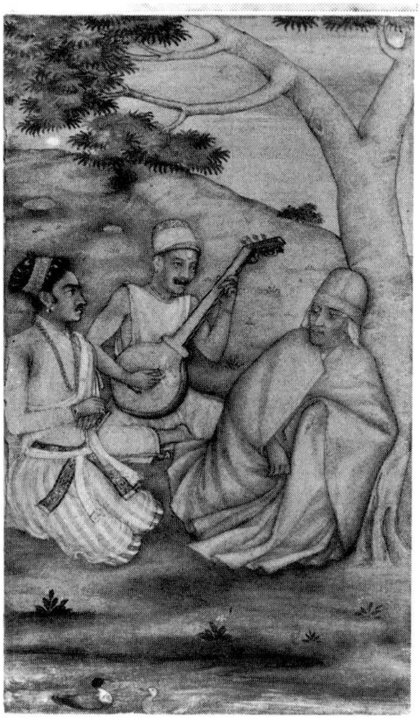

110. Dara Shikoh and a Holy Man. Mughal, ca. 1635

in the *Padshahnama* accession darbar (fig. 96), and Govardhan's portrait of circa 1638 (fig. 106) is only one of several that further proclaim the inseparability of father and son. Dara is allowed occasionally to be shown with a halo, until then a distinctively imperial insignia in Mughal painting. In several scenes, it is uncertain whether Shahjahan or his son is shown, so interchangeable have the portraits become.

Works related to Shahjahan's sons are more varied in subject and style than those of the emperor. Matching portraits of Dara and Shah Shuja, his next younger brother, were made about 1633, the year both were married. *Lovers on a Terrace* (fig. 111), by Balchand, shows Shuja with his consort. It is a dulcet, romantic scene, with the lovers gazing adoringly at each other. The distant landscape helps create a mood of revery, which emphasizes the gentleness of the emotions portrayed. We also admire the fabrics as we would real cloth, and the realism of the bolsters or the wine bottles. Balchand has recreated an intensely human encounter, a world which other Mughal painters were beginning to leave behind. *Two Musicians* (fig. 112), by Hashim, is another sketch which shows the imperial painters' continuing ability to depict personalities and human characteristics with great intensity, even when images were not intended to make an official statement.

Shah Shuja Hunting Nilgae (fig. 113) also shows an intimate encounter. The

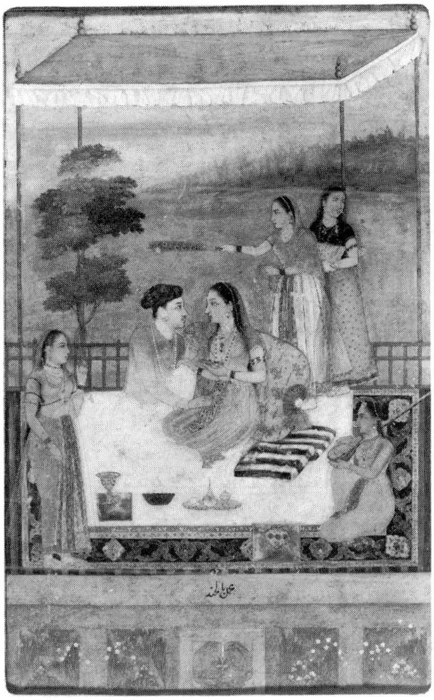

111. Lovers on a Terrace. Attributed to Balchand; from the Leningrad Album, Mughal, ca. 1633

beauty and alertness of the deer, and the lovingly detailed landscape, create a scene in which there is neither wildness nor danger. The scene is emotionally and visually opulent, and the immensely sympathetic depiction of the deer reveals talents that painters could seldom incorporate into scenes of court ceremonial. *A Nilgae* (fig. 114) has virtually isolated and magnified one detail from the hunting scene. Thanks to the quoted account by Jauhar (see page 15), our first evidence for Mughal painting was a reference to an animal study; and here, close to the end of the great phase of Mughal painting, the interest remains undiminished.

The emperor's clear favoritism for Dara Shikoh, together with his protection of the prince, who was seldom given military or political responsibilities away from the court, assured the elder youth of the loathing of his brothers. In 1657, during an illness when Shahjahan's death was anticipated, a series of battles among the four siblings began when Shah Shuja moved to attack the imperial troops. He was met at Bahadarpur (near Benares) by Suleiman Shikoh, the son of Dara Shikoh, and their encounter is recorded in a drawing (fig. 115). Shuja – here shown as the seated and haloed figure, suggesting that the painter was in his employ – was turned back, then at the later Battle of Samugarh, Aurangzeb emerged as victor over both Dara and the younger Murad. The massing of troops seen in the drawing is similar to figures found in the almost contemporary engravings of the French artist Jacques Callot (fig. 116), as well as in the sketches of the English adventurer Peter Mundy,[29] who was in India in the 1630s. Some European traits were certainly transmitted by such amateur artists.

After the battle of Samugarh, the victorious Aurangzeb imprisoned his father in Agra Fort and proclaimed his own rule – after arranging for the deaths of his brothers. Dara, for example, was tried by an Islamic court for apostasy and convicted. Aurangzeb, the direct opposite of Akbar in temperament, left no doubt of his orthodoxy. He persecuted Hindus and Hindu shrines, and soon abandoned any pretense of interest in the arts. He spent much of his time trying to bring the Deccan under control, copying out Qurans, and arranging for the building of mosques. He is shown soon after his accession in *Darbar of Aurangzeb* (fig. 117). It is virtually identical in style to *Shahjahan and His Sons* (fig. 108), and both have been attributed here to the same artist, Hashim. Thus, at the very beginning of the new reign, there was once again no major stylistic upheaval.

The sense of a court petrified by opulence and ritual is very evident in the darbar scene. The contemporary *Darbar of Sultan Ali Adil Shah II of Bijapur* (fig. 118), painted in the Deccan at Bijapur about 1660, on the other hand, is enlivened by the unknown artist's ability to make active and energetic patterns from the textiles or the architecture, and to present portraits at once convincingly individualized and exaggeratedly generalized. If the depiction of Aurangzeb suggests stillness and suffocation, the Bijapur work is immensely lively. And the comparison is not unjust, for Mughal art was now an artistic tradition at the end of its life.

[29] See plates in P. Mundy, *Travels in Europe and Asia, 1608–1667*, edited by Sir R. C. Temple, Cambridge, 1907–1936.

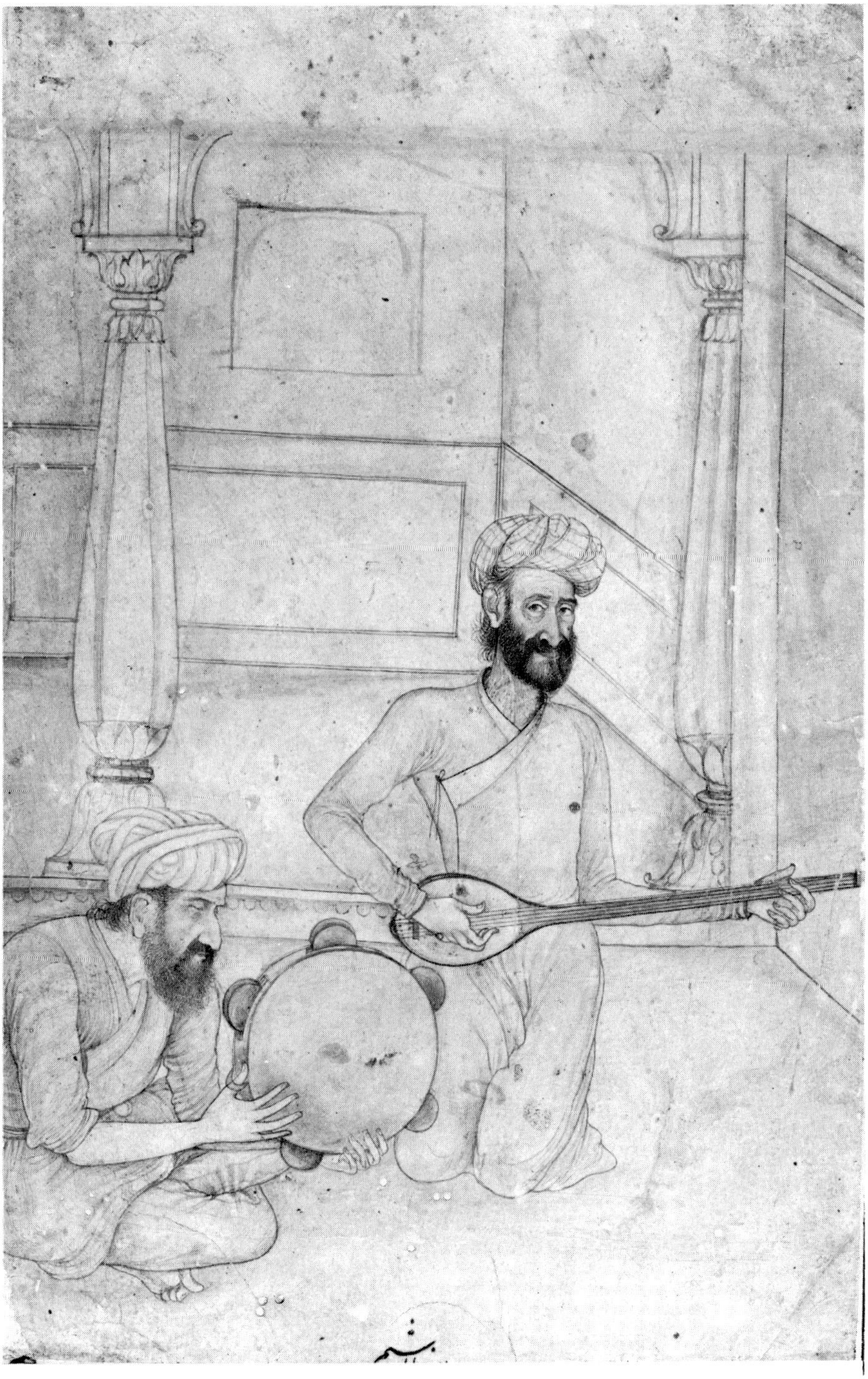

112. Two Musicians. By Hashim; Mughal, ca. 1630

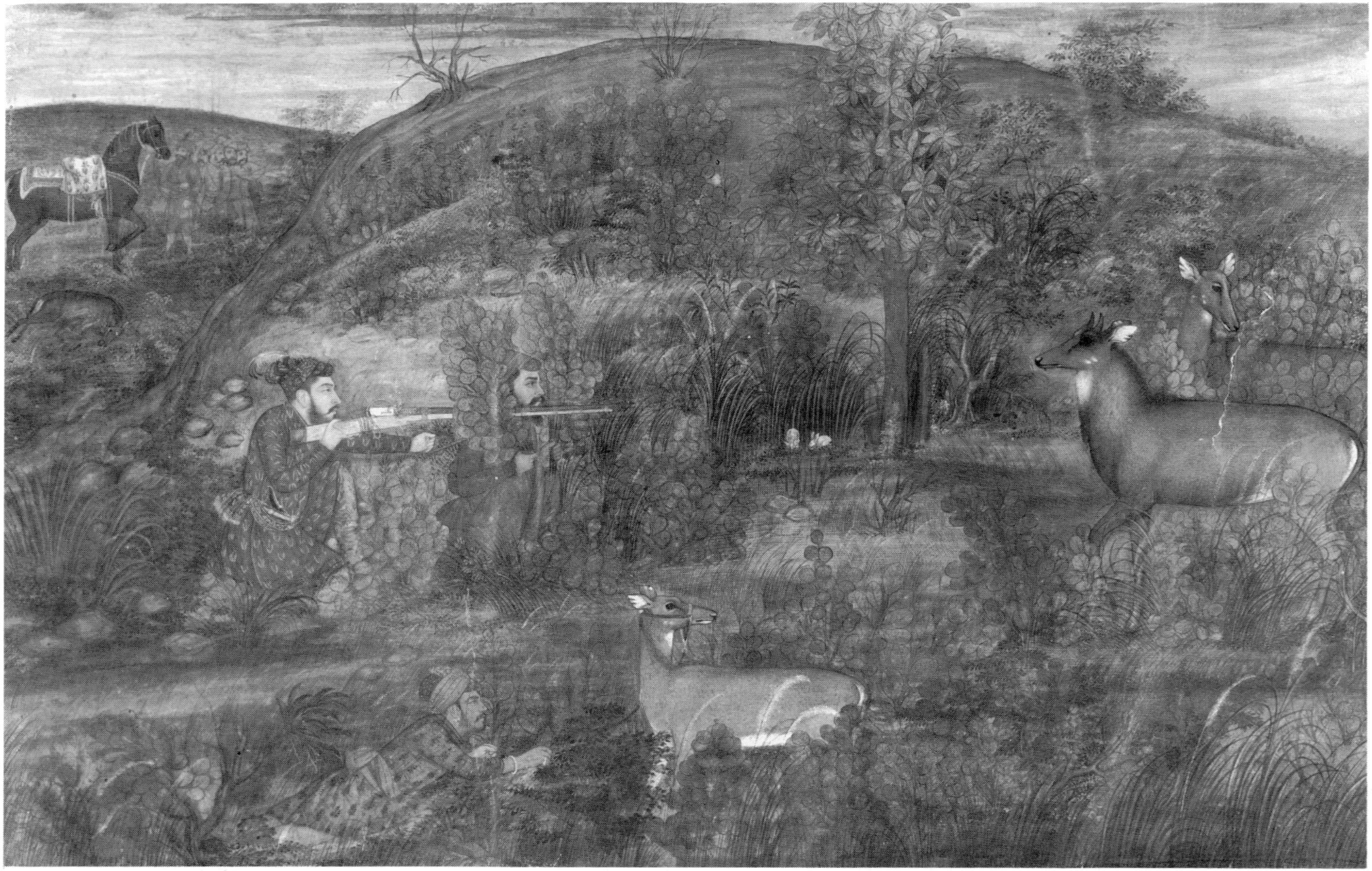

113. Shah Shuja Hunting Nilgae. Attributed to Payag; Mughal, ca. 1650

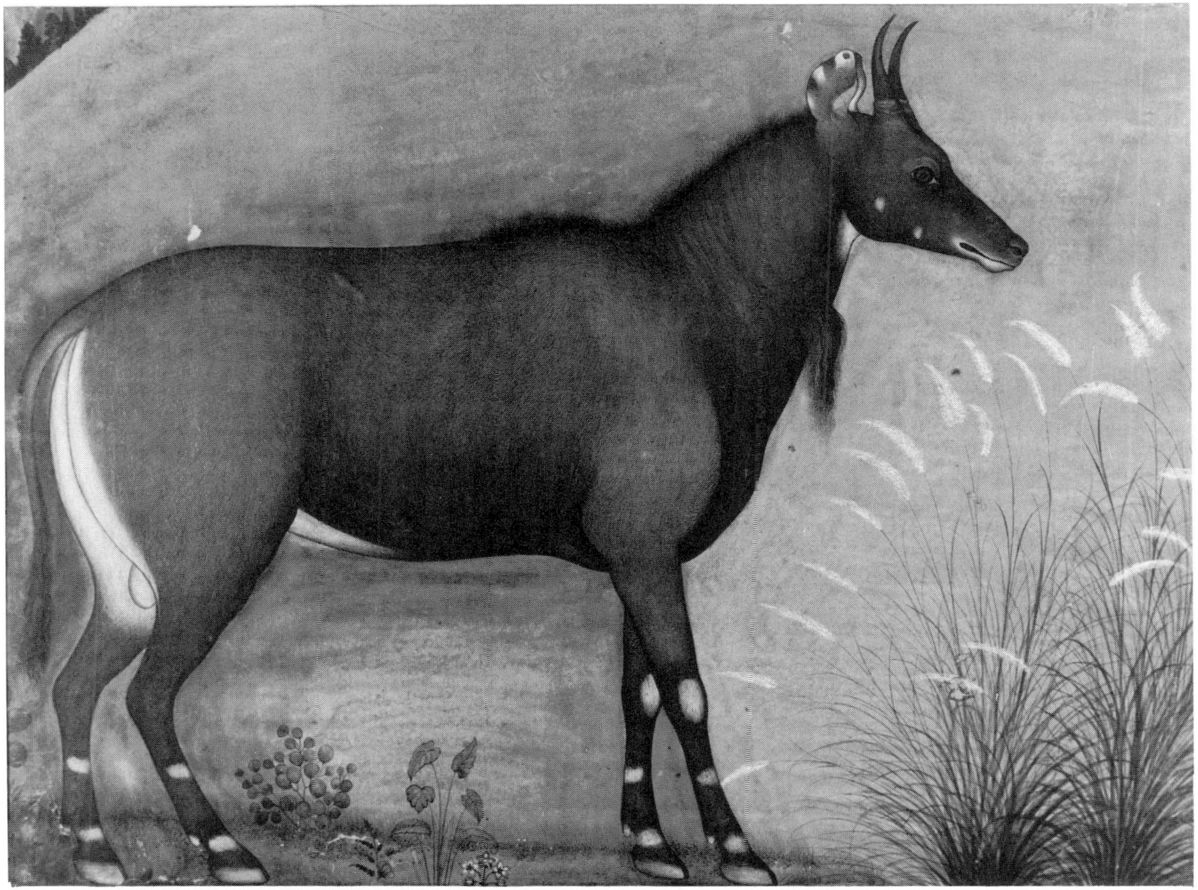

114. A Nilgae. Mughal, ca. 1650

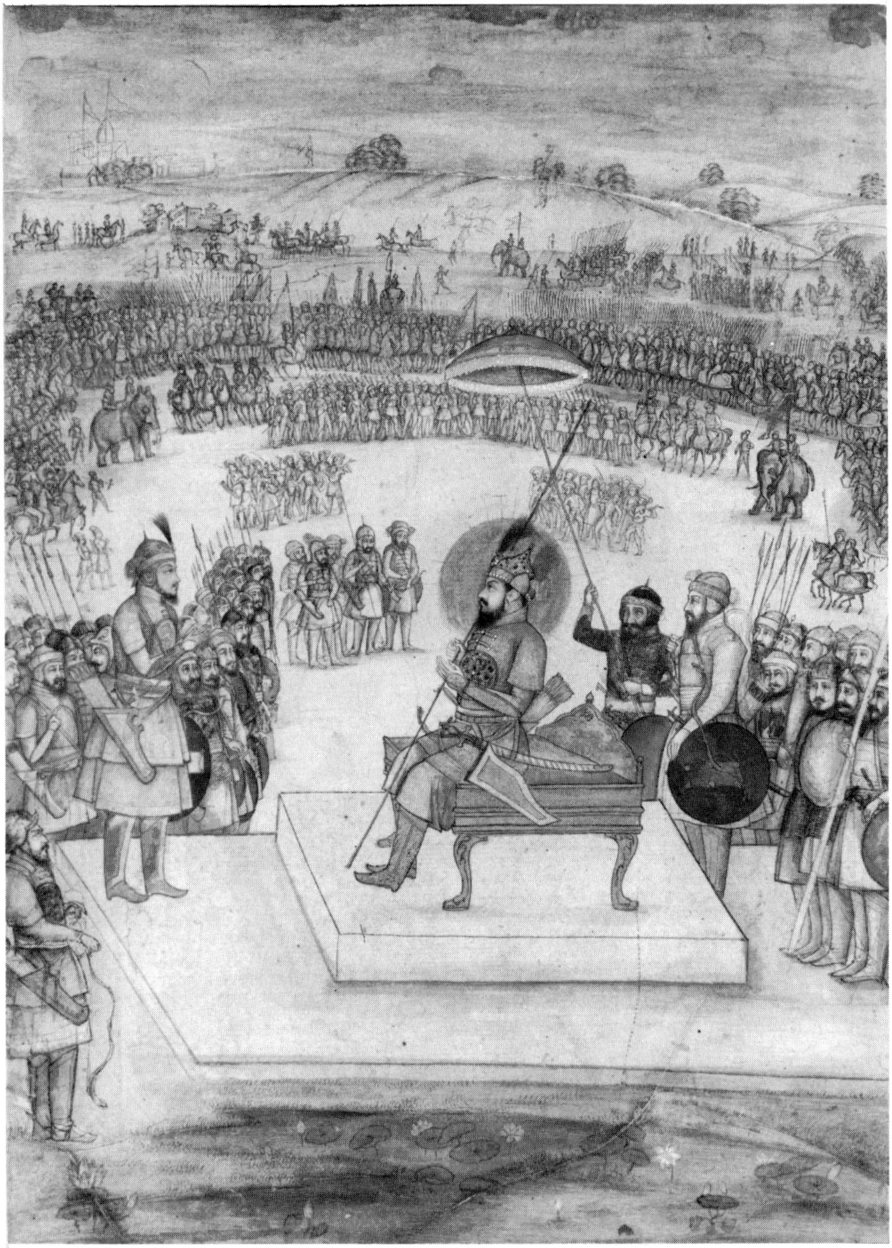

115. Sultan Shuja at the Battle of Bahadarpur. By Ilyas Khan; Mughal, ca. 1658

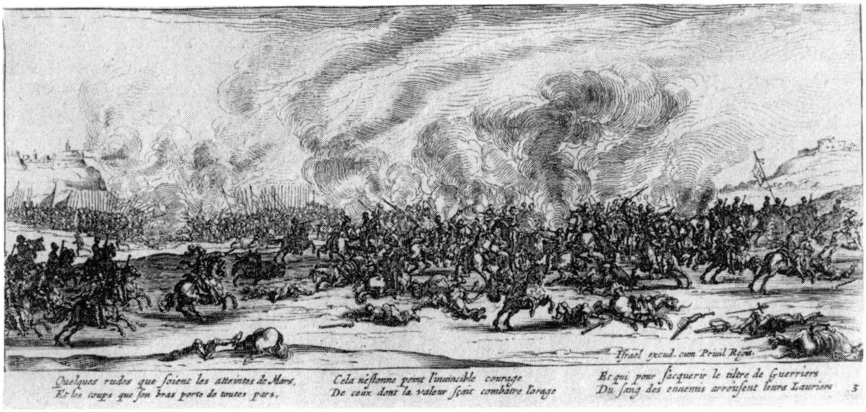

116. Jacques Callot. From *The Miseries of War*, French, 1633

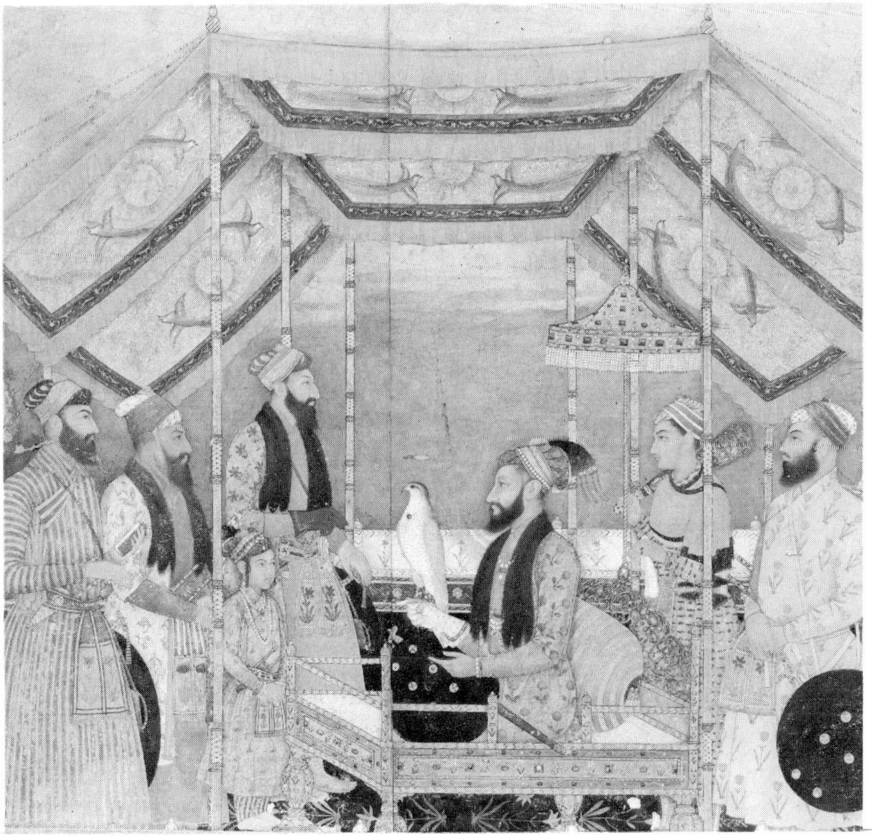

117. Darbar of Aurangzeb. Attributed to Hashim; Mughal, ca. 1660

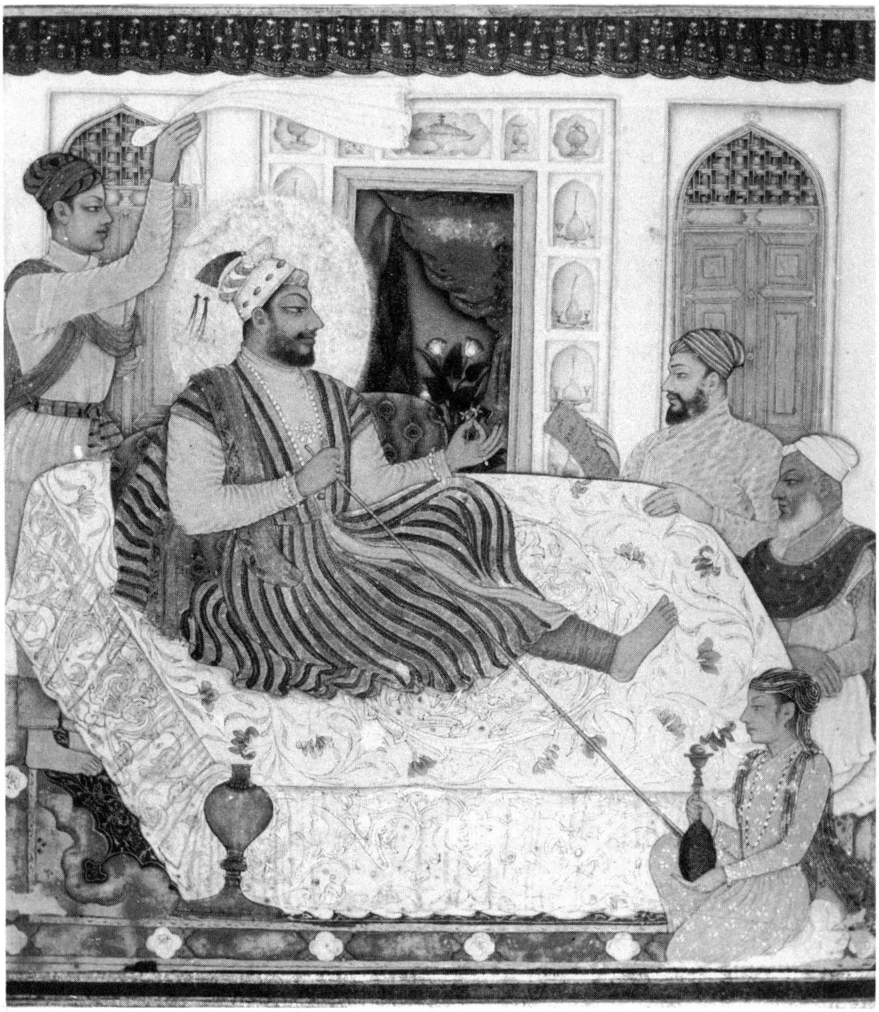

118. Darbar of Sultan Ali Adil Shah II of Bijapur. Deccani, at Bijapur, ca. 1660

CHAPTER 5

1660–1700: THE GROWTH OF LOCAL STYLES

Until the eighteenth century, painting for Rajput patrons was almost completely confined to the illustration of familiar, traditional texts – although we have already seen exceptions. *Ragamalas*, together with episodes from the god Krishna's life (usually adapted from the *Bhagavata Purana*), were the most popular subjects for Rajput painters. The standard *Ragamala* (garland of ragas) is a set of thirty-six paintings depicting possible relationships between a man and a woman, categorized according to the emotional potential of different times of day (for example dawn or sunset) or seasons of the year (pre-monsoon heat, for example, or the rainy season). Each of these is a separate *raga*, or its variant, a *ragini*. *Vasanta Raga* (plate H), for example, shows the man and woman dancing together in spring. Their physical union is foreshadowed by wild jungle plants, whose rich buds and blossoms are emblems of divine creativity. Nature is still used in such works to intensify the human situation, not to provide a spatial backdrop.

The text of the *Ragamala* illustrates an element of Hinduism known as *bhakti*, devotionalism. This is a system whereby the worshipper exists in a direct relationship with a god possessing personal attributes. In both literary and visual presentations, as noted above, this takes the form of romantic, often explicitly sexual, imagery: the worshipper (Lover) longs for union with the divine (the Beloved), and the obliteration of all sense of individuality. By the sixteenth century, numerous *bhakti* texts had been written in vernaculars, for this was a reactionary movement against priestly control of access to the gods through rituals in Sanskrit.

A second facet of the religious background to Rajput painting is Vaisnavism, the worship of the god Vishnu. This had become overwhelmingly influential in north India by the sixteenth century. Krishna, the favorite incarnation of Vishnu, is a form of the god sent to earth to release men from the power of evil forces – mythologically presented as the demonic King Kamsa. Vaisnavism and devotionalism had become so intertwined that such non-Vaisnavite, *bhakti* texts as the *Ragamala* often show Krishna as the male figure, as in *Vasanta Raga* (plate H). We shall see that Krishna is often celebrated through literary texts of great sensuousness, and in the popular imagination he became the archetypal Beloved.

While many states in Rajasthan developed distinctive local artistic traditions, different courts in the same geographic area (Bikaner and Jodhpur, for example, or Sirohi and Mewar) usually shared general traits. This allows us to develop also a sense for broad regional styles. Mewar, bordered by Sirohi on the west, was also adjoined by the central Indian kingdom of Malwa to the southeast. Malwa painting, too, in the seventeenth century, finds its closest parallel in works from Mewar.

Mewar and its neighbors, and the Rathor States (Jodhpur and Bikaner), have been mentioned because they represent two extremes in the range of Rajput styles during the later years of the seventeenth century. (These variations are defined in part by differing tolerances of Mughal influence.) Sirohi, in the southwest corner of Rajasthan bordering Gujarat as well as Mewar, seems to have developed a highly recognizable style by about 1680. *Sarang Ragini* (plate I) is from one of several related and almost identical Sirohi *Ragamala* sets of the period. All show even less interest in Mughal developments than did Mewar, where the most comparable style was practiced. *Sarang Ragini* presents us with a completely flat surface pattern, in which the forms are crisply and cleanly defined. The architecture is obviously freely drawn, neither traced nor measured, giving a spontaneity and vivacity to the execution that matches the extraordinary vibrancy of the color. The palette – bright, and dominated by red, green, white, and saffron yellow – is close to that of the pre-Mughal *Bhagavata Purana* (plate B), as is the tight compartmentalization of the composition. The figures are modelled by shading along the outlines, for example, although this increases their vividness, not their three-dimensionality. (This is a technique known in Buddhist cave paintings at sites such as Ajanta more than a millennium earlier.) There is nothing illusionistic in the scene. It is a brilliant and powerful image. We can trace a few works that seem to show an evolution of the style, although as late as 1740 it remained substantially intact; and it was patronized by Jains as well as Hindus.

Sirohi is a useful example of the problems continually encountered in attempting to assign provenances to some recognizable Rajasthani styles. While for Bikaner we have thorough (even if unstudied) contemporary documentation, and for Mewar enough inscriptions to be sure of the broad outlines of development, there is no extant inscriptional evidence to connect the style of *Sarang Ragini* to Sirohi specifically. The attribution is based on the shaky foundation of one dealer's claim to have once seen an inscription on a now lost *Ragamala* series naming the place of origin as Vasantgarh, the summer capital of the Sirohi maharaos. Yet as the closest parallels to the style occur in inscribed paintings from the towns of Nadol, Desuri, and Bijapur, nearby in the same region of Rajasthan, the claim seems plausible and has been repeated. We must admit, however, that at present it is only a useful conjecture.

Similar space and architecture to that of *Sarang Ragini* (plate I) is found in a contemporary *Ragamala* attributed to Malwa, from which a quite different interpretation of the same subject is reproduced. *Sarang Ragini* (fig. 119) shows

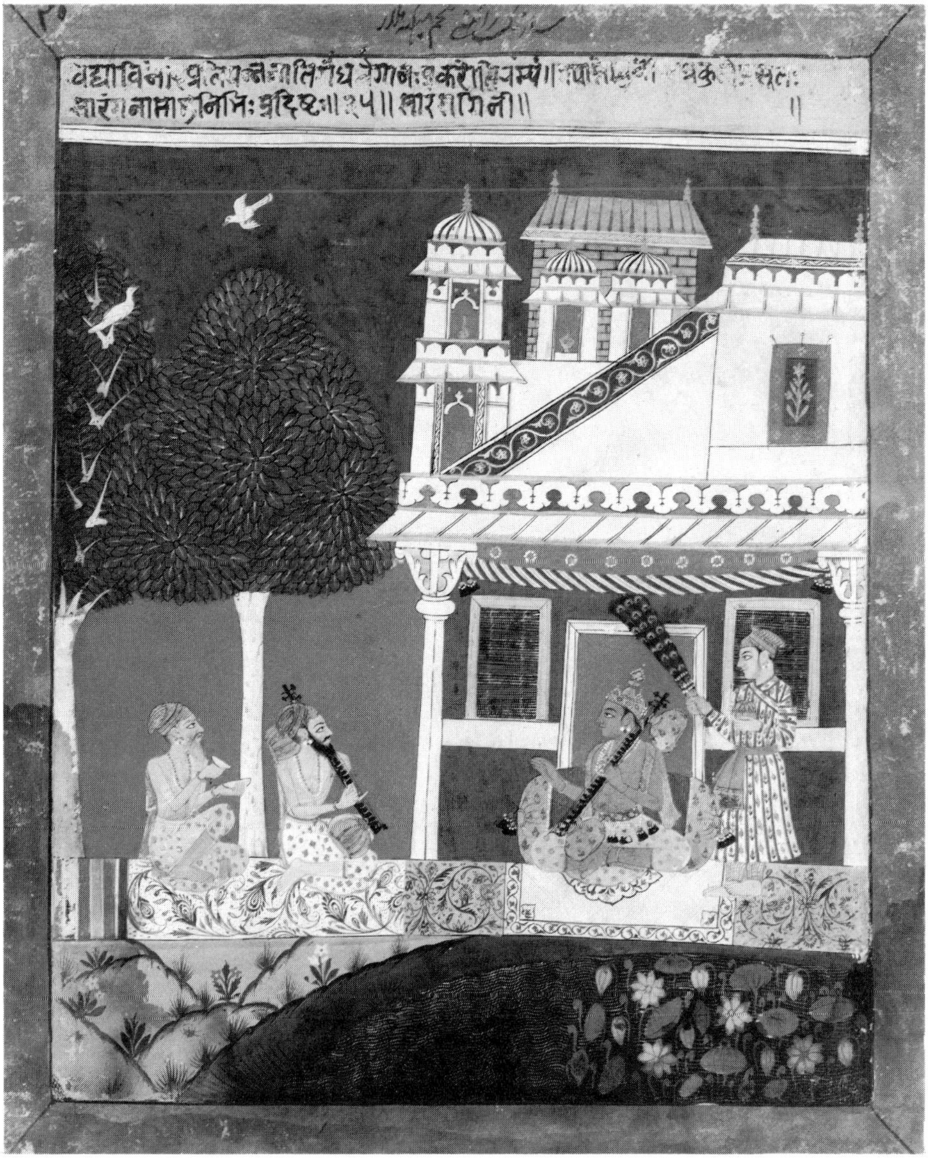

119. Sarang Ragini. From a *Ragamala* series, Rajput, Central India, ca. 1680

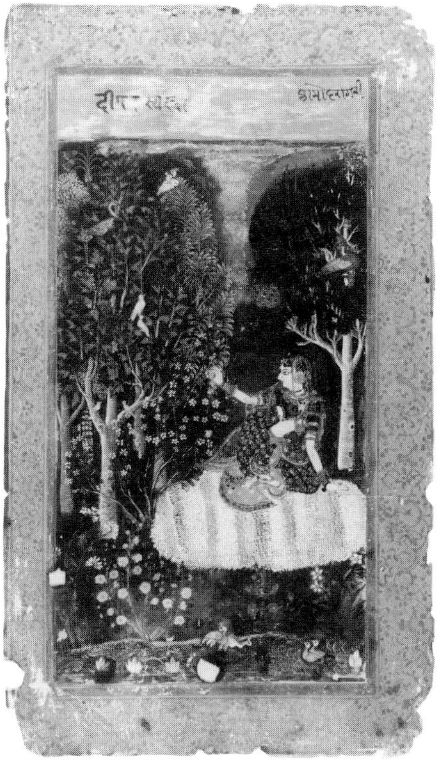

120. Kamod ragini. From a *Ragamala* series, Rajput or sub-imperial Mughal, at Chunar, dated 1591

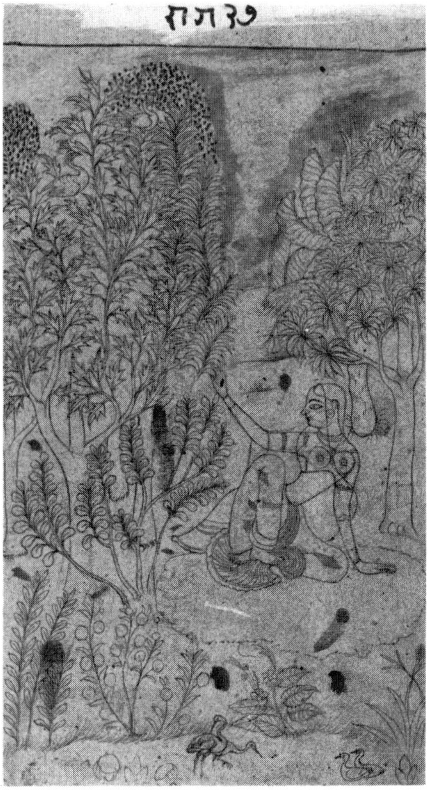

121. Kamod ragini. From a *Ragamala* series, Rajput, Rajasthan at Bundi, ca. 1600

no greater spatial sophistication than that found in ragamalas painted in the same region four decades earlier (fig. 90), although the work is visually more detailed, and the descriptively specific passages soften its impact. Areas of pattern in the architecture and the textiles; the small, even forms used to define the foliage; the landscape and evenly patterned lotus pond, all draw and hold our attention. We can perhaps see this simultaneous enrichment (through details) and taming (by softer forms and colors) of the surface as Mughal traits. Certainly the turban of the man at the right, and his floral *jama* (robe) and *kamarband* (sash), are inspired by Mughal fashion.

Bundi and Kota were bordered by Malwa to the south and Mewar on the west, and it is no surprise that the ragamala tradition at the two courts relates closely to *Ragamalas* from Mewar, Sirohi, and Malwa. By 1680 the Bundi style, having undergone almost a century of development, was mature and

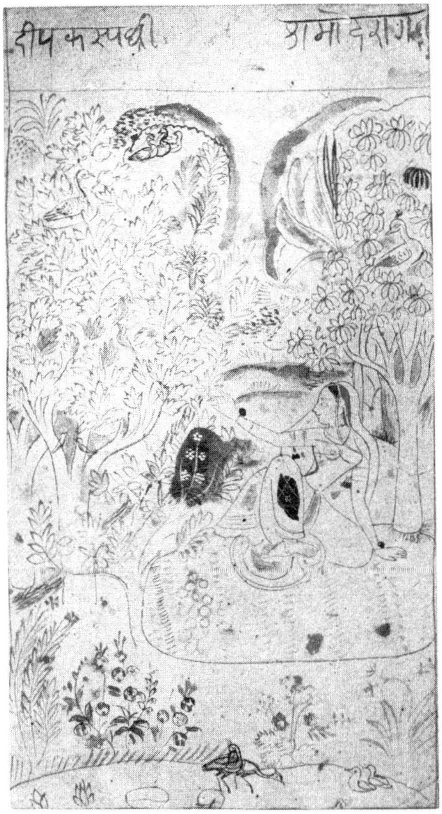

122. Kamod ragini. From a *Ragamala* series, Rajput, Rajasthan at Bundi, ca. 1660

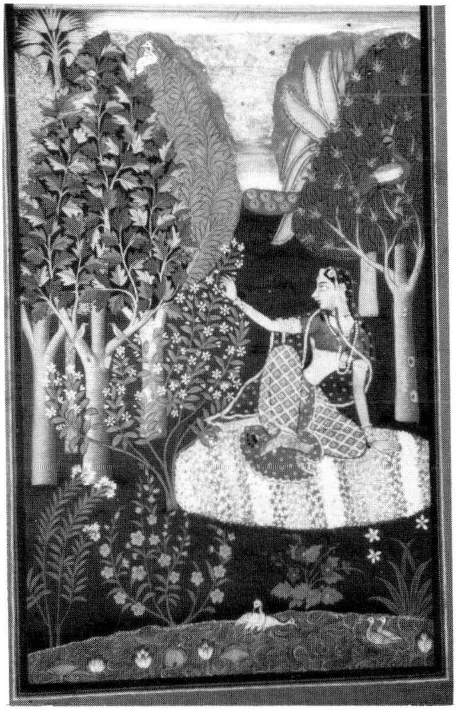

123. Kamod ragini. From a *Ragamala* series, Rajput, Rajasthan at Bundi, ca. 1680

distinctive. A *Ragamala*, datable to about 1680, is the best known example of Bundi workmanship at the time. Like other pages from that series, *Kamod Ragini* (fig. 123) uses the identical composition found first in the earlier Chunar *Ragamala* (fig. 120) of 1591. Among his stock of supplies, a painter would have had tracings of standard and often-requested compositions, and such artists' patterns for *Kamod Ragini* (figs. 121 and 122) are known. The painter would use such drawings, which also indicate appropriate colors, to create fresh but faithful renderings of favorite subjects. The system obviously made no allowance for conscious artistic initiative, yet the circa 1680 *Ragamala* (fig. 123) is quite different in effect, if not in composition, from its prototype of 1591 (fig. 120). Repetition has removed the vigor, even the wildness, of the earlier illustration (which may be the original set to use this specific iconography). And whereas the Chunar series cannot be discussed without reference to Mughal painting (see pages 45–47), the 1680 series betrays no obvious Mughal influence.

The two drawings for the subject help further to define and explain this evolution. Clearly of different dates, one (fig. 121) is closely related in style to the Chunar *Kamod Ragini* (fig. 120) because of the figural proportions and the controlled brushwork, while the second (fig. 122), with its different female type, is best compared to the later Kanoria painting (fig. 123). Let us assume that the earlier drawing (fig. 121) was a copy of the original scene (fig. 120), and that it was itself copied in the later drawing (fig. 122), upon which the painting of circa 1680 (fig. 123) was based. (This is, of course, pure conjecture, but it does illustrate general working methods.)

Note now the area at the top right where trees and sky meet. In the earliest drawing, wet pigment is lightly brushed against the outline of the trees to simulate the atmospheric night sky seen in the 1591 *Ragamala*. The artist of the second drawing chose to abbreviate this darker area, and it became a simple strip of color. Were one not to know the original work, it would be difficult to know what is being described; in fact, it now looks like a distant tree. This hard-edged form – no longer clearly part of the sky – is repeated in the circa 1680 *Kamod Ragini* painting, where it remains ambiguous. The painter was copying his model literally, without knowing the meaning of the forms presented to him.

There are two important conclusions to make. First, when Mughal influence diminished at Bundi, for whatever reason, interest in naturalism lessened and the style simply reverted back to recognizable and established Rajput traits. In a sense, it is as if the earlier Mughalized phase of the style never existed, for while the Chunar set did establish the composition and iconography that were continued in the later scenes, the relative realism of spatial setting, or the physical volume and presence of the figures – important Mughal *stylistic* innovations – vanished. We saw this as well at Udaipur, for the 1649 *Ramayana* scene (fig. 89) did not incorporate any of the carefully (if minimally) naturalistic observations noted in the 1628 *Ragamala* page (fig. 88). And the same general direction was noted too at Jodhpur (see figs. 93 and 94).

There is therefore not the same cumulative linear stylistic development in these Rajput schools that we found basic to the Mughal style from the mid sixteenth century to the reign of Aurangzeb. And this leads to a second point. Judging from the chronological progression of the Bundi *Ragamala* scenes, major stylistic change within the Rajput tradition is not necessarily the result of conscious artistic initiative. This is hardly surprising in a tradition where artistic fulfillment comes first from faithful performance, and only secondarily from invention. We cannot therefore expect changes of style in Rajput painting always to be as significant as in the Mughal tradition, for they are far less the product of conscious choice and individual initiative.

Ragamalas and other traditional subjects invariably represent the most conservative aspect of any Rajput school, for once compositional models were established, artistic initiative was not expected. It is instead the intrusion of new subjects that forced artists to be inventive. For the Rajputs, portraiture was such a novelty, and it developed in response to Mughal artistic fashion. *Maharao Jagat Singh of Kota in a Garden* (fig. 124), for example, is based on a compositional type established under Jahangir (fig. 125). It is the finest surviving portrait of the dark-skinned Rajput. He is centrally positioned on a platform in a geometrically laid out garden seen from bird's-eye view. Rarely has a symmetrical garden seemed more jungly, however. Yellow, orange, and pink blossoms burst out from a tangle of dark foliage, and there is no sense whatsoever of the rigid garden pattern that actually underlay the visible growth. Jagat Singh's expression is lively, and even the lines of his skirt swirl with abandon. Unlike the virtually contemporary Mughal *Darbar of Aurangzeb* (fig. 117), which was meticulously planned and executed, *Maharao Jagat Singh of Kota in a Garden* seems to have been painted in a series of spontaneous gestures. The observation can be made equally validly of the earlier *A Royal Hunt* (fig. 92), as well as of *Vasanta Raga* (plate H), where the artist has treated a stock composition as if it were a fresh invention. Such vivacity must be seen as particularly characteristic of Kota works.

Vasanta Raga presents a dancing Krishna full of rhythm and energy, against a brilliant floral jungle. The intense, saturated colors, the awareness of how expressive pure color can be, the clear gestures, and the flat space, are all elements we have related to the "pure" Rajput style. The series was probably commissioned by Maharao Jagat Singh (r. 1657–1684), who must now be recognized as one of the greatest Rajput patrons.

Daulatabad Besieged (fig. 126) includes Jagat Singh among forces approaching the citadel. (He is at the upper left, riding an elephant.) As in *A Royal Hunt*, the artist presents us with a wide vista, and a dynamic placement of the opposing elements; the line is swift, as well, and the artist builds rhythms by the repetition of forms – in this case the horses. The drawing is both minutely descriptive and full of technical and expressive innovations. Among the horsemen at the bottom, we find figures seen in both frontal and rear views, a spatial experimentation rarely seen even in Mughal paintings. And broad washes of dark pigment surround the fortress, suggesting both storms and the smoke of battle. The work is directly comparable in style to the almost contemporary *Sultan Shuja at the Battle of Bahadarpur* (fig. 115), or to the closely related *Battle of Samugarh*.[1] The Kota artist has betrayed no interest in those European techniques of modelling or spatial recession that so fascinated his Mughal counterpart, however.

[1] Beach, *Grand Mogul*, no. 65.

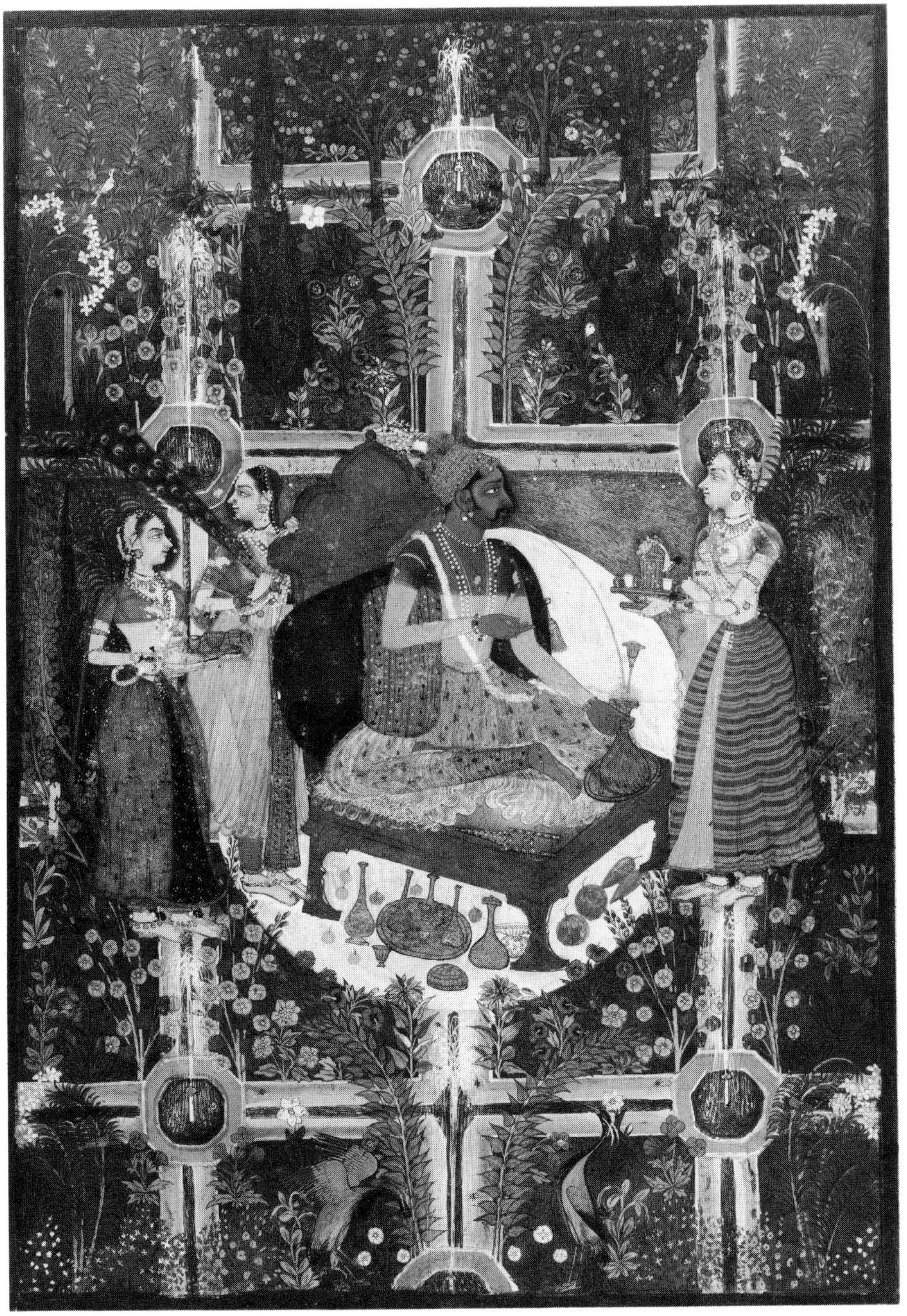

124. Maharao Jagat Singh of Kota in a Garden. Rajput, Rajasthan at Kota, ca. 1660

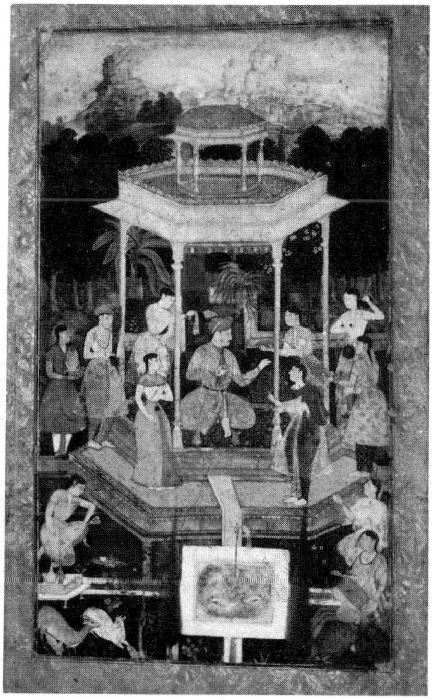

125. Jahangir in a Garden. Mughal, ca. 1605

Maharao Ram Singh I of Kota Pursuing a Rhinoceros (fig. 127) seems unrelated initially to the miniaturistic *Daulatabad Besieged*. It is the most monumental and dramatic Rajput image we have seen, yet here too color and line are isolated against an unpainted surface; and the line, rather than simply charting the boundaries of forms, takes on an independent expressiveness. This emphasis on linearity has already distinguished Kota painting.

While the overwhelming vitality of the elephant suggests that it too was a fresh invention of the artist, perhaps the most surprising aspect of the drawing is that an identical composition of elephant and rider is found in the earliest identifiable Kota drawing, *A Royal Hunt* (fig. 92), dated about 1630. As in the most traditional *ragamala* subjects, therefore, the artist was working within the confines of pre-determined compositional elements. (Or rather, once a satisfactory depiction of an elephant was produced, it instantly became a model for other artists to copy.) As we noted, the earlier drawing is very large within the Rajput context, so even the monumental scale of the rhinoceros hunt has been anticipated. However, the artist of *A Royal Hunt* has filled the scene with landscape and additional figures, diminishing the central elephant's impact, while the line does not yet have the rapid, whiplash quality of Ram Singh I's mount. These hunting scenes, together with the portraits of Maharao Jagat Singh, make

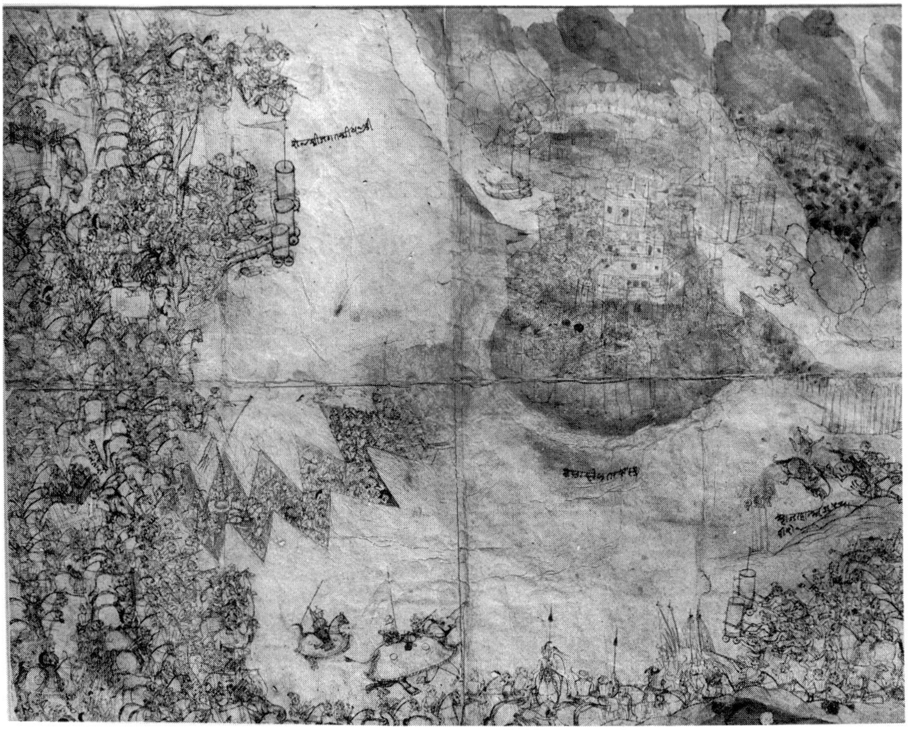

126. Daulatabad Besieged. Rajput, Rajasthan at Kota, ca. 1660

it unquestionable that Kota was the most inventive and experimental Rajput school in the seventeenth century, a position it will hold throughout much of its history.

In contrast to the styles of southern Rajasthan and Central India, court paintings from the region of Jodhpur show a quite different sensibility. Few seventeenth-century works from Jodhpur itself have survived (see figs. 93 and 94), but paintings from the nearby kingdom of Bikaner are known in quantity. Like Jodhpur, Bikaner was ruled by members of the Rathor family. It had been established in 1459 by Bika, the sixth son of Rao Jodha (r. 1453–1489) of Jodhpur, but relations between the two branches of the family were seldom amicable. Rao Kalyan Mal (r. 1539–1571) submitted to Akbar in 1570, and his brother's daughter was married to the emperor. Rai Singh (r. 1571–1612) succeeded to the throne, and in 1586 his daughter married Prince Salim. Bikaner too, therefore, was an important and early presence at the Mughal court, and this certainly affected the artistic taste of the state's rulers.

Vishnu with Lakshmi and Attendant Ladies (plate J) is by Ruknuddin, the

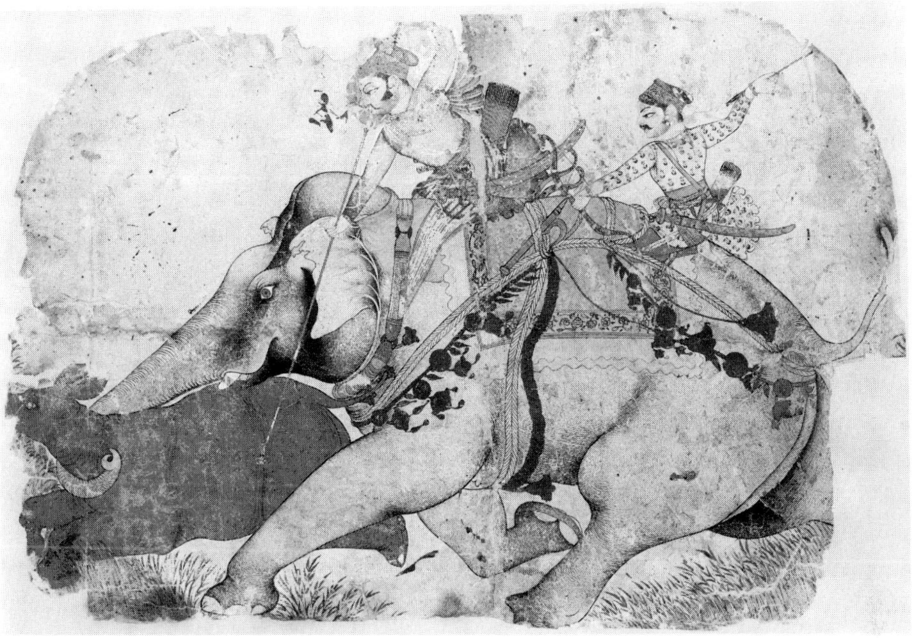

127. Maharao Ram Singh I of Kota Pursuing a Rhinoceros. Rajput, Rajasthan at Kota, ca. 1690

most famous of all Bikaner painters, and is dated 1678. When the scene is compared to other Rajput works of the same decade (for example plates H, I, and K; figs. 119 and 123), its Mughal affiliation is obvious, whether due to its airy space, the specificness of the architecture, the careful attention to fabric patterns, or the precise and diminutive figures of the women. The latter are immediately comparable to the women in *Festivities at the Wedding of Dara Shikoh* (figs. 97 and 98), from the *Padshahnama*, or the two ladies in *An Old Man Rebukes a Young Girl* (fig. 104), from the 1629 *Bustan* of Sa'di. This latter manuscript is especially important as illustration of a type of source for the Bikaner style. From a category of manuscript probably made to be given as state gifts, it was not of the highest imperial quality, and therefore represented a level of manuscript production most accessible to Rajput courtiers. Among Rajasthani schools, Bikaner painting remained closest to the Mughal style for the longest period of time.

The evolution of Bikaner painting, however, remains unstudied, although scenes of a similarly Mughalized type are known through specifically dated works as early as the mid seventeenth century. On the whole, Bikaner painting has thorough contemporary documentation: inscriptions are frequently found giving the artist's name, his father's name, and the date. Such historical interests are clearly another link with Mughal attitudes.

To the north of Rajasthan, in the Punjab Hills, foothills to the Himalayas, was a cluster of thirty-five princely states. It was – and, of course, remains – a wild and dramatic setting. Snow-covered mountains, roaring torrents, and secluded, fertile valleys make us more than usually aware of nature's intimate involvement in daily life; and certainly inspired local artists to create some of the most powerful and expressive landscapes in Indian painting. The terrain, with its natural walls and divisions, framed and contained the kingdoms, whose rulers were therefore less able to contest or easily extend existing boundaries. Nature unified the states culturally, so that painting here has a different character from the Rajput schools of Rajasthan; it also helped to minimize outside influences. It was, after all, physically difficult to travel in the hills.

While none of the ruling houses was as powerful, or as closely allied to the Mughal court, as Amber, Bikaner or Jodhpur, hill chiefs did serve in the imperial armies, and such rulers as Bhupat Pal (r. 1595–1635) of Basohli became intimates of the imperial circle. Until very recently, there had been no evidence for painting in these *pahari* (of the hills) states before about 1660, the date ascribed to a *Rasamanjari* series (figs. 128 and 149) and related works. And while these illustrations were attributed to a Basohli provenance, they were certainly not in a Mughal-derived style. The *Rasamanjari*, a series of paintings illustrating a fourteenth-century Sanskrit text by Bhanudatta, again presents physical relationships as metaphoric of devotional states. *Stupor* (fig. 128) illustrates the following verse, words which the heroine's confidante addresses to the waiting lover:

> The bracelet on her hand is producing no sound; the garment on her bosom is not waving; the gaze of her pupils is fixed; and her ear-rings are dancing no more. There is no difference between her and one painted [in a picture] . . . unless a ripple of thrill is awakened in her on her hearing your name.[2]

A second, related series of works, illustrating an unidentified text about the tantric goddess Bhadrakali, has recently appeared. *Devi Worshipped by Brahma, Vishnu, and Shiva* (plate K) is wilder in spirit than any but the earliest images from Rajasthan.

Dated between 1660 and 1670, both this series and the *Rasamanjari* compare to paintings from Sirohi (plate I), for example, rather than those of Bikaner (plate J). The composition is an assemblage of compartments, each backed by a flat plane of brilliant color. Figures are angular, and gestures clear. Expressions are intense, emphasized by large heads and enormous eyes, and the impact is instantaneous – meaning that its effect is strongest at first glance. Much of the

[2] M. S. Randhawa and S. D. Bhambri, "Basohli paintings of Bhanudatta's *Rasamanjari*," *Roopa Lekha*, vol. 36, nos. 1–2, p. 119.

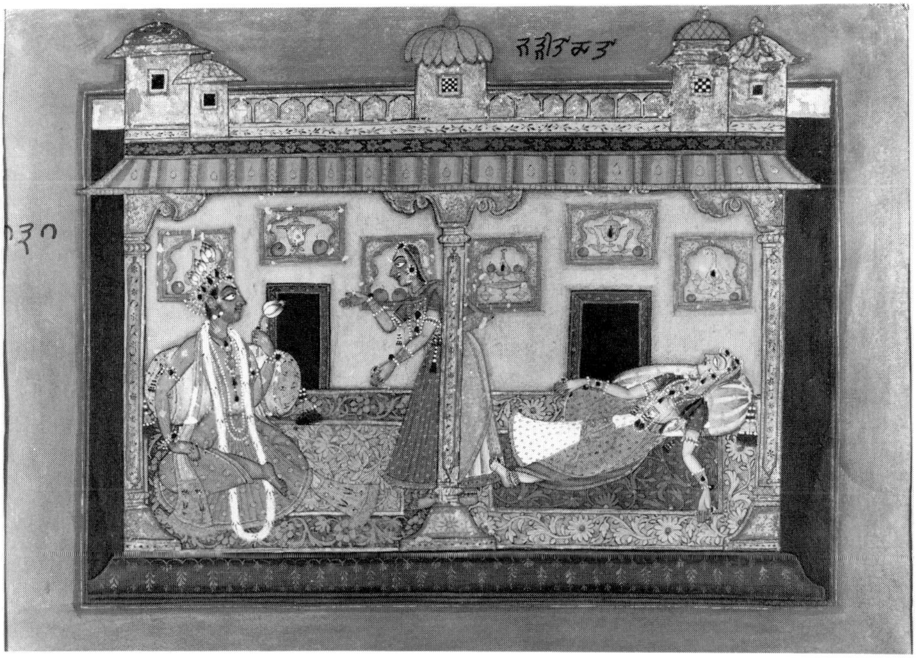

128. Stupor. From a *Rasamanjari* series, Rajput, Punjab Hills, ca. 1660–1670

impact of these extraordinary paintings is due to a vividness and seeming simplicity that initially allies them to pure Rajput traditions. It is the refinements, however, that focus the power of the works and make us aware of the artists' pictorial sophistication and experience. The flat background colors, for example, are not only intense in hue, they are smoothly burnished and reflective, and the effect is opulent. There is facial modelling, but not allied to effects of light and shade. Instead, it is used to strengthen contour lines, to emphasize shapes, and thus to intensify the effect of the dramatically distorted forms. These distortions are coupled with a technique that is extremely precise. There is none of the roughness of the pre-Mughal *Bhagavata Purana* (plate B), to which the *Rasamanjari* is in other ways directly comparable, and no sense of sometimes unanticipated effects. Every detail is carefully planned, and this early pahari series thus combines wildness with elegance. (Note, in particular, the use of cut and applied beetle wing-cases to simulate large emeralds, dramatically placed among the cascades of jewels.) If this is the first known painting from the Punjab Hills, it nonetheless demands a considerable antecedent tradition.

How and even where this style developed is presently unknown. It certainly came out of the same basic background as the Rajasthani schools, for it seems in many ways just another regional variant and historical continuation of the

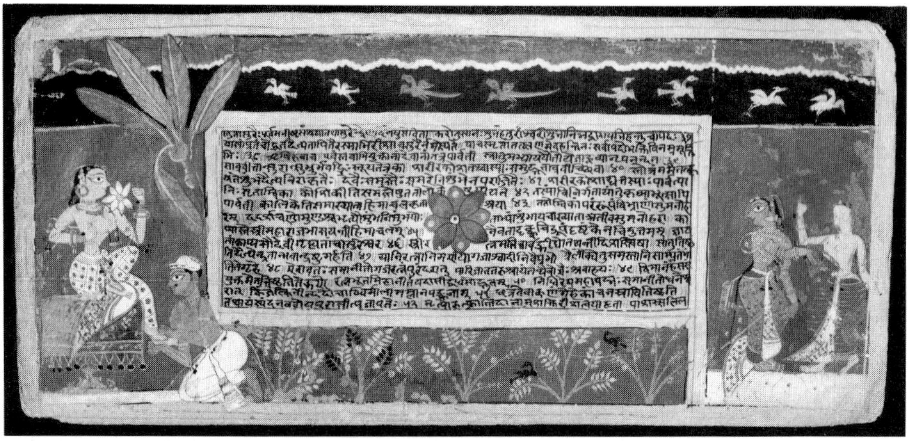

129. Subdued by Beauty. From a *Devi-mahatmya* series, possibly from the Punjab Hills, dated 1552(?)

Chaurapanchasika style (fig. 4), rather than a wholly different tradition. It is possible that a variant of the pre-Mughal *Bhagavata Purana* style was practiced in the hills in the sixteenth century or earlier, as suggested by a recently discovered (and controversial) *Devimahatmya* manuscript of 1552 (fig. 129), which contains inscriptions in a local hill script. There are also strong correspondences to Rajasthani styles in other, even more distant, hill regions. *The Birth of Buddha* (fig. 130), from an *Astasahasrika Prajnaparamita* manuscript made under the Nepalese Raja Srinivasa Malla in 1682, shows strong affinities to works from southern Rajasthan as well as to the *Devimahatmya*. We must constantly remember, therefore, that books and artists traveled and stylistic alternatives were thus available to painters with relative ease. The general vocabulary of the works we have been discussing was found throughout north India, however, and represented accepted traditional attitudes.

A major group of illustrations, including a *Ramayana* and a *Bhagavata Purana*, have recently been attributed by Catherine Glynn to the hill state of Mandi about 1640, as have a number of portraits.[3] The style of the works is closely related to imperial Mughal painting of the Shahjahan period, and they may hold a place in the pahari regions similar to that of the Kota School *Bhagavata Purana* in Rajasthan. The attributions to Mandi are disputed, although one would expect Mughal influences to have made clear inroads into the region (as it had elsewhere) by the early seventeenth century. This would help to explain the pictorial and technical brilliance and sophistication of the Basohli *Rasamanjari* series, but it makes the vigor and primitiveness of that style at such a relatively late date all the more puzzling. Also, there is no

[3] See Catherine Glynn, "Early Painting in Mandi," *Artibus Asiae*, vol. 44, no. 1, pp. 21–64.

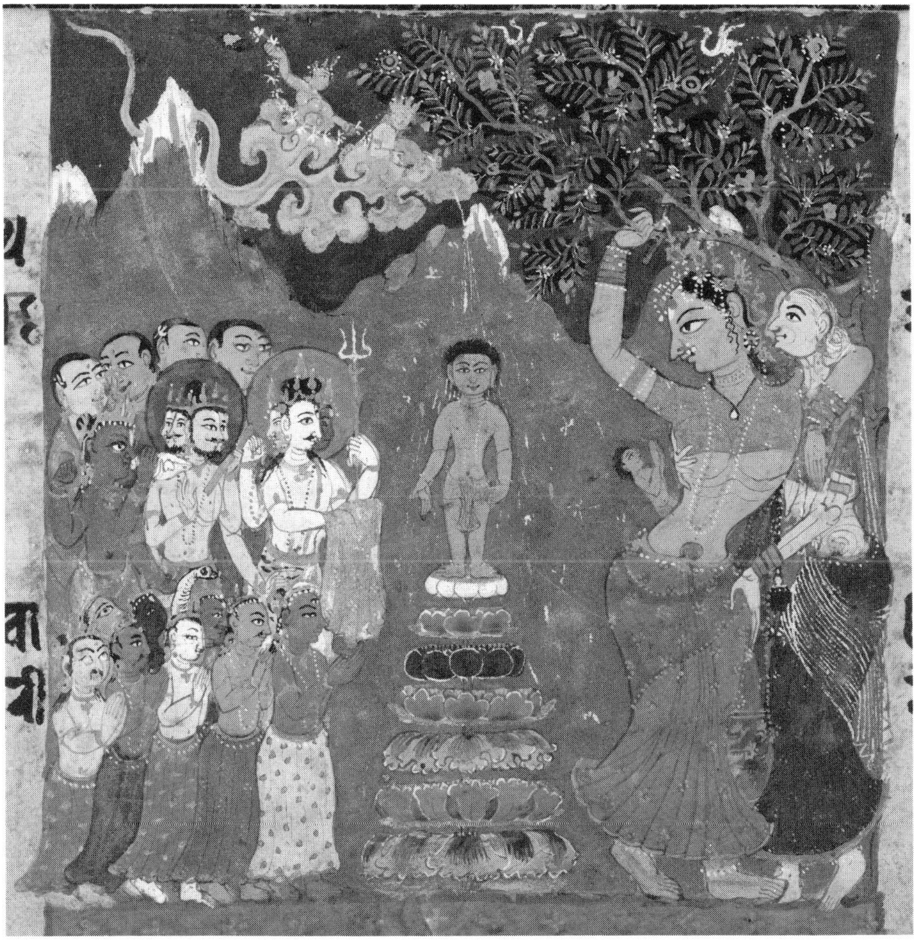

130. The Birth of the Buddha and The First Seven Steps. From an *Astasahasrika Prajnaparamita* manuscript, Nepal, dated 1682

immediate explanation for the disappearance of such well-understood and thoroughly assimilated Mughal innovations as those that we find in these series. Nonetheless, the assumption that painting in the hills began about 1660 may have been so strong that we have simply failed to recognize contrary evidence. The *Rasamanjari* is uninscribed, and the oft-quoted fact that many of the works in this style were found at Basohli is not sufficient by itself to confirm that state as the source of the illustrations. More useful is the direct relationship of these pages to a second *Rasamanjari* series, made for Raja Kirpal Pal of Basohli and dated 1695 (see Appendix).

Another major variant of this pahari style is a spirited set of *Ramayana* illustrations. *The Gods Are Born as Monkeys* (fig. 131) is immediately comparable to the first *Rasamanjari* series because of colors, compartmentalization, and the intricacy, vivacity, inventiveness, and character of the architectural detail. Whereas the earlier set is extremely precise and controlled in both composition and technique – and these are important aspects of its style – this *Ramayana* series seems almost haphazard: horizontals waver as they cross the page, and while the proportions of the figures are large and dramatic, they can also often be justly termed lumpish and ungainly. As with any large series – there were more than 270 pages when the paintings were recently rediscovered – different artists would have worked on the project and there is consequently a wide range of quality. But the best pages are full of life, with vivid colors, and bold gestures. In *The Gods are Born as Monkeys*, even the roof line seems alive, its domes like luxuriant tropical plants or enormous nesting birds. The wildness of the earliest *Rasamanjari* remains more intact here than in many other series.

There is no colophon yet known on any of these *Ramayana* pages. Local traditions attribute its production to Kulu, and it was found in the collection of the Raja of Shangri, a territory that separated from Kulu to become an independent state in the mid nineteenth century. B. D. Goswamy and Eberhard Fischer, however, have recently argued that the works were executed instead at the state of Bahu, because a known series of portraits of Bahu rulers was in the same distinctive style. The study of pahari painting is continually hampered by the lack of inscriptional documentation or other factual material from which a solid framework for judgments can be formed.

In contrast to the vitality of Rajput painting in the second half of the seventeenth century, Mughal painting instead declined. In the *Muntakhabu-l Lubab* of Muhammad Hashim Khafi Khan, the atmosphere of the imperial court is indicated by remarks within the narrative for the eleventh regnal year (1668–1669):

> Prohibitions were promulgated against intoxicating drinks, against taverns and brothels, and against . . . fairs, at which on certain dates countless numbers of Hindus, men and women of every tribe, assemble at their idol temples . . . The minstrels and singers of reputation in the service of the Court were made ashamed of their occupation . . . public proclamations were made prohibiting singing and dancing . . . [4]

It had been a life of sensual and aesthetic pleasures that had motivated Mughal art into the period of Shahjahan's rule; we see this reflected in style, materials, and subject matter. Under the abstemious and orthodox Aurangzeb, however, imperial patronage withered. At the beginning of his reign, painters continued

[4] Quoted in Sir H. M. Elliott and John Dowson, *The History of India as Told by Its Own Historians*, Allahabad, 1964 (reprint), vol. VII, p. 283.

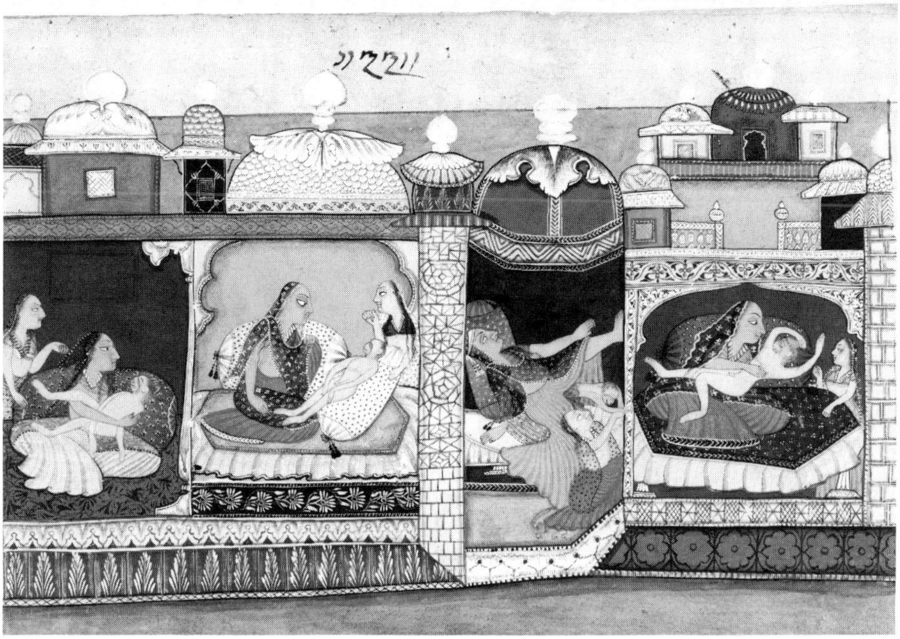

131. The Gods Are Born as Monkeys. From a *Ramayana* series, Rajput, Punjab Hills (at Kulu?), ca. 1700

to work as if Shahjahan were still their patron (fig. 117), but this did not last. Formal portraits of the emperor and the nobility remained in demand, but they were created through the successful – although increasingly mechanical – repetition of long established formulas. Images were now made for ceremonial purposes, not for pleasure. Individual interpretations were of little interest to the emperor, and artists were not encouraged to be inventive. Under these conditions, the separation of Mughal and Rajput artistic ideals was increasingly obliterated. Mughal court art in effect adopted the quite different standards which we have here related to art made for religious or temple use. Many painters must have left the imperial workshops to seek other employment, taking with them the styles and formulas learned at court. At its new homes in Rajput territories, eastern India, or the Deccan, Mughal style was exciting and new, and it sometimes inspired local artists in novel and challenging ways. Later emperors showed greater interest in the arts than Aurangzeb, as we will see, but the historical continuity of a distinctively Mughal painting style had ended.

CHAPTER 6

1700–1800: THE DOMINANCE OF RAJPUT PAINTING

By 1700, Rajput palaces contained gardens, courtyards, pavilions, and darbar halls in the Mughal fashion; court dress and manners often followed Mughal standards; and, in the arts, many painters used finer pigments to paint subtler perceptions of the natural world in softer colors and more experimental styles. Neither architects nor painters working for Rajput patrons adopted anything more than this superficial appearance of Mughal taste, however. Even when painting portraits – a Mughal-inspired subject – the Rajput artist showed no sustained interest in the visual specificity, or individual psychological comprehension, that was so distinctive a Mughal contribution to Indian art. Figures remained types. The regard for human portraiture so remarkable in the works of such Mughal artists as Govardhan or Hashim is found virtually nowhere in Rajput painting; compare, for example, figs. 117 and 124. This is, of course, a matter determined by the context of patronage. Some of the greatest Mughal painters were Hindus by personal faith, but the demands of the patron took precedence over the artist's individual cultural affiliation. In fact, throughout the history of Indian painting, artists took jobs where they were available, and whether or not they were for patrons with whom they shared religious beliefs.

This difference of attitude is nowhere more obvious than in the treatment of space. A sense of spatial depth – whether or not successful by European terms – is basic to the mature phase of Mughal painting (for example fig. 111). By creating a visual equivalent for empty space, in which solid forms are carefully located, the boundaries and thus the inherent separateness of these forms is affirmed. Hindu artists working for Hindu patrons sought to show instead the inseparability of forms, and found it more effective to use a less scientific space, even to deny the concept of empty space. In *Maharaja Jaswant Singh of Jodhpur Listening to Music* (fig. 94), or *Maharao Jagat Singh of Kota in a Garden* (fig. 124), for example, the background is as aesthetically expressive and assertive as the human figures.

The individual uniqueness of physical forms is denied also in other ways. Hindu poetry continually presents forms and shapes as metaphors and symbols evoking other, quite different sensations. One example would be the heroines (or *nayikas*) who populate many Hindu devotional texts. The beauty of one of these women has been described as follows:

> Her brow is like the moon, her shapely eyebrows like a bow. Her tremulous, bewitching eyes are like the sharp arrows of Kamadeva [the God of Love]. Her breath has the fragrance of a lotus bud. Her teeth are like pearls and her laughter flashes like lightning. Her belly is shaped like a betel-leaf, her feet like lotuses, and her gait graceful like a swan's.[1]

These sometimes relentless poetic images serve to open out, to universalize, the subjects portrayed by showing their likeness to other forms, qualities, or aspects of existence. Hindu paintings too, although far less concretely, seek to generalize. No artist would actually use plant forms for a woman's face, of course. Yet even in *Raja Savant Singh of Kishangarh on a Terrace* (fig. 141), a picture which otherwise is so close to Mughal taste, the stance of the ruler describes pride more than a specific physiognomy, and the forms of Krishna's skirt in fig. 142 are more closely allied to plant life than to the texture of cloth. This metaphoric quality can be compared to the physical descriptiveness of mature Mughal works, or to the unearthly quality found in Deccani work of the early seventeenth century – the period when its character is most distinctive.

At the opening of the eighteenth century, therefore, Rajput painting remains recognizably different in intent from traditional Mughal attitudes. The two complexes show different patterns of historical development as well. We have already mentioned that painting at Mewar and Bundi during the seventeenth century does not show the clear or seemingly logical stylistic progression seen in Mughal painting between 1560 and 1660, for example. That situation is made more obvious by a series of energetic portraits, chiefly of Maharana Amar Singh II (r. 1698–1716) of Mewar. *Equestrian Portrait of Rana Amar Singh II of Mewar* (fig. 132) is almost completely in *grisaille* (tones of grey). While the subject, the portrait of a specific ruler and his retainers, is still relatively novel at Udaipur – there are few seventeenth-century portraits known from that state – it is the style that is most surprising. A finished painting, rather than a drawing, it lacks major color. This, plus the use of stippled greys to create or imply highlights and shading, is totally unanticipated in earlier Mewari works. The technique almost certainly originated in the modelling formulas found in European prints, and it was popular elsewhere in India at the same time. Here, once again, however, it is reinterpreted in a more traditionally Indian way. Lines of shading in the clothing do not follow the effects of light, but repeat and reinforce the linear definition of the drapery outlines and folds. We have seen this use of contour shading in the Buddhist paintings of Ajanta (fig. 2), as well as in Rajasthani *ragamala*s (plate I). While it gives to forms a sense of weight and mass, it also emphasizes the way those forms fit together with other shapes on the picture surface; it integrates, rather than separates, forms. Once again,

[1] M. S. Randhawa, *Kangra Paintings on Love*, New Delhi, 1962, p. 38.

the European source was used in a way totally compatible with traditional sensibilities and techniques.

This particular style is a major element in the definition of Mewar painting around 1700, yet it does not evolve organically from earlier painting in the region. And it disappears after a generation, leaving little trace of its presence. Such sudden shifts, reflecting momentary enthusiasms or the availability of painters working in novel styles, are familiar within Rajput sequences, although they are not always so clear or dramatic. To a degree, Mughal influence on Rajput artists is itself a similar phenomenon.

An exciting narrative depiction of *The Emperor Visits Tulsi Das* (plate L) can be dated to about 1710. Completely unlike the contemporary and more exotic grisaille style (fig. 132), this is a work whose impact relies on color. Like the earliest Rajput illustrations, it is clearly organized into compartments, although here more subtle and justifiable in terms of naturalistic description. Below is a scene in which a Mughal emperor (probably Bahadur Shah, who ruled between 1707 and 1710) is shown as if visiting the great sixteenth-century poet Tulsi Das. Various scenes taken from the life of Vishnu, together with scenes of Vishnu worship, are above. These are all separately defined by architecturally enclosed compartments, and the effect of the picture comes from this rectilinearity and containment (unlike the Kota hunting scenes, which seemed free from all such constraint). While the compartmentalization and limited palette ally it to the earliest works from Mewar, and even to pre-Mughal traditions, the observation of tree types, for example, or of gestures, is far more acute. It is perhaps because of the strength of pre-Mughal traditions in Mewar that the inherent energy and vigor of the school – and of Rajput art in general – is intensified, rather than diminished, by greater refinement of perception and technique. It is a bold, immediate, flat composition, which is nonetheless as informative about daily life as any Mughal work. In the eighteenth century, portraits and visual records of daily events were the subjects about which painters were most enthusiastic. *Maharana Ar Singh Performing Puja in Badi Mahal* (fig. 133) is a further example. Unlike the *Ragamala* sets, which continued to be made in abundance as necessary components of dowries or for use as official gifts, compositions for specific – even if historically impossible – events were frequently invented afresh, and painters often made acute comments about their subjects.

Krishna Fluting (fig. 134), one of the greatest Rajput pictures, was painted in either Udaipur or central India about 1700. It is a visually vibrant work, despite a very limited number of colors and a rigidly symmetrical composition. It compares most directly with a late Mughal imperial portrait, *Muhammad Shah Viewing a Garden* (fig. 136), of about 1730. The clearly silhouetted plant forms, the solid, patterned foliage of the trees, and the choice of hues are directly related. In both, white is also used to set off and increase our awareness of

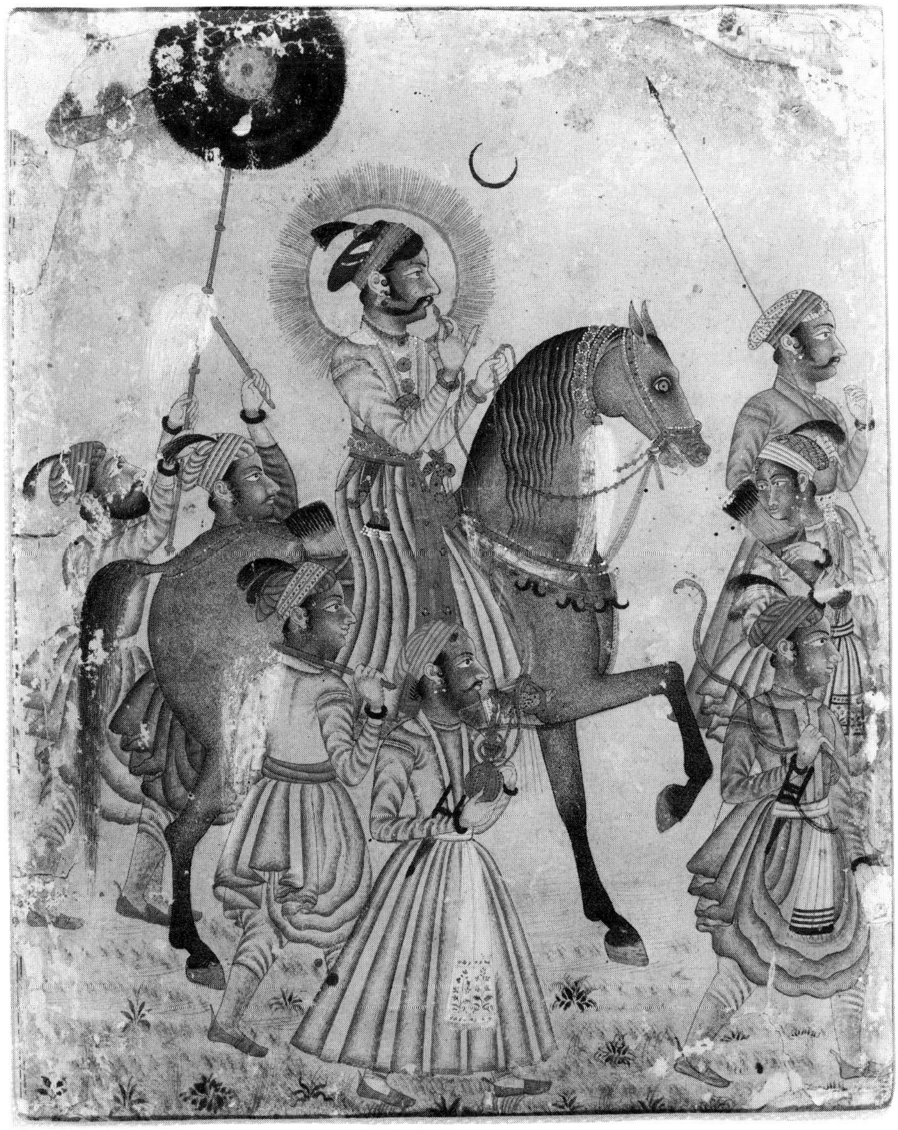

132. Equestrian Portrait of Rana Amar Singh II of Mewar. Rajput, Rajasthan at Udaipur, ca. 1700

individual colors and patterns. (In earlier Rajput works, the sheer quantity of unrelieved color made us less aware of individual color areas than of cumulative effect.) It is therefore subject more than style that ultimately separates these two works. In fact, at this point, the stylistic distinction of Rajput illustrations and the few contemporaneous imperial Mughal works overall is no longer obvious. The distinctive characteristics of earlier imperial works, the qualities which seemed to separate them from the mainstream of traditional Indian art, were no longer of interest to Mughal artists or patrons.

In the early eighteenth century, when Aurangzeb's successors again occasionally employed artists, Mughal painting was simply one among many regional Indian styles. Moreover, *Krishna Fluting* is compositionally and conceptually close to The *Miracle at Sravasti* (fig. 135), a sandstone panel from the east gateway of the Great Stupa at Sanchi, dated to the first century A.D.; the scenes share flat space, for example, and the shapes and placement of the trees. It is possible, therefore, to see in both *Krishna Fluting* and *Muhammad Shah Viewing a Garden* yet another reinterpretation of deep-seated and traditional Indian artistic attitudes towards space and human figures.

During the eighteenth century, painters working at Kota continued to explore further the innovations that had begun almost a century earlier, and hunting scenes remained those which prompted the greatest results. *Rao Bhoj Singh of Bundi Slays a Boar* (fig. 137), painted at Kota about 1740, develops directly from earlier works. (Bhoj Singh, who ruled from 1585–1607, was a common ancestor to the Kota and Bundi ruling families.) Here a wide variety of brush-strokes are placed against plain paper, and the work delights in exploring varieties of foliage patterning. *Rao Bhoj Singh of Bundi Slays a Boar* is large in size and full of large-scale forms, and the effect is ebullient, virtually bursting with energy. Here, for the first time in Rajput painting, we sense the spaciousness and power of nature – one of the great contributions of Kota artists. The size of the image, therefore, was not increased to pack in greater quantities of detail, as we sense in *A Royal Hunt* (fig. 92), but because the dynamism and energy which the artist found in the scene could not be contained within a traditional Rajput format.

The Bhoj Singh hunting scene is an important work for understanding painting at Kota. Its large size and scale, and the free and sketchy technique, are clear developments from earlier illustrations, but it also sets the standard for later hunting scenes, which are more derivative than innovative. *Maharao Umed Singh of Kota Hunts a Lion* (fig. 138), by Gumani and dated 1779, is set in the jungle south of Kota City, along the ridge separating Kota from Malwa. The scene is the annual Spring Hunt, and one lion, driven towards a rope enclosure, has turned to attack his pursuers. The scene is once again packed with descriptive details, both of the action and of the landscape. The

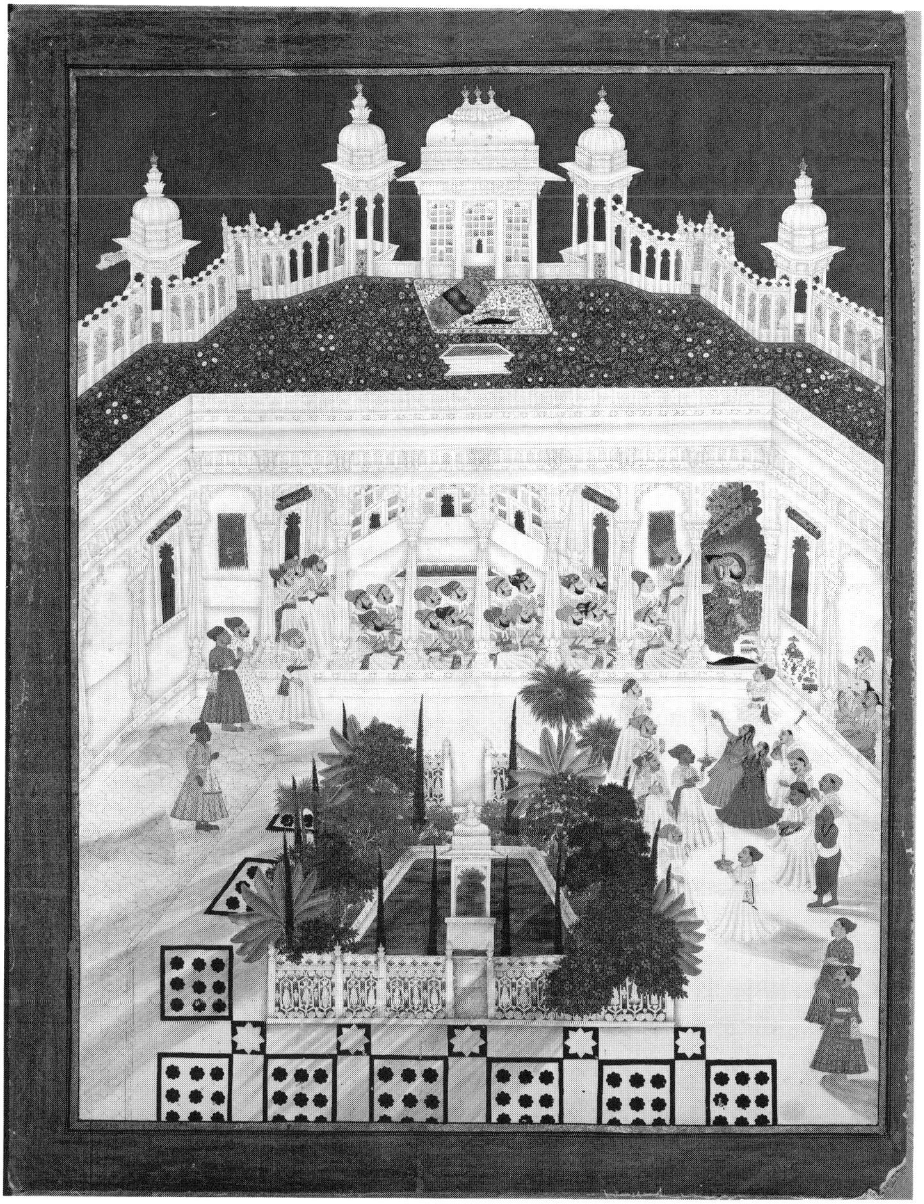

133. Maharana Ar Singh Performing Puja in Badi Mahal. Rajput, Rajasthan at Udaipur, dated 1764

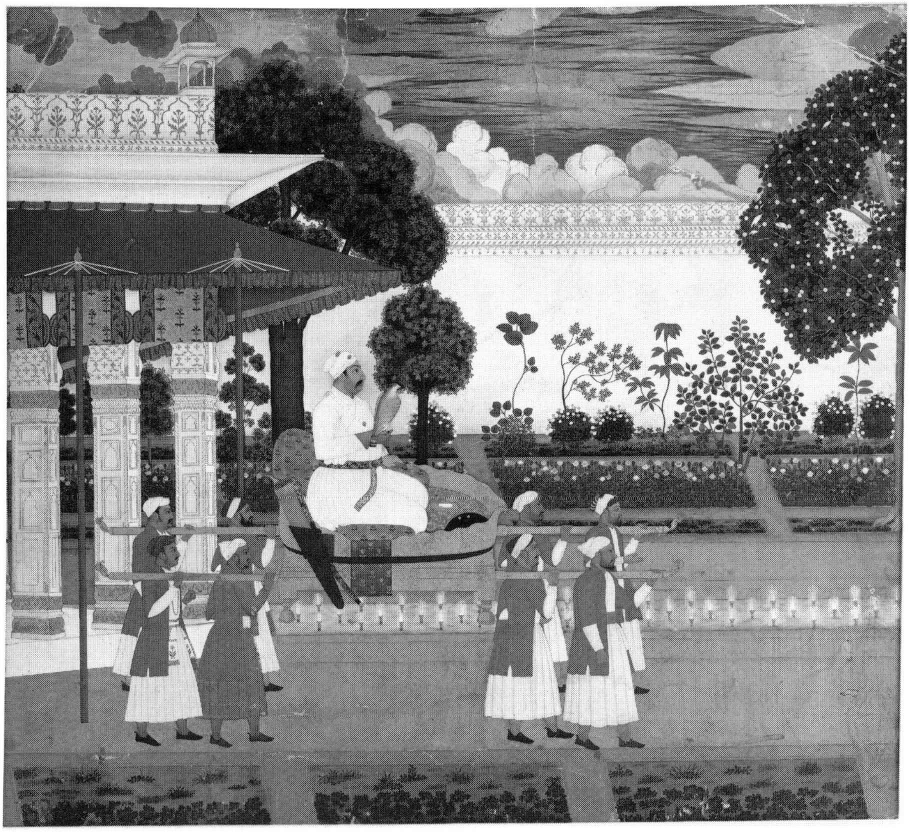

136. Muhammad Shah Viewing a Garden. Mughal, ca. 1735

aspects of the tradition that do change or that betray individual or historically innovative artistic qualities. It is the traditional subjects such as *Ragamalas* that were created in greatest abundance, however; they were the basic and necessary output of the workshops and the importance of the artistic attitudes they illustrate should not be ignored.

A work from the Rathor state of Kishangarh re-evokes (or is derived from) Mughal painting of almost a century earlier. In *Raja Savant Singh of Kishangarh on a Terrace* (fig. 141), the prince stands in a garden seen in bird's-eye view, and while weightless, he is drawn with imperial precision. It is the extremity of his arched back, perhaps, or the angularity of his elbows that gives him a Rajput character. And the work – which should be compared in composition, technique, and mood to *Lovers on a Terrace* (fig. 111) – repays close attention. In the small screened pavilion over the raja's head, one could easily miss the form of a woman watching, and in the doorway to the left there is the

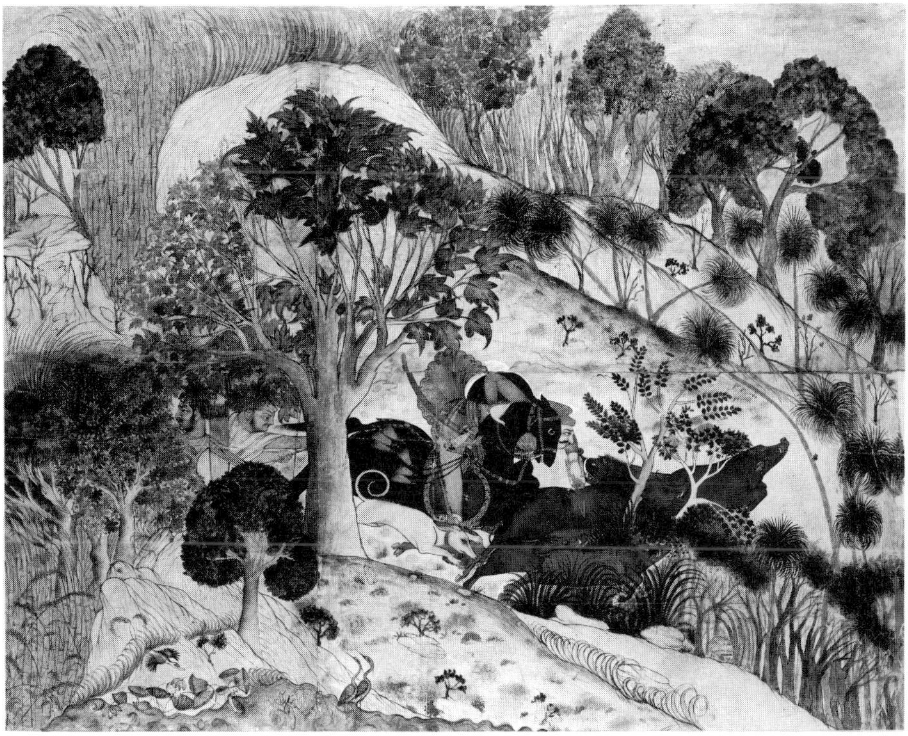

137. Rao Bhoj Singh of Bundi Slays a Boar. Rajput, Rajasthan at Kota, ca. 1740

barest indication of a female profile and the extension of a hand holding a flower. Not a simple portrait, this is a subtle presentation of the physical opulence, romance, and intrigue present at a princely court.

Raja Savant Singh of Kishangarh on a Terrace is inscribed on the reverse with a date given as the "twenty-fifth regnal year of the Emperor Muhammad Shah," equal to 1745. That the Mughal reign date is given instead of the usual Hindu era is further important evidence of Kishangarh's ties to the Mughal court. By the later eighteenth century, the slight formal exaggerations seen in this early work have become a distinctive stylistic mannerism. In *Krishna and Radha* (fig. 142), the sharp profiles, extremely elongated eyes, outlandishly arched backs, or the elegant hair style suggest that the court was intensely conscious of style and fashion. (The strength of the profiles or eyes as shapes, and their formulaic repetition, does evoke attitudes to figures used in the pre-Mughal *Bhagavata Purana* seen in plate B.) These traits – like those distinctive devices used in hunting scenes at Kota – have become specific trademarks of Kishangarh.

Kishangarh was formed as a state in 1613, when lands near Ajmer were granted to Kishan Singh Rathor, a son of Mota Raja Udai Singh (r. 1583–1594) of Jodhpur. The earliest identified paintings from the state are of the late seventeenth century, and include drawings of hunting scenes set in similarly low, wooded hills. By tradition, the greatest patron of painting at Kishangarh was Raja Savant Singh (r. 1748–1764), who under the name of Nagari Das was also an active poet, writing intensely devotional verse in praise of Krishna. His love for a court singer, Bani Thani, became legendary in Rajasthan. The two were often likened to Krishna and Radha, and the affair may have been one inspiration for many of Kishangarh's effusively romantic paintings.

Like Kishangarh, Bikaner was also an offshoot of the Rathor state of Marwar, and its rich and inventive tradition of painting during the seventeenth century has already been mentioned. By 1700, Bikaner artists were producing works fully as elegant and sophisticated as any Mughal painting: colors were subtle and varied, precision of craftsmanship was expressively important, and scenes continually evoked the worldly atmosphere of court life. Even Krishna was painted wearing jewelry and the finest silks. The Bikaner style, however, was also distinctive and unique. Whereas *Raja Savant Singh of Kishangarh on a Terrace* of 1745 differs only minutely from mid seventeenth century Mughal attitudes to naturalism, *A Prince Shooting Herons* (fig. 143), by Ustad Murad and from Bikaner, could never be mistaken for an imperial work. Technically, this is as precisely painted as any seventeenth-century Mughal illustration, yet its color scheme of green, silver, and lilac betrays a taste deeply affected by painting in the Deccan, the source also for the delight in pattern – note especially the herons – and the extreme refinement of the forms and personages portrayed. This is not the real world, but a fantasy realm, and the Deccani link is hardly surprising. Anup Singh (r. 1674–1698) of Bikaner served under the Mughals at Aurangabad, Bijapur, and Golconda, and it was for his bravery at Golconda in 1687 that his rank was raised to that of Maharaja. Bikaner rulers continued to defend imperial policies in the Deccan through the early decades of the eighteenth century.

The most inventive and distinctive period of activity at Bikaner was in the years around 1700, for by the middle of the eighteenth century the technical finesse and unanticipated color combinations of the greatest works had been replaced by a more mainstream pan-Rajasthani style. In later works, it is more frequently details than overall compositions that are most pleasing.

Painting from Amber (later Jaipur) was immensely prolific in the eighteenth century, but it too has been little studied. An important *Ragamala* series is among the most significant documents, for an inscription gives the date of 1709 and names Maharaja Jai Singh (r. 1700–1744) as patron. *Kanhra Ragini* (fig. 144) is from a second but uninscribed *Ragamala* in identical style. It is a highly conservative work, which allows us more easily to identify its source. It

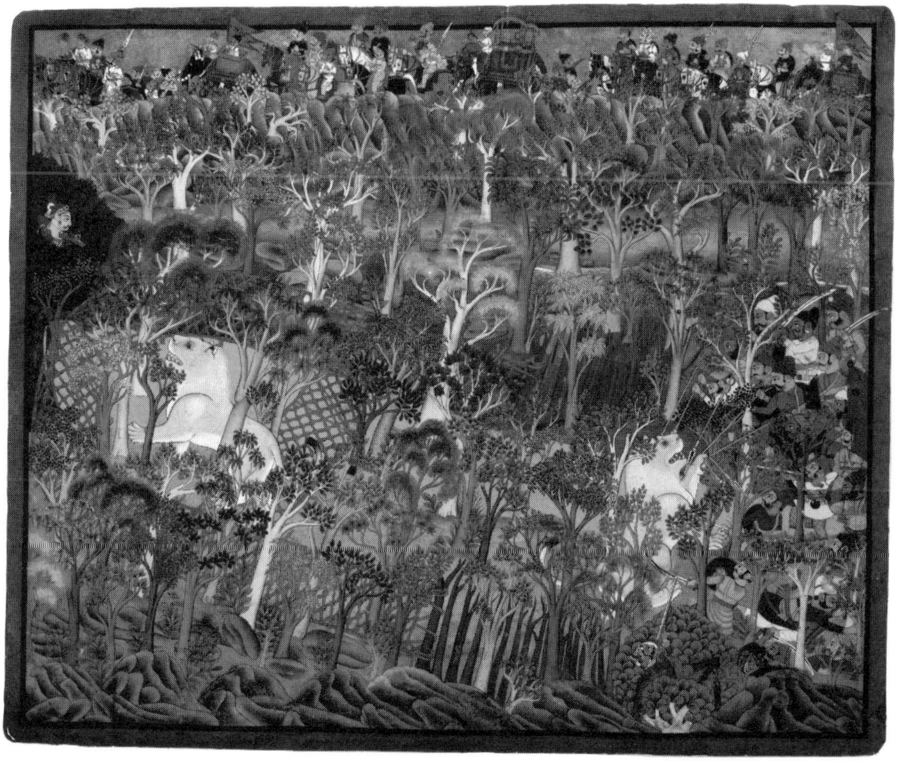

138. Maharao Umed Singh of Kota Hunts a Lion. By Gumani; Rajput, Rajasthan at Kota, dated 1779

derives directly from a well-known *Rasikapriya* series usually dated to about 1630 and heretofore termed "sub-imperial" Mughal.[2] *Sri Raga* (fig. 145), from a closely related set, shows an ascetic and musician performing before a raja. The proportions of the figures are identical to those in *Kanhra Ragini*, and the architecture, too, is almost unchanged – note especially the column brackets. Since architectural experimentation was intense throughout the seventeenth century, this suggests a consistent pictorial tradition connecting the two series, and one in which painters took few liberties. It is very likely, therefore, that the *Rasikapriya* and related works represent early seventeenth-century styles at Amber.

Political power or importance was no guarantee of the originality or vitality of a local style of painting. Artistic excellence was instead completely the result of

[2] Ananda K. Coomaraswamy, *Catalogue of the Indian Collections at the Museum of Fine Arts, Boston, Part VI: Mughal Painting*, Cambridge (Mass.), 1930, nos. X–XXXVIII.

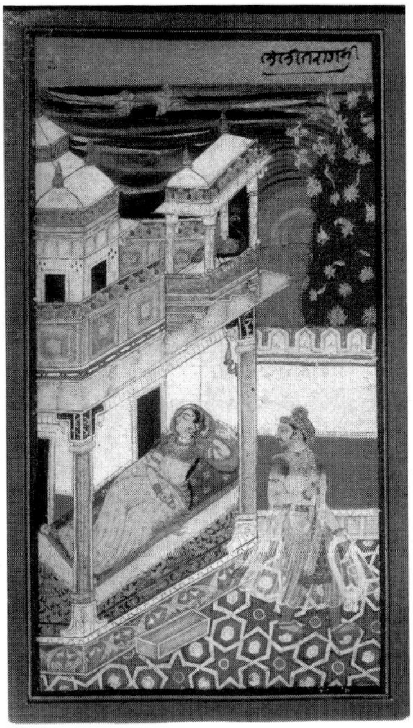

139. Lalita ragini. From a *Ragamala* series, Rajput, Rajasthan at Kota, ca. 1680

the personal interest of a patron, of the availability of good artists, and of the chemistry between painter and patron – often combined with the strength of a continuing local tradition. So far we have been discussing only works that can be located to major ruling states, but our assumption that the rulers themselves were inevitably the only patrons is often supposition; more information is needed. Certainly some smaller states and subservient landholders (the equivalent of barons, perhaps) were also highly active patrons.

The tiny state of Sawar, near Ajmer, for example, produced a superb series of paintings between the late seventeenth and early nineteenth centuries, although the early and late phases are in quite separate, seemingly unrelated styles. In each case, the works are attributable to the state because of portrait inscriptions naming known rulers.

Raj Singh of Sawar Visiting a Yogi in a Garden (fig. 146) presents one of the rulers, together with attendant nobles and musicians, meeting with a holy man. It is dated by inscription to 1714, and shows the taste for sketches or lightly colored compositions that we have already seen during these same years at Udaipur and Kota. Many works attributable to this same (anonymous) artist are known, and all present similarly uncluttered, childlike compositions. This simplicity allies the work to folk or village art traditions, or at least to types of painting that did not seek (or were not able) to impress by richness of

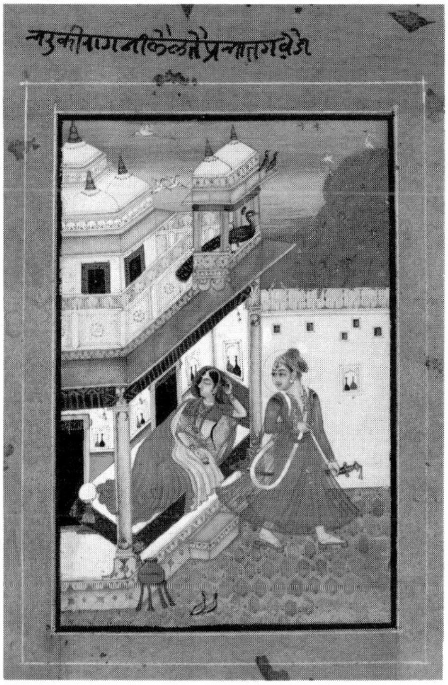

140. Lalita ragini. From a *Ragamala* series, Rajput, Rajasthan at Kota, ca. 1760

materials or workmanship. An example is *Rama Enthroned with Sita, Lakshman, and Hanuman* (fig. 147), from a *Ramayana* series dated 1723. Lacking the refined draftsmanship of the Sawar portrait, it is nonetheless a lively work more closely allied in spirit to the Sawar court scene than to paintings from the major Rajput courts.

The later Sawar style related to the artist Pemji, and extends over about two decades beginning in 1780. His works, fully painted, show the lively informal character of this unpretentious court, where nobles tuck flowers into their turbans and nap under shrubs. *A Wild Party in a Garden* (fig. 148) shows Kunvar Ajit Singh at Raj Bagh and has almost every person neatly labelled – a trait of Pemji's work. Figures often appear several times, for it is a cluster of events rather than a single moment that is being recorded. Like *The Emperor Visits Tulsi Das* (plate L), the surface is organized into compartments, and the color is bright and strong. It is a much less sophisticated work artistically, however, for the definition of the forms is rough and basic – but therein lies the painting's power. Like his unknown earlier predecessor at Sawar, Pemji is also able to create brilliant patterns which are both uncomplicated and unpredictable, and the directness of the work is a revitalization of the original Rajput aesthetic.

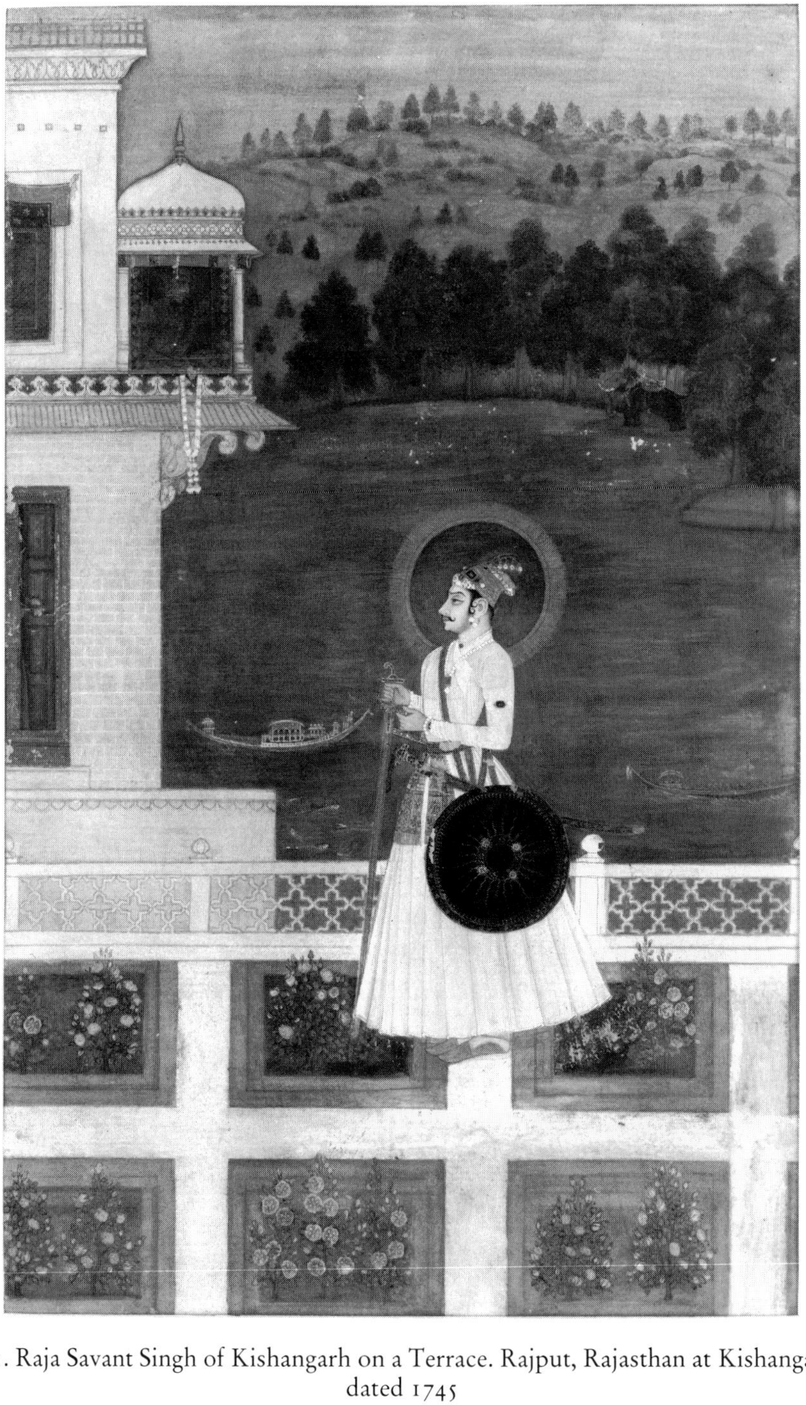

141. Raja Savant Singh of Kishangarh on a Terrace. Rajput, Rajasthan at Kishangarh, dated 1745

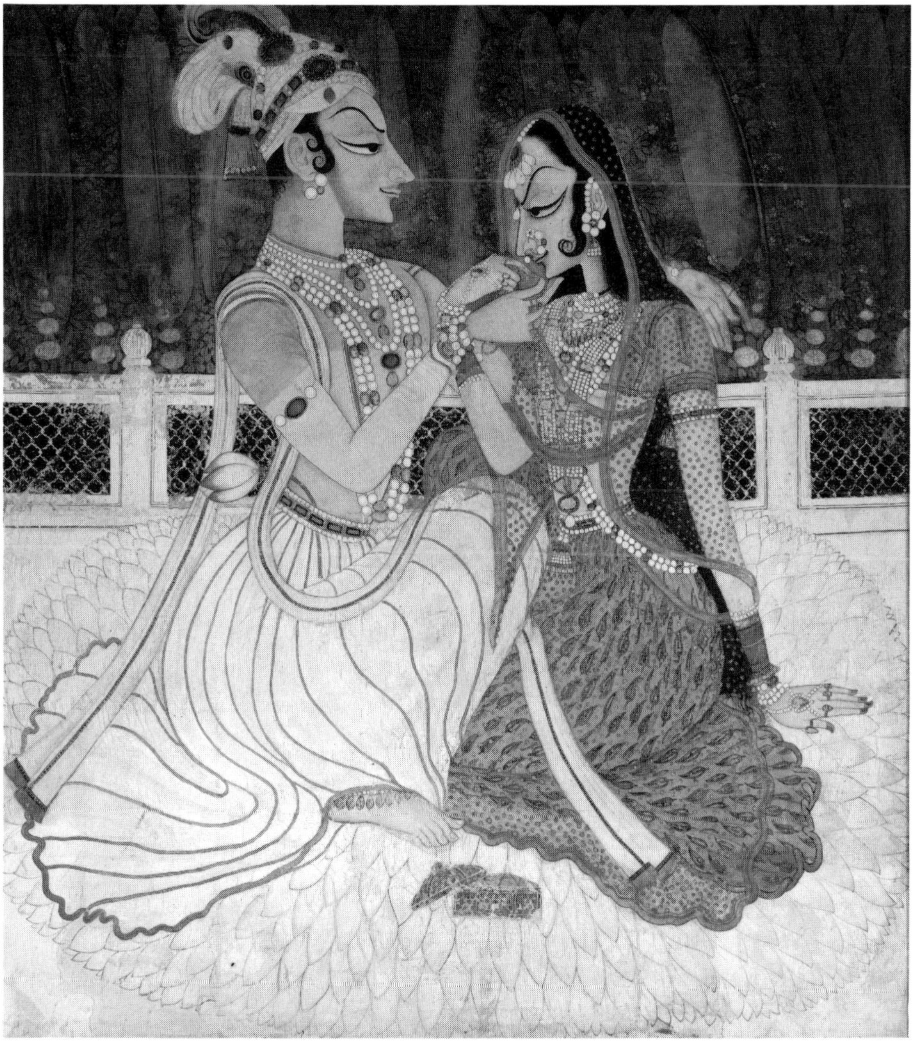

142. Krishna and Radha. Rajput, Rajasthan at Kishangarh, late eighteenth century

There is no evidence of patronage between these two flourishings of painting at Sawar, however, and no transitional style. The concept of a consistent, ongoing local style, therefore, is irrelevant. It is only when workshops were of sufficient size and when patronage was continuous that stylistic continuity becomes an important factor.

In many ways, there is greater stylistic unity and direction among the various schools of painting at courts in the Punjab Hills, but here there were different factors at work. The first important dated pahari series in the eighteenth century illustrates the *Gita Govinda* (Song of the Lord), a devotional poem to Krishna. Unlike the 1695 *Rasamanjari* by Devidasa mentioned earlier, no provenance is given in the inscription in this particular copy.

The *Gita Govinda* text, written in Sanskrit by the twelfth-century poet Jayadeva, is among the most sensuous of all Hindu devotional works, and celebrates Krishna's amorous adventures with the women (gopis) of Brindaban. The poem is historically important too, for it consolidates changes in the attitude towards Krishna that had occurred over the preceding two or three centuries. It stresses his role as the archetypal lover or Beloved, for whom the gopis forsake their husbands, children, and family responsibilities – just as one must abandon all worldly ties to be united to the Divine. The fervancy of the devotional sentiment expressed in these verses is deeply rooted in Hindu India, where erotic and sexual imagery has always held great importance.

Radha and a Confidante (plate M) places Krishna's beloved in an intensely beautiful spring landscape at dusk, and she discusses the god with someone to whom she can speak with complete freedom. The setting describes physical beauty and the time of day suggests pleasures to come, but the effect is nonetheless of controlled rather than uncontrolled passion. The uninhibited emotions of the earliest *Rasamanjari* paintings (for example figs. 128 and 149) have here been tamed and civilized; and because two of the key series in the stylistic sequence established by these first pahari works are dated (1694 and 1730), it can be implied that the difference is, at least partially, chronological.

An inscription on the *Gita Govinda* cites the painter Manaku, who in other sources is termed Manaku of Guler. He was a son of Pandit Seu, a Guler native, and elder brother to Nainsukh, an artist to whom we shall later and continually refer. Guler was therefore his family home, although this is no evidence of where the *Gita Govinda* was painted. That there are so few signed or dated pahari pictures, forces scholars to examine or justify carefully any attributions that are made. In turn, we are led to question why the situation here is different than in Rajasthan, where there is copious contemporary inscriptional documentation; what this might tell us about the character of the patronage; and whether the establishment of provenances provides us with as significant information as it does in other Rajput areas.

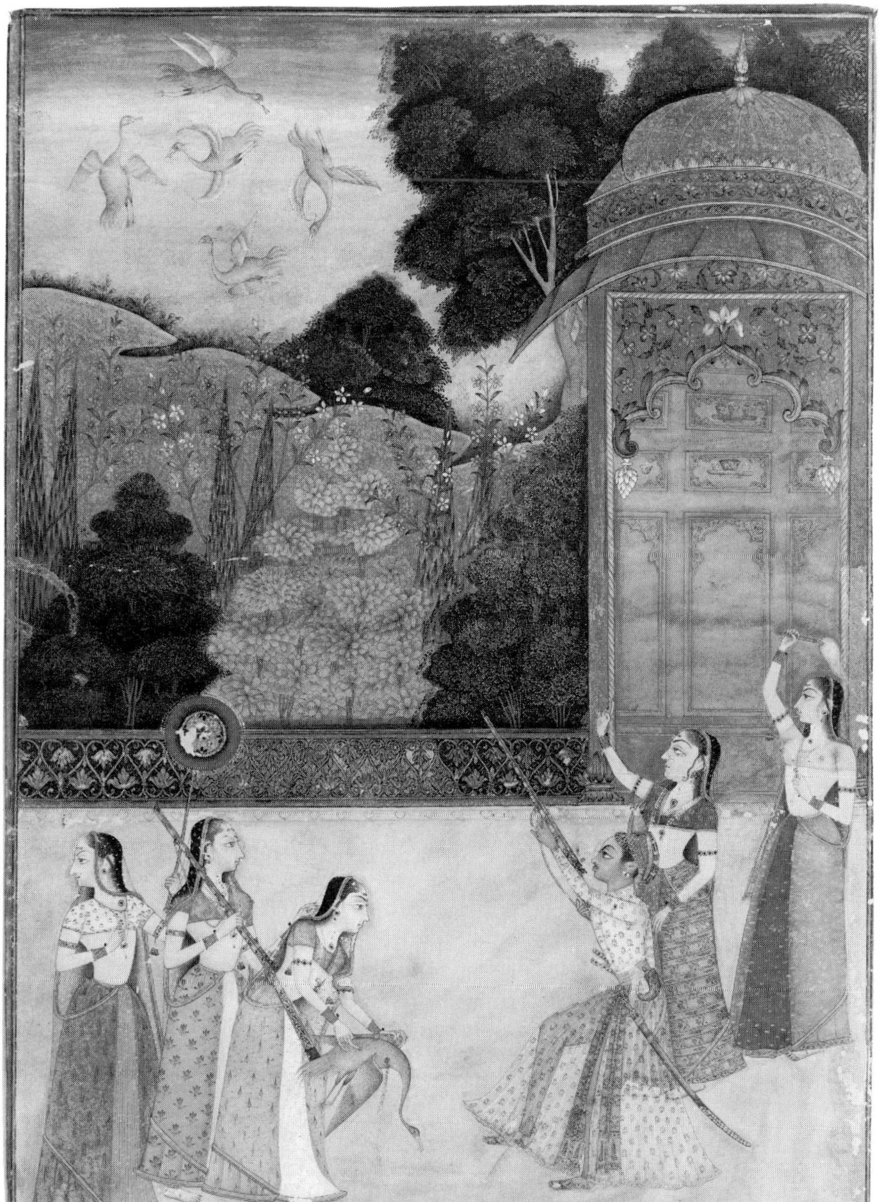

143. A Prince Shooting Herons. By Ustad Murad; Rajput, Rajasthan at Bikaner, dated 1701

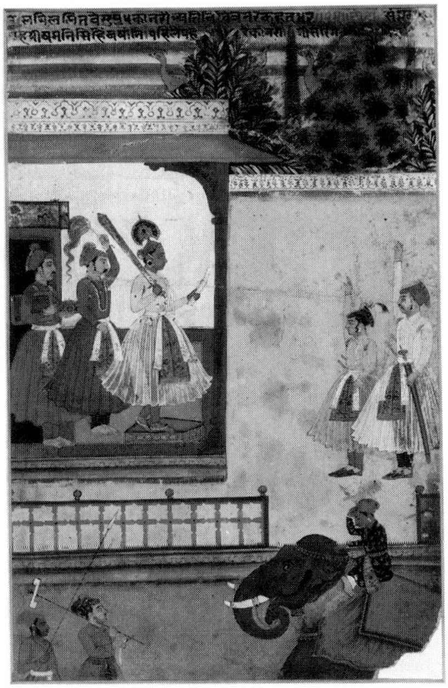

144. Kanhra Ragini. From a *Ragamala* series, Rajput, Rajasthan at Amber, ca. 1710

There is a generic development in pahari painting that should be outlined, to provide a framework for further discussion. This can be done by comparing four hill pictures, dating from the mid seventeenth to the mid eighteenth centuries and not necessarily from one workshop tradition. The first, *Satha Nayaka* (fig. 149) comes from the circa 1660–1670 *Rasamanjari*. Its style has been discussed (see page 168). In subject and basic composition it is similar to *Lovers on a Terrace* (fig. 111), the Mughal portrait of about 1633. Both works stress emotion and mood. The styles, however, are totally different, and this points out important characteristics of both traditions. Whereas the imperial work is dulcet and gentle, the Rajput painting is unrestrained and impassioned. Balchand's couple gaze quietly and deeply at each other, whereas the Rajput lovers are in a trance, as if possessed by the onrush of their desire. There is attention to detail (bolsters, bottles, the textures of fabrics) in the Mughal work, while the *Rasamanjari* uses light and color to heighten the emotions, not to describe surfaces. The background in the pahari scene is solid, framing and intensifying our concentration on the couple, whereas *Lovers on a Terrace* diffuses our focus by opening up a vast expanse of empty space. Quiet, and a slow delectation of objects and emotions or line and color, is contrasted in the Mughal image to clear, vivid expressions and gestures, and emotional turbulence in the Rajput work.

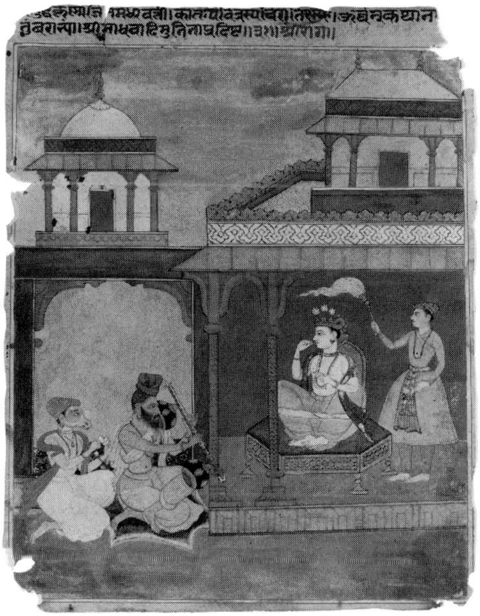

145. Sri Raga. From a *Ragamala* series, probably Rajput, Rajasthan at Amber, ca. 1630

The second pahari painting is *Ahiri Ragini* (fig. 150), from a *Ragamala* of circa 1710. The composition is simpler than in *Satha Nayaka*, and less dramatic. The work depicts a woman passing the time waiting for her lover by feeding milk to cobras, their twisting and writhing bodies mirroring her own emotional turmoil. Nonetheless, the faces here are less intense, but this is not a qualitative comparison. Both works are strong, vital paintings; but the profiles are less angular, and the eyes not as wildly expressive.

Lady Bathing (fig. 151), of about 1740, is a further development. Colors are now truly muted. The background, for example, is a neutral tan, as if the artist had wished to reduce the impact and strength of the earlier backgrounds without knowing yet what to put in their place, and the women wear clothing of pink and lilac – colors more familiar from Deccani works than from antecedent hill traditions. The figures, finely and exactly painted, are self-consciously graceful, drawn with long, curving lines quite different from the relatively angular outlines of the *Rasamanjari* or even the *Ragamala* figure. A comparison of faces in the three illustrations shows how much more delicately the features are drawn in later works; note especially the hairlines.

All of these trends culminate in *Vilaval Ragini* (fig. 152). Datable to about 1770, the bodily proportions and textures are more visually naturalistic.

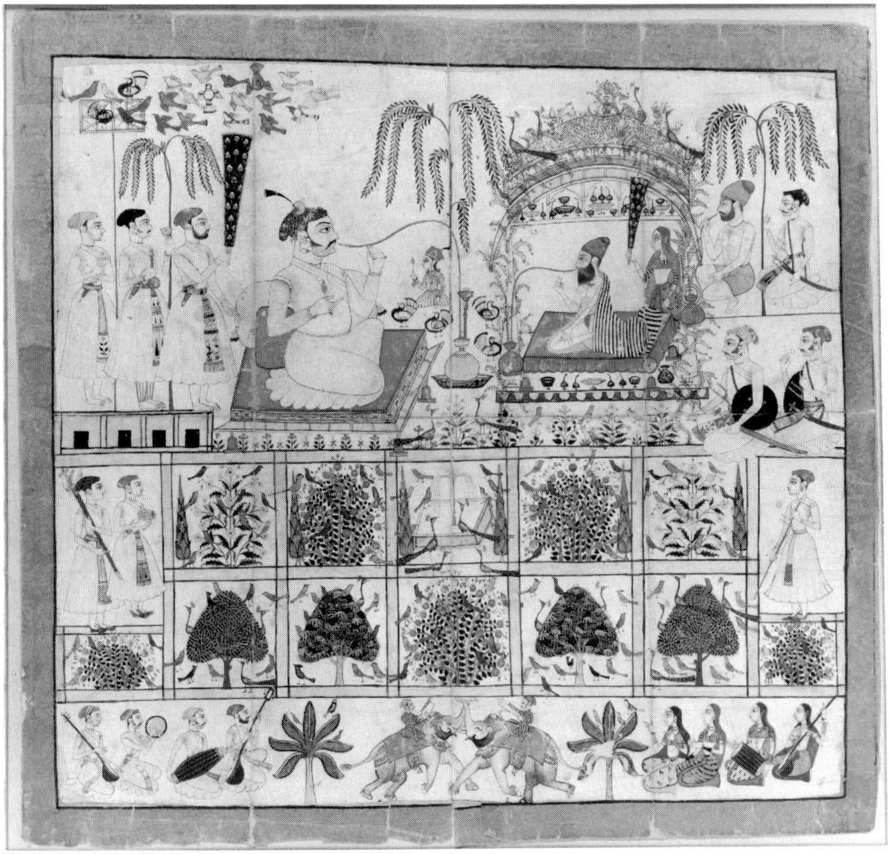

146. Raj Singh of Sawar Visiting a Yogi in a Garden. Rajput, Rajasthan at Sawar, dated 1714

Gestures are graceful, and faces, convincingly natural, reveal very human emotions. The background, with figures and forms diminishing in size according to distance, is carefully descriptive, and certainly indebted to Mughal style. When compared to *Satha Nayaka* (fig. 149), at the beginning of this developmental sequence, one sees that the painters' intentions have dramatically changed. *Vilaval Ragini* is clearly much closer to the Mughal *Lovers on a Terrace* (fig. 111) in both mood and style. Yet it could never be mistaken for a second work by Balchand, where every element stresses the physical characteristics of the subject. The cloth of the Mughal work has the texture of real fabric, whereas in the Rajput painting the long lines of the skirts are a visual metaphor for the gracefulness of cloth, rather than a description of how it falls.

The most dramatic change in the sequence, which shows a steady replacement of the passion and wildness of pure Rajput taste by Mughal refinement

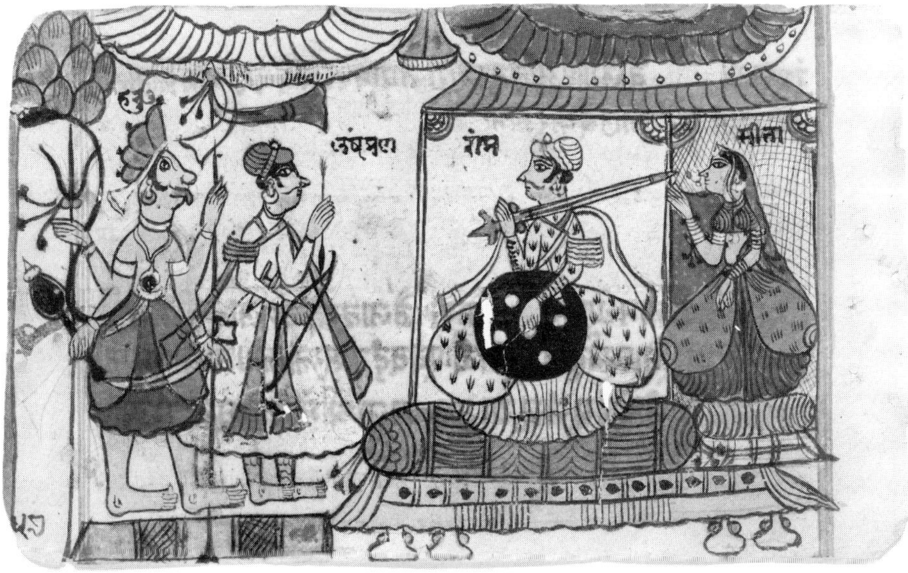

147. Rama Enthroned with Sita, Lakshman, and Hanuman. From a *Ramayana* series, Rajasthan, Jodhpur area, dated 1723

and elegance, occurs after 1740, with the intense, and new, interest in naturalism and convincingly organic representations of personalities and physical appearance. It is an important change, and one which lamentably sweeps away the barbaric splendor of the earlier style.

The development of portraiture in the hills further refines our understanding of these changes. Early pahari portraits tend to show individual figures arranged into strongly defined abstract shapes, and painted in solid, bright colors. In *Raja Medini Pal of Basohli* (fig. 153), the seated ruler (who ruled between 1722 and 1736) is enormous, out of scale with both the architecture and the attendant figure at the right; his face, and the architecture, are only a slight modification of the formulas used in the seventeenth-century *Rasamanjari* series. He holds a lotus bud in one hand and a huqqa stem in the other, its shape strong enough to balance visually the raja at the left. It is a work made powerful by its distortions, and this style has long been identified with the Basohli court.

A quite different portrait tradition can be examined through the works of the painter Nainsukh, brother of Manaku. His studies of a Raja Balwant Singh are among the most sympathetic of all Rajput portraits. The ruler is shown in innumerable and routine daily events: inspecting a horse, listening to musicians, having his beard trimmed, writing a letter, preparing himself for bed. Presented as a gentle, rather lonely man, he observes but seldom interacts

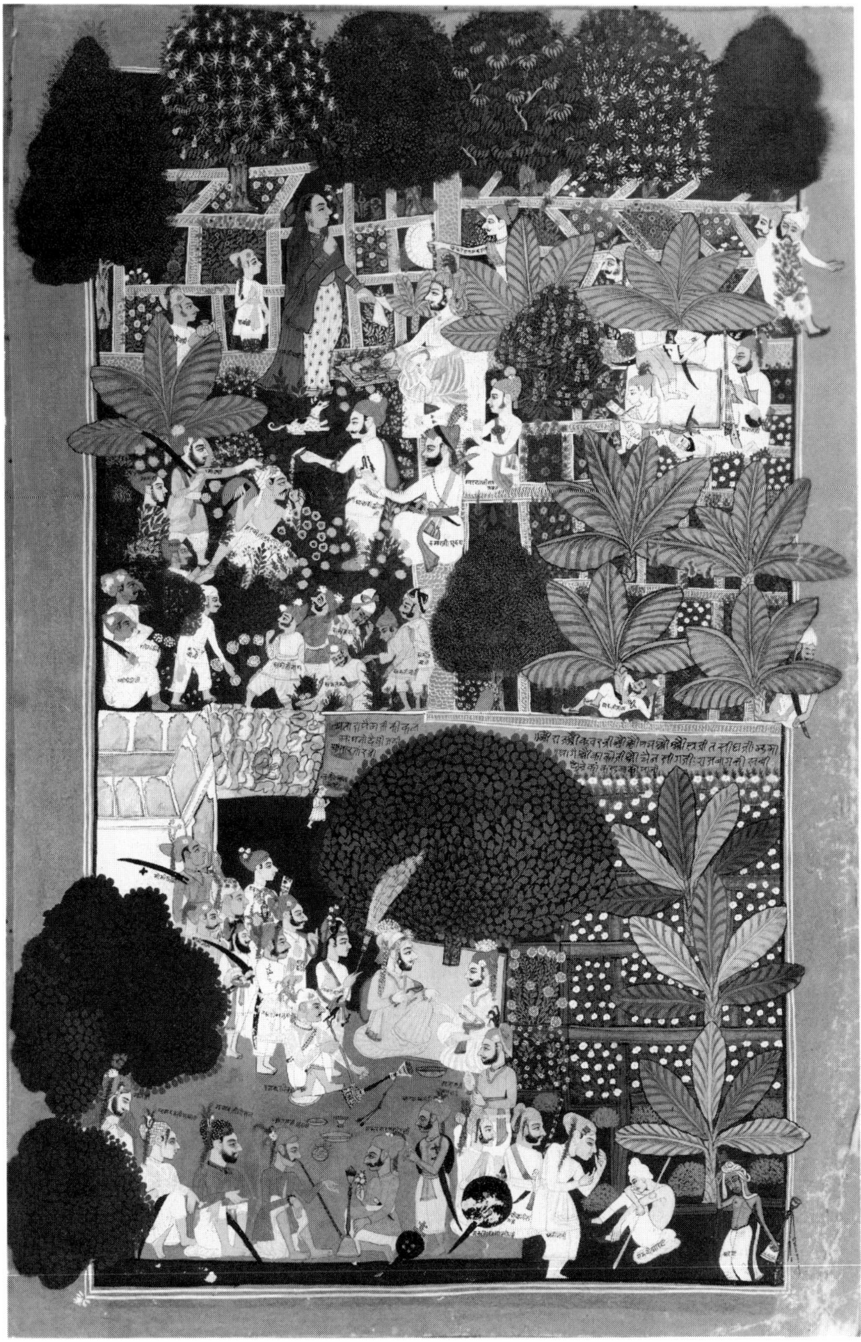

148. A Wild Party in a Garden. By Pemji. Rajput, Rajasthan at Sawar, ca. 1780

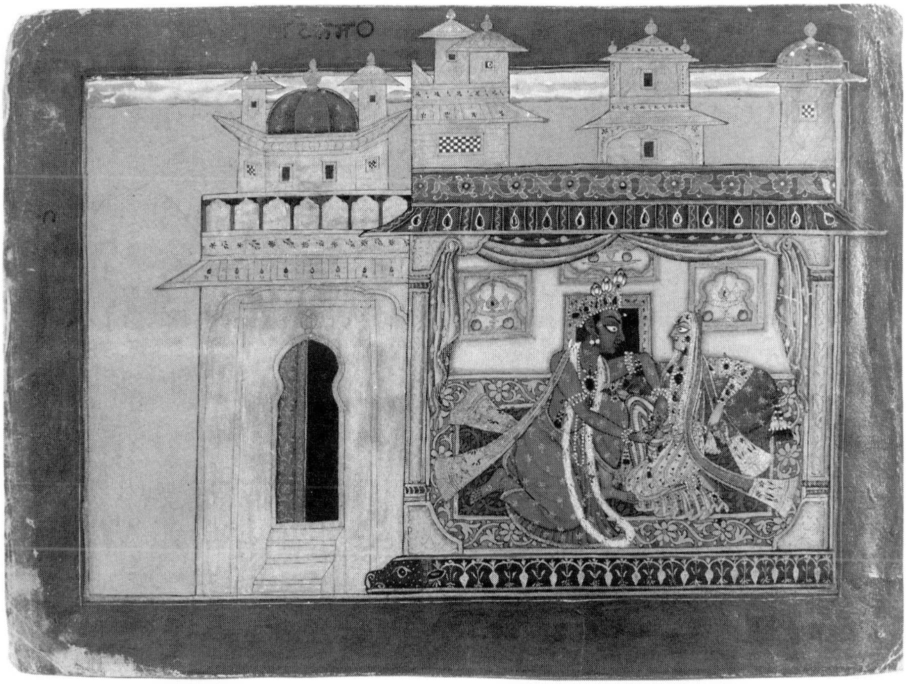

149. Satha Nayaka. From a *Rasamanjari* series, Rajput, Punjab Hills, ca. 1660–1670

with those around him. His rapport with Nainsukh, however, was such that together – painter and patron – they helped transform painting throughout the pahari region.

Raja Balwant Singh Performing His Toilet Before Retiring (plate N), by Nainsukh, has none of the manipulations of scale, form, or color found in *Raja Medini Pal of Basohli*. It is an obviously controlled, carefully assembled illustration, dominated by the three evenly spaced archways of a building seen from the front. This formality forces us to be acutely conscious of any variations in the basic symmetry (such as the patterns of the *jalis*, or pierced screens), while the white walls set off the shapes and patterns of such details as the striped curtains. The presentation of architecture, architectural decoration (including textiles), and human beings in the Balwant Singh scene is factually justifiable. Unlike the *Rasamanjari* series, where architecture is simply a setting to coordinate the colors and shapes that might best heighten the mood of the situation, this is a highly informative scene. It is a specific palace building.

Nainsukh's style is a dramatic shift from works of a generation earlier, or even from the 1730 *Gita Govinda* (plate M), painted by his brother Manaku. While Manaku's style evolved from earlier Basohli traditions, the portraits of Balwant Singh reveal nothing of that initial Basohli manner. The closest

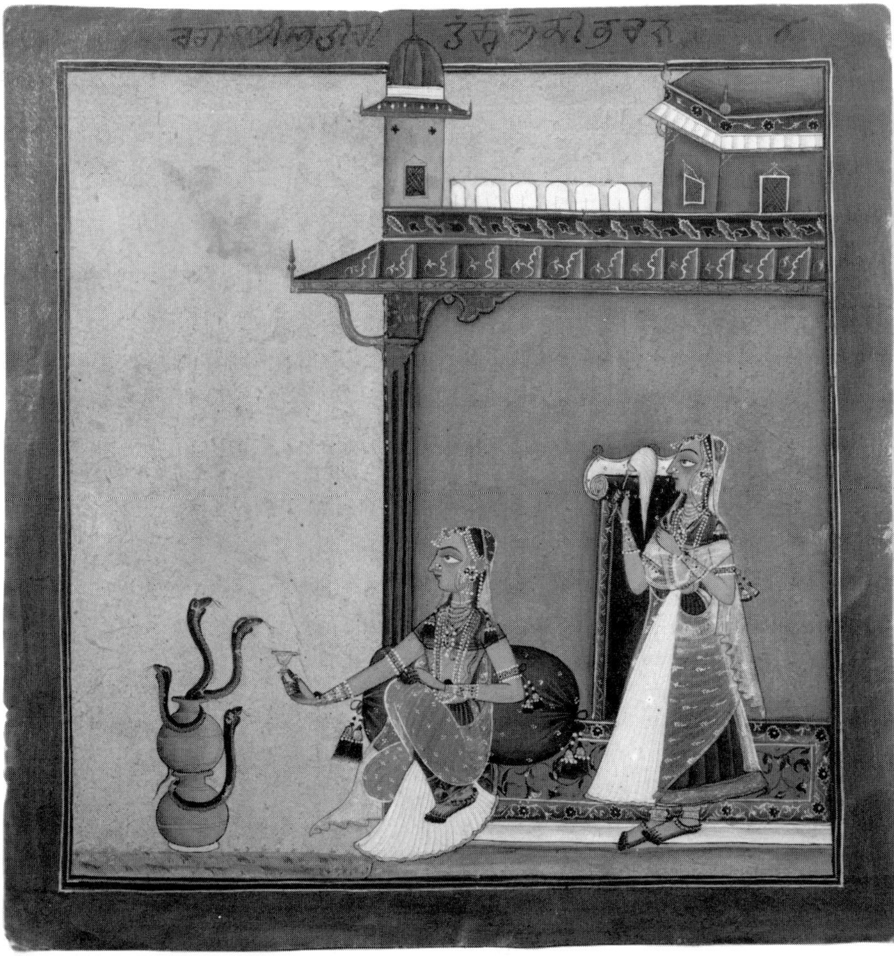

150. Ahiri ragini. From a *Ragamala* series, Rajput, Punjab Hills, ca. 1710

stylistic parallel is not from the hills at all, in fact, but from the Mughal court. *Muhammad Shah with Courtiers* (plate O) is also organized around broad architectural areas which emphasize the patterns of hanging fabrics, formal figural arrangements, and portraiture. *Muhammad Shah Viewing a Garden* (fig. 136), discussed earlier, is equally comparable for its precise patterning, and for areas of bright color carefully isolated against a white background, characteristics important also to Nainsukh's style.

The brief re-emergence of an important imperial portrait tradition under the Emperor Muhammad Shah (r. 1719–1748) cannot be predicted by the few known Mughal paintings of the earlier eighteenth century. Nor are there any stylistic traits to separate these imperial images from works made for Hindu

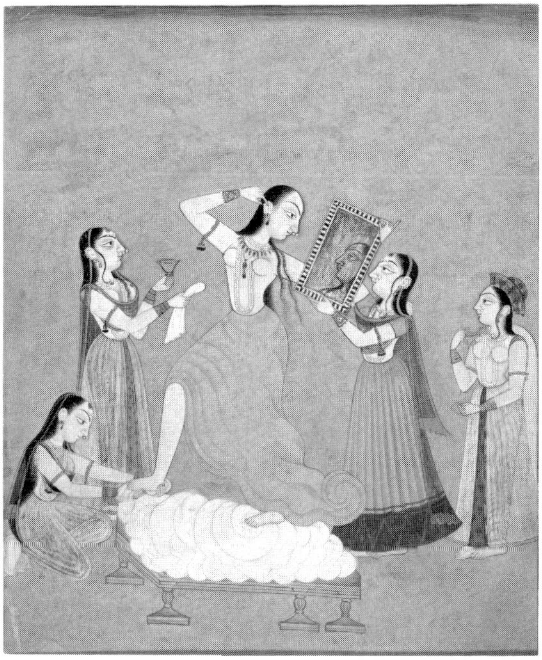

151. Lady Bathing. Rajput, Punjab Hills, ca. 1740

rulers. It seems probable that the emperor's personal interest in the arts led him to revitalize the imperial workshops by hiring painters whose talents might otherwise have found appropriate outlet at a Rajput court. The comparability of paintings for Muhammad Shah and those of Nainsukh is therefore not – as sometimes suggested – proof of renewed Mughal influence on Rajput painting, but simply evidence that both traditions now drew from a common vocabulary and sensitivity.

Balwant Singh almost certainly lived in the hill state of Jasrota. When the prince died, the painter took employment at Basohli with Raja Amrit Pal (r. 1757–circa 1778) until his own death in 1778. Nainsukh had four sons and Manaku two, and painting was the family profession. There is firm evidence that other family members were eventually employed at Basohli, Chamba, Guler, Jammu, and Kangra – and many additional hill states also supported Pandit Seu's offspring. Each of the artists had been trained initially in a common family style, for even Manaku eventually adopted his brother's manner. This family style, therefore, spread throughout the hills, and there is no other comparably influential painter family known in either the pahari area or Rajasthan. B. N. Goswamy – upon whose research this knowledge is based – has argued that the specific geographic provenance of the paintings they made is therefore of little significance; that a painting made at Basohli by one family

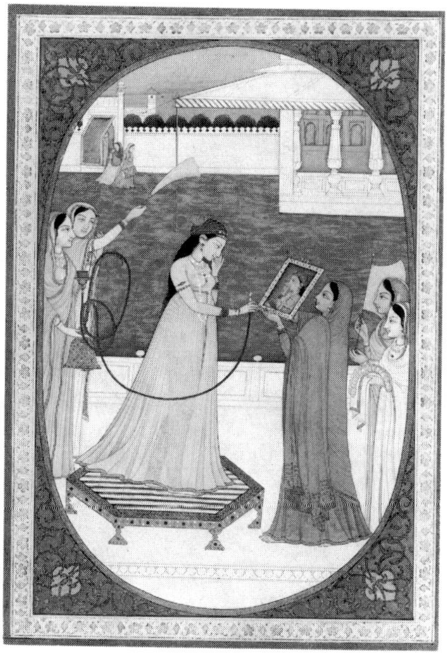

152. Vilaval Ragini. From a *Ragamala* series, Rajput, Punjab Hills, ca. 1770

member is more like a painting from Kangra by a cousin than either would be to works by artists from different families working in the same state. This does not preclude there being consistent, parallel local styles as well, however.

The *Gita Govinda* of 1730 (plate M), by Manaku and his assistants, represents the most advanced pahari style of its time, a role played by Nainsukh's portraits (plate N) about a decade later. Several works help define this important transitional period, in which we see older artists struggling with, and then mastering, the new manner so effortlessly adopted and developed by the young Nainsukh. *Samvara Receives the Fish* (fig. 154), from a *Bhagavata Purana* series, can be attributed to Manaku about 1750. The architecture here manages to be both specific and spacious, and the faces are far more carefully modelled and expressive than those in Manaku's earlier *Gita Govinda*. This *Bhagavata Purana* series has a large number of illustrations; other pages from the series are close to the 1730 *Gita Govinda* in style, while a further group is almost fully in the Nainsukh manner. It is the most important single work for defining the historical evolution of hill painting between 1730 and 1760, and it seems to indicate that the stylistic changes it charts were the result of Nainsukh's influence.

A shrewdly observant and humorous illustration, *Dancing Villagers* (fig. 155), is also a transitional work. The characterizations are witty, and

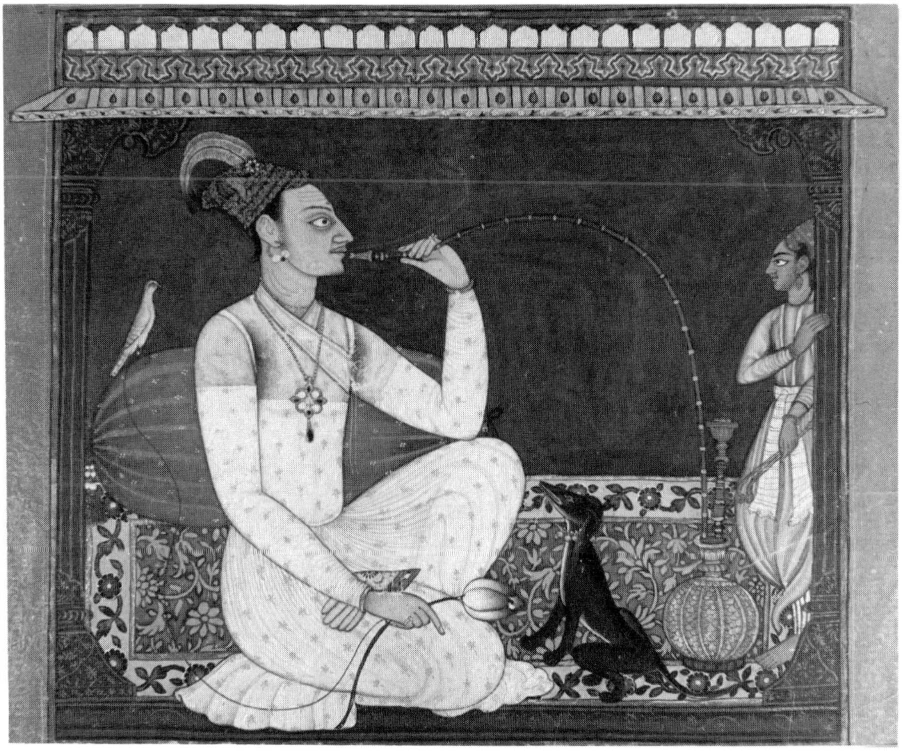

153. Raja Medini Pal of Basohli. Rajput, Punjab Hills at Basohli, ca. 1730

almost certainly based on actual people; their personalities and their interrelationships are important expressive elements of the work. Were it not for a solid, burnished red background, and a narrow band indicating sky at the top, this work would have seemed totally independent of the earlier *Rasamanjari* style. Only further study will isolate the sources of the innovations by which Nainsukh so transformed pahari painting. One drawing by the artist, *Incident During a Hunt* (fig. 156), has so many stylistic and narrative parallels with imperial Mughal works of the earlier seventeenth century that Mughal contacts with the hill regions must be better understood.[3]

The fully mature pahari style of the later eighteenth century is recognizable in a large series of *Nala-Damayanti* drawings, named for a hero and heroine whose love story they narrate. These several preparatory illustrations would eventually have been fully colored, had the series been completed. B. N.

[3] See A. A. Ivanova, O. F. Ashmushkina, T. Grek, and L. T. Gyuzalyana, *Albom Indiyskikh i Persidskikh Miniatyur XV–XVIII v.v.*, Moscow, 1962, nos. 64 and 65; or f. 134v in the Windsor Castle *Padshahnama* (unpublished).

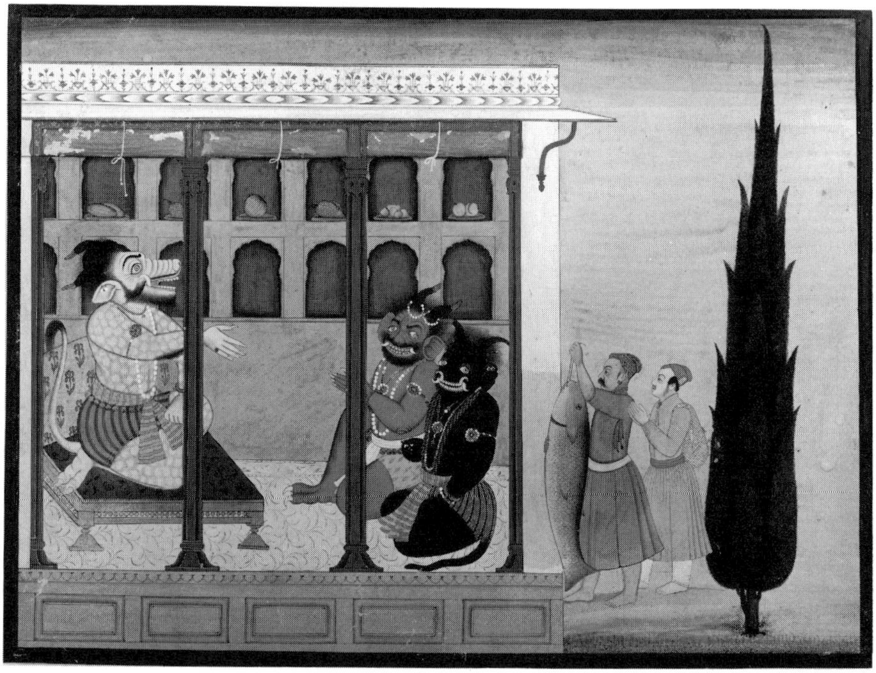

154. Samvara Receives the Fish. From a *Bhagavata Purana* series, Rajput, Punjab Hills, ca. 1750

Goswamy has extensively studied the works, and considered their relationship to a group of preliminary sanguine ink drawings (*namoonas*). These latter are from an earlier stage of the same project, and are the initial plans for the final compositions. What is of major interest in Goswamy's study is his discovery that written notes on the surface record the reactions of Hindu pandits, religious and linguistic scholars who examined the compositions to make sure that the important details of the text were properly emphasized before final versions were copied. It is evidence of the continuing importance of painting as the accurate illustration of established texts, or as a devotional rather than simply artistic activity.

The Departure of Damayanti for Nisadha (fig. 157) illustrates the moment when the new bride leaves her own home for that of her husband. Like *Balwant Singh Performing His Toilet Before Retiring* (plate N), this is a picture full of information about an actual – or seemingly actual – event. The weeping women following the palanquin, the elderly man (at the lower right) clearing the gateway for the procession, the man rolling aside the cloth enclosure so that the women might leave, all place the mythical event within the world of a contemporary Rajput court. Here is a visual declaration that the world of gods and the world of men are identical.

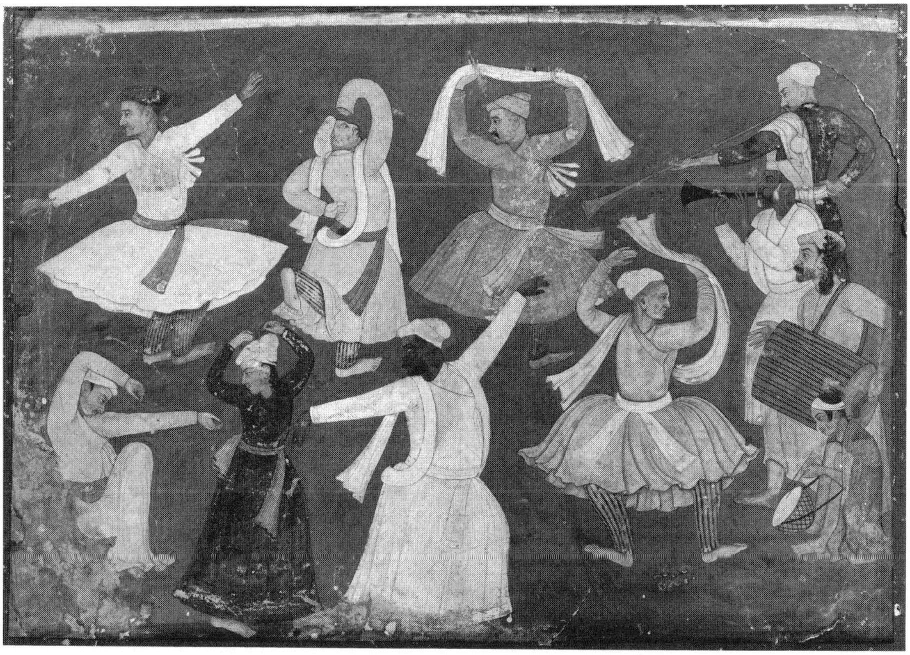

155. Dancing Villagers. Rajput, Punjab Hills, ca. 1730

The Departure of Damayanti for Nisadha is spatially far more complex than any previous pahari illustration. Elephants, chariots, and men on foot all cover a distant hillside and carry Damayanti's wedding gifts to her new home. The figures also diminish in scale as they recede in depth. The clear movement of the procession of women across the page is even more complicated. Having come through an arched doorway into a screened courtyard, they are about to enter a gateway through which a group of men is already passing – some of them visible in rear view. No longer a screen or frame for figures, architecture is an active participant in the scene.

Another *Bhagavata Purana* may be the greatest of all the later pahari series, for it reinterprets a favorite text using new stylistic developments. *The Gopis Search for Krishna* (fig. 158) shows a moment when the god has disappeared from the banks of the Ganges, and the gopis, his romantic partners, go in search of him. The series is perhaps most notable for its landscape scenes, which develop further the use of nature in the *Nala-Damayanti* drawings (although not the example reproduced here). The trees, the extraordinary blossoming branches, and even the riverbank are as graceful as the gestures of the women. There is nothing unruly here. Everything in the picture tells of the seductive beauty of Krishna's world.

In *The Death of Putana* (fig. 159), datable to about 1800, landscape has been

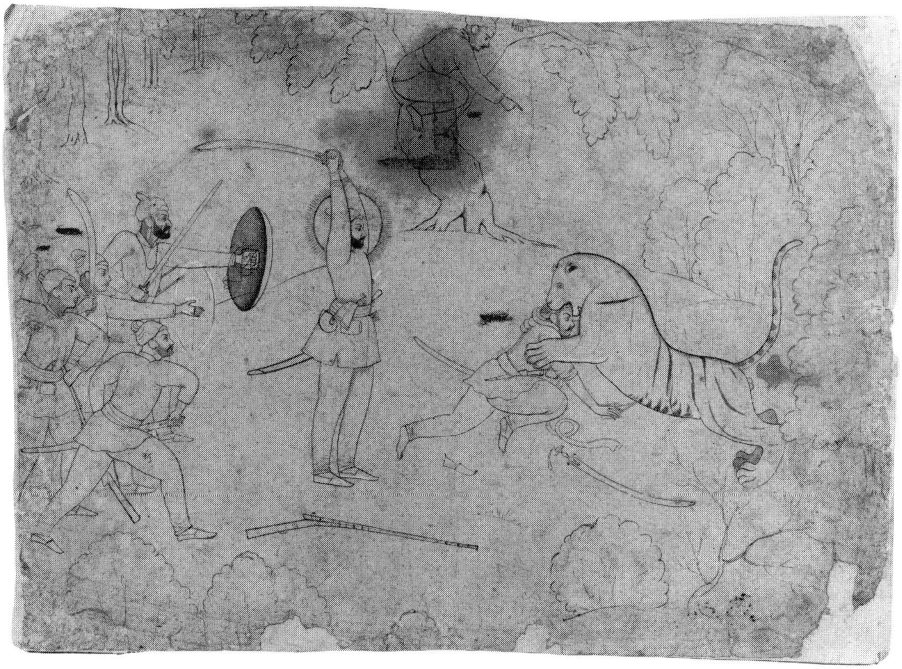

156. Incident During a Hunt. Attributed to Nainsukh; Rajput, Punjab Hills at Jasrota, ca. 1750–1755

reduced to a single tree – although one which follows the formula developed in *The Gopis Search for Krishna*. The ladies and children are a familiar cast of characters and, since they represent general types, appear in many later hill paintings. Here they are formed into a tightly interwoven series of surface rhythms; there is no background to distract us. The lines of the arms at the right evoke a virtual aureole around Krishna and the demoness whose poisoned breasts he sucks, for example. The forms of her body and clothing create richly rewarding shapes, expressive of her torment and agony as Krishna pulls the life from her body.

In later pahari painting, the grace and sweetness of expression which is so remarkable in such illustrations as *The Gopis Search for Krishna* also becomes as much a formula as the shapes used to define people or the landscape. A trait initially delightful for its freshness thus becomes cloying, unless relieved – as it is in *The Death of Putana* – by visual complexity. This development is still within the tradition established by Nainsukh, and works in the later stages of the style are signed by, or still attributable to, his descendants.

Painting in the Kulu region, if we accept the traditional provenance for *The Gods are Born as Monkeys* (fig. 131), was closely related to the Basohli style in

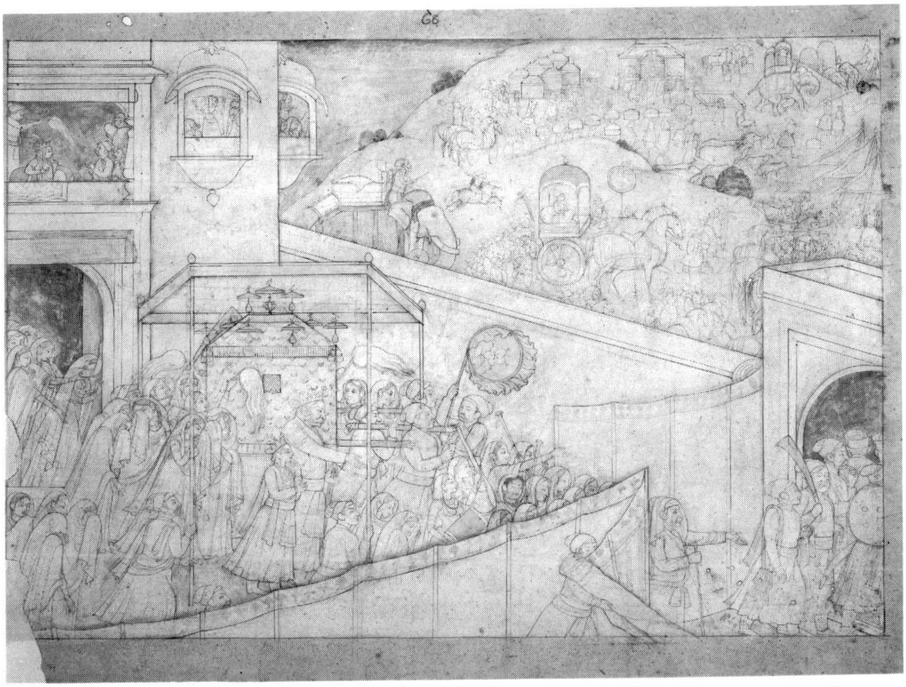

157. The Departure of Damayanti for Nisadha. From a *Nala-Damayanti* series, Rajput, Punjab Hills, ca. 1780

the early seventeenth century, although with a strong individual character, especially in figure types. By the late eighteenth century, Kulu artists were adapting the mainstream pahari style, again giving it a unique character. *The Insects Attack* (fig. 160) illustrates an episode in a *Madhu-Malati* series dated 1799. The flat pattern made by the figures provides an even, abstract rhythm; it bears no relation to spatial relationships experienced visually. Colors, too, are flat and unshaded. The impact of the work lies in its simplicity and directness – once again a reassertion of the earliest and most potent Rajput artistic values.

Painting at nearby Mandi adopted the metropolitan hill style during the reign of Raja Isvari Singh (r. 1788–1826). The majority of works painted in the state during the eighteenth century are rough, almost folk-level illustrations, however. *Shiva* (fig. 161) places the grey-skinned god against a neutral background. The figure is almost caricatured, as in a child's drawing. There is nothing elegant here, nothing consciously made beautiful for its own sake. It is instead a broadly, almost crudely, humorous and highly expressive work, full of rich visual contrasts. The Shiva is pot-bellied and silly, as if the painter were purposely avoiding grace and sweetness, the cliches of pahari style – rather an accomplishment considering how pervasive they were to become.

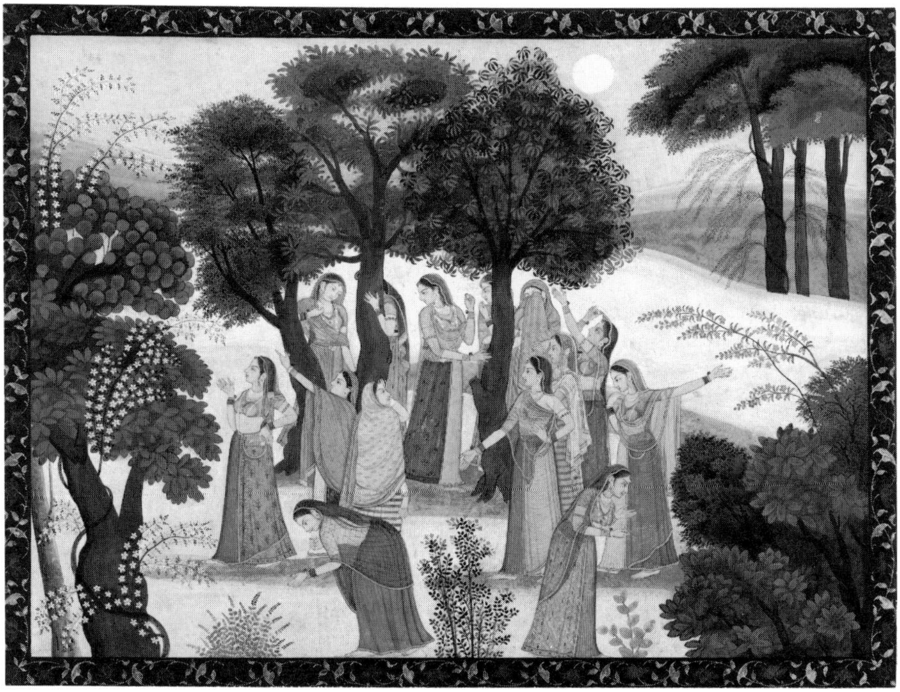

158. The Gopis Search for Krishna. From a *Bhagavata Purana* series, Punjab Hills, ca. 1780

Painters throughout India were exceptionally productive during the eighteenth century. Many artistic centers – those of Orissa, for example, or Gujarat – were little affected by Mughal influence, or by court levels of taste. A *Bhagavata Purana*, probably made at Surat (in Gujarat) about 1720, illustrates the links that developed between manuscript illustration and the important local textile industry. *Krishna and Radha Exchange Roles* (fig. 162) is dominated by a large tree of fanciful and varied blossoms which grows from a small hillock. This "tree of life" motif was basic to contemporary Gujarati textiles, and even if the same designers worked in both media, it was the aesthetic of textiles that dominated. The provenance and date of the illustration can be established by a *Devi-mahatmya* manuscript (fig. 163), dated 1719, in identical style.[4] On the other hand, a *pichchhawai* (fig. 164), made to hang behind an image of Krishna

[4] Also identified as a *Durgashaptasati* ms., another page is reproduced in Moti Chandra and Umakant P. Shah, "New Documents of Jaina Paintings," *Shri Mahavir Jaina Vidyalaya Golden Jubilee Volume*, Part I, Bombay, 1968, fig. 28. A stylistic precursor, dated 1659 and also from Surat, is reproduced in the same article as fig. 34.

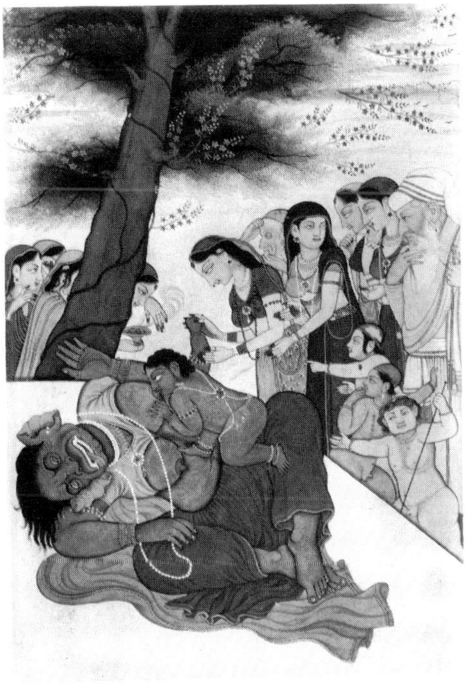

159. Death of Putana. Rajput, Punjab Hills, ca. 1800

in a temple, is in full court style, and may come from Bikaner. Textile production there in this case was subservient to painting, and textile designs were really paintings on cloth. This is true too of a *rumal* (cloth often used for wrapping a gift or ceremonial object) from the Punjab Hills. *The Abduction of Rukmini* (fig. 165), datable to about 1820, was certainly designed by a painter. The various episodes of the story could be details from a sequence of narrative scenes, here arranged decoratively over the surface of the cloth. Painters, after all, were seen as craftsmen capable of applying their talents to a variety of tasks.

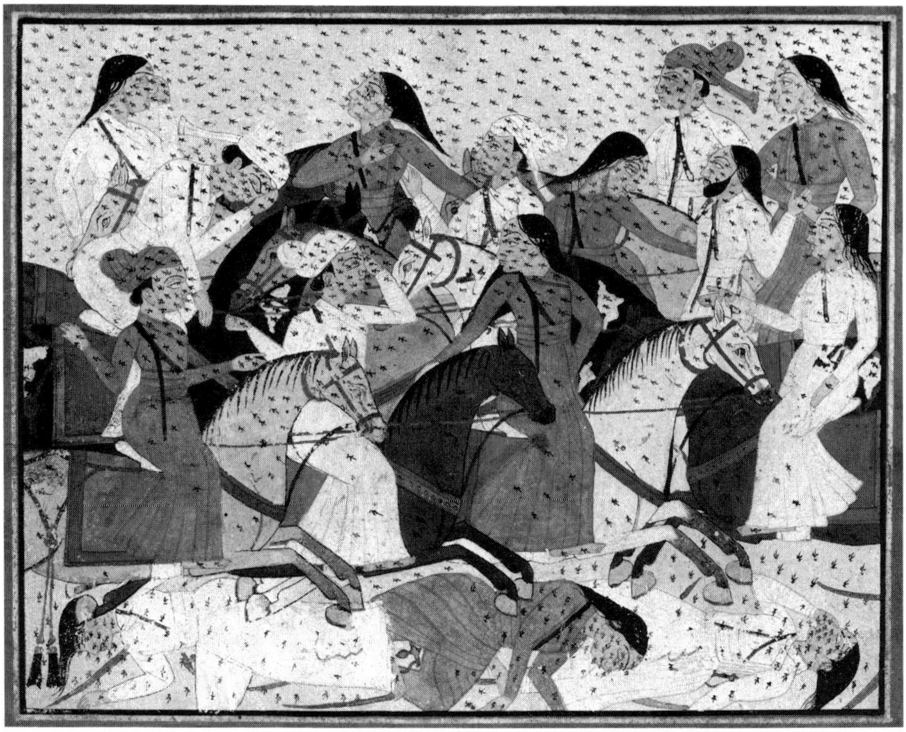

160. The Insects Attack. By Bhagwan; from a *Madhu-Malati* manuscript, Rajput, Punjab Hills at Kulu, dated 1799

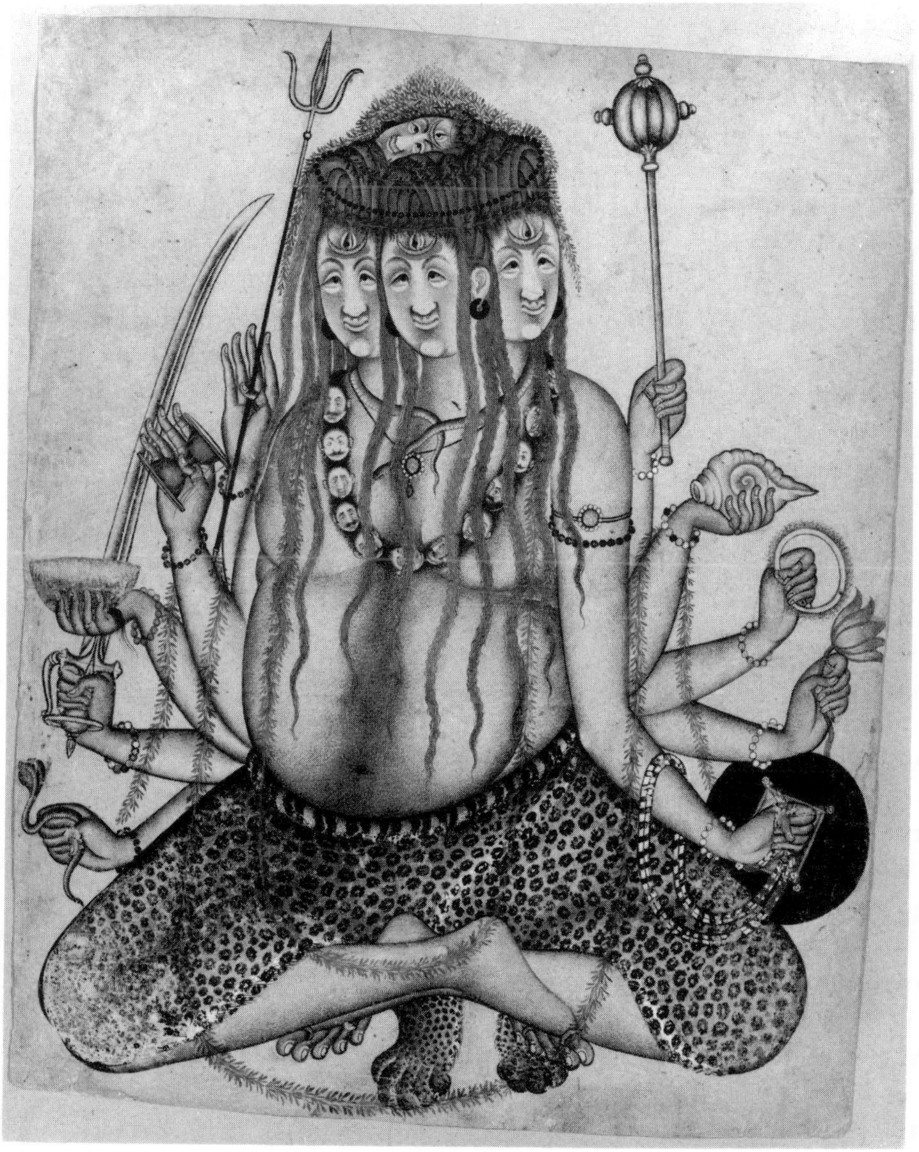

161. Shiva. Rajput, Punjab Hills at Mandi, ca. 1700–1725

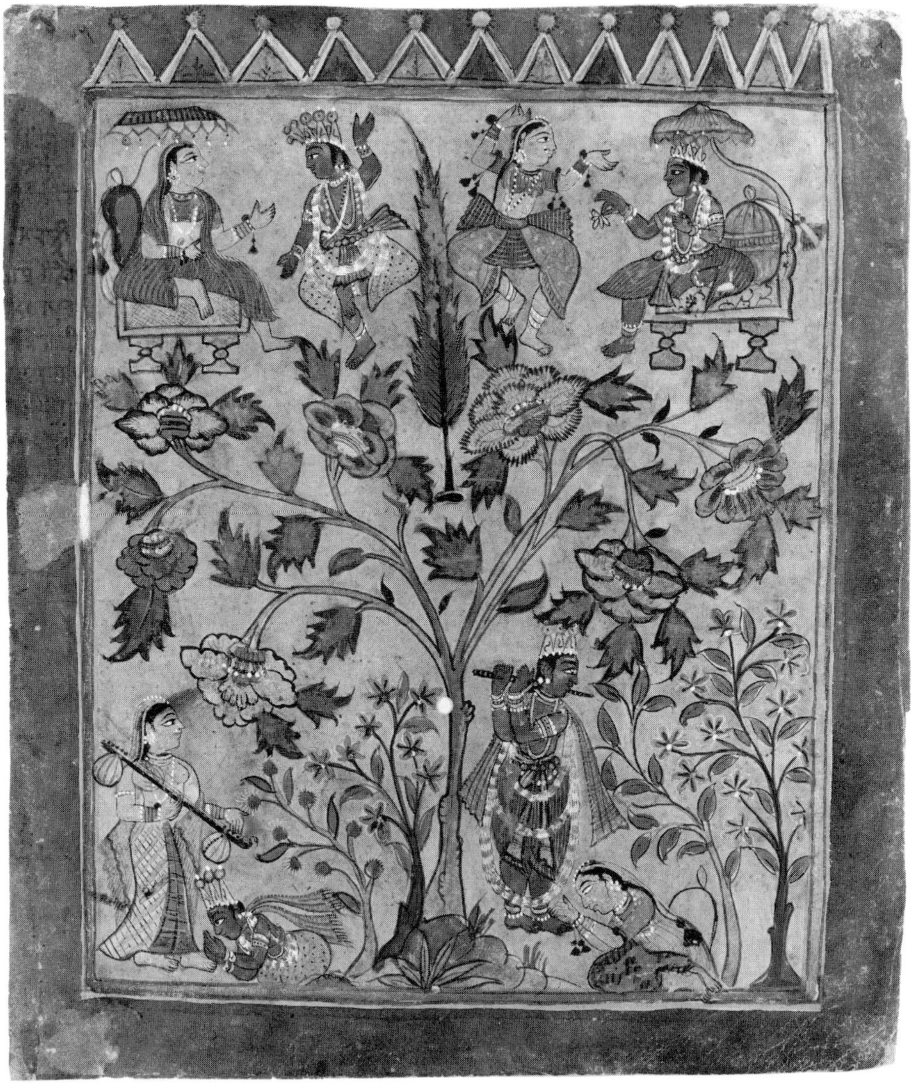

162. Krishna and Radha Exchange Roles. From a *Bhagavata Purana* series, Gujarat, probably at Surat, ca. 1720

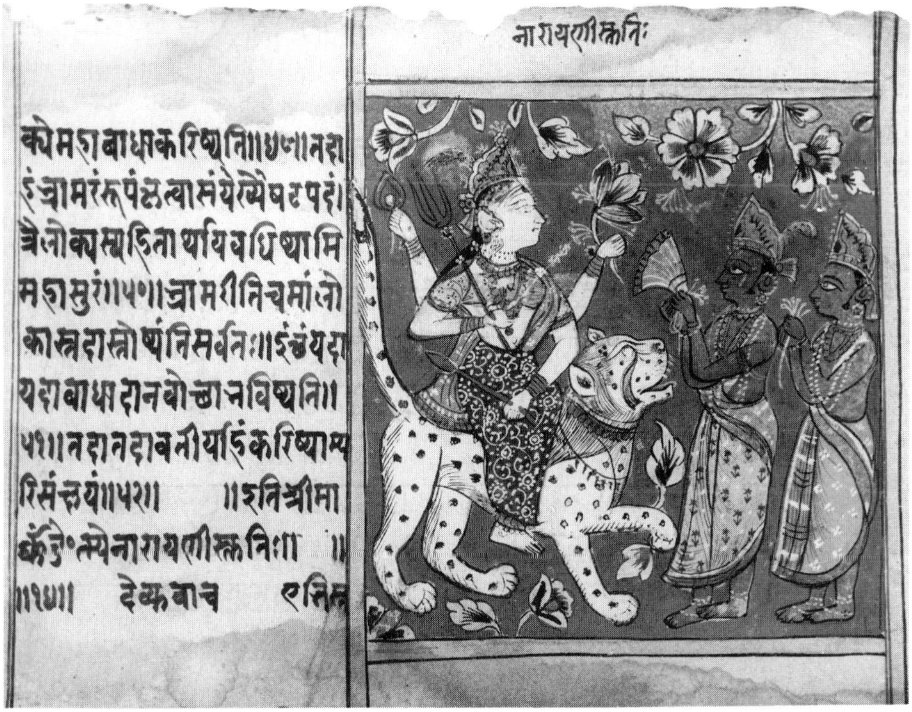

163. Durga. From a *Devi-mahatmya* ms., Gujarat, probably at Surat, dated 1719

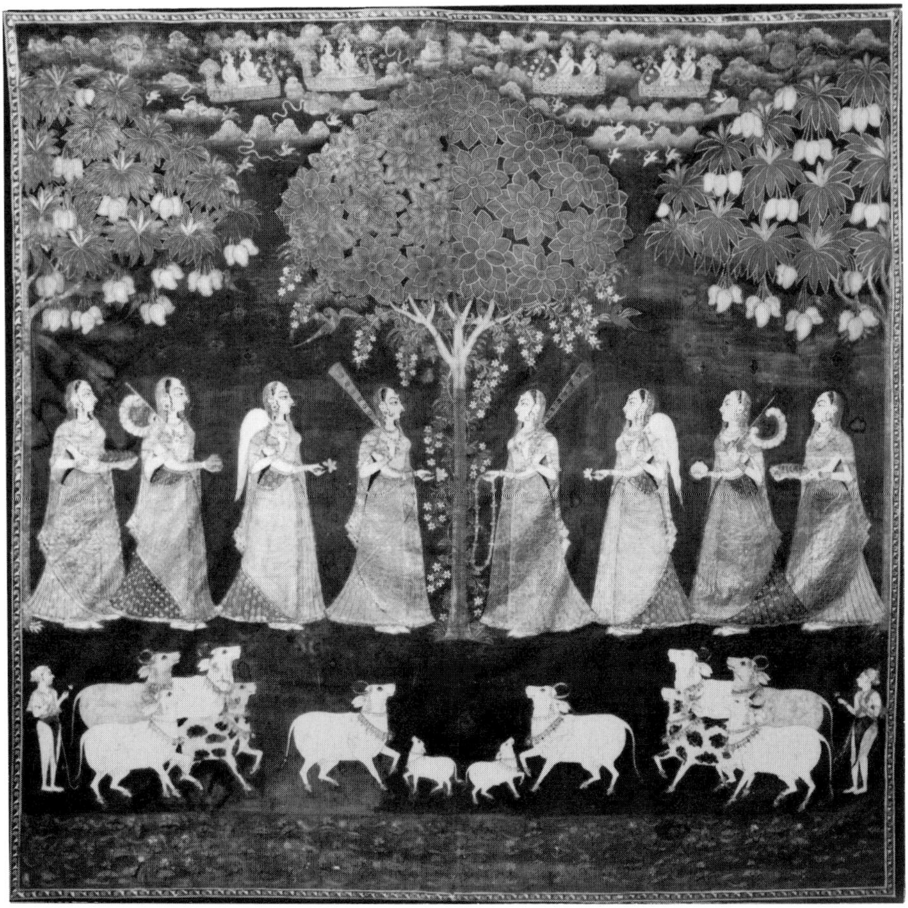

164. Pichchhawai. Rajasthan, perhaps at Bikaner, late 18th century

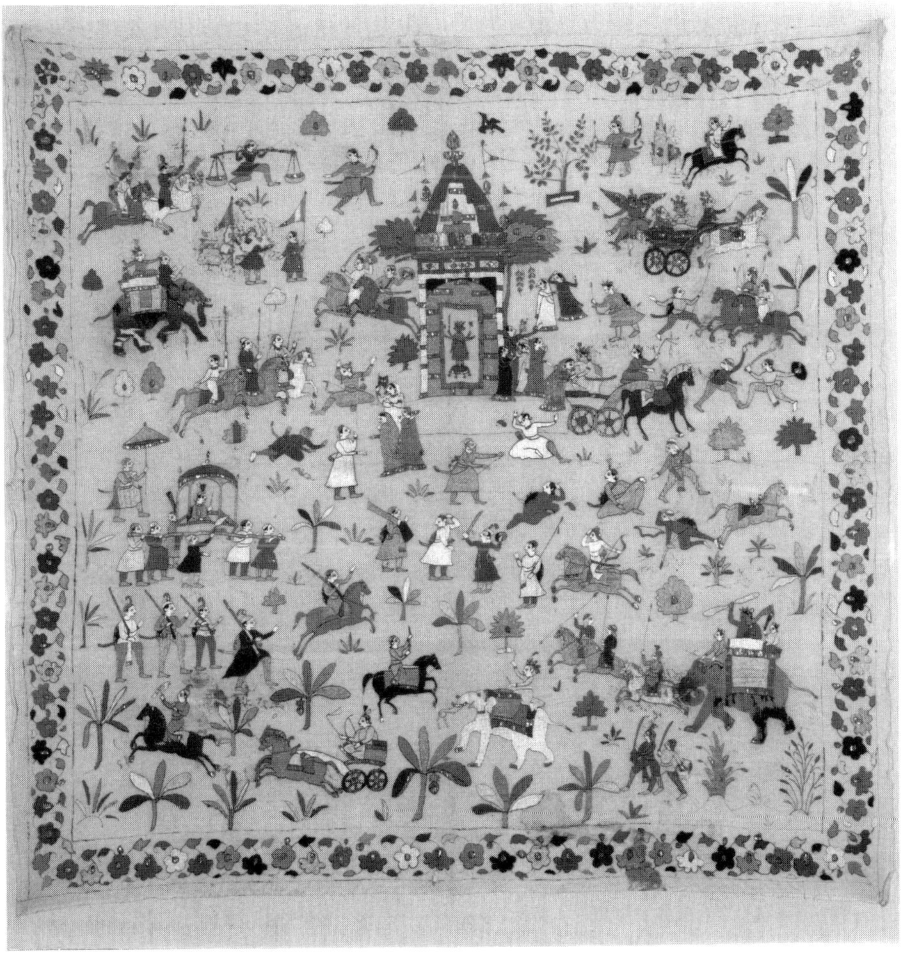

165. The Abduction of Rukmini. Rajput, Punjab Hills, ca. 1820, embroidery on cotton

CHAPTER 7

1800–1858: TRADITIONALISM AND NEW INFLUENCES

Whether we are dealing with imperial Mughal paintings during Jahangir's reign, the Rajput style at Jodhpur, or pahari traditions, periods of innovation are followed by the resurgence of conservative, continually valid, pan-Indian artistic values. Two paintings from the pahari region are especially useful in defining these values. In *Raja Sansar Chand of Kangra with His Small Son and Courtiers* (fig. 166), the architectural setting and the arrangement of the people derive directly from *Raja Balwant Singh Performing his Toilet Before Retiring* (plate N), painted by Nainsukh more than half a century earlier, and the Mughal *Muhammad Shah with Courtiers* (plate O). The painting could not have been executed without these prototypes. Nonetheless, the dancing women and the foreground soldiers – hierarchically less important figures – are very much smaller in scale than the courtiers, and they in turn are dominated by the massive raja. As in the allegorical portraits of Jahangir which changed the direction of Mughal painting about 1615, we have been transferred back to a world of symbolism and hierarchy.

Arjuna and His Charioteer Lord Krishna Confront Karna (fig. 167) is in an even more conservative style. Like *The Departure of Damayanti for Nisadha* (fig. 157), this depicts an episode described in the *Mahabharata*. However, the earlier work placed the gods firmly on earth, inhabiting palaces and courtyards in which the patrons of the paintings would themselves have felt comfortable. The only space in the scene of Arjuna and Krishna, however, is flat on the surface; the confrontation is expressed through strong, formal surface patterns, flat shapes, and proportions based even more obviously on hierarchy rather than nature. Ten feet long and on paper, the illustration is equivalent in size to a wall painting, and its scale accentuates the impact of this pattern. The faces, too, are far less differentiated than in *The Departure of Damayanti for Nisadha*. The portraitlike distinctions which Nainsukh and his followers allowed even to the figures in mythological scenes are disappearing. Human figures are again general types.

Kumbhakarna Asleep (fig. 168), painted at Basohli by Ranjha, son of Nainsukh, is dated 1816. Its links to the family manner are clear; there is neither a visible holdover from the earlier, distinctive *Rasamanjari* style of Basohli nor the re-emergence of those traits we have seen in *Arjuna and His Charioteer Lord Krishna Confront Karna*. As a line drawing, it is as graceful and descriptively effective as *Incident During a Hunt* (fig. 156) or *The*

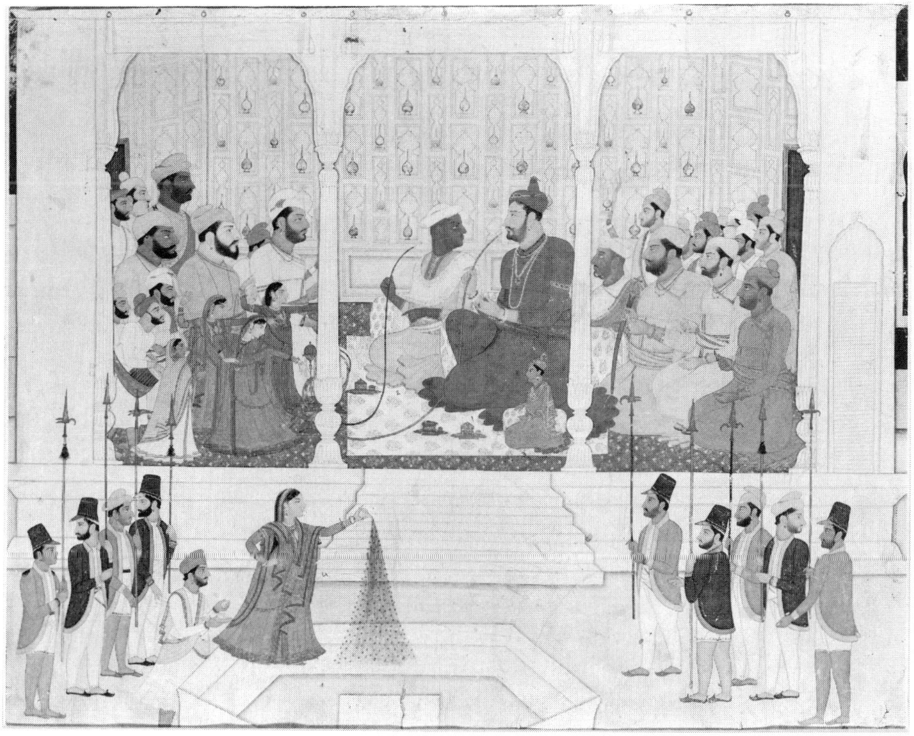

166. Raja Sansar Chand with His Small Son and Courtiers. Rajput, Punjab Hills, ca. 1800

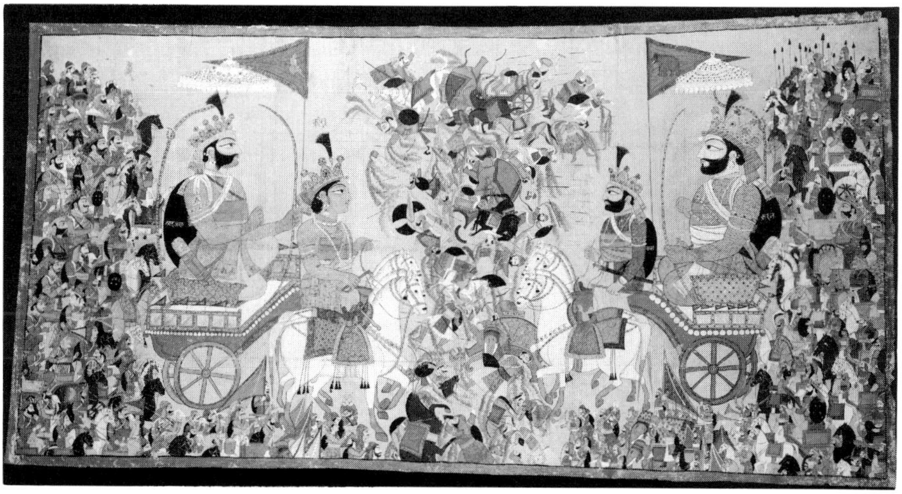

167. Arjuna and His Charioteer Lord Krishna Confront Karna. Punjab Hills, ca. 1820

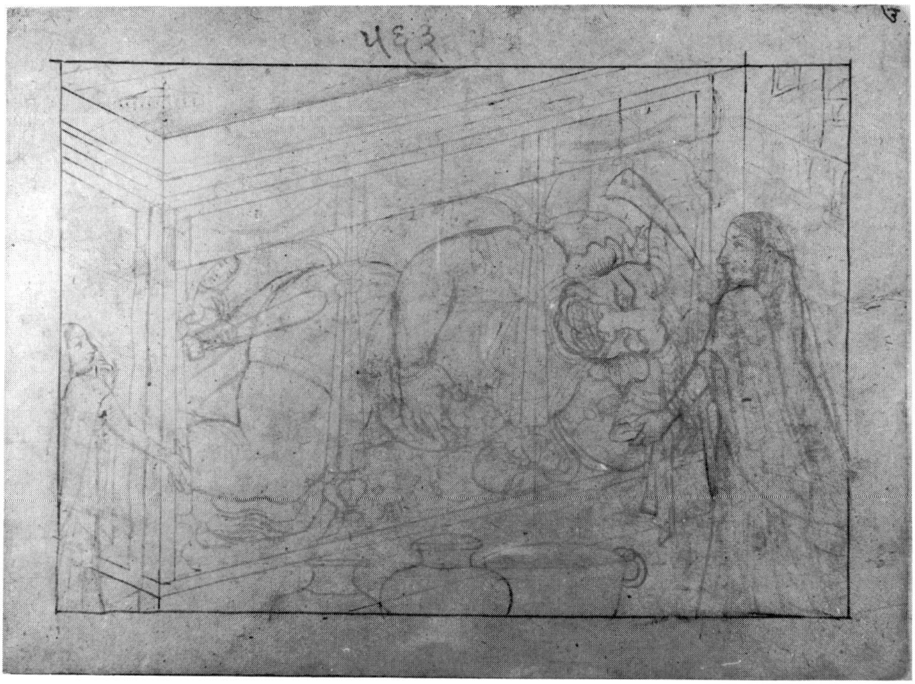

168. Kumbharkana Asleep. By Ranjha; from a *Ramayana* series, Rajput, Punjab Hills at Basohli, dated 1816

Departure of Damayanti for Nisadha. Family allegiance to Nainsukh's style, however, could not hold back the re-emergence of indigenous sensibilities into the mainstream of Rajput painting.

Developments parallel to those in the Punjab Hills are seen also in Rajasthani painting. *Maharana Jawan Singh of Mewar Hunting Boar* (fig. 169) contains neither the visual excitement nor the narrative energy of *Rao Bhoj Singh of Bundi Slays a Boar* (fig. 137). In fact, the man and the animals are immobile, and so carefully fitted between the evenly spaced clumps of vegetation that nothing moves. The scene is painted according to formula, for the clumps of grass, the trees, and the low bushes each use a single shape repeated and decoratively arranged. (In Kota, this use of formula began to assert itself in hunting scenes by the 1780s, as was noted above.) The execution, too, is rough and swift, quite different from the precise miniaturism which defines the landscape in a work such as *Raja Savant Singh of Kishangarh on a Terrace* (fig. 141). It would be difficult here to argue that the painter was concerned with an actual event, or with specific personalities. This is an iconic presentation of a warrior, not an examination of the psychology of blood sports.

Many of the most exciting paintings from Mewar State were created not for the Maharana, but at the *thikana* (barony) of Devgarh. A particular group of

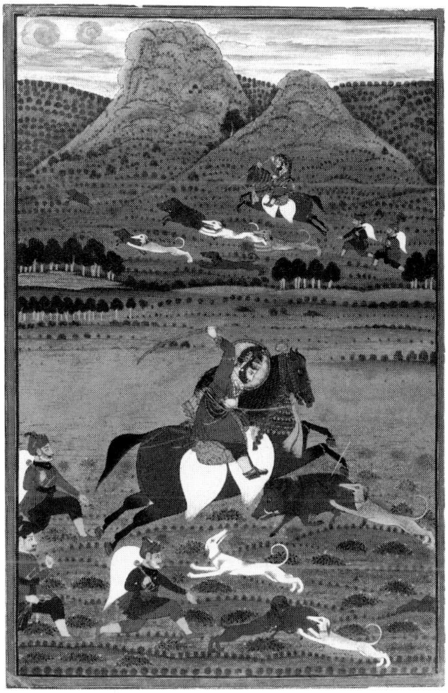

169. Maharana Jawan Singh of Mewar Hunting Boar.
Rajput, Rajasthan at Udaipur, dated 1835

artists worked at that court, and included at least four members of one family – although the men also worked for periods of time elsewhere. *Rawat Gokul Das of Devgarh at a Lake Palace* (plate P) was painted by Bagta and dated 1808. It is full of movement. The landscape writhes and billows, and the edge of the central lake leads the eye on a swift tour of the entire surface. It is a large painting, 21½ by 31½ inches, and we are more immediately affected by the enormous shapes and broad rhythms than by the tiny figures that enliven the terrain. Nature dominates and controls man (as it does, albeit in a different way, in the Mewar boar hunt shown in fig. 169), and in this tumultuous setting a large range of activities is shown. Gokul Das (r. 1786–1821) is found hunting, both on land and from the lake palace, where he is surrounded by his harem, their closed purdah carriages neatly lined up on shore. There are fishermen, *dhobis* (laundrymen), grooms, courtiers, and varieties of animals and plants, giving a thorough survey of contemporary life.

The figures in *Maharaja Man Singh II of Jodhpur on a Ferris Wheel* (fig. 170) are also reduced to types, again with strong profiles and large eyes, while even the clouds are merely white curlicues evenly spaced at the top. The scene is full of energy, with strong contrasts of color and strong rhythmic movements, unlike the languid exaggerations more typical at Kishangarh. Perhaps more

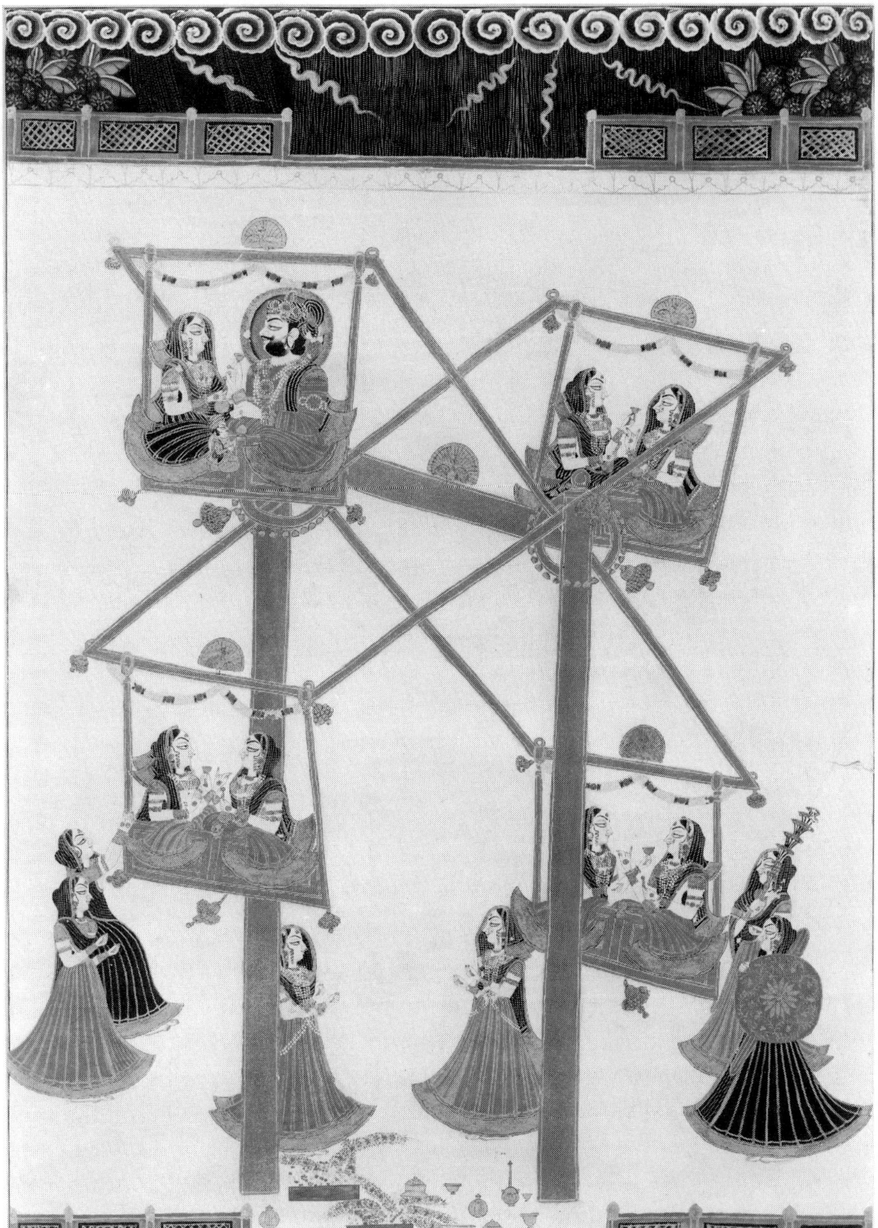

170. Maharaja Man Singh II of Jodhpur on a Ferris Wheel. Rajput, Rajasthan at Jodhpur, ca. 1840

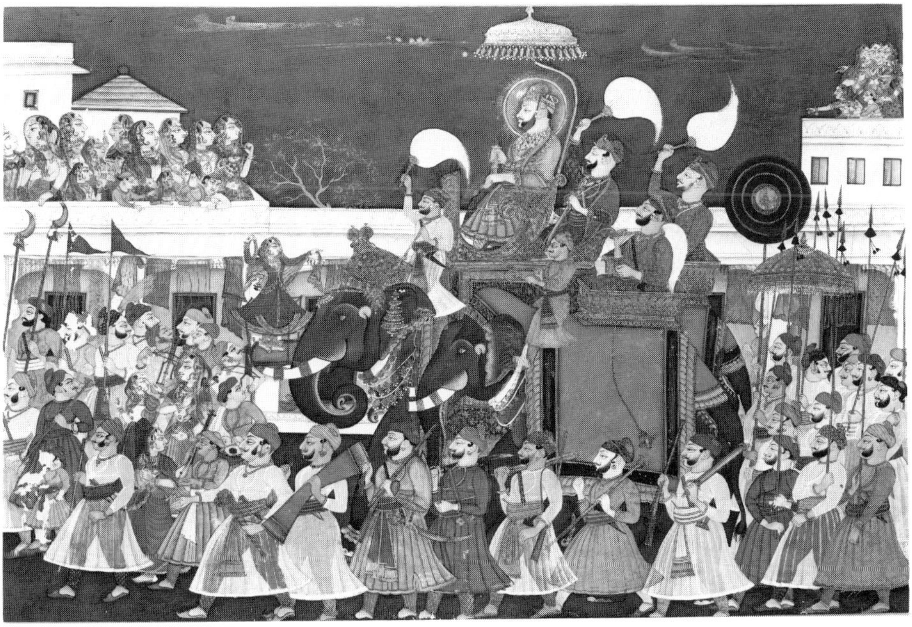

171. Maharao Ram Singh II of Kota in Procession. Rajput, Rajasthan at Kota, ca. 1830

than any other Rajput school, Jodhpur has moved from an intense identification with the Mughal style to a revival of the strong, flat shapes, bright colors, and clear patterns of the pre-Mughal Rajput style. This development continues a trend seen already in two seventeenth-century works from Jodhpur (figs. 93 and 94).

In *Maharao Ram Singh II of Kota in Procession* (fig. 171), the ruler is seated under a gold parasol, with fly-whisks waving about him as he moves through the city; and lest he be even momentarily bored, a dancing girl – strategically placed on a platform supported by the elephant's tusks – provides constant amusement. Colors are solid and strong. The deep blue sky, for example, reduces the fly-whisks to silhouettes and creates a wonderfully dancing surface rhythm which continues in the men evenly lined up along the front. Their white muslin skirts are translucent and reveal colored trousers (*paijamas*) beneath. It is not three-dimensionality or the texture of cloth that is thereby emphasized; instead, the translucence simply allows a greater density of flat patterns.

At Kota, painted scenes were distributed to worshippers from the region who came to the Vaisnavite shrine to Sri Nathji installed within the palace. *The Worship of Sri Nathji* (fig. 172) shows Dauji II (act. 1797–1826), chief priest of the temple at Nathadvara, at a ceremonial invocation of the god. Such paintings made at Kota, or at any of several other such subsidiary shrines of the central temple at Nathadvara (in Mewar State), followed common formats, but local painters would execute the works. They were certainly the same artists who painted court scenes for the local rulers, and the continuing vitality of Rajput painting was a result of this ability of the painters to communicate with – and draw from – different artistic needs and expectations. Mughal art had maintained no such ties to taste outside the court circle.

At all the Rajput schools of painting in Rajasthan and the Punjab Hills, Mughal standards and taste had become influential and then declined, although according to very different schedules. And in every case indigenous traits reasserted themselves. The British were deeply entrenched in the Lucknow region and around Calcutta, however, so Mughal and European influence both continued to be strongly felt in the nineteenth century in northeastern India. As the central imperial court declined, the provincial courts in eastern India claimed power and accumulated wealth – including studios of painters able to evoke an imperial style. An increasingly strong political and cultural presence throughout eastern India, the English too began to patronize painting. Indian rulers in the region, in turn, looked to European objects and stylistic references to increase their prestige with the English as well as to counter any feelings of provincialism.

A few major imperial portraits are also known from these years. *Shah Alam II* (fig. 176) shows the elderly emperor, who reigned between 1759 and 1806, at the end of his life. He is seated on a reconstruction of the Peacock Throne that had been stolen by Nadir Shah in 1739, and he is blind – the result of a particularly brutal attack by the Rohilla Ghulam Qadir in 1788. While it conforms to a traditional portrait compositional type, it is an extraordinarily moving work. This is not only because of the historical circumstances, but because of such details as the courtier at the left; in a space that seems hushed and empty, the nobleman looks quietly but with great compassion on the now powerless emperor. *Bahadur Shah II with His Sons* (fig. 177) depicts the last of the Mughal emperors seated on a makeshift platform placed over the interior water-channel, the Stream of Paradise, in the palace at Delhi. Contemporary accounts by European visitors state that the palace was a shambles by the early nineteenth century, for it was much too large to be maintained by a court powerless to collect taxes and tribute. Nonetheless, the image suggests – probably inaccurately – that the emperor's dignity remained intact. Few imperial works of such quality and power are known from these last years. Those that exist certainly reflect the momentary skills of single painters rather than the ongoing strength of a tradition.

If the court at Delhi was in eclipse, the cities of Oudh were bursting with wealth and activity. Colonel Antoine Louis Henri Polier (1741–1795) joined

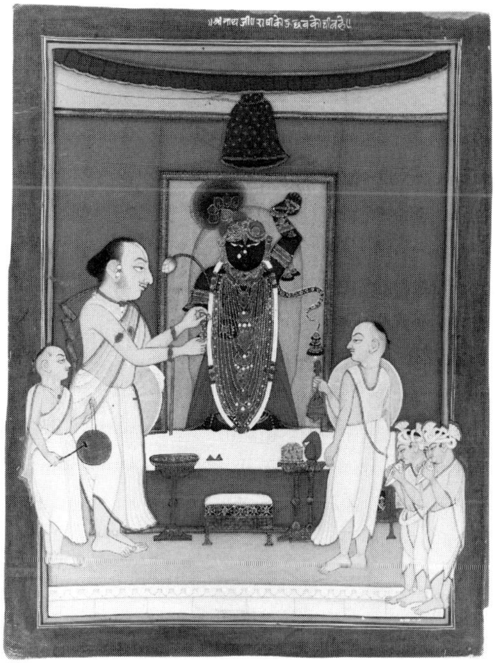

172. The Worship of Sri Nathji. Rajasthan at Kota, ca. 1820

the entourage of Shuja ad-Daula (r. 1753–1775), the Nawab of Oudh, and supported artists and performers. *Colonel Polier's Nautch Party* (fig. 173), by Mihr Chand, is set on a terrace by a river beyond which fireworks are displayed. It immediately recalls the composition of *Festivities at the Wedding of Dara Shikoh* (figs. 97 and 98), except that Polier sits on a European settee. Polier collected and commissioned Indian pictures and calligraphies, as did many other resident and visiting Europeans. *A Gingi Vulture* (fig. 175), typical of the natural history studies made for the British wherever they travelled, is directly related to the studies of animals found in the *Baburnama* manuscripts (fig. 42) or even *Squirrels in a Plane Tree* (fig. 65), and the common documentary intent behind all these works made it easy for Indian artists to adapt to English patrons.

Acrobats on a Terrace (fig. 174), by Faizullah, is a contemporaneous work, almost certainly painted for an Indian patron. It recalls eighteenth-century prints of French gardens, except that the space is totally misunderstood; there are several vanishing points, and an alternate horizon line within the central arch. On the other hand, nowhere in Mughal painting, including works of the early seventeenth century, is space used in a way consistent with European Renaissance theory. This was not a concept useful to Mughal painters. Instead,

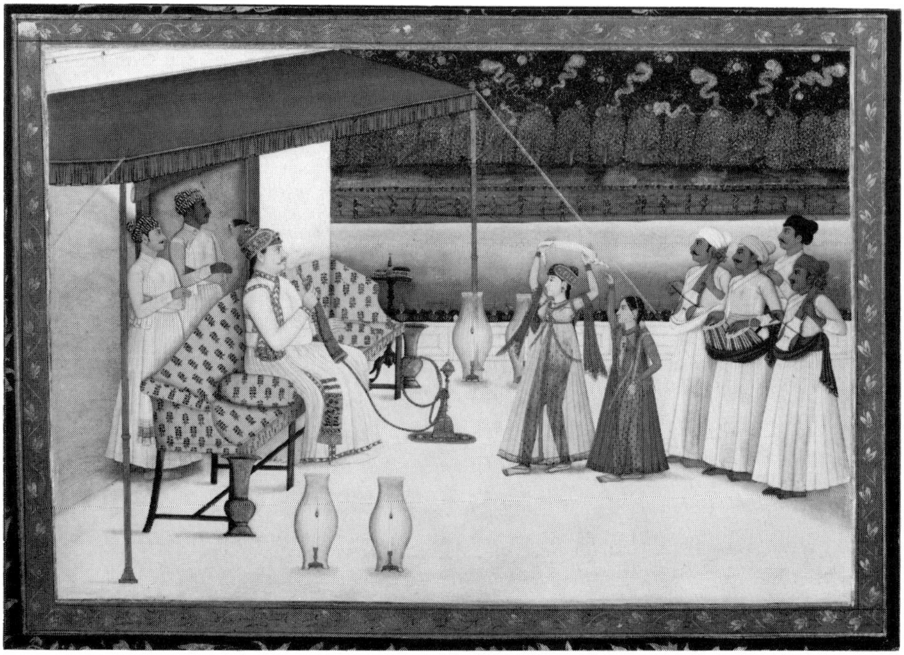

173. Colonel Polier's Nautch Party. By Mihr Chand; Oudh, ca. 1780

space was added to a picture when it could effectively animate or accentuate a particular detail or section of the surface. The spatial inconsistencies seen in *Acrobats on a Terrace* are therefore more obvious, but not different in kind, than those in earlier Mughal works.

One of the most extraordinary figures of this period was Ghazi-ud-din (r. 1814–1827) of Oudh, given the title King of Oudh by the British. The decadence of his court is somehow communicated in *Ghazi-ud-din Entertains Europeans at Dinner* (fig. 178). There is no decorum in evidence; courtiers and entertainers crowd the king and his guests, and to compound the spatial claustrophobia, fireworks once again fill the sky. The artist is intent on packing the composition with details: European silverware, and a clock about to be presented by a man wearing eyeglasses; chandeliers; jewelry and fashionable hair styles on the women; elephants and distant armies. There is no dignity here. It is an entertaining illustration, but the taste it reveals is coarse, and it perfectly confirms the verbal portrait of Oudh presented in *The Private Life of an Eastern King*, written anonymously by "a member of the household of his Late Majesty, Nussir-u-deen, King of Oudh [son of Ghazi-ud-din]." In complete contrast to the works made for Shahjahan – or even the portrait *Shah Alam II* (fig. 176) – this scene reveals a world out of control. It is also a world out of touch with traditional India.

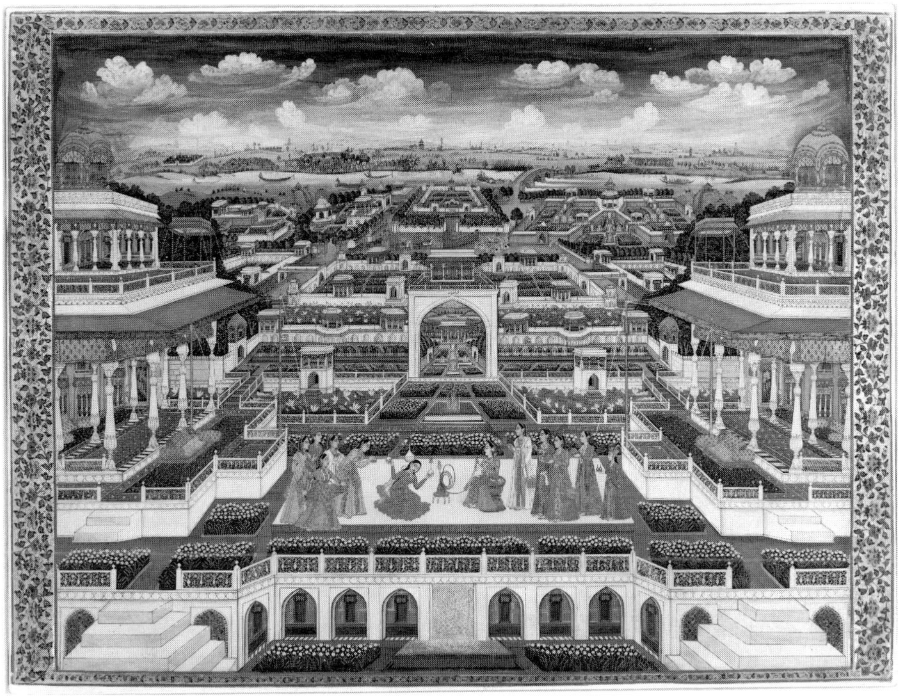

174. Acrobats on a Terrace. By Faizullah. Oudh, ca. 1770

If *Ghazi-ud-din Entertains Europeans at Dinner* is one extreme among paintings from India, the other might be represented by the exactly contemporary *Arjuna and His Charioteer Lord Krishna Confront Karna* (fig. 167). They represent conflicting ideals that have continually confronted each other during the period under study. Whether expressed as Muslim versus Hindu, Mughal versus Rajput, foreign versus indigenous, or secular versus sacred, painting in India cannot be understood without an awareness of the tensions created by these various opposites.

The portrait of Ghazi-ud-din has no counterpart in India outside the Mughal courtly tradition – of which it is a late, provincial, and isolated reflection. *Arjuna and His Charioteer Lord Krishna Confront Karna*, a Rajput court work from the Punjab Hills, on the other hand, can immediately be compared to *A Battle of Snakes and Mongeese* (fig. 179), from a series of *Mahabharata* illustrations made for the use of village story-tellers in Maharashtra. (There are several similar sets of illustrations that have survived, and some are on European watermarked paper specifically datable to between 1830 and 1880.) This work therefore represents artistic attitudes of wide geographic and social acceptability. The common compositional clarity of the narratives – each of

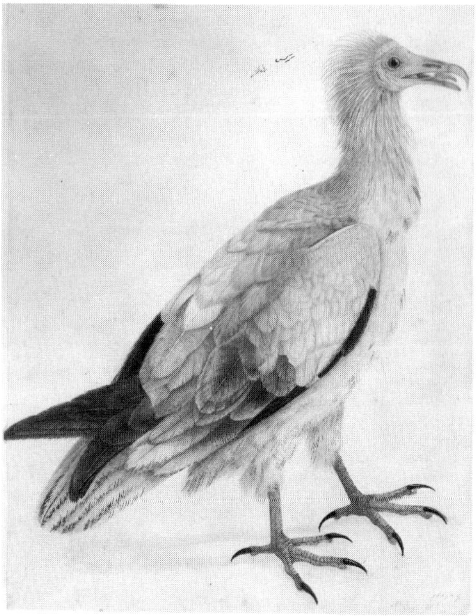

175. A Gingi Vulture. Company School at Barrakhpur, ca. 1805

which shows a direct confrontation – is easily explained by the village work: it is from a sequence of scenes held up by storytellers as they sang and recited the tales illustrated. Aesthetic subtleties worked against the effectiveness of any scene. What was necessary instead was to have instantly legible compositions that isolated and quickly communicated the essential aspect of any chosen subject through immediately recognizable figural formulas and strong color. The power of the narrative was never lost, or replaced, by importance given to the painting as a financially valuable physical object – an important aspect of Mughal workmanship. These same characteristics had defined the pre-Mughal *Bhagavata Purana* series of about 1540 (plate B), and they remained intact for centuries at the village level, no matter what momentary interest in other styles or purposes occurred at Rajput courts.

That Rajput rulers and their artists both remained in touch with the relatively unchanging traditions of Indian village imagery is a situation that provided stylistic continuity to Rajput art. *Maharaja Man Singh II of Jodhpur on a Ferris Wheel* (fig. 170), for example, like *Arjuna and His Charioteer Lord Krishna Confront Karna*, is a variation on these traditions more than a comment on – or even a development of – Mughal style. It shows no evidence or even awareness of the earlier interest in Mughal art shown by Jodhpur court painters (for example fig. 93). As in the early *Bhagavata Purana* scenes, figures are once again constructed by repetition of stock formulas. This is, however, an

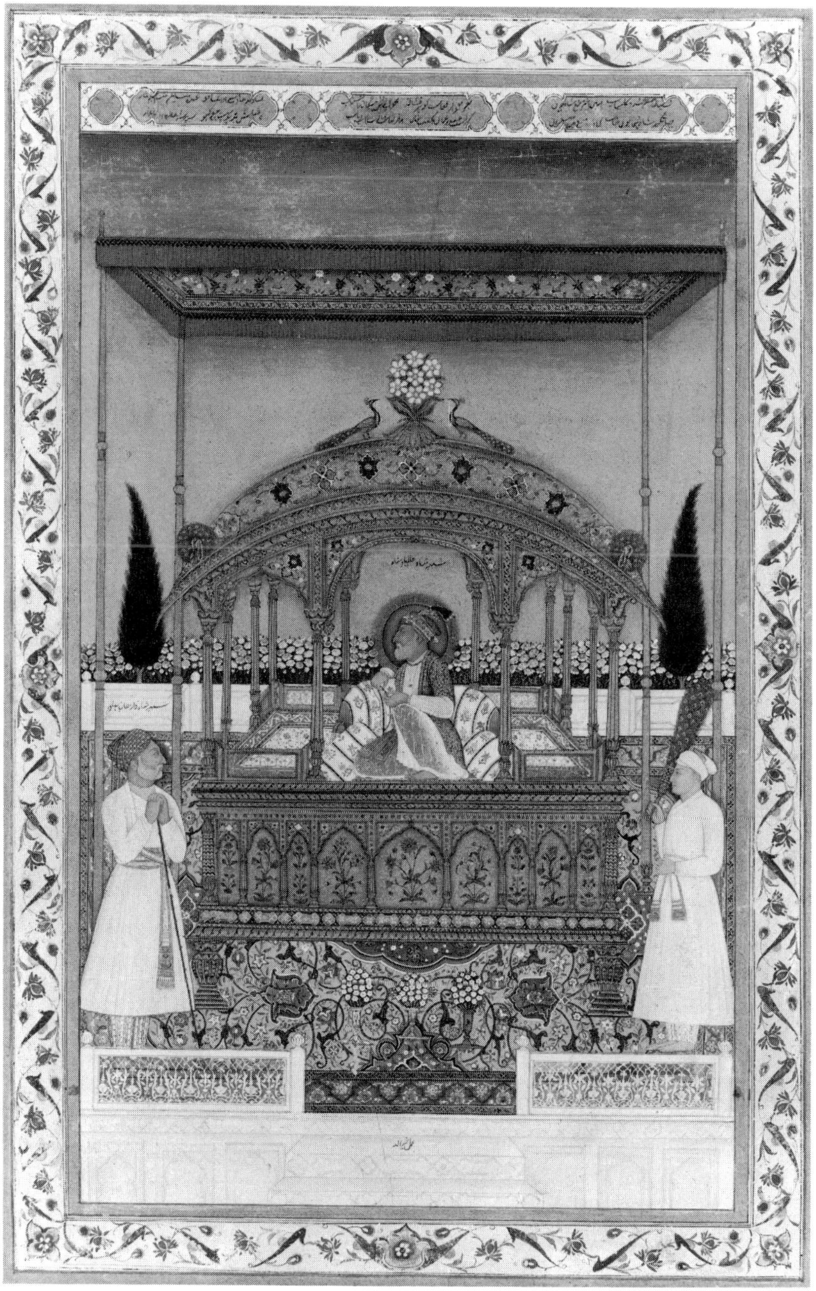

176. Shah Alam II. By Kheirallah; Mughal, ca. 1800

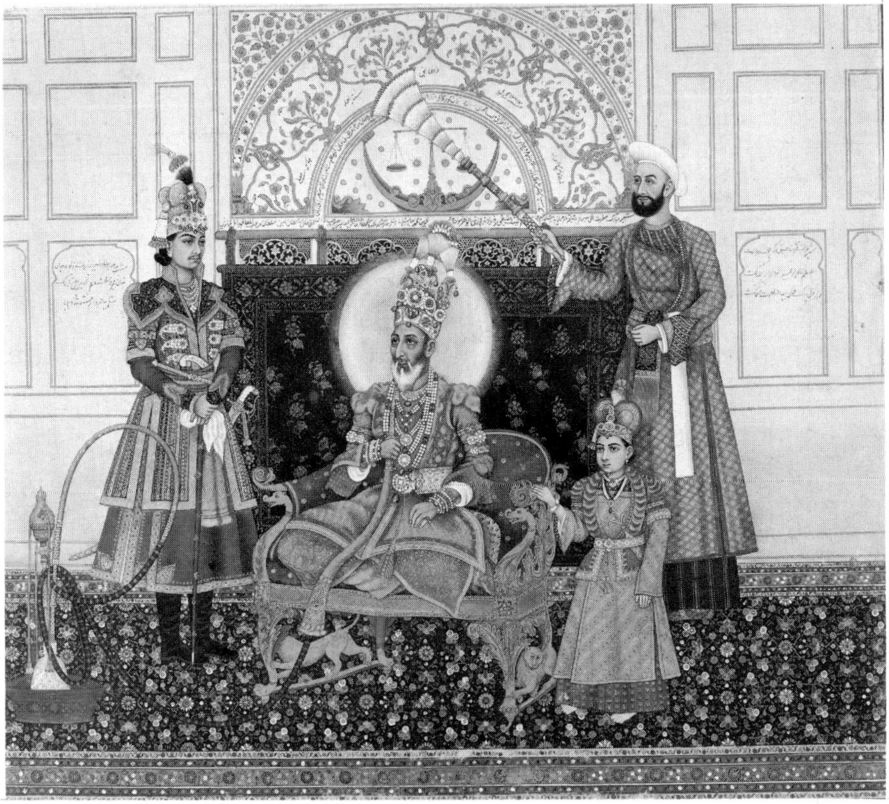

177. Bahadur Shah II with His Sons. Mughal at Delhi, dated May 1838

unusual art-historical situation, and it confirms what we have seen continually at individual Rajput court workshops. After periods of novelty and change, Rajput artists inevitably returned to reaffirm the importance of those pictorial qualities from which they had earlier departed. This is in strong contrast to the evolution of Mughal styles, in which – at least between about 1550 and 1650 – there was continual change and a probing progression in the understanding of the subjects portrayed. In Mughal art, stylistic phases, once abandoned, did not again come into fashion, and the study of Mughal painting is therefore a chronicle of changing perceptions and constant challenges to the status quo. The situation answers the need of the historian who "is interested in the inception of styles, not in their perpetuation," to quote a major European scholar of Asian art. "The importance of a work from the historian's point of view . . . depends largely on his insight into its one-time stylistic newness."[1] It

1 Max Loehr, "Some Fundamental Issues in the History of Chinese Painting," *Journal of Aesthetics and Art Criticism*, Fall 1965, p. 39.

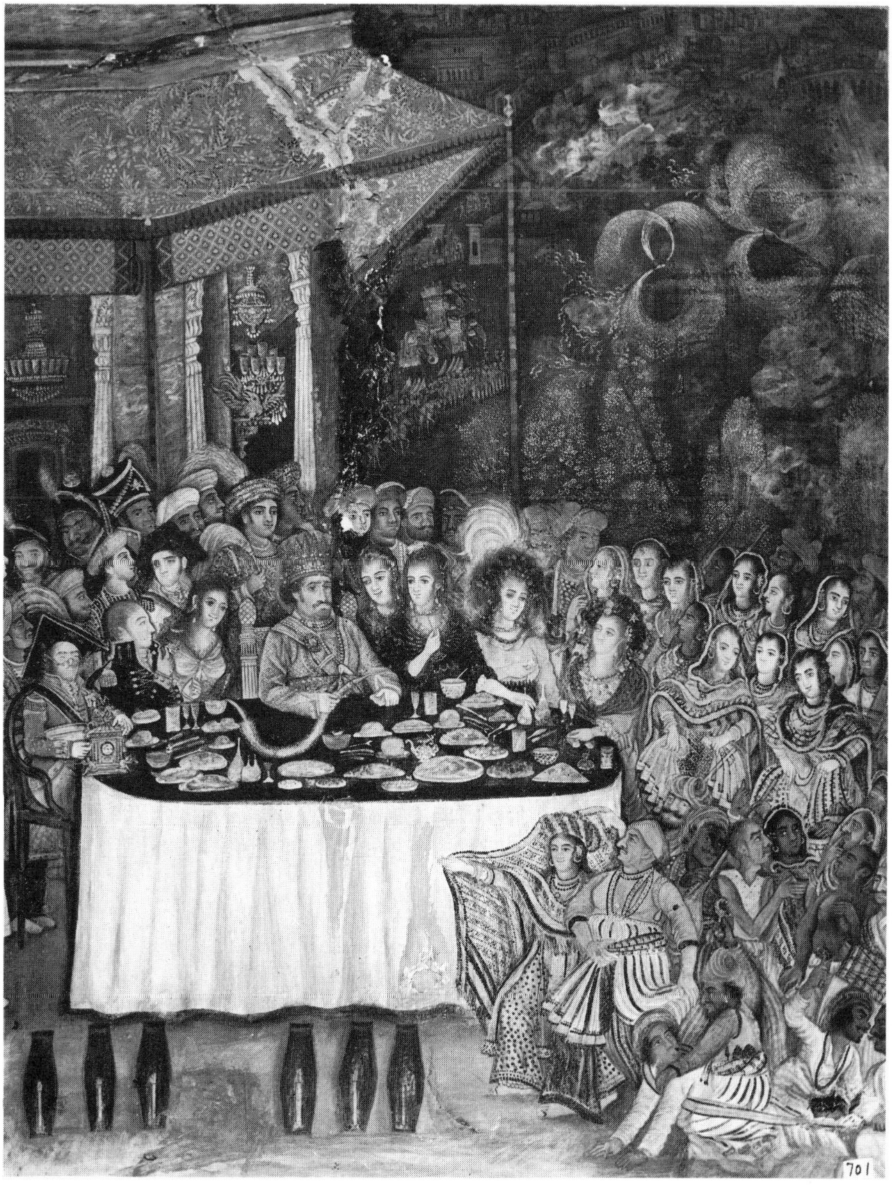

178. Ghazi-ud-din Entertains Europeans at Dinner. Oudh, ca. 1820

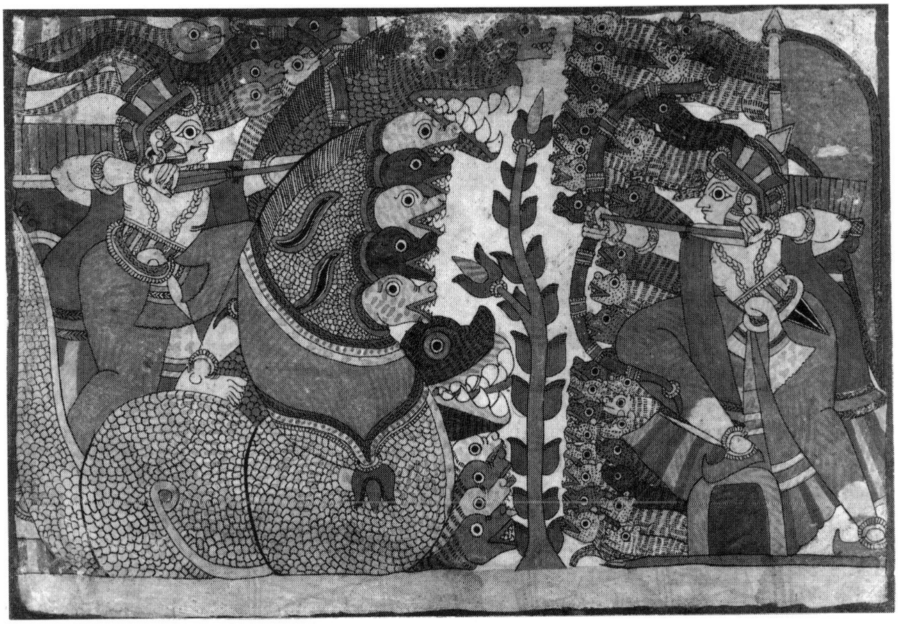

179. A Battle of Snakes and Mongeese. From a *Mahabharata* series, Maharashtra, ca. 1880

should be no surprise, therefore, that Mughal painting has been so extensively studied outside of India.

Rajput art, however, used novel visual ideas – those introduced by Mughal taste, for example – for opposite purposes: to explore and extend the expressive possibilities of established and unquestioned pictorial values. Rajput painters continually confirmed the richness and universality of inherited artistic styles. This profoundly Indian attitude was eventually accepted even by Mughal painters, who had begun already in Jahangir's reign to emphasize the universal aspects of the emperors, rather than their unique qualities, and to diminish the importance of the individualistic, innovative styles practiced by specific painters. What has been termed the decline of imperial Mughal art when viewed with the criteria of the European historian is also evidence of the assimilation finally of Mughal painting into the Indian artistic mainstream. The study of Rajput and Mughal images from north India – and the works reproduced here – should convince us of the power and validity of this central tradition and the ideas it embodies.

APPENDIX

Colophons and brief references for dated and/or inscribed Indian manuscripts or series mentioned in the text.

1411 *Kalpasutra* and *Kalakacharyakatha*
Arthur M. Sackler Gallery, Smithsonian Institution, Washington, D.C. (s85.0002)
Ref.: Milo C. Beach, "A volume of homage: a Jain manuscript, 1411," *Asian Art*, vol. 1, no. 3, pp. 38–56
Plate A

The colophon, on folio 118, states that "in the year 1468 2 krsmapaksa of Asadha [= July 7, 1411], it was copied here in Karkara," and that the manuscript was presented to the Kharataragachchha after having been caused to be copied by Mayanalladevi, the wife of Mula, son of Bhamharapala, in the lineage of Lunadulha, together with her sons Bhima, Hidana, Talhana, Devaraja, and Mahiraja. (Translation and summary by David Pingree.)

1439 *Kalpasutra*
Copied at Mandu
National Museum of India, New Delhi (49.175)
Refs.: Karl Khandalavala and Moti Chandra, "A consideration of an illustrated ms. from Mandapadurga (Mandu) dated 1439 AD," *Lalit Kala* 6, pp. 8–29; Pramod Chandra, "Notes on the Mandu *Kalpasutra*," *Marg*, vol. XII, no. 3, pp. 51–54

As given in Khandalavala and Chandra, the colophon reads:
"At the fort of Mandapagarh in the Samvat year 1496 [= 1439–1440] in the reign of King Mahmud, Sri Kshemahamsagani, the foremost disciple of the master reciter Sri Kshemakirtigani, glorified by the presents of the reciters and venerable monks Somadhvajagani, Bhavarajagani, Kshemarajagani, got this illustrated ms. written for his own reading. May the text impart pleasure for a long time."

1441 *Adipurana*
Copied at Gwalior
Private collection
Ref.: *Masterpieces of Jain Painting*, edited by Saryu Doshi, Bombay, 1985, p. 63, fig. 36

1451 *Vasanta Vilasa*
Copied at Ahmedabad
Freer Gallery of Art, Smithsonian Institution, Washington, D.C. (32.24)
Ref.: N. C. Mehta, *Studies in Indian Painting*, Bombay, 1926, pp. 15–21; W. Norman Brown, *The Vasanta Vilasa*, New Haven, 1962.

According to a colophon, the manuscript was copied by Acharya Ratnagar for Shah Sri Chandrapal, son of Shri Shah Depal.

1454 *Yashodara Charitra*
Probably copied at Gwalior
Shri Shantinath Shvetambara Mandir, Delhi
Ref.: Doshi, *Masterpieces*, p. 145, fig. 23

1465 *Kalpasutra*
Copied at Jaunpur, and illustrated by Venidasa
Narasimhaji Pol na Jnanabhandara, Baroda
Ref.: Karl Khandalavala and Moti Chandra, "An illustrated *Kalpasutra* painted at Jaunpur in AD 1465," *Lalit Kala* 12, pp. 9–15

As given in the reference listed above, the colophon reads:
"In the Samvat year 1522 [= 1465] on Friday the second of the bright half of the month of Bhadrapada, in the reign of Huseyn Shah of Jaunpur, Sravika Harshini, the daughter of the merchant Sahasaraja and the wife of Sanghavi Kalidasa, of Srimali caste with their son Dharmadasa got this *Kalpasutra* written, and revised by the Upadhyaya Kalamasamyama by the order of Sri Jinachandra-suri, an ornament of the sacred seat of Sri Jinabhadrasuri of Kharataragachchha; it was painted by the Kayastha Venidasa, son of Pandita Karmasimha Gauda. For the welfare of all."

1516 *Aranyaka Parvan*
Copied at Yoginipura by Gauda Bhavanidasa
Asiatic Society of Bombay (Ms. 966)
Ref.: Karl Khandalavala and Moti Chandra, *An Illustrated* Aranyaka Parvan *in the Asiatic Society of Bombay*, Bombay, 1974

As given in the reference listed above, the colophon reads:
"In the *Samvat* year 1573 [= 1516] on Monday the 9th [or 8th?] day of the dark fortnight of the month of Sravana. At that time, in the city of Yoginipura, during the victorious reign of Sultan Sikandar . . . At that time in the water [river] fort of Kachhauva, inhabitants of Chaudrapuri were residing there. Chaudhuri Kalha, the reputed son of Chaudhuri Vinaya. His [Chaudhuri Kalha's] son, a Vaishnavite, Chaudhuri Bhanadasa. [By him] this Aranyaparava of Mahabharata was gotten written for his own hearing. It was written by the Kayastha called Gauda Bhavanidasa, the son of Lakhansai, so it has been heard."

1540 *Mahapurana*
Executed at Palam (near Delhi)
Sri Digambara Jain Atisaya Kshetra, Jaipur

Ref.: Karl J. Khandalavala and Moti Chandra, *New Documents of Indian Painting – A Reappraisal*, Bombay, 1969, plates 17–19 and figs. 143, 144, 148, 150, 151, 154; Doshi, *Masterpieces*, figs. 6, 7, 9–18, 20–22, 24, 26–28

As given by Khandalavala and Chandra, the colophon reads:
"[This work was written] on Tuesday, the 13th day of second fortnight of the month of Phalgun in Vikrama Samvat 1597 [= 1540]. It was the time when the great fort of Joginipura [Delhi] situated in Kuru was under the rule of Badshah Sultan Shah 'Alam (Sher Shah), at the sacred place called Palamva [modern Palam] . . . one Dharmadasa . . . who got the Mahapurana Adikhanda consisting of eight thousand *slokas* to be written for the destruction of his *karmas*. Raimal got it illustrated. This was done by Kayastha Harinatha, with his family. Written by the Brahmana Vishnudasa."

1552 *Devi-mahatmya*
Himachal Pradesh State Museum, Simla
Ref.: B. N. Goswamy and Eberhard Fischer, *Pahari Meister – Hofische Malerei aus den Bergen Nord Indiens*, Zurich, 1990, pp. 16–27 and plates 1–6; B. N. Goswamy, V. C. Ohri, and Ajit Singh, "A *Chaurapanchasika* style manuscript from the Pahari area, notes on a newly discovered Devi Mahatmya in the Himachal Pradesh State Museum, Simla," *Lalit Kala* 21, pp. 9–21.
Fig. 129

Full information on the colophon is given in Goswamy and Fischer.

1568 *Deval Rani Khizr Khan*
Copied by Sultan Bayazid ibn Nizam
National Museum of India (L.53–2/7)
Ref.: Jeremiah P. Losty, *The Art of the Book in India*, London, 1982, no. 56
Fig. 18

As given in National Museum of India, *Manuscripts from Indian Collections – Descriptive Catalogue*, New Delhi, 1964, p. 96, the colophon names the scribe for the manuscript, and gives its date:
"The miserable wretch, the sinner, Sultan Bayazid, son of Mir Nizam, known as Dawri. Dated Muharram 976 [= 1568]."
(Translated by Wheeler M. Thackston; and see Cl. Huart, *Les Calligraphes et les Miniaturistes de l'Orient Musulman*, Paris, 1908, p. 233 for a further reference to the calligrapher.)

1570–1571 *Nujum-ul-Ulum*
A. Chester Beatty Library, Dublin (Ms. 2)
Ref.: T. W. Arnold and J. V. S. Wilkinson, *The Library of A. Chester Beatty – A Catalogue of the Indian Miniatures*, Dublin, 1936, vol. 1, ms. 2

The date H 978 [= 1570–1571] is given separately on three different folios of the manuscript.

1571 *Anwar-i-Suhaili*
Copied by Muhibb-Ali b. Hasan
School of Oriental and African Studies, University of London (Ms. 10102)
Ref.: Losty, *Art of the Book*, no. 57
Figs. 19 and 54

As translated here by Wheeler M. Thackston, the colophon reads: "*[Tammat] al-kitāb ni-'awn al-malik al-wahhāb fī tārikh 22 shahr rabī' al-ākhar. Ḥarrahu'l-faqīr al-mudhnib Muḥibb- 'Ali ibn Ḥasan Sirrī, ghafara 'llāhu dhunūbahu sanat 978.*" ["The book was completed with the help of the All-Bestowing King on the date of 22 Rabi II. Written by the poor sinner Muhibb-Ali, son of Hasan Sirri (may God forgive the sins of both of them). Year 978 (= 29 April 1571)."]

1582–1594 *Tarikh-i-Alfi*
Dispersed
Ref.: Milo C. Beach, *The Imperial Image – Paintings for the Mughal Court*, Washington, D.C., 1981, pp. 91–99

According to contemporary historical sources cited in the reference above, the writing of this text was commissioned in H 990 [= 1582–1583], with a final copy presented to the emperor in H 1002 [= 1593–1594].

1582–1586 *Razmnama*
Maharaja Sawai Man Singh II City Palace Museum, Jaipur
Ref.: M. A. Chagatai, "The illustrated edition of the Razm Nama," *Bulletin of the Deccan College Research Institute* 5, 1943–1944, pp. 281–329; Robert Skelton, "Mughal paintings from Harivamsa manuscript," *Yearbook of the Victoria and Albert Museum* II, p. 48; Beach, *Imperial Image*, pp. 68–71; 215–218.
Fig. 23

The text of this manuscript was commissioned in 1582, according to references cited in Beach, while Skelton has found separate dates on some paintings from 1585 and (perhaps) 1586.

1583 *Kitab-i-Saat*
Copied at Hajipur by Muhammad Yusuf for Khan-i-Azam al-Mashhur Mirza Aziz Koka on 21st Shawwal, H 991 (= November 7, 1583)
Collection of Hashem Khosrovani
Ref.: P. & D. Colnaghi and Co. Ltd., *Indian Painting*, 1978, no. 5
Fig. 43

1588 *Ramayana*
Maharaja Sawai Man Singh II City Palace Museum, Jaipur
Ref.: A. K. Das, "An introductory note on the Emperor Akbar's *Ramayana* and its miniatures," in Robert Skelton (ed.), *Facets of Indian Art*, New Delhi, 1987, pp. 94–104

According to Dr. Das, the manuscript was completed on 28 Zu'l-hijja, H 997 [= November 1588]. For information about a related *Ramayana* made for Abd ar-Rahim *Khan-i khanan*, see Beach, *Imperial Image*, pp. 128–155.

1588 *Diwan* of Anwari
Copied at Lahore
Harvard University Art Museums (Arthur M. Sackler Museum) (1960.117.15)
Ref.: Stuart Cary Welch and Annemarie Schimmel, *Anwari's Diwan: A Pocketbook for Akbar*, New York, 1983
Fig. 34

As given in Welch and Schimmel, the colophon reads:
"This elegant copy was completed at the hand of the sinful slave who hopes for God's mercy . . . [name obliterated] . . . in the city of Lahore at the beginning of Dhu'l-qa'da 996 [= September 22, 1588]."

1589 *Baburnama*
Dispersed
Ref.: Ellen Smart, "Four illustrated Mughal Babur-nama manuscripts," *Art and Archaeology Research Papers*, no. 3, pp. 54–58
Plate D and figs. 41 and 42

This appears to be the manuscript referred to by Abu'l Fazl in the *Akbarnama* as having been presented to the Emperor in 1589 (Abu'l Fazl, *Akbar Nama*, vol. III, p. 862).

1591 *Ragamala*
Painted at Chunar
Dispersed
Ref.: Milo C. Beach, *Rajput Painting at Bundi and Kota*, Ascona, 1973, pp. 6–10; Robert Skelton, "Shaykh Phul and the origins of Bundi painting," *Chhavi* 2, Banaras, 1981, pp. 123–129; Karl Khandalavala, "Editorial comment on the Chunar Ragamala," *Lalit Kala* 22, pp. 71–72
Figs. 27 and 120

As translated here by Wheeler M. Thackston, the colophon reads: "*Huwa 'llāh ta'ālā. Kitāb-i Rāg Mālā tayār shud roz-i chahārshamba ba-waqt-i peshin dar maqām-i Chunār. Shāgirdān-i Mīr Sayyid 'Alī Nādir al-Mulk Humāyūnshāhī wā Khwāja 'Abdul-Samad Shīrīn-Qalam banda Shaykh 'Ali wa Shaykh Hātam* [?] *walad-i Shaykh Bah[l]ūl Chisti. Maḥarrar fī'l-tārīkh 29 māh-i Rabī' al-āxar sana 999. Katabahu banda Dāūd walad-i Sayyid Qapū* [?]." ["The book of Ragamala was prepared [finished] on Wednesday noon in Chunar. Pupils of Mir Sayyid-Ali Nadirulmulk Humayunshahi and Khwaja Abdul-Samad Shirin-Qalam, the slave Shaykh Hasan and Shaykh Ali and Shaykh Hatam [?] son of Shaykh Bahlul [?] Chisti. Written on the 29th of Rabi' II 999 [= September 22, 1591]. Inscribed by the slave Daud, son of Sayyid Qapu [?]."]

See also the reading by Simon Digby given in Beach, *Rajput Painting*, p. 9.

1596 *Yashodara Charitra*
Probably at Idar (Gujarat)
Private collection
Ref.: Doshi, *Masterpieces*, figs. 19, 21

1597 *Akbarnama*
British Library, London (Or. 12988), Chester Beatty Library, Dublin (Ms. 3), and dispersed
Refs.: T. W. Arnold and J. V. S. Wilkinson, *The Library of A. Chester Beatty – A Catalogue of Indian Miniatures*, London, 1936, ms. 3; Jeremiah P. Losty, *The Art of the Book in India*, London, 1982, nos. 70–71; John Seyller, "Scribal Notes on Mughal Manuscript Illustrations," *Artibus Asiae*, vol. 48, nos. 3/4, pp. 261–275
Fig. 45

The dating has been established by Seyller, based on marginal annotations.

1596–1597 *Anwar-i-Suhaili*
Copied at Lahore by Abdul-Rahim Harawi
Bharat Kala Bhavan, Varanasi
Ref.: Rai Krishnadasa, "A Fable Book for Akbar," *Times of India Annual*, 1966, pp. 1–40
Fig. 55

As translated here by Wheeler M. Thackston, the colophon reads: "*Tammat 'alā yad al-faqīr al-mudhnib 'Abdul-Raḥīm al-Harawī satara 'llāhu 'uyūbahu wa-ghafara dhunūbahu. Bi-Dār al-salṭana Lāhor marqūm gasht sana 1005 tamm.*" ["Finished by the hand of the poor sinner Abdul-Rahim Harawi (may God cover his faults and forgive his sons). Written at the Seat of the Sultanate Lahore in the year 1005 [= 1596–1597]."]

1597–1598 *Khamsa* of Amir Khusrau Dihlavi
Copied by Muhammad Husayn Zarrin-Qalam
Walters Art Gallery, Baltimore (w.624)
Ref.: Losty, *Art of the Book*, no. 66; Barbara Brend, "Akbar's *Khamsah* of Amir Khusrau Dihlavi, a reconstruction of the cycle of illustration," *Artibus Asiae*, vol. 49, nos. 3/4, pp. 281–315
Figs. 38 and 39

As translated here by Wheeler M. Thackston, the colophon lists the scribe and the date: "*al- 'abd al-mudhnib al-faqīr al-ḥaqīr Muḥammad Ḥusayn Zarrīn-Qalam fī tārīkh-i sana-i 42 bi-itmām rasīd.*" ["The poor, miserable, sinning slave Muhammad Husayn Zarrin-Qalam in the [regnal] year 42 [= 1597–1598]."]

1598 *Razmnama*
Dispersed
Ref.: M. A. Chagatai, "The illustrated edition of the Razm Nama," *Bulletin of the Deccan College Research Institute* 5, 1943–1944, pp. 281–329; John Seyller, "Model and copy: the illustration of three *Razmnama* manuscripts," *Archives of Asian Art* 38, 1985, pp. 37–66
Figs. 24 and 25

1598 *Baburnama*
Dispersed
Ref.: Ellen Smart, "Four illustrated Babur-nama manuscripts," *Art and Archaeology Research Papers* 3, 1973, pp. 54–58.

The date of completion of the manuscript is given in Abu'l Fazl, *Akbar Nama*, vol. III, p. 862.

1604–1605 *Nafahat al-uns*
Copied at Agra by Abdul-Rahim Shirin-Qalam Akbarshahi
British Library (Or. 1362)
Ref.: Losty, *Art of the Book*, no. 69
Fig. 46

As translated here by Wheeler M. Thackston, the colophon reads: "*Itmām yāft u anjām pazīruft īn kitāb-i-girāmī bi-rasm-i khizāna-i kutub u kitābkhana-i 'ali-i bandagān-i ḥaḍrat-i khilāfat-panāh shāhanshāh Jalāl al-Dīn wa'l-Dunyā Akbar Bādshāh khallada 'llāhu ẓilāla salṭanatihi wa-iqbālihi kamtarīn-i khānazādān 'Abd al-Rahīm kātib shīrīn-qalam-i Akbarshāhi. Satara 'llahu 'uyūbahu wa-ghafara dhunūbahu bi-Dār al-Khilāfa Agra sana-i 49.*" ["This book completed for the exalted treasury of books and library of the slaves of His Majesty Refuge of the Caliphate King of Kings Jalaluddin . . . Akbar Badshah (may God make the shadow of his reign and good fortune continue forever). The least of slaves 'Abdul-Rahim Shirin-Qalam Akbarshahi copyist . . . at Agra, [regnal] year 49 [= 1604–1605]."]

1604–1610 *Anwar-i-Suhaili*
British Library (Add. 18579)
Ref.: J. V. S. Wilkinson, *The Lights of Canopus: Anwar i Suhaili*, London, 1929; Losty, *Art of the Book*, no. 75
Figs. 48–49 and 56

While the completion of the manuscript is dated in the colophon to H 1019 [= 1610–1611], two folios bear independent dates of H 1013 [= 1604–1605].

1605 *Bustan* of Sa'di
Copied at Agra by Abdul-Rahim *Ambarin-Qalam*
Soudavar Collection
Ref.: Ivan Stchoukine, "Un Bustan de Sa di illustre par des artistes Moghols," *Revue des Arts Asiatiques*, vol. 11, pp. 68–75
Plate F

As translated here by Wheeler M. Thackston, the colophon reads: "*Tammat 'alā yad-al 'abd al-mudhnib al-faqīr al-haqīr 'Abd al-Raḥīm al-Harawī 'Anbarīn-Qalam-satara 'llāhu 'uyūbahu wa-ghafara dhunūbahu-fī shuhūr sanat arba' 'ashar wa-alf min al-hijriyya* [sic] *al-nabawiyya taḥrīran bi-baldat Āgra.*" ["Completed by the sinful slave, the poor, miserable Abdul-Rahim al-Harawi Anbarin-Qalam ['ambergris pen'] – may God cover his faults and forgive his sins – in the year 1014 [= 1605–1606] of the hegira, written in Agra."]

Ref.: Ralph Pinder-Wilson, "Three illustrated manuscripts of the Mughal period," *Ars Orientalis* 2, pp. 418–422
Fig. 105

1669 *Meghaduta*
Copied at Asani
L.D. Institute of Indology, Ahmedabad
Ref.: Moti Chandra and Umakant P. Shah, "New documents of Jaina Paintings," in *Sri Mahavir Jaina Vidyalaya Golden Jubilee Volume*, Part 1, Bombay, 1968, p. 370

The authors identify the site of Asani with a town near Jaunpur (U.P.). Instead, on stylistic grounds, it is more probably from the Asani near Jodhpur (in Rajasthan).

1682 *Astasahasrika Prajnaparamita*
Nepalese
Museum of Fine Arts, Boston, and Arthur M. Sackler Museum, Harvard University
Fig. 130

As translated by Ian Alsop, the inscription, in Newari script, records the finishing of the manuscript on Friday, the seventh of the bright half of the month of Magha, in the year of Nepal Samvat 802 [= January–February 1682], during the reign of King Srinivasa Malla.

1695 *Rasamanjari*
Painted at Basohli by Devidasa
Dispersed
Refs.: W. G. Archer, *Indian Paintings from the Punjab Hills*, London, 1973, pp. 43–46

As translated by H. Sastri and published by W. G. Archer, the inscription reads: "In order to see the creation of God and to realize the hollowness of the world this [*Chittarasamanjari*], containing many pictures, [which are] the wealth [i.e., creation] of mind, was caused to be prepared by Raja Kirpala Pal. [It was completed] on the auspicious day, the seventh *tithi* of the bright fortnight of Magha [January–February] in the Vikrama year [which is] counted by the eyes [two], the arrows [five], the sages [seven] and the moon [one] [i.e., s 1752 = 1695] in the town called Vivashthali [the modern Basohli] which lies on the beautiful banks of the Airavati [the modern Ravi], by Devidasa, who is well-versed in the art of painting."

1709 *Ragamala*
Painted at Amber; text written by Ramakrishna mahatma
Ref.: Shridhar Andhare, "A dated Amber Ragamala and the problem of provenance of the eighteenth century Jaipuri paintings," *Lalit Kala* 15, pp. 47–51

As given by Andhare, the colophon reads: "In the year Samvat 1766 [= 1709] in the month of Jetha vadi 3 on a Saturday written by Ramakrishna mahatma in the fort of Amber during the reign of Jai Singh."

1723 *Gita Govinda*
Painted at Aurangabad
Rajasthan Oriental Research Bureau, Udaipur
Unpublished

1730 *Gita Govinda*
Dispersed
Ref.: Archer, *Indian paintings*, pp. 46–48
Plate M

As published by W. G. Archer, the inscription reads: "In the Vikrama year corresponding to the sages [seven], the gems [eight], the mountains [seven] and the moon [one] [i.e., s 1787 or 1730], the Lady Malini who was famed for her good conduct and was skilled in the Malini meter, who was referred by the virtuous and was devoted to the Unborn [i.e., Vishnu] had this picture [book] of the *Gita Govinda*, graced by charming calligraphy, made by the [male] painter, Manaku."

1799 *Madhu Malati*
Painted at Raghunathpur (Kulu) by Bhagvan
Dispersed
Ref.: Archer, *Indian Paintings*, p. 339
Fig. 160

As translated by B. N. Goswamy and published by Archer, the inscription reads: "In the city of Raghunathpur, in the reign of Sri Pritam Singh, the painter Bhagvan made this *kalasa* [auspicious object] and presented it. The month was Bhadra [August-September], the date the fifth, the day Wednesday, the scribe Sagara, the painter the servant Bhagvan. In the revered samvat year 1856 [= 1799]."

1816 *Ramayana*
Painted at Basohli by Ranjha, son of Nainsukh
Bharat Kala Bhavan, Banaras
Ref.: B. N. Goswamy, "The artist Ranjha and a dated set of *Ramayana* drawings," *Chhavi* 1, 1971, pp. 224–231; Archer, *Indian Paintings*, pp. 52–53
Fig. 173

As translated by Goswamy, the inscription reads: "In the *vikrama samvat*, calculated by Rama [three], Rishi [seven], Vasu [eight] and Bhu [one] [i.e., 1873 [= 1816]] in the dark half of the month of Shravan, on Wednesday the 7th, in the town of Basohli, during the reign of Sri Raja Bhupendra Pal, the learned Sudarshan, born in the family of Kashmiri [Brahmins], composed according to his best understanding, this *bhasha* for the artist Ranjha who gave visual form to the verses. This rendering of the *katha* [story] of the *Ramayana* is blessed by Rama himself; it enables all to cross the world of misery and absolves them of a multitude of sins. May [this *bhasha*] be conducive to the prosperity, happiness, long life and well-being of the whole world."

BIBLIOGRAPHICAL ESSAY

PAINTING BEFORE 1540

Few recent studies of Indian painting have considered the established traditional Indian styles out of which Sultanate, Rajput, Mughal, and Deccani painting developed and in the context of which they should more frequently be seen. Douglas Barrett and Basil Gray, *Indian Painting*, Geneva, 1963, did discuss the earlier traditions of wall-painting, and their discussion provides a framework for very necessary future studies; otherwise, however, their survey study – although the best currently available – has long been out of date. *Ajanta Murals*, edited by A. Ghosh, New Delhi, 1967; C. Sivaramamurti, *South Indian Paintings*, New Delhi, 1968; Amancharla Gopala Rao, *Lepakshi*, Hyderabad, 1969; and C. Sivaramamurti, *Vijayanagara Paintings*, New Delhi, 1985, all provide important information about and reproductions of earlier wall-paintings at major sites.

Several studies provide an overview of the various regional styles of manuscript painting that immediately preceded the advent of Mughal influence. The most thorough survey, and the best introduction to the subject, remains Karl Khandalavala and Moti Chandra, *New Documents of Indian Painting – A Reappraisal*, New Delhi, 1969. Many of the ideas presented there are further expanded in Moti Chandra, *Studies in Early Indian Painting*, London, 1974. Pramod Chandra, *The Tuti-Nama of The Cleveland Museum of Art and the Origins of Mughal Painting*, Graz, 1976, thoroughly discusses how these pre-Mughal styles affected and directed early Mughal manuscript illustrations. It is essential reading.

These books are the first to isolate and define sultanate styles alongside the more familiar Hindu and Jain paintings, although the identification of many specific sultanate works remains under dispute. Irma L. Fraad and Richard Ettinghausen have argued that several manuscripts, once considered provincial Persian, were actually sultanate Indian. Their article "Sultanate painting in Persian style," *Chhavi – Golden Jubilee Volume, Bharat Kala Bhavan, 1920–1970*, Banaras, 1979, pp. 48–66, is still controversial in detail, for there is considerable disagreement about those variations of Persian style that might indicate an Indian origin. The principle that those two authors established, that various patrons in India demanded works very close in style to those of Iran, is well accepted now, however. Simon Digby has explored textual sources for sultanate art in "The literary evidence for painting in the Delhi sultanate," *Bulletin of the American Academy of Benares*, Volume One, Varanasi, 1967, pp. 47–58, thereby providing a model for several later anthologies of literary evidence, an enormously important source of documentation.

There are so many dated Jain manuscripts that understanding of the historical development of this tradition provides few problems, or surprises. Dr. Saryu Doshi in *Masterpieces of Jain Painting*, Bombay, 1985, has nonetheless assembled new material of great interest, including many works which help to relate Jain illustrations to those done for other communities, and her study includes an essential bibliography. She also has proved that Jain painters responded to local artistic traditions. Additional less well-known material is included in Moti Chandra and Umekant P. Shah, "New documents of Jaina paintings," *Sri Mahavira Jaina Vidyalaya – Golden Jubilee Volume*, Bombay, 1968. Older, encyclopedic surveys are also essential to understanding these distinctive manuscripts, and they provide important documentary information; the most important are Moti Chandra, *Jain Miniature Paintings from Western India*, Ahmedabad, 1949; Sarabhai M. Nawab, *Masterpieces of the Kalpasutra Paintings*, Ahmedabad, 1956; and Sarabhai M. Nawab, *The Oldest Rajasthani Paintings from Jain Bhandars*, Ahmedabad, 1959.

The following additional studies of pre-Mughal manuscript illustration are especially important: Barbara Brend, "The British Library's *Shahnama* of 1438 as a sultanate manuscript," in Robert Skelton (ed.), *Facets of Indian Art*, New Delhi, 1987, pp. 87–93; W. Norman Brown, *The Vasanta Vilasa*, Washington, 1962; Saryu Doshi, "An illustrated Adipurana of 1404 A.D. from Yoginipur," in *Chhavi*, pp. 382–391; Richard Ettinghausen, "The Bustan manuscript of Sultan Nasir-Shah Khalji," *Marg*, vol. 12, no. 3, pp. 42–43; B. N. Goswamy, *A Jainesque Sultanate Shahnama*, Zurich, 1988; Goswamy, "A pre-Mughal *Shahnama* from Jaunpur," in Karl J. Khandalavala (ed.), *An Age of Splendour: Islamic Art in India*, Bombay, 1983; Goswamy, "In the sultan's shadow: pre-Mughal painting in and around Delhi," in R. K. Frykenberg (ed.), *Delhi Through the Ages – Essays in Urban History, Culture and Society*, Delhi, 1986, pp. 129–142; Goswamy, V. C. Ohri, and Ajit Singh, "A 'Chaurapanchasika style' manuscript from the pahari area," *Lalit Kala* 21, pp. 9–21; Karl Khandalavala, Moti Chandra, Pramod Chandra, and Parmeshwari Lal Gupta, "A new document of Indian painting," *Lalit Kala* 10, pp. 45–54; Anand Krishna, "An illustrated manuscript of the Laur-Chanda in the Staatsbibliothek," in *Chhavi* 2, Banaras, 1981, pp. 275–289; Robert Skelton, "The Ni'mat nama: A landmark in Malwa paintings," *Marg*, vol. 12, no. 3, pp. 44–50; Robert Skelton, "The *Iskandar Nama* of Nusrat Shah," in P. & D. Colnaghi and Co., Ltd., *Indian Painting*, London, 1978, pp. 135–152.

RAJPUT AND RELATED PAINTINGS FROM RAJASTHAN

There is no single, authoritative survey of Rajput and related paintings, for the subject has never accommodated itself to – or rewarded – the established disciplinary methods of European art-historical scholarship. Some reasons for this are proposed in Milo Cleveland Beach, "The context of Rajput painting," *Ars Orientalis* 10, pp. 11–18, which also discusses in theoretical terms the interrelationship of Rajput, Mughal, and Deccani works. This is explored too in an important exhibition catalogue by Vishakha Desai, *Life at Court: Art for India's Rulers, 16th–19th Centuries*, Boston, 1985, as well as in Milo C. Beach, *The Art of India and Pakistan*, Durham, North Carolina, 1985.

Historically, it was the ground-breaking study by Ananda K. Coomaraswamy, *Rajput Painting*, London, 1916, that launched interest in the field and encouraged the collecting of Rajput works in Europe and America. The historical information given there, however, and the attributions, are no longer valid. Sherman E. Lee, *Rajput Painting*, New York, 1960, served as catalogue to the first major exhibition of Indian painting in the United States. It includes brief text that renewed interest in the subject and encouraged a new generation of collectors. Since then the major quantity of literature on Rajput painting has appeared in exhibition or collection catalogues, a category of publication not comprehensively listed here.

However, there are important exceptions. Andrew Topsfield, *Paintings from*

Rajasthan in the National Gallery of Victoria, Melbourne, 1980, presents a fine, if brief, overview of painting at Udaipur in Mewar State through a catalogue of works formerly in the collections of the maharanas. It is the first major new contribution to our understanding of this school since Hermann Goetz, "The first golden age of Udaipur: Rajput art in Mewar during the period of Mughal supremacy," *Ars Orientalis* 2, pp. 427–438, and it was quickly followed by Topsfield's "Sahibdin's *Gita-Govinda* illustrations," *Chhavi* 2, pp. 231–238. His "Ketelaar's embassy and the farangi theme in the art of Udaipur," *Oriental Art*, vol. 30, no. 4, pp. 350–367, discusses a particular group of works which show members of the Dutch East India Company who traveled through Mewar in 1711. Shridhar Andhare, "Mewar painters, their status and genealogies," in Skelton, *Facets*, pp. 176–184 provides initial identification of some specific artists.

Perhaps most interesting about Udaipuri painting is its relation to works from other Mewari schools. One of the most distinctive and artistically prolific subsidiary courts in Mewar was Devgarh, and many of its paintings are well documented historically. Shridhar Andhare, "Painting from the thikana of Deogarh," *Bulletin of the Prince of Wales Museum of Western India* 10, pp. 43–54, first isolated these works, and subsequent studies include Milo Cleveland Beach, "Painting at Devgarh," *Archives of Asian Art* 24, pp. 23–35; and Shridhar Andhare and Rawat Nahar Singh, *Deogarh Painting*, Bombay, 1977. It is clear from these discussions that painting at Devgarh was in no way inferior artistically to works from the court of the maharana. Nathadvara, another town in Mewar, was the site of an important Vaisnavite temple, where several hundred painters worked to decorate the temple rooms and make painted images for purchase. Robert Skelton, *Rajput Temple Paintings of the Krishna Cult*, New York, 1976, gives an overview of this tradition, but Amit Ambalal, *Krishna as Srinathji – Rajasthani Paintings from Nathadvara*, Ahmedabad, 1987, is a more thorough survey. It should be read in conjunction with Renaldo Maduro, *Artistic Creativity in a Brahmin Painter Community*, Los Angeles, 1976. This latter work is an anthropological and psychological study of Nathadvara painters, and its concerns can be extended through G. Morris Carstairs, *The Twice-Born*, Bloomington, 1957, a psychoanalytic study of a thikana community in Mewar. It provides interesting evidence of the perceived ascending cultural hierarchy of Hindu, Muslim, and European that helps to explain interactions among artistic styles, in which some influences come from cultural groups thought to be superior in rank. Bhilwara and Shahpura, other important Mewari towns, have long been the home of an active tradition of village painting: the Pabuji and Dev Narayan *padhs*, or painted narrative scrolls. They are closely related to early, pre-Mughal styles from Mewar, and their study can further illuminate both chronological and social developments. These works have barely been published and need serious study; but see Jyotindra Jain and Aarti Aggarwala, *National Handicrafts and Handlooms Museum, New Delhi*, Ahmedabad, 1989, pp. 112–113. The varied readings about painting in Mewar listed here, if taken together with more conventional publications listed in the bibliographies they include, can help inspire a new methodology for the study of Rajasthani painting. It is essential that the interrelationship of court and non-court styles be dealt with; the painters, after all, easily moved from one such patronage group to another.

Painting in the states of Bundi and Kota has recently been the subject of important new studies. The historical literature on these painting traditions begins with W. G. Archer, *Indian Painting in Bundi and Kotah*, London, 1959, and Pramod Chandra, *Bundi Painting*, Delhi, 1959. Milo Cleveland Beach, *Rajput Painting at Bundi and Kota*, Ascona, 1974, provided additional material and argued for an earlier origin and distinctive character for Kota works; that study also isolated and discussed related styles found in the territories of Uniara and Raghugarh. Elements of all these early studies have been superseded by the research of such scholars as Joachim Bautze, as found in his "A contemporary and inscribed equestrian portrait of Jagat Singh of Kota," in *Deyadharma – Studies in Memory of Dr. D. C. Sircar*, Delhi, 1986, pp. 47–64; "Mughal and Deccani influence on early 17th-century murals of Bundi," in Skelton, *Facets*, pp. 168–175; *Drei "Bundi"-Ragamalas – Ein Beitrag zur Geschichte der Rajputischen Wandmalerei*, Stuttgart, 1987; and "Portraitmalerei unter Maharao Ram Singh von Kota," *Artibus Asiae*, vol. 59, nos. 3/4, pp. 316–350. The latter article reproduces for the first time a photograph of Maharao Ram Singh II, whose face has long been familiar from countless paintings. It is a startling discovery, and allows very useful comparisons. Dr. Bautze's greatest contributions, however, are based on publication of important wall-paintings within the palace complexes in both states. See also Robert Skelton, "Shaykh Phul and the Origins of Bundi Painting," *Chhavi* 2, pp. 123–129; Carisse Beaune, "The mural paintings of Bundi and Kota," *Orientations*, June 1985, pp. 30–44; and a study by Maharaj Kumar Brijraj Singh, *The Kingdom that was Kota*, New Delhi, 1985.

Among additional studies of Rajasthani painting must be listed Hermann Goetz, *The Art and Architecture of Bikaner State*, Oxford, 1950, still a very important work. Despite the massive amount of inscriptionally signed and dated material which has appeared since this investigation – Bikaner has probably the best documentary source materials of all Rajput schools – there has been no recent monographic publication. Very important Bikaner works, including several inscribed portraits of artists, are included in Karl Khandalavala, Moti Chandra, and Pramod Chandra, *Miniature Painting – A Catalogue of the Exhibition of the Sri Motichand Khajanchi Collection Held at the Lalit Kala Akademi, 1960*, New Delhi, 1960; and see also Naval Krishna, "Bikaneri miniature painting workshops of Ruknuddin Ibrahim and Nathu," *Lalit Kala* 21, pp. 23–27. This school would be a particularly fruitful topic for future research.

Eric Dickinson and Karl Khandalavala, *Kishangarh Painting*, New Delhi, 1959, and M. S. Randhawa and D. S. Randhawa, *Kishangarh Painting*, Bombay, 1980, both explore an especially individualistic school at a court near Ajmer; the books, however, are essentially picture books with text. Painting at Sawar (also near Ajmer) and Isarda (a dependency of Jaipur) is discussed in Indar Pasricha, "Painting at Sawar and at Isarda in the 17th century," *Oriental Art*, vol. 28, no. 3, pp. 257–269. Jaipur itself must have been one of the most prolific schools of painting in Rajasthan. That virtually nothing has been written about the artistic traditions of that court is further evidence of the substantial work that needs to be done on Rajasthani art. The early studies of various Rajput artistic traditions by Hermann Goetz were posthumously republished under his name as *Rajput Art and Architecture*, Wiesbaden, 1978, a volume edited by Jyotindra Jain and Jutta Jain-Neubauer. While these articles are no longer always up-to-date, they remain very substantial contributions to the field, and are essential reading. Rose Maria Cimino, *Vita di Corte nel Rajasthan*, Florence, 1985, is an exhibition catalogue that includes previously unpublished material and an extensive survey text.

PAINTINGS FROM THE PUNJAB HILLS

Writings about specific schools of painting in the hill regions are far more plentiful than those for Rajasthan. These were the works most lauded in the Coomaraswamy study of Rajput painting published in 1916, although the interest of W. G. Archer, first shown in his *Indian Painting in the Punjab Hills*, London, 1952, has been far more influential. (Karl Khandalavala, *Pahari Miniature Painting*, Bombay, 1958, soon provided a more comprehensive survey, but many of his assertions – based on conjecture and all too colorful local traditions – could not be accepted.) Archer wrote voluminously on the hill schools, ending with his great, two-volume *Indian Paintings from the Punjab Hills*, New York, 1973. There he exhaustively examined the historical and visual evidence for attributions to each hill court, arguing that each such school had a distinctively local visual character. His work is an important methodological statement for the study of all Rajput, perhaps even all Indian, painting.

B. N. Goswamy, "Pahari painting: the family as the basis of style," *Marg*, vol. 21, no. 4, pp. 17–62, had already seriously challenged Archer's seemingly straightforward approach. Goswamy's theory was further developed in his "Of patronage and pahari painting," in Pratapaditya Pal (ed.), *Aspects of Indian Art*, Leiden, 1972. He argued that styles were determined by family training, not by the court at which the painter eventually worked, and his evidence is strong. Together with Eberhard Fischer, he has provided specific further information about individual artistic personalities in *Pahari-Meister: Hofische Malerei aus den Bergen Nord-Indiens*, Zurich, 1990, and an exhaustive study of the painter Nainsukh is forthcoming. In any case, an awareness of the implications of the different organizational principles used by Archer and Goswamy is necessary to future art-historical studies of Rajput works.

Archer's 1974 study provides a superb bibliography, to which the only additions can be those few works published since. (The thoroughness of Archer's *magnum opus* has acted to discourage, rather than inspire, further studies of pahari painting, however, a situation which needs to end. It is time to examine the conflict between the Archer and Goswamy theories.) Especially important citations in Archer include B. N. Goswamy, "The problem of the artist 'Nainsukh of Jasrota'," *Artibus Asiae*, vol. 28, no. 2, pp. 205–210, which centers on the greatest painter from the family of Pandit Seu, the most influential artistic family in the hills. The same author's *Pahari Paintings of the Nala-Damayanti Theme*, New Delhi, 1975, discusses various phases in the preparation of a major series of illustrations, and notes that priests and pandits were frequently called upon to approve or correct compositions to assure ritual or textual accuracy. This gives rare insight into the artistic process and the all-important role of established tradition – often religious tradition – in determining acceptable artistic results.

Two recent articles have together suggested that understanding of the earliest phases of painting in the hills has been misunderstood. Catherine Glynn, "Early painting in Mandi," *Artibus Asiae*, vol. 44, no. 1, pp. 21–64, argues that a group of paintings hitherto attributed to Bikaner about 1680 should instead be assigned to Mandi about 1640. They show a strong Mughal stylistic influence which is later not so clearly evident, and her theories, while disputed, are important. B. N. Goswamy, V. C. Ohri, and Ajit Singh, "A 'Chaurapanchasika style' manuscript from the pahari area," *Lalit Kala* 21, pp. 9–21, proposes a sixteenth-century tradition of painting in the hill areas.

Materials for a future substantial exploration of the relation of text to image are especially copious for hill painting. Several publications by M. S. Randhawa should be mentioned: *Kangra Paintings of the Bhagavata Purana*, New Delhi, 1960; *Kangra Paintings on Love*, New Delhi, 1962; *Kangra Paintings of the Gita Govinda*, New Delhi, 1963; and *Kangra Ragamala Painting*, New Delhi, 1971, all present specific images along with the text passages they illustrate. A comparative study of *Ragamala* illustrations from all periods is provided in Klaus Ebeling, *Ragamala Painting*, New Delhi, 1973; and see also Pratapaditya Pal, *Ragamala Paintings in the Museum of Fine*

Arts, Boston, Boston, 1967. For images of Krishna in painting and their relationship to works in other media, see P. Banerjea, *The Life of Krishna in Indian Art*, New Delhi, 1978; and Walter M. Spink, *Krishnamandala – A Devotional Theme in Indian Art*, Ann Arbor, 1971.

MUGHAL PAINTING

The origin and definition of early Mughal painting continue to be disputed. The most thorough study is Chandra, *Tuti-nama*. It concentrates on a manuscript central to the period, and relates it to all the major known comparative material. Important alternate interpretations are provided in Anand Krishna, "A reassessment of the Tuti-nama illustrations in the Cleveland Museum of Art (and related problems on early Mughal painting and painters)," *Artibus Asiae*, vol. 35, no. 3, pp. 241–263; and Karl J. Khandalavala and Jagdish Mittal, "An Early Akbari Manuscript of Tilasm and Zodiac," *Lalit Kala* 14, pp. 8–20. Milo Cleveland Beach, *Early Mughal Painting*, Cambridge, Mass. and London, 1987, argues for an active tradition of painting under Humayun, attributing to him subjects and styles thought by others to be the result of Akbar's patronage. All these studies discuss the *Hamzanama* ms., which is most thoroughly published in Gerhard Egger, *Hamza-nama*, two volumes, Graz, 1974 and 1982; and Heinrich Gluck, *Die indischen Miniaturen des Hamzae-Romanes im Österreichischen museum fur Kunst und Industrie in Wien und anderen Sammlungen*, Vienna, 1925. The two directors of the *Hamzanama* project have been further and more recently studied. For Abd as-Samad, see Martin Dickson and Stuart Cary Welch, *The Houghton Shahnameh*, Cambridge, Mass., 1981, vol. II, pp. 192–200; Richard Ettinghausen, "'Abdu 's-Samad," *Encyclopedia of World Art*, vol. I, New York, 1960, pp. 15–20 and plates 14–17. Mir Sayyid Ali is also discussed in Dickson and Welch, *Shahnameh*, vol. I, pp. 178–191.

Scholarly survey source books of Mughal painting include Milo Cleveland Beach, *The Imperial Image – Paintings for the Mughal Court*, Washington, D.C., 1981, and the same author's *The Grand Mogul – Imperial Painting in India 1600–1660*, Williamstown, Mass., 1978. These books list and discuss the major imperial manuscripts and artists active between 1550 and 1660, and give extensive bibliographical references. Further important information is found in Michael Brand and Glenn D. Lowry, *Akbar's India: Art from the Mughal City of Victory*, New York, 1986; Asok Kumar Das, *Mughal Painting During Jahangir's Time*, Calcutta, 1978; and Joseph M. Dye III, "Artists for the Emperor," in P. Pal, J. Leoshko, J. M. Dye III, and S. Markel, *Romance of the Taj Mahal*, Los Angeles, 1989, pp. 88–127. Stuart Cary Welch, Annemarie Schimmel, Marie L. Swietochowski, and Wheeler M. Thackston discuss the Kevorkian Album, a major Shahjahani anthology, in *The Emperor's Album*, New York, 1987. It establishes a new methodology for studying and reassembling dispersed Mughal album pages. Jeremiah P. Losty, *The Art of the Book in India*, London, The British Library, 1982, is also a basic reference source for the period, but includes much non-Mughal material as well.

Questions regarding the importance of workshop procedures, and of the individual artist, to the determination of style, are subjects that are discussed in three important articles by John Seyller, "Model and copy: the illustration of three *Razmnama* manuscripts," *Archives of Asian Art* 38, pp. 37–66; "The School of Oriental and African Studies *Anvar-i Suhayli*: the illustration of a de luxe Mughal manuscript," *Ars*

Orientalis 16, pp. 119–51; and "Scribal notes on Mughal manuscript illustrations," *Artibus Asiae*, vol. 48, nos. 3–4, pp. 247–277. These are studies which have introduced a new category of evidence to Mughal manuscript studies, and they should be supplemented by Marianne Shreve-Simpson, "The production and patronage of the *Haft Aurang* by Jami in the Freer Gallery of Art," *Ars Orientalis* 13, pp. 93–120, which throws into question the reliability of colophons on Islamic manuscripts in the determination of provenance.

Many further studies have investigated the role of European influences in the development of Mughal style. The best historical background material has long been known: Edward Maclagan, *The Jesuits and the Great Mogul*, New York (reprint), 1972; *Akbar and the Jesuits – An Account of the Jesuit Missions to the Court of Akbar by Father Pierre du Jarric, S.J.*, translated by C. H. Payne, London, 1926; *Jahangir and the Jesuits – With an Account of the Travels of Benedict Goes and the Mission to Pegu from the Relations of Father Fernao Guerreiro, S.J.*, translated by C. H. Payne, London, 1930. All provide important contemporary references to European art and artists. General discussions of artistic influences specifically are found in Brand and Lowry, *Akbar's India*; and Beach, *The Grand Mogul*. The identification of European source materials is given in Milo Cleveland Beach, "A European source for early Mughal painting," *Oriental Art*, vol. 22, no. 2, pp. 180–188; Beach, "The Mughal painter Abu'l Hasan and some English sources for his style," *Journal of the Walters Art Gallery*, vol. 38 (1980), pp. 7–33; Beach, "The Gulshan Album and its European sources," *Bulletin of the Museum of Fine Arts, Boston* 332, pp. 63–91; Richard Ettinghausen, "New pictorial evidence for Catholic missionary activity in Mughal India," *Perennitas*, Munster, 1963; Ettinghausen, "The emperor's choice," *De Artibus Opuscula XL: Essays in Honor of Erwin Panofsky*, edited by Millard Meiss, New York, 1961, pp. 98–120; J. V. S. Wilkinson, "Indian Paintings in a Persian Museum," *Burlington Magazine* 66, 1935, pp. 168–171; Ernst Kuhnel and Hermann Goetz, *Indian Book Painting from Jahangir's Album in the State Library, Berlin*, London, 1926. These discussions together establish European sources, their effects, and the routes of contact.

Sub-imperial works of the early seventeenth century have been discussed by Pramod Chandra in "Ustad Salivahana and the Development of Popular Mughal Art," *Lalit Kala* 8, pp. 25–46. For later paintings from courts in eastern India, see Mildred Archer, *Patna Painting*, London, 1948; Robert Skelton, "Murshidabad painting," *Marg*, vol. 10, no. 1, pp. 10–22; Edwin Binney 3rd, "Later Mughal painting," in Pal, *Aspects*, pp. 118–123. While these are valuable studies, much new material has become available in recent years.

Non-art-historical studies of particular importance include S. A. A. Rizvi, *Religious and Intellectual History of the Muslims in Akbar's Reign*, Delhi, 1975; J. F. Richards, "The formulation of imperial authority under Akbar and Jahangir," in J. F. Richards (ed.), *Kingship and Authority in South Asia*, Madison, 1978; and Abdul Aziz, *The Imperial Library of the Mughals*, Delhi, 1974.

OTHER REGIONAL STYLES

Painting in the Deccan was first studied in Stella Kramrisch, *A Survey of Painting in the Deccan*, London, 1937, and subsequently in D. E. Barrett, *Painting of the Deccan*, London, 1958. Mark Zebrowski, *Deccani Painting*, London, 1983, is a thorough new survey of painting in this region and introduces many previously unknown works together with new historical information.

The interplay of local and imported traditions in Western India is discussed in B. N. Goswamy and A. L. Dallapiccola, *A Place Apart – Painting in Kutch, 1720–1820*, Delhi, 1983. Unlike the courtly Deccani and Kutch schools, painting in Maharashtra is primarily concerned with village traditions. Recent publications include Valentina Stache-Rosen, "Story telling in Pinguli paintings," *Artibus Asiae*, vol. 45, no. 4, pp. 253–286; Anna L. Dallapiccola, *Die Paithan Malerei*, Wiesbaden, 1981; and Eva Ray, "Documentation for Paithan paintings," *Artibus Asiae*, vol. 40, no. 4, pp. 239–282. Jyotindra Jain, *Painted Myths of Creation – Art and Ritual of an Indian Tribe*, New Delhi, 1984, helps to define a type of workmanship not discussed in this volume. His description of working procedures, and of the importance of the artist's communal identity in tribal situations, may prove important in helping to improve understanding of non-court workshop methods as they also existed in other social communities. A village tradition from Bihar is explored in Mary C. Lanius, "Mithila painting," in Michael W. Meister (ed.), *Making Things in South Asia*, Philadelphia, 1988, pp. 134–145; Upendra Thakur, *Madhubani Painting*, Atlantic Highlands, N.J., 1982; and Yves Vequaud, *The Women Painters of Mithila*, London, 1977. The Kalighat paintings of Bengal are studied in Hana Knizkova, *The Drawings of the Kalighat Style*, Prague, 1975; and W. G. Archer, *Kalighat Paintings*, London, 1971. Joanna Williams, "A painted *Ragamala* from Orissa," *Lalit Kala* 23, 1988, pp. 14–19; and Joanna Williams and J. P. Das, "Raghunatha Prusti: an Oriya artist," *Artibus Asiae*, vol. 48, nos. 1–2, pp. 131–159, discuss a strong and persistent local style in eastern India. Mildred Archer, *Indian Popular Painting*, London, 1977, is just one of the majesterial volumes produced by a great scholar of Indian painting, and it serves as a fine survey. Manuscripts were also produced in Kashmir in great numbers. Karuna Goswamy, *The Glory of the Great Goddess*, Zurich, 1989, and her "Itinerant Kashmiri artists: notes on the spread of a style," in Meister, *Making Things*, pp. 86–95, are among the first serious studies of a tradition that approached mass production. All of these works help to define the artistic context in which Rajput and Mughal painters worked.

PAINTING OF THE BRITISH PERIOD

Mildred Archer is the greatest authority on British period (or Company) painting, and a bibliography of her individual studies is far too vast to be included here. Many are listed in her major studies: *Company Drawings in the India Office Library*, London, 1972; *British Drawings in the India Office Library*, London, 1969; *Natural History Drawings in the India Office Library*, London, 1962; and, together with her husband W. G. Archer, *Indian Painting for the British 1770–1880*, London, 1955. With Toby Falk, she has also published *India Revealed – The Art and Adventures of James and William Fraser, 1801–35*, London, 1989, which discusses the Fraser Album. While exhibition catalogues have been only sparingly referred to in this bibliographic essay, two should be mentioned here: Pratapaditya Pal and Vidya Dehejia, *From Merchants to Emperors: British Artists and India, 1757–1930*, Ithaca and London, 1986; and Stuart Cary Welch, *Room for Wonder – Indian Painting During the British Period 1760–1880*. They reproduce and discuss unusual and otherwise little known works.

C. SITES

D. PERSONS

THE NEW CAMBRIDGE HISTORY OF INDIA

I The Mughals and their Contemporaries

John F. Richards, *The Mughal Empire*
*M. N. Pearson, *The Portuguese in India*
Catherine B. Asher, *Architecture of Mughal India*
*Milo C. Beach, *Mughal and Rajput Painting*
Bruce B. Lawrence, *Indian Sufism and the Islamic World*
*Burton Stein, *Vijayanagara*
Richard M. Eaton, *Social History of the Deccan*

II Indian States and the Transition to Colonialism

*C. A. Bayly, *Indian Society and the Making of the British Empire*
*P. J. Marshall, *Bengal: The British Bridgehead*
Stewart Gordon, *The Maratha Empire*
Om Prakash, *The Northern European Trading Companies and India*
Richard B. Barnett, *Muslim Successor States*
*J. S. Grewal, *The Sikhs in the Punjab*
David Washbrook, *South India*

III The Indian Empire and the Beginnings of Modern Society

F. Conlon, *Modern Maharashtra*
Sugata Bose, *The Agrarian Development of Modern Bengal*
David Ludden, *Agriculture in Indian History*
Susan Bayly, *Caste in South Asia*
B. R. Tomlinson, *Economic Growth, Change and Stagnation*
Thomas R. Metcalf, *Ideologies of the Raj*
*K. W. Jones, *Socio-religious Reform Movements in British India*
B. N. Ramusack, *The Indian Princes and their States*
Gordon Johnson, *Government and Politics in India*

IV The Evolution of Contemporary South Asia

*Paul R. Brass, *The Politics of India since Independence*
Anil Seal, *The Transfer of Power and the Partition of India*
Raj Chandavarkar, *The Urban Working Classes*
Geraldine Forbes, *Indian Women in the Twentieth Century*
Francis Robinson, *Islam in South Asia*
Gyan Pandey, *Peasants and Politics*
Shahid Amin, *Economy, Society and Culture*

**Already published*